The Princeton Review®

AF776516

Paying for College

2027 Edition

By Kalman A. Chany with Geoff Martz

PrincetonReview.com

Penguin Random House

The Princeton Review
110 East 42nd St., 7th Floor
New York, NY 10017
princetonreview.com
penguinrandomhouse.com

Published in the United States by Penguin Random House LLC, New York.

ISBN: 979-8-217-23070-9
eBook ISBN: 979-8-217-23071-6
ISSN: 1944-3781

Editor: Aaron Riccio
Production Artist: Deborah Weber

Manufactured in the United States of America

10 9 8 7 6 5 4 3 2 1

2027 Edition

EU Contact:
Penguin Random House Ireland
32 Nassau Street
Dublin D02 YH68
https://eu-contact.penguin.ie

For customer service, please contact **editorialsupport@review.com**, and be sure to include:

- full title of the book
- ISBN
- page number

Acknowledgments

Geoff Martz and I are most grateful to those who have helped with this and prior editions of the book.

We would first like to thank Robert Franek, Deborah Weber, Laura Rose, and Aaron Riccio at The Princeton Review as well as Tom Russell and Alison Stoltzfus at Penguin Random House.

Special thanks to Jeanne Krier, who has served as our publicist for more than twenty-five years. Her understanding of the many complex issues surrounding financial aid and college funding as well as her keen suggestions for future editions have been an ongoing source of help and support. Her skill as a public relations expert and the high regard that many members of media have for her professionalism have also contributed significantly to the success of this project.

We are also grateful to Jonathan Goodsell, Victoria Malone, Michele Brown, Anita Gross, Daria Adams, and Jeanne Saunders at the U.S. Department of Education as well as Susan McCrackin, Jessica Bernier, Ami Boshardt, and Vanessa DeShane at the College Board who have been a tremendous source of help for many editions of this book.

I would also like to thank Isidore Matalon, my longtime friend and a constant source of new ideas; Steven Levine of the accounting firm of Lederer & Levine in Lyndhurst, New Jersey, for his helpful suggestions regarding tax law; Catherine O'Connor, my associate at Campus Consultants without whom I could never have managed; Robert Weinerman, Director of Training at Iron Bridge Resources, LLC, for his keen insights related to federal student aid regulations; the high school counselors and independent college consultants who have entrusted students and their parents to me over the years; and my own parents, who somehow managed to pay for my college education without the benefit of having read a book like this.

Last but not least, I would like to thank my clients who have provided me with the opportunity to prove that financial aid planning really works.

—Kal Chany

Contents

Get More **(Free)** Content

at **PrincetonReview.com/guidebooks**

As easy as *1•2•3*

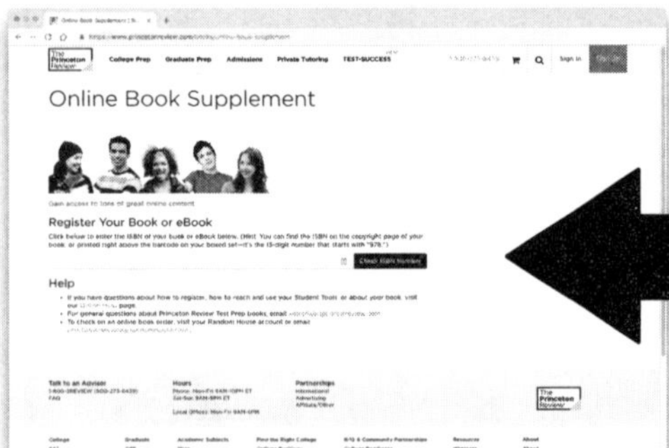

1 Go to PrincetonReview.com/guidebooks or scan the **QR code** and enter the following ISBN to register your book:
9798217230709

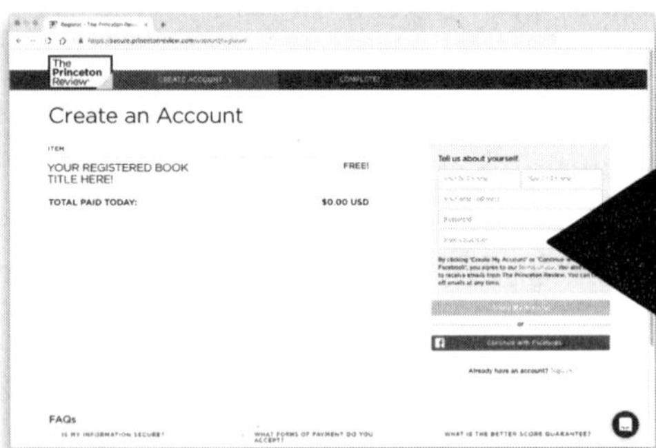

2 Answer a few simple questions to set up an exclusive Princeton Review account. *(If you already have one, you can just log in.)*

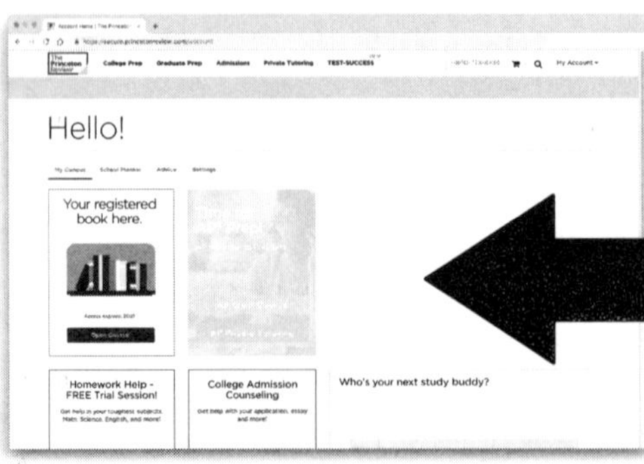

3 Enjoy access to your **FREE** content!

Once you've registered, you can...

- Take a full-length practice SAT or ACT.
- Get valuable advice about the college application process.
- Use our searchable rankings of *The Best 392 Colleges* to find out more information about your dream school.
- Access any errata pertaining to this book or the 2027–2028 forms.

Need to report a potential **content** issue?

Contact **EditorialSupport@review.com** and include:

- full title of the book
- ISBN
- page number

Need to report a **technical** issue?

Contact **TPRStudentTech@review.com** and provide:

- your full name
- email address used to register the book
- full book title and ISBN
- Operating system (Mac/PC) and browser (Chrome, Firefox, Safari, etc.)

Look For This Icon Throughout The Book

Each edition of this book attempts to provide the most accurate and up-to-date information available when we finalize the copy in late June. However, the delayed release of clear policy guidance from the U.S. Department of Education regarding the FAFSA and other federal student aid matters often leads to issues that are not resolved by that point. The following icon indicates such a situation for the accompanying text, alerting you that such information may well change.

INFORMATION STILL PENDING

Introduction

A college education has long been considered part of the American Dream. But given its high cost, that dream has become a financial nightmare for an ever-increasing number of parents and students. This book is designed to help you minimize your out-of-pocket costs and reduce your anxiety. It will answer many of your questions, including those you never thought to ask, like those having to do with the FAFSA Simplification regulations affecting federal student aid—which are anything *but* simple.

If College Is So Good for Me, Why Does This Feel So Bad?

The total cost of a four-year private college education, including tuition, fees, food, and housing has passed the $400,000 mark at some schools, which is enough to cause even the most affluent parent to want to sit down and cry. The public Ivies—state schools with excellent reputations—largely keep raising their charges for tuition, fees, and room and board as well, so much so that some of them have sticker prices for out-of-state students that are now comparable to those at many private colleges. This year, an out-of-state student living on campus will have to pay almost $80,000 to attend the University of Michigan for one year.

Colleges are also facing a "demographic cliff," a significant decline that corresponds with a decreasing birthrate, in the number of high-school seniors heading to college. This drop-off in university enrollments, which may last several years, along with recent federal legislation affecting student aid, ongoing deficits that have reduced university endowments, and cuts to the education budgets of many state governments, has created a crisis in higher education. Many colleges have had to slash their budgets, eliminate programs, lay off faculty, consolidate with other colleges, or even close permanently.

The Joy of Aid

If there is a bright side to all this, it is that in spite of all the bad news, there is still a great deal of financial aid available—and we are talking *billions* of dollars. With so much money on the table, almost every family now qualifies for some form of assistance. Many parents don't believe that a family that makes $250,000 a year, owns their own home, and holds substantial assets could possibly receive financial aid. These days, that family—provided it is presented in the right light—almost certainly does at a large number of schools. Many parents who make $60,000, rent their home, and have no assets, don't believe they can afford to send their child to any type of college at all. They almost certainly can—in fact, they may find to their surprise that with the financial aid package some schools can put together for them, it may cost less to attend an "expensive" private school than it would to go to a "cheaper" state school.

Who Gets the Most Financial Aid?

You might think that the families who receive the most financial aid would be the families with the most need. In fact, this is not necessarily true. The people who receive the most aid are the people who best understand the aid process.

Some years ago, we had a client who owned a $1 million apartment in New York City and a stock portfolio with a value in excess of $2 million. Her daughter attended college—with a $4,000-a-year need-based grant.

Is This Fair?

No. But lots of things in life aren't fair. In that particular case, we were able to take advantage of a financial aid loophole involving the way state aid is computed in New York. There are lots of financial aid loopholes.

Is This Legal?

You bet. All of the strategies we are going to discuss in this book follow the law to the letter.

Is This Ethical?

Let us put a hypothetical question to you: If your accountant showed you a legal way to save $4,000 on your income tax this year, would you take it?

The parallels between taxes and financial aid are interesting. Both have loopholes that regularly get exploited by the people who know about them. But more important, both also involve adversarial relationships. In the case of your taxes, the IRS wants as much money from you as it can get. You, in turn, want to give the IRS as little as possible. This pas de deux is a time-honored tradition, a system of checks and balances that everyone understands and accepts. And as long as both sides stick to the rules, the system works as well as anyone can expect.

In the case of college, it is the job of the financial aid officer (known in college circles as the FAO) to get as much money from you as possible. In the pursuit of this task, the FAO will be much more invasive than the IRS ever is, demanding not just your financial data but intimate details of your personal life such as medical problems and marital status. The FAO wants to protect the college's assets and give away as little money as possible, as this helps with rankings. Let the financial aid officers do their job—believe us, they're very good at it. In the meantime, you have to do *your* job—and your job is to use the rules of financial aid to make your monetary contribution to college as small as possible.

Parents who understand these rules get the maximum amount of financial aid they are entitled to under the law. No more and no less.

Besides, You've Already Paid for Financial Aid

Whether you know it or not, you've been contributing to financial aid funds for years. Each April 15, you pay federal taxes, a piece of which goes straight to the federal student aid programs. You pay state taxes, part of which goes directly to state schools and to provide grant programs for residents attending college in-state. You may even make contributions to the alumni fund-raising campaign at your own college.

Your son or daughter may not go to your alma mater, may not attend a school in your state, may not even go to college, but you have paid all these years so that *someone's* son or daughter can get a college education.

You may now have need of these funds, and you should not be embarrassed to ask for them.

Is This Only for Rich People?

Many people think that tax loopholes and financial strategy are only for millionaires. In some ways, they have a point: the rich often reap the greatest benefits under the tax code.

But financial aid strategy is for everyone. Whether you are just getting by or are reasonably well off, you still want to maximize your aid eligibility.

A College Is a Business

Despite the ivy-covered walls, the slick promotional videos, and a name that may intimidate you, a college is a business like any other. It provides a service and must find customers willing to buy that service.

You may have heard of an education scam that's been cropping up in different parts of the country in which bogus "trade schools" provide valueless educational courses to unwary consumers. While not to be confused with legitimate trade schools that have been providing valuable educational training to students for years, these schools scam students into paying for their "courses" by taking out government-guaranteed student loans. The schools pocket the money, the student receives very little in the way of education, and then must spend the next 10 to 25 years paying off the loan. Or not paying off the loan, in which case the taxpayer must pick up the tab.

Higher education sometimes seems like a slightly more genteel version of the bogus "trade school" scam. The colleges need warm bodies to fill their classrooms. Many of these warm bodies qualify for federal aid (including grants and student loans), which helps keep the colleges afloat. Meanwhile, the financial aid officers do their bit by trying to get as much money from the student and her family as possible.

Although public ones do it less often than private ones, a significant number of universities of both types engage in financial aid leveraging, the practice of determining how little aid they can award while still getting the student to enroll.

The Ivy-Covered Bottom Line

Of course there is a great deal more to college than merely a business selling a service—there is the value of tradition, the exploration of new ideas, the opportunity to think about important issues, the chance to develop friendships that will last for the rest of a student's life—but do not lose sight of the bottom line. Colleges stand accused by many experts of wasting a good part of their endowment through sloppy management, misguided expansion, and wasteful expenditures. A college tuition would cost much less today if the colleges had been run in a businesslike manner over the past twenty-five years.

If colleges are in trouble right now, there are many who would say it is their own doing, and that they will be better off once they have lost some of the excess fat they allowed themselves to gain during the past few decades. Certainly it is not your responsibility to pay for their mistakes if you don't have to.

But the FAOs have their own bottom line to consider.

An Uneducated Consumer Is Their Best Customer

It is not in the FAO's best interest for you to understand the nuances of the aid system. The more you know about it, the more aid they will have to give you from the school's own coffers. You can almost *feel* the FAO's reluctance to let the consumer know what's going on when you look at the standardized financial aid applications (known as need analysis forms), which are constructed in consultation with the colleges. These forms (unlike the federal tax forms that allow you to calculate your own taxes) require you to list your information but do not allow you to calculate the amount of money you will be required to pay to the college. This calculation is done by the aid form processors and the colleges. Mere parents are not allowed to know how the formula is constructed. We are going to show you that formula and much more.

Understanding and Taking Control of the Process

In this book we will first give you an overview of the process of applying for aid, and then show you how to begin to take control of that process. We will discuss long-term investment strategies for families that have time to plan, and short-term financial aid strategies for families about to begin the aid process. We have devoted an entire chapter to a step-by-step guide to filling out the standardized need analysis forms to your best advantage, because the decisions the colleges will make on the basis of these forms are crucial to your ability to pay for college. Once you have received your aid packages from the schools, you will want to compare them.

Part 4 of this book, "The Offer," shows you how to do that, as well as discussing how to negotiate with the colleges for an improved package.

The majority of our readers are parents planning for their children's education, but this book is also for older students who are continuing their own studies. Most of the financial aid strategies to increase your eligibility for aid are essentially the same.

A Word of Caution

Some of the aid strategies we will discuss in this book are complicated, and because we do not know the specifics of your financial situation, it is impossible for us to give anything but general advice. Nor can we cover every eventuality. We recommend that you consult with a competent professional about your specific situation before proceeding with a particular strategy. In Chapter 11, we discuss how to find a good financial aid consulting service.

Unfortunately, because of the volume of correspondence, we can't answer individual mail or give specific advice over the telephone. If we did, we'd have no time for our private clients—or for the daunting task of preparing next year's edition of *Paying for College*.

The New (But Not-so-Improved) Financial Aid Landscape

As you may have heard, after years of delays the U.S. Department of Education finally fully implemented its overhaul of the college financial aid system. Its rollout of the updated Free Application for Federal Student Aid form—known as the FAFSA—in 2024–2025 was little short of a disaster.

Millions of families had problems accessing the form online. There were inexcusable delays in processing applications, data was lost, erroneous calculations were made that required many forms to then be re-processed, and certain workarounds to fix known problems did not work. College aid offices had to struggle with constantly changing guidance from the U.S. Department of Education as well. The result of what was to be "simplification" produced instead massive complications that were soon labeled the "FAFSA Fiasco" by the media and aid professionals. Perhaps the most terrible result of all is that more than one million fewer students applied for federal financial aid though the first week of June 2024 than they had by June 2023.

It gave us absolutely no pleasure that we had predicted this mess in June 2023, when we sent the 2024 Edition of this book to print.

While perhaps the *worst* of the kinks of the new federal student aid system are likely behind us, we are still not sure there will be smooth sailing when the 2027–2028 application season begins. In Part 3 of this 2027 edition, we have included practical time-tested tips to help you navigate these waters.

Keeping You Up-to-Date

One reason we initially resisted writing this book was our reluctance to put out a book that might be bought after it was out of date. In the world of financial aid, things change rapidly. We agreed to do this book only after getting a commitment from our publisher that there would be a new edition every year.

However, even within the space of a year, things can change: tax laws can be amended, financial aid rules can be changed. While we've done our best to include the most accurate information, the icon that appears in the margin of this paragraph will be used to alert you about some information that, at the time of printing, may well change or be clarified.

Late Breaking News

The first draft of the 2027–2028 FAFSA was released in February 2026 and had a 60-day period in which the public could leave comments about it. Several dozen comments were submitted both by individuals (including the author of this book) and prominent financial aid and/or student advocacy organizations. Many of these comments focused on issues with the way parent and student incomes and assets were treated, and the United States Department of Education (USDOE) published 125 pages of responses in May 2026. Unfortunately, many of these responses resulted in additional issues being raised, and as we went to press in late June 2026, the 45-day Public Comment Period for the second draft of the 2027–2028 version of the FAFSA was just ending. This means that it is possible that the USDOE may have made further adjustments to the final version of the 2027–2028 FAFSA based on those comments.

Additionally, as we went to press, many provisions of the budget reconciliation law passed by Congress and signed into law by President Trump on July 4, 2025, were just becoming effective on July 1, 2026. This piece of legislation, known to some as the One Big Beautiful Bill Act (or OBBBA or OBBB or OB3), contained many changes to federal student aid, especially the federal student loan programs. While the law was passed over a year ago, there were still a number of questions involving the implementation of the legislation that had not yet been answered. Furthermore, some provisions affecting student loans are not to be fully implemented until sometime in 2027 or 2028.

The USDOE has not made it easy to follow their policies, let alone for us to provide guidance on them. That's because ever since this whole FAFSA Fiasco began in January 2024, the USDOE has had a habit of issuing guidance, only to retract it shortly thereafter. That is why we have placed icons throughout the book to indicate items that have not been 100% resolved.

To access any such updated information, register your book online and check your student tools. That's where we'll add any new planning strategies for certain situations as well as updated guidance on how to complete certain questions on the 2027–2028 aid forms to your best advantage. Turn to page vi (right before the Introduction), and under the heading "Get More (Free) Content," you'll find instructions on how to access this (and any other) information as it becomes available.

However, please be aware that with any updates, we will only cover issues that have been fully resolved as we will not speculate or provide guidance until all the fine print has dried. This is because the USDOE since the time of the FAFSA Fiasco that began in January 2024 has had a habit of issuing policy guidance, only to retract it shortly thereafter. So keep in mind that if an update icon appears next to any text, that does not necessarily mean than we will post any new updated information if the issue in question is still not properly resolved.

A Final Thought

Depending on which survey you read, between 70% and 80% of all college-bound high school students were accepted by their first-choice college last year. Nowadays, the problem is not so much how to get into college, but how to pay for it once you are there.

In the following pages we will show you how to pay for college. This is not about ripping off the system, or lying to get aid you don't deserve. This is about empowering students and parents with the information they need to get the maximum amount of aid they are entitled to receive under the law and to minimize their out-of-pocket costs.

Part One

Understanding the Process

Chapter One

Overview

How the Aid Process Works: Paying for College in a Nutshell

Ideally, you began this process many years ago when your children were quite small. You started saving, at first in small increments, gradually increasing the amounts as your children got older and your earning power grew. You put the money into a mixture of growth investments like stock funds, and conservative investments like treasury bonds, so that now, as the college years are approaching, you are sitting pretty with a nice fat college fund, a cool drink in your hand, and enough left over to buy a vacation home in Monte Carlo.

However, if you are like most of us, you probably began thinking seriously about college only a few years ago. You have not been able to put away large amounts of money. Important things kept coming up. An opportunity to buy a home. Taxes. Braces. Soccer camp. Taxes.

If you are foresighted enough to have bought this book while your children are still young, you will be especially interested in our section on long-term planning. If your child is already a senior in high school just about to apply for college, don't despair. There is a lot you can do to take control of the process.

Most people cannot afford to pay the full cost of four years of college. Financial aid is designed to bridge the gap between what you can afford to pay for school and what the school actually costs. Parents who understand the process come out way ahead. Let's look at the aid process in a nutshell and see how it works—or at least how it's supposed to work. Later on, we will take you through each step of this process in greater detail.

The Standardized Need Analysis Forms

While students start work on their admissions applications, parents should be gathering together their records in order to begin applying for financial aid.

At a minimum, you need to fill out a standardized need analysis form called the Free Application for Federal Student Aid (FAFSA). This form is available in two formats: (1) online or (2) as a printable PDF. These two versions are expected to be available for filing after September 30th of the student's senior year of high school.

Many private colleges and some state-supported institutions may require you to electronically complete the CSS/Financial Aid Profile Form as well. This form is developed and processed by the same organization that brings you the SAT—The College Board.

A few schools will require other forms as well—for example, the selective private colleges often have their *own* financial aid forms. For students whose two biological or adoptive parents are no longer living together, the situation gets more complicated. To find out which forms are required by a particular college, consult the individual school's financial aid office website or printed information.

All of the forms ask the same types of invasive questions: How much did you earn last year? How much money do you have in the bank? What is your marital status? A hundred or so questions later, the need analysis company will have a very clear picture of four things:

1. the parents' available income
2. the parents' available assets
3. the student's available income
4. the student's available assets

The processor of the FAFSA form uses a federal formula (called the *federal methodology* or FM) to decide what portion of your income and assets you get to keep and what portion you can afford to put toward college tuition this year. This amount (which prior to the 2024–2025 award year was called the Expected Family Contribution, or EFC) is now called the calculated Student Aid Index (SAI), and will most likely be more than you think you can afford.

However, some schools do not feel that the SAI generated by the FAFSA gives an accurate enough picture of what the family can contribute to college costs. Using the supplemental information on the CSS Profile (which is analyzed using a formula called the *institutional methodology* or IM, that is developed by the College Board) and/or using their own individual forms, these institutions perform a separate need analysis to determine eligibility for aid that those schools control directly.

A Family's "Need"

Meanwhile, the admissions offices of the different colleges have been deciding which students to admit and which to reject. Once they've made their decision, the financial aid officers (known as FAOs) get to work. Their job is to put together a package of grants, work-study, and loans that will make up the difference between what they feel you can afford to pay and what the school actually costs.

The total cost of a year at college includes:

tuition and fees
food and housing
personal expenses
books and supplies
travel

The difference between what you can afford to pay and the total cost of college is called your "need."

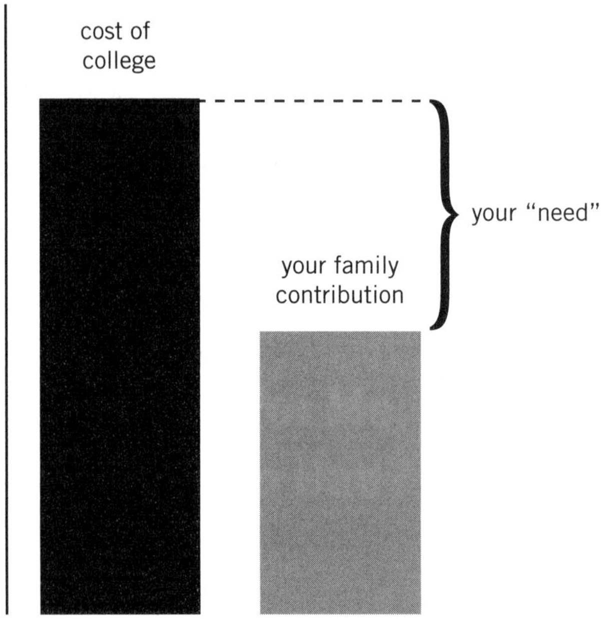

In theory, your Student Aid Index will be approximately the same no matter what schools your child applies to. If your SAI is calculated to be $20,300 and your child is accepted at a state school that costs $30,300, you will pay about $20,300, and the school will make up the difference—in this case $10,000—with an aid package. If you apply to a prestigious Ivy League school that costs $90,000, you will still pay about $20,300 and the school will make up the difference with an aid package of approximately $69,700.

In theory, the only difference between an expensive school and a cheaper school (putting aside subjective matters like the quality of education) is the amount of your need. In some cases, depending on how badly the college wants the student, parents won't pay a penny more for an exclusive private college than they would for a state school.

This is why families should not initially rule out any school as being too expensive. The "sticker price" doesn't necessarily matter; it's the portion of the sticker price that you have to pay that counts. Parents are often under the impression that no matter what type of school their child attends—be it a very expensive private college, an expensive out-of-state public institution, or their local state university—they will receive the same amount of aid. In fact, as you saw from the previous example, the amount of aid you get is in part determined by the cost of the school you choose.

Theory vs. Reality

Of course, the reality is slightly more complicated. Because some schools are using supplemental data (such as home equity) to determine eligibility for their private aid, your expected contribution at a more selective university will most likely be different, and in some cases higher. In later chapters we'll be talking about what factors can cause the schools to adjust the SAI calculated under the federal methodology, and more important, we'll be showing you how to minimize the impact of these adjustments. But for now, we are going to introduce you to some basic core concepts and terms related to financial aid. If you correctly learn these basics now, the more-detailed material in those later chapters will be easier to grasp.

A "Snapshot" of Your Financial Picture

Each year your son or daughter is in college, the school will ask you to fill out a form reporting income and assets—in effect a snapshot of your overall financial picture. You've probably noticed that snapshots can be very misleading. In one picture, you may appear like your ideal self; in another, you may look like you just crawled out of bed. Perhaps neither photograph is exactly correct. Of course, when you are deciding which picture to put in the scrapbook, the choice is easy: throw away the one you don't like and keep the one you do.

In choosing which financial snapshot to send to the colleges, the object is a little bit different: send them the worst-looking picture you can find.

To be very blunt, the single most effective way to reduce the family contribution is to make your income and your assets look as small as possible.

Well, This Is Not Revolutionary Advice

After all, you've been trying to do this for years.

We're sure you and your accountant are generally doing a fine job of keeping your taxes to a minimum. However, certain long-term tax strategies that normally make all kinds of sense can explode in your face during college years. Neither you nor your accountant may fully grasp how important it is to understand the ins and outs of the financial aid formulas.

How College Planning Affects Tax Planning

There are two reasons why tax planning has to change during college years.

First, the FAOs (unlike the IRS) are concerned about only *four years* of your financial life. Using strategies we will be showing you in the next few chapters, you may be able to shift income out of those four years, thus increasing your financial aid.

Second, financial aid formulas *differ* from the IRS formulas in several key ways. Certain long-term tax reduction strategies (shifting income to other family members, for example) can actually *increase* the amount of college tuition you will pay. However, astute parents who understand these differences will find that there are some wonderful, legal, logical alternatives they can explore to change the four snapshots the college will take of their income and assets.

Tax accountants who do not understand the financial aid process (and in our experience, this includes most of them) can actually hurt your chances for financial aid.

The First Base Year Income

Colleges and the government normally base your ability to pay *this* year's tuition *not* on what you made this year or even what you made *last* year, but on what you made the year before *that*. This may seem like ancient history, but the colleges have their complicated reasons (which we'll go into later). Thus the first financial aid scrutiny you will undergo will not be directed at the calendar year during which your child will start her freshman year of college, *but two years before*. That year is called the first base income year and is the crucial one.

The base income year (shaded in the diagram that follows) extends from January 1 of your child's sophomore year in high school to December 31 of your child's junior year in high school. This is when first impressions are formed. The college will get an idea of how much you are likely to be able to afford, not just for the first year of school, but for the remaining years as well. First impressions are likely to endure and are often very difficult to change. Thus it would be helpful to remove as much income as possible from this calendar year.

Aug. | Sept. High School Sophomore Year Begins	Oct.	Nov.	Dec.	Jan.	Feb.	Mar.	Apr.	May	June	July
Aug. | Sept. High School Junior Year Begins	Oct.	Nov.	Dec.	Jan.	Feb.	Mar.	Apr.	May	June	July
Aug. | Sept. High School Senior Year Begins	Oct.	Nov.	Dec.	Jan.	Feb.	Mar.	Apr.	May	June	July
Aug. | Sept. College Begins	Oct.	Nov.	Dec.	Jan.	Feb.	Mar.	Apr.	May	June	July

What If I'm Already Past the Base Income Year?

If you are reading this book and your son or daughter is already in the spring term of junior year in high school, then you have probably missed the chance to make adjustments to your income for the base income year—but don't despair. First of all, there are three other years still to go; the strategies we outline below can be used to lower the appearance of income in the years to come. And second, you haven't missed the chance to make adjustments to your assets. *That* snapshot gets taken on the day you fill out the forms. We'll talk about assets a little later in this chapter.

What If I'm In the Middle of the Base Income Year?

If you are reading this book and you are still in the base income year, there are a bunch of very specific things you can do to minimize the appearance of income.

What If My Income Has Radically Changed Between the Base Income Year and Now?

If your income has gone *up* since the base income year, that's great. No need to report the change, unless you are asked to by an individual college. However, if your income has gone markedly *down* since the base income year, you can always write to the colleges and explain. We'll describe this process, called an "appeal," in Part Four, "The Offer."

The Aid Package

About the time your child receives an offer of admission from a particular college, you will receive an award letter. This letter will tell you what combination of aid the FAO has put together for you in order to meet your need. The package will consist of three different types of aid:

Grants and Scholarships—These are the best kinds of aid, because they don't have to be paid back. Essentially, a grant is free money. Some grant money comes from the federal government, some comes from the state, and some comes from the coffers of the college itself. Best of all, grant money is almost always tax-free. If you are in the 35% combined tax bracket, a $5,000 grant is the equivalent of receiving a raise of $7,692.

Scholarships are also free money, although there may be some conditions attached (academic excellence, for example). Contrary to popular wisdom, scholarships are usually awarded by the schools themselves. The amount of money available from outside scholarships is actually quite small.

Federal Work-Study (FWS)—The federal government subsidizes this program, which provides part-time jobs to students. The money earned is put toward either tuition or living expenses.

Student Loans—These loans, usually taken out by the student rather than the parents, are often subsidized (and guaranteed) by state or federal governments. The rates are usually much lower than regular unsecured loans. In most cases, no interest is charged while the student is in school, and no repayment is required until the student has graduated or left college.

Preferential Packaging

The FAOs at the individual colleges have a lot of latitude to make decisions. After looking at your financial information, for example, they might decide your SAI should be lower or higher than the need analysis processor originally computed it.

More important, the package the FAOs put together for a student will often reflect how badly the admissions office wants that student.

If a school is anxious to have your child in its first-year class, the package you will be offered will have a larger percentage of grant money, with a much smaller percentage coming from student loans and work study. If a college is less interested, the award will not be as attractive.

Your award will also reflect the general financial health of the college you are applying to. Some schools have large endowments and can afford to be generous. Other schools are financially strapped, and may be able to offer only the bare minimum.

If the school is truly anxious to get a particular student, it may also sweeten the deal by giving a grant or scholarship that isn't based on need. A non-need scholarship may actually reduce your family contribution.

Unmet Need

In many cases, you may find that the college tells you that you have "unmet need." In other words, they were unable to supply the full difference between the cost of their school and the amount they feel you can afford to pay. This is bad news. What the college is telling you is that if your child really wants to attend this college, you will have to come up with even more money than the aid formulas determined you could contribute.

Usually what this means is that you will have to take on additional debt. Sometimes the colleges themselves will be willing to lend you the money. Sometimes you will be able to take advantage of other loan programs such as the Federal Parent Loans for Undergraduate Students (PLUS), which is a partially subsidized loan to parents of college students. The terms are less attractive than the subsidized student loans but still better for most parents than unsecured loans you would get from banks if you walked in off the street.

Sifting the Offers

The week on which acceptance and award letters arrive can be very tough, as you are confronted with the economic realities of the different schools' offers. The school your child really wants to attend may have given you an aid package you cannot accept. The week will be immeasurably easier if you have taken the financial aid process into account when you were selecting schools to apply to in the first place.

Just as it is important to select a safety school where your child is likely to be accepted, it is also important to select what we call a "*financial* safety school" that is cheap enough to afford out of your own pocket (or with minimal aid and, more important, with minimal loans) in the event that the more expensive schools you applied to do not meet your full need. In some cases, the admissions safety school and financial safety school may be the same. If a student is a desirable candidate from an academic standpoint, she is likely to get a good financial aid package as well. However, you should also consider the economic health of the schools you are applying to as well as the past history of financial aid at those schools. This information can be gleaned from many of the college guides (including The Princeton Review's *The Best 392 Colleges*, 2027 edition) available at bookstores and online booksellers.

It is also vital to make sure that there is a reasonable expectation that the package will be available for the next three years as well. How high do the student's grades have to be in order to keep the package intact? Are any of the grants or scholarships they gave you one-time-only grants? Once you've received an offer, these are questions to ask the FAO.

Negotiating with the FAOs

Even if a school's award letter has left you with a package you cannot accept—perhaps the percentage of student loan money in your package is too high; or perhaps your need was not fully met—you may still be able to negotiate a better deal.

Over the past few years we have noticed that the initial offer of aid, especially at some of the more selective schools, seems to have become subject to adjustment. In many cases, if you just accept the first offer, you will have accepted an offer that was not as high as the FAO was willing to go.

Many parents feel understandably hesitant to go back to the table. However, if the aid package is actually too low for you to be able to send your child to that school, you have little to lose by asking for more. And most FAOs will appreciate learning that they are about to risk losing a qualified applicant solely because of money.

The key in these negotiations is to be friendly, firm, and in control. Know what you want when you talk to the FAO and be able to provide documentation. In some cases, the FAO will alter the aid package enough to make it possible for you to afford to send your child to the school.

There is an entire section of this book devoted to the award letter—how to compare award letters, how to negotiate with FAOs, and how to apply for next year.

Same Time Next Year

The financial aid package you accept will last only one year. You will have to go through the financial aid process four separate times, filling out a new need analysis form or forms each year until your child reaches the senior year of college. If your financial situation were to stay *exactly* the same, then next year's aid package would probably be very similar to this year's. We find, however, that most parents' situations do change from year to year. In fact, after you finish reading this book, there may be some specific changes you'll *want* to make.

How the Aid Process Really Works

Parents and students who understand how to apply for financial aid get more. It's that simple. We aren't talking about lying, cheating, or beating the system. We're talking about understanding the system and utilizing the rules to get the best deal.

In Part Two, you will learn how to take control of the process. For those parents who are starting early, Chapter Two covers long-term investment strategies that minimize taxes and maximize aid eligibility. For those parents who have children in high school, Chapter Three through Chapter Six will show you how to use the financial aid formulas to save money. We'll explain in detail how the different parts of your finances and family situation affect what you will be expected to finance—and what adjustments you can make to boost your aid eligibility. In addition, we discuss how to pick colleges that will give the best aid packages, how to apply for state aid, and—very important—what the *student* can do.

In Part Three, we provide step-by-step guidelines for handling the financial aid application process, along with detailed strategies for completing the two most commonly used standardized financial aid forms for the 2027–2028 award year.

In Part Four, we discuss the offer. What does an award letter look like? What are the different types of aid you may receive, in detail? How do you compare award letters? How do you negotiate with the FAOs to get an improved package?

In Chapter Seven, we talk about innovative payment options and in Chapter Eight, we discuss managing student loans during and after school. In Chapter Nine, we cover in more detail some special topics such as divorced and separated parents, graduate students, minority students, independent students, and other topics that may be of interest to some of our readers. In Chapter Ten, we'll discuss some important information involving educational tax benefits. For those who feel they need individualized guidance, Chapter Eleven provides tips on how to find a good financial aid consultant. In Chapter Twelve, future trends regarding financial aid and educational financing are covered, as well as some helpful tips for paying for college in these tough economic times.

In Part Five, you will find worksheets for calculating the Student Aid Index for the federal methodology, a draft version of the 2027–2028 FAFSA, as well as copies of Pages 1 and 2 of the 2025 IRS Form 1040 and Schedule 1 of the 2025 IRS Form 1040.

At the end of this book, there is a Glossary of common college financing and financial aid terms.

Part Two

How to Take Control of the Process

If you have read Part One of this book, then you now know the basics about how the financial aid process works. Now, it's time to start figuring out how to take control of that process—and prevent the process from taking control of you.

Understanding What's Going On

The college FAOs don't really want you to understand all the intricacies of the financial aid process. This benefits the colleges, as it means that parents won't ask questions that schools don't want to have to answer and will accept whatever the FAOs tell them instead.

We know of one case in which a financial aid officer from a private college told a parent who had called asking for an increase in aid that "our hands are tied. Federal regulations prevent us from giving you any more money." The parent, not knowing any better, accepted this as the truth. In fact, it was a bald-faced lie. Almost all colleges (and this one was no exception) hand out their own grants, which are privately funded and not regulated by federal law at all.

Another thing parents are often too willing to accept at face value is the initial financial aid offer by the college. In a recent trend, many schools (particularly the most competitive) have begun to build some bargaining room into their initial offers. They expect you to ask for more. In many cases, accepting that first offer means taking a lower number than the FAO was willing to give. These are just two examples of the facts you will learn in the next few chapters—facts that will enable you to understand and begin to take control of the financial aid process.

Parents whose children are several years away from college will find the next chapter on long-term planning particularly useful. In it, we will show you how to begin building a fund for college that will take advantage of both tax law and financial aid law. Families who are getting ready to apply to college should skip long-term planning and go directly to Chapter Three on short-term strategies. There we will begin to show you how linking your income tax strategies and your financial aid strategies can save you big bucks. We will show you how the colleges assess your income, expenses, assets, and liabilities, and how to influence these assessments to your advantage.

Don't Let the Terminology Intimidate You

A word of caution before we begin. In the course of counseling thousands of families, we've seen how confusing financial aid jargon can be to the nonprofessional. Just remember, the FAOs don't mind if you are a little confused. In fact, they would prefer it. And since they have a large influence on the instructions that come with the aid forms you will have to fill out, it shouldn't surprise you to learn that the instructions to the forms are confusing and full of unfamiliar terminology as well. The introduction to one particularly confusing financial aid form states that some questions are "self-explanatory, and therefore no instructions are given."

Don't worry. By the time you finish reading this book, the jargon will be second nature. At the back of this book is a comprehensive glossary; feel free to refer to it at any time.

To avoid confusion, we have taken care to use the same terminology used by the need analysis companies and the IRS. Even though it seems a little ridiculous to refer to certain deductions as "Adjustments to Income," we did so anyway, just so that you will know what the terms mean once you start completing the forms and negotiating with the FAOs.

Chapter Two

Long-Term Strategies for Paying for College

Congratulations! If you are reading this section you've had the foresight to begin planning early for the expense of paying for college. What do we mean by early? We will be presenting strategies for parents with children who are three years away, five years away, ten years away, and 15 years away from their first year of college.

The point of this chapter is not to make specific investment recommendations or tout individual stocks or investment instruments, but rather to show you the ways and means to begin a long-term college fund for your children. Our purpose is not to be your financial planner, for no financial planner could responsibly set up a 10-year plan without being around to administer it (and obviously, we can't do that). Things change. Investment opportunities come up suddenly. Interest rates go up or they go down. Tax laws are amended; financial aid laws are revised. We are going to outline some general strategies, but we advise you to invest cautiously, perhaps with the aid of a financial planner whom you can consult day to day.

If your child is applying for college next month, we recommend that you skip this section. Seeing a variety of techniques that are too late to implement at this point will only frustrate you. Instead, skip to the next chapter, where we begin talking about short-term strategies. We think you will be pleased.

How Much Should We Save Every Month?

Any realistic long-term plan is more of an educated guess than an exact prediction. There are so many unknown factors—how much will college cost in ten years? Or 15 years? What will the inflation rate average over the next decade? Will stocks continue to be the best long-term investment as they have for the past 40 years, or will some unforeseen trend make real estate or bonds a better investment?

Any financial planner who says you have to save exactly $937 per month to reach your goal is being unrealistic—in part because you don't even know with certainty what that goal will be. We think the main thing such pronouncements do is scare parents into paralysis. "We don't *have* that kind of money," clients wail to us on the phone after they hear these figures. "What are we supposed to do?"

The Important Thing Is to Start

It is easy to get so paralyzed by the projection of the total cost of a four-year college education that you do nothing. The important thing is to begin saving *something* as early as possible, as regularly as possible. It doesn't matter if you can't contribute large amounts. The earlier you start, the longer you give your investments to work for you.

If you have not saved the total cost of four years' tuition at a private college (and very few parents ever have), all is not lost. That is why there is financial aid.

So Why Bother to Save at All? If We Don't Have Any Money, We'll Just Get More Financial Aid

This is partly true, but only partly. A poor family without the means to pay for college will find concerned FAOs ready to look in every corner of their coffers to come up with the aid necessary to send that family's child to college. An affluent family that has lived beyond their means for years and is now looking for the college to support this lifestyle with financial aid will find the FAOs to be very unsympathetic and tightfisted.

An honest attempt to save money and a willingness to make sacrifices can make a large impression on the FAOs. These men and women have broad powers to increase or decrease your family contribution, to allocate grants, and to meet your family's *entire* need—or just part of it.

Trust us, you will be much happier if you have saved for college. Who can say whether in five years there will be many colleges left that can afford to continue "need-blind" admissions policies? Perhaps by the year 2040 virtually *no* colleges will be able to meet a family's full remaining need—meaning that if you are without resources, your child will simply not be able to attend college at all. If you still aren't convinced, think about this: a significant proportion of financial aid packages comes in the form of loans. You have the choice of saving now and *earning* interest, or borrowing later and *paying* interest. Earning interest is more fun.

Finally, under the aid formulas, colleges will assess parents' assets at a top rate of only 5.65%. In other words, if you have managed to build up a college fund of say, $40,000, as long as it is in the parents' name, the colleges will assess up to approximately five and a half cents of each dollar of that fund each year. We'll be discussing the pros and cons of putting money in your child's name later. You can certainly spend more if you like, but it is important to understand that having money in the bank does not mean the colleges get to take it all.

Money in the Bank Gives You Options

A college fund, even a small one, gives you control over your own destiny. What if the college your child really wants to attend doesn't fully meet your need? What if you lose your job just as the college years are approaching? By planning a little for the future now, you can ensure that you'll have options when the college years are upon you.

How Much Will a College Education Cost in *X* Years?

Every year, the price of a college education goes up. In the past couple of years, the rate of increase at private colleges has actually slowed, the result in part of market forces: families have been turning to state schools in greater numbers, forcing the private colleges to cut their prices, or at least to slow the increase of their prices. Partly in response to increased demand and partly because state budgets have been slashed, the rate of tuition increase at state schools has risen dramatically—especially for out-of-state students who must pay extra. Will these trends continue? The best we can do is make broad predictions based on current trends. Let's look at some numbers.

The Cost of a Private College

The average cost of a year's tuition, room and board, and fees at a private college last year was $60,920 (according to the College Board). Many experts predict that the cost of private college will increase at a rate of about 3.75% per year. Here is a chart of what the average cost of a year of private college would be over the next 15 years, based on 3.75% yearly growth:

Average Annual Cost of a Private College in			
2026	$63,205 (today)	2034	$84,850
2027	$65,575	2035	$88,032
2028	$68,034 (2 years)	2036	$91,333 (10 years)
2029	$70,585	2037	$94,758
2030	$73,232	2038	$98,312
2031	$75,978 (5 years)	2039	$101,998
2032	$78,827	2040	$105,823
2033	$81,783	2041	$109,792 (15 years)

Of course, if your child decides on one of the most prestigious private schools, the cost will be even more. This year, many of the top colleges have crossed the $90,000-a-year barrier. In five years, at 3.75% growth per year, that will be approximately $108,190.

The Cost of a Public University

The average cost of a year's tuition, room and board, and fees at a public university last year was $25,850 (according to the College Board). Many experts predict that the cost of public university will also increase at a rate of about 3.5% per year over the next decade. Here is a chart of what the average cost of a year of public university could cost over the next 15 years, if the experts are right:

Average Annual Cost of a Public University in			
2026	$26,755 (today)	2034	$35,231
2027	$27,691	2035	$36,464
2028	$28,660 (2 years)	2036	$37,740 (10 years)
2029	$29,663	2037	$39,061
2030	$30,702	2038	$40,428
2031	$31,776 (5 years)	2039	$41,843
2032	$32,888	2040	$43,308
2033	$34,040	2041	$44,824 (15 years)

Of course, if you are attending one of the "public Ivies," such as the University of Michigan, as an out-of-state resident, the cost right now is approximately $80,000. In five years, at a 3.5% growth rate per year, that would be close to $95,000.

How Much Money Will You Need?

If your child is 15, 10, or even five years away from college, she has probably not even begun to think about what kind of school she would like to attend. Since you can't ask your child, ask yourself: what kind of college could you picture your son or daughter attending?

If you have picked a private college of average cost, and your child is ten years away from college, look up the price on the first chart we gave you above. Rather than concentrating on the cost of freshman year, look at the cost of junior year, two years further on. Whatever this number is, multiply it by four. This is a rough approximation of an average college education at that time.

If you picked an average public university, and your child is five years away from college, look up the price on the second chart above. Count two years more and multiply that number by four. This is a rough approximation of a college education at an average public university at that time. Of course, if costs increase faster than the experts are projecting, the figure could be more.

If you wish to be even more precise, find a guide to colleges and look up the current price of a particular school you are interested in. Let's choose Spelman College, a private Historically Black College for women, which has a current price of about $53,716, and let's say your daughter is going to be ready to go to college in five years. Multiply the current price by our assumed rate of increase:

$$\$53{,}716 \times 1.0375 = \$55{,}730$$

The new number is the price of that school next year. To find out the projected price of Spelman in five years, just repeat this operation four more times ($55,730 × 1.0375 = $57,820; $57,820 × 1.0375 = $59,988; etc.). For 10 years, repeat the operation nine more times.

Of course, these will only be rough estimates since no one has a crystal ball. If your daughter were to start Spelman five years from now, the first year would cost roughly $66,993. By the time she is a junior, the projected cost would be $72,112. To figure out the grand total, multiply the cost of junior year by four. This is a rough projection of the cost of a four-year education. At Spelman five years from now, a college education will cost about $288,447. At Stanford or Yale, the bill will most likely exceed $475,000.

Now don't faint just yet. This is a great deal of money, but first of all, there's a lot of financial aid out there—and the majority of this book will be devoted to showing you how to get that financial aid. Second of all, you still have time to plan, save, and invest—and because of the joys of compounding, your investments can grow much faster than you might believe possible. Third, your earning power will most likely increase over time.

In the rest of this chapter, you will find investment strategies for saving money for college. Try not to obsess about the total projected cost. The important thing is to begin.

When Do You Begin Saving?

Right now. The more time you give your investments to multiply, the better. Even if you can manage only a small amount each month, you will be surprised at how much you have put away by the end of the year, and even more surprised at how quickly that money multiplies.

The Joys of Compound Interest

Let's say that you had a pretty good year this year and were able to save $5,000. Sound like too much? Okay, let's say $4,000. You invest this money in a high-yield mutual fund. Some of these funds have been averaging a return of over 8% a year, but let's be more conservative and say you get a 7% rate of return, which you plow back into the fund. Don't like mutual funds? That's fine. If you are uncomfortable with this level of risk, we'll be discussing other investment vehicles a little later. This is just an example to show you how investments grow.

The calculation is actually the same one we used to figure out what college would cost in the future. To find out how much $4,000 would earn in one year at 7%, multiply $4,000 times 1.07.

$$\$4,000 \times 1.07 = \$4,280$$

To find the value of the investment over five years, repeat this calculation four more times ($4,280 × 1.07 = 4,580; $4,580 × 1.07 = $4,900; etc.) In five years, your original $4,000 will be worth $5,610. In 10 years, it will have grown to $7,869. Not bad, especially when you consider that this comes from only one year of saving.

Of course, this example is a little simplified. One or two of those years might be bad years and the fund might not pay 7%. Other years might be extremely good years and the yield could be much higher. There are tax implications to consider as well. However, $7,869 is a reasonable forecast of what one $4,000 investment could be worth in ten years.

And if you continued to invest another $4,000 each year for the next ten years, with the same rate of return—well, now we're talking real money. At the end of ten years, you would have a college fund in excess of $59,134.

A Young Couple Just Starting Out

Let's take the fictional couple David and Carmen, who have a daughter who is now seven years old. David and Carmen are pretty young, and they can't afford to save much, but they decide they can manage $1,000 a year. They invest the $1,000 in a mutual fund with an average return of 8%, which they reinvest in the fund. By the time their daughter is ready to go to college in ten years, that first $1,000 has become $2,159. Each year, they invest another $1,000. The money they invest the second year has only nine years to grow, but it is still worth $1,999 by the time their child is ready for college. The money they invest the third year has only eight years to grow, but is still worth $1,850.

If Carmen and David invest $1,000 a year in this manner for ten years, they will have built a college fund of $15,645. Of course this is not enough to pay the entire cost of college, but there are several factors we haven't taken into account yet:

- No one is asking them to pay the entire amount. If David and Carmen aren't earning big money by the time the college years arrive, they may qualify for significant amounts of financial aid.

- David and Carmen might begin earning more money over the next ten years. Promotions and/or raises could allow them to save more than $1,000 per year as time goes on.

- The couple may have been able to make other investments as well (such as buying a house), against which they can borrow when their daughter is in college.

- During the college years, David and Carmen may be able (in fact are expected) to pay some of the cost of college from their current income.

Timing

Because of the way compounding works, it would be better, in theory, to make your largest contributions to a college investment fund in the early years when the investment has the most time to grow. Unfortunately the reality of the situation is that a couple just getting started often doesn't have that kind of money.

If you get a windfall—an inheritance, a large bonus, a year with a lot of overtime—by all means put that money to work for you. However, for most parents, it will be a matter of finding the money to invest here and there.

Many financial advisors recommend an automatic deduction plan, in which a certain amount of money is automatically deducted from your paycheck or your bank account each month. Parents often find that if the money simply disappears before they have time to spend it, the process of saving is less painful.

Should Money Be Put in the Child's Name?

One of the most important decisions you will have to make is whether to put the college fund in your own name or in your child's name.

There are some tax advantages to putting the money in your child's name, but there can also be some terrible financial aid disadvantages. Let's look at the tax advantages first.

Each year a parent is allowed to make a gift of up to $19,000 per parent per child. Depending upon the state in which you live, funds in such "custodial accounts" will be governed by the Uniform Gift to Minors Act (UGMA) or the Uniform Transfer to Minors Act (UTMA). Thus, if you live in a two-parent household, you can give up to $38,000 per year to your child, without gift-tax consequences. This is not a $38,000 tax deduction for you, but neither is it $38,000 in taxable income to the child. You have merely shifted money from you to your child. From now on, some of the interest that money earns will be taxed not at the parents' rate, but at the child's rate, which is almost always much lower.

The child is not allowed to have control over the account until the age of 21 (or 18 in some states). By the same token, you are not allowed to take that money back either. The money can be spent only on behalf of the child. You could use the money to pay for an SAT prep course, or braces, say, but not on the rent or a vacation to Hawaii—even if you took the child along.

Of course, if this gift is being made as part of a fund for college, this should be no problem. You don't plan to touch it until your son or daughter is ready to enroll anyway. You can shift the money between different investments, or even give it to a financial planner to invest.

Years ago, many parents and other relatives—especially those in the higher tax brackets—found it beneficial to shift their funds into a child's name so that the unearned income (i.e., interest, dividends, and capital gains) would be taxed at the child's presumably lower tax rate. To thwart this income-shifting strategy, Congress passed legislation that would tax some of this unearned income of younger children at a parent's rate once such unearned income in a given tax year passed a certain threshold amount. In the tax years 2006 and 2007, this tax on the unearned income of a minor child at the parent's tax rate—often referred to as the "Kiddie Tax"—applied to children under the age of 18 at the end of the tax year. For a child 18 and older, none of the money in the custodial account was taxed at the parent's rate. (Prior to 2006, age 14 was the magic number. But Congress tinkered with the rules to prevent more families from shifting unearned income into a lower tax bracket.) To avoid the kiddie tax rules, many parents invested custodial account money in growth stocks, which would presumably appreciate in value but pay small dividends. Then, after the child reached the age when the rules no longer applied, they would sell the stock and generate a capital gain which would then be taxed solely at the child's rate. In years past, this was a very effective strategy, especially since capital gains have been taxed recently at a lower rate than most other types of income. However, when Congress realized that the tax rate on capital gains (and qualified dividends) would drop to zero in 2008 for those in the lowest tax bracket, they passed a new (and far more complicated) kiddie tax in May 2007 that became effective January 1, 2008, in order to close this loophole. Then in 2017, Congress tinkered with rules again, taxing the excess above the threshold using the trust and estate tax rates, only to revert back in 2019 to the pre-2017 rules beginning with the 2020 tax year. So that's the backstory. Here are the latest rules:

For a child under the age of 18 at the end of the year: As long as the custodial account generates less than $1,350 per year in interest or dividend income and there is no other income, there will be no income tax due at all. As long as the custodial account generates less than $2,700 in income and there is no other income, the excess over $1,350 will be taxed at the child's rate (0% to 10% federal depending on the type of unearned income). Once the child's unearned taxable income exceeds the $2,700 cap, the excess will be taxed at the parents' higher rate, which can go up as high as 37% federal. State and local taxes will push this even higher.

For a child who is age 18 at the end of the year: The same rules apply as with younger children, though it is possible to avoid the kiddie tax if the child has earned income (e.g., wages, salary, income from self-employment) that exceeds half of her support.

For a child who is age 19 to 23 at the end of the year: If the child is unable to meet the "more than half support" rule, the kiddie tax will still apply if the child is a full-time student for at least five months during the year. (While there may still be some clarification before the end of the year about what constitutes a "month," other provisions of the tax code related to months of attendance in school have viewed enrollment for even one day in a particular month to be considered the same as if the student is enrolled for the entire month.) Given this increased age limit, it is possible that some students—including younger graduate students—who escaped the kiddie tax for a few years due to their age may again be subject to it. And if the child has not yet reached age 24 by the end of the year, it makes no difference whether the child is claimed as a dependent or not on a parent's tax return.

So if you wish to avoid the kiddie tax, you would want to have some investments generate a little less than $2,700 in income per year, and the remaining funds allocated to investment instruments that generated little or no income. For example: if your child's college fund was paying 4% interest, the fund could contain $67,500, and the interest the money earned would still be taxed at the child's rate. As the fund gets larger than $67,500, some of the interest would begin to be taxed at your rate. It is important to note that there are other rules that apply if the child has both earned and unearned income.

Even with these new, more restrictive rules, it is still possible to achieve some tax savings by putting money in the child's name. Unfortunately, because of the regulations under which financial aid is dispensed, putting any money in the kid's name can be a very expensive mistake.

If You Have Any Hope of Financial Aid, *Never* Put Money in the Child's Name

When you apply for financial aid, you will complete a need analysis form, which tells the colleges your current income, your child's income, your assets, and your child's assets. The colleges will assess these amounts to decide how much you can afford to pay for college. Under the federal formula, your income will be assessed up to 47%. Your assets will be assessed up to 5.65%.

However, your *child's* income will be assessed at up to 50% and your *child's* assets will be assessed at a whopping 20%. A college fund of $40,000 under *your* name would be assessed (as an asset) for up to $2,260 the first year of college. That is to say, the college would expect you to put as much as $2,260 of that money toward the first year of school.

The same fund under your child's name would be assessed for $8,000.

That's a big difference. You might say, "Well that money was supposed to be for college anyway," and you would be right—but remember, the colleges aren't just assessing *that* money. They will assess 20% of *all* of the child's assets, up to 5.65% of the parents' assets, up to 50% of the child's income, and up to 47% of the parents' income. By putting that money in the child's name, you just gave them a lot more money than you had to.

We've already noted the similarities between a college financial aid office and the IRS. Both see it as their duty to use the rules to get as much money as possible from you. It is up to you to use those same rules to keep as much money as possible away from them. It is an adversarial relationship, but as long as both sides stick to the rules, a fair one.

If you are going to qualify for financial aid, you should never, ever put money in the child's name. It is like throwing the money away. You've worked too hard to save that money to watch it get swallowed up in four giant gulps. By putting the money in the parents' name, you keep control over it. If you choose to, you can use it all, or not use it all, on your timetable.

The College Board made a number of significant changes to the Institutional Methodology (IM) starting with the 2000–2001 academic year. The maximum assessment rates under the IM for the 2024–2025 award year were as follows: 25% of the child's assets, up to 5% of the parents' assets, up to 46% of the child's income, and up to 46% of the parents' income. However, since the 2024–2025 academic year, the College Board no longer makes such rates public. It seems though that these percentages will still be applicable.

What If You're Pretty Sure You Won't Qualify for Aid?

If you are certain you won't qualify for aid, then you're free to employ every tax-reducing strategy your accountant can devise, including putting assets in the kid's name. But be very certain. People are often amazed at how much money you have to make in order NOT to qualify for aid.

In the introduction we told you about a family who received financial aid despite huge assets. Parents always want to know exactly what the cutoff is. Unfortunately, it is not as simple as that. Each family is a separate case. Don't assume that just because your friend didn't qualify for aid that you won't either. There are so many variables it is impossible to say the cutoff is precisely *X* dollars. It just doesn't work that way.

If you are close to the beginning of the college years and you want to figure out if you qualify for aid, read the rest of this book and then use the worksheets in Part Five to calculate your Student Aid Index. There is really no shortcut. We have seen articles that give you a simple chart on which you can look up your SAI. These charts are much too simplistic to be of any real use. We've also seen a number of websites with errors.

And as you'll soon discover, there are strategies you can employ to increase your chances of receiving aid.

What If You Aren't Sure Whether You'll Qualify for Aid?

If your child is a number of years away from their first year of college, your dilemma is much more difficult. How can you predict how much you'll have in 5 years or 15 years? For safety, it would be better to avoid putting large sums of money in the child's name until you are sure you won't be eligible for aid.

Once the money is put into the child's name, it is extremely difficult to put it back in the parents' name. If you set up a custodial account sometime in the past and have come to regret it, consult a very good financial consultant or tax lawyer who is also knowledgeable about financial aid.

Now that you've decided whose name to put the money under, let's talk about what kind of investments you can make.

What Types of Investments to Choose for a College Fund

The key to any investment portfolio is diversity. You will want to spread your assets among several different types of investments with varying degrees of risk. When your child is young, you will probably want to keep a large percentage of your money in higher-risk investments in order to build the value of the portfolio. As you get closer to the college years, it is a good idea to shift gradually into less volatile and more liquid investments. By the time the first year of college arrives, you should have a high percentage of cash invested in short-term treasuries, CDs, or money market funds.

To stay ahead of inflation over the long term, there is no choice but to choose more aggressive investments. Despite the recent declines, most experts still agree that the stock market is your best bet for long-term high yields. However, as we saw in 2022 and 2026, there can be significant volatility with stock prices. Yet it is worth noting that over the past 40 years, in spite of various bear markets, recessions, crashes, and acts of God, stocks have, on average, outperformed every other type of investment.

Stock Mutual Funds

Rather than buying individual stocks, you can spread your risk by buying shares in a mutual fund that manages a portfolio of many different stocks. You can go online to check how mutual funds are performing. In general, we recommend no-load or low-load funds that charge a sales commission of 4.5% or less. The minimum investment in mutual funds varies widely, but often you can start with as little as $1,000. Many of the large mutual fund companies control a few different funds and allow you to switch from one type of fund to another or even to a regular money market fund without charge. In this way, you can move in and out of investments as events change, just by making a phone call.

You can spread your risk even further by purchasing stock mutual funds that specialize in several different areas. By putting some of your money into a blue-chip fund and some into whatever you think will soon be hot, you can hedge your bets.

It should be noted that over the past several years, individuals who never invested in the stock market before have been putting money into mutual funds in an effort to earn a higher return than the current rates offered on CDs and savings accounts. We would just like to add our cautionary voice to the chorus of experts who have been warning the public that investing in mutual funds is not the same thing as having money in the bank.

High-Yield Bonds

Another aggressive investment to consider is high-yield bonds. For high yield, read "junk." Junk bonds, which pay a high rate of interest because they carry a high level of risk, helped to bring the boom-boom decade of the 1980s to its knees. However, if purchased with care, these bonds can get you a very high rate of return for moderate risk. The best way to participate in this market is to buy shares in a high-yield bond fund. The bonds are bought by professionals who presumably know what they are doing, and again, because the fund owns many different types of bonds, the risk is spread around.

Normal-Yield Bonds

If you want less risk, you might think about buying investment-grade bonds (rated at least AA) which can be bought so that they mature just as your child is ready to begin college. If you sell bonds before they mature, the price may vary quite a bit, but at maturity, bonds pay their full face value and provide the expected yield, thus guaranteeing you a fixed return. At present, the total annual return on this type of bond, if interest is reinvested, can top 4.0%.

One way of avoiding having to reinvest interest income is to buy zero-coupon bonds. You purchase a zero-coupon at far below its face value. On maturity, it pays you the full face value of the bond. You receive no interest income from the bond along the way; instead the interest you would have received is effectively reinvested at a guaranteed rate of return. You still have to pay tax every year on the "imputed interest," but the rate of return on zero-coupons can be substantial.

EE Savings Bonds

If you don't earn too much money, Series EE Savings Bonds offer an interesting option for college funds as well. The government a few years ago decided that if an individual over 24 years of age with low to moderate income purchases EE Savings Bonds after 1989 with the intention of using them to pay for college, the interest received at the time of redemption of the bonds will be tax-free. The interest earned is completely tax-free for a single parent with income up to $101,800 or a married couple filing jointly with income up to $152,650. Once you hit those income levels, the benefits are slowly phased out. A single parent with income above $116,800 or a married couple with income above $182,650 is not eligible for any tax break. All of these numbers are based on 2026 tax rates and are subject to an annual adjustment for inflation. EE Savings Bonds are issued by the federal government, and are as safe as any investment can be. They can also be purchased in small denominations without paying any sales commission.

However, EE Savings Bonds have several drawbacks. One is their low rate of return. You might do better with a taxable investment that pays a higher rate, even after taxes. It is also hard to predict in advance what your income level will be when you cash in the bonds. If your income has risen past the cutoff level for the tax break, your effective rate of return on the bonds just plunged into the low single digits. To make it worse, the IRS adds the interest from the bonds to your income *before* they determine whether you qualify for the tax break. Finally, whether the interest from these bonds is taxed or untaxed, it will still be considered income by the colleges and will be assessed just like your other income.

Tax-Free Municipal Bonds

Those families that are in the 22% income tax bracket (or higher) may be tempted to invest in tax-free municipal bonds. If you factor in the tax savings, the rate of return can approach 6%. As usual, you can reduce your risk by buying what is called a tax-free muni fund. These come in different varieties, with different degrees of risk.

One thing to be aware of is that while the IRS does not tax the income from these investments, the colleges effectively do. Colleges call tax-exempt interest income "untaxable income" and assess it just the way they assess taxable income. If you're eligible for aid, the real effective yield of munis will be pushed down by these assessments.

Trusts

Establishing a trust for your child's education is another way to shift assets and income to the child. Trusts have all the tax advantages of putting assets in the child's name—and then some; they allow more aggressive investment than do custodial accounts; they also give you much more control over when and how your child gets the money.

The drawbacks of trusts are that they are initially expensive to set up, costly to maintain, and very difficult to change—more important, they also jeopardize your chances of qualifying for financial aid.

If you have no chance of receiving aid, a trust fund can be an excellent way to provide money for college. There are many different kinds of trusts, but all involve you (called the grantor) transferring assets to another party (called the trustee) to manage and invest on behalf of your child (called the beneficiary). Typically, the trustee is a bank, financial advisor, or a professional organization chosen by you. You can design the trust so that your child will receive the money in a lump sum just as she enters college, or so that it is paid out in installments during college, or so that the child receives only the interest income from the trust until she reaches an age selected by you. Trusts must be set up with care to envision all eventualities because once they are in place, they are almost impossible to change. When you create the trust, you essentially give up the right to control it.

The tax advantage of a trust over a simple custodial account is that the trust pays its own separate income tax at its own tax bracket. Not the child's bracket. Not yours. This is especially useful when the child is under the age of 24: a regular custodial account of any significant size would most likely be taxed at the parents' higher rate due to the "kiddie tax."

The investment advantage of a trust is that there is no limit on the type of investment instrument that may be used. Unlike custodial accounts, which are not allowed to invest in certain types of instruments, a trust can dabble in real estate, junk bonds, or any newfangled scheme the investment bankers can invent.

Obviously, trusts must be set up with care, and you have to find a suitable trustee; someone you can, well, trust. Parents should never try to set up a trust on their own. If you are considering this strategy, consult a good tax attorney.

Financial Aid and Trusts

For various reasons, financial aid and trusts do not mix. It is partly the "rich kid" image that trust funds engender in the FAOs, and partly certain intricacies of the financial aid formulas, that we will describe in more detail in Chapter Three of this book. A trust of any size may very well nix any chance your family has of receiving aid.

Qualified State Tuition Programs (529 Plans)

Forty-nine states—all except Wyoming—and the District of Columbia now offer special programs that are designed to help families plan ahead for college costs. These Qualified State Tuition Programs, which are more commonly called Section 529 plans (after the relevant section of the Internal Revenue Code), come in two basic forms: tuition prepayment plans and tuition savings accounts. Most states offer one type or the other, but a number of states offer or will soon offer both. Some plans have residency requirements for the donor and/or beneficiary. Others (like California) will allow anyone to participate. While some states limit who can contribute funds to the plan (usually the parents and grandparents), other states have no such restrictions. And with some plans, it is possible for the contributor to name herself as the beneficiary as well.

With some states, the buildup in value is partially or entirely free of state income taxes (provided the beneficiary is a resident of that state). Most plans allow you to make payments in a lump sum or on an installment basis. In some states, these payments can be automatically deducted from your bank account—or even your paycheck, provided your employer agrees to participate.

With some plans, contributions are partially tax-deductible for the donor as well. For example, New York gives its residents up to a $5,000 deduction (up to $10,000 for joint filers) on the state income tax return for amounts contributed during a particular tax year. Many states have added some unique features to their plans.

Years ago, the prepaid tuition plans used to be a rotten deal as the funds could only be used in-state and normally only for public colleges and universities. Otherwise, you got your money back with little or no interest. But now, many of these state-sponsored plans have become more flexible, letting you take money out-of-state or to a private university in your own state. A major benefit of these prepayment plans is the peace of mind that comes from knowing that no matter how much tuition inflation there is, you've already paid for a certain number of course credits at the time of purchase. This peace of mind was rather costly during the Wall Street boom when returns on stocks far exceeded the rate of tuition inflation. However, given the recent volatility in the stock market and the reduced rates of return on CDs and bonds, the prepaid plans have regained some of their luster. So while many investment advisors still tell families they are better off avoiding these prepaid plans and funding the college nest egg using other investment vehicles which are likely to earn a higher rate of return, the prepaid plans are something to consider if the student will start college in the next few years.

Under the old tax laws, you had to pay federal income taxes on the difference between the initial investment and the value of the course credits when they were redeemed, but such investment income was taxed at the beneficiary's presumably lower tax rate. Starting in 2002, there are no longer any federal income taxes involved, provided the funds are used to cover qualified higher education expenses (i.e., tuition and fees as well as allowances for room and board) at a federally accredited school, which includes most U.S.-based four-year colleges and universities, many two-year programs and vocational schools, and even some foreign schools.

Note: Given the high rate of tuition inflation at public universities, some prepaid plans have temporarily or permanently stopped accepting contributions or have added a premium onto the current price for each credit purchased.

Unlike the prepaid plans, the state-sponsored tuition savings accounts do not guarantee to meet tuition inflation. A major benefit over traditional investment options is that earnings in these accounts grow tax-deferred from a federal standpoint. Just as with the prepaid plans, withdrawals from these accounts for qualified educational expenses are now also completely free of federal income taxes. (Under the old law, the prorated share of the withdrawal that represented investment income—and not the original investment—was subject to tax at the beneficiary's rate.) The funds in these plans are invested by professional managers. But if you choose to put some or all of the funds into any equity-based investment option that is offered, you could lose part of your initial investment. Just as with the prepaid plans, a number of states do not consider part or all of the earnings as income on a resident beneficiary's state tax return.

Most of these tuition savings plans offer the choice of an age-based asset allocation model to determine how your funds will be invested. This means that the younger the child, the greater the percentage of the principal is invested in equities. As the child grows older, the percentage of equities falls, and the percentage of assets in bonds, money markets, and other fixed-income investments increases. The allocation models can vary tremendously from plan to plan. Besides the age-based models, most plans have other investment options that vary in the degrees of risk.

Most prepaid plans and tuition savings accounts allow you to change beneficiaries—which just means you can switch money you might have earmarked for one child to another child—or even to another family member. You'll need to read the fine print if you envision actually trying this, because there are tax consequences if the new beneficiary is of a different generation. With the savings plans, you'll also want to find out whether or not the asset allocation model will change to reflect the age of the new beneficiary. For example, if your oldest child decides not to go to college and you decide to transfer the funds to her kid brother, you would want to be sure that the mix of investments will be changed to reflect the age of the younger beneficiary. Otherwise, your nest egg may be invested mostly in money market funds for a number of years.

Another benefit of these Section 529 plans, from an estate-planning standpoint, is that a person can contribute up to $95,000 in one lump sum to any one beneficiary's plan, provided you do not make any further gifts to that person for the next five years (and provided the state's plan permits contributions of this size). So, in effect, you are being allowed to use the $19,000 annual gift allowance for the next five years and accelerate it into one lump sum. This allows a contributor to remove up to five years' worth of income and growth on the contributed funds from her estate. Of course, if the contributor dies before the five-year period has elapsed, there could be estate tax consequences.

Coverdell ESAs

These special educational savings accounts were originally called Education IRAs, even though they were never really retirement accounts. While contributions to these accounts (currently up to $2,000 per year per child under age 18) are not tax deductible, any withdrawals used for post-secondary education will be totally tax-free. While there are income limits that affect your ability to contribute to such an account—for 2025, this benefit phases out between $190,000 and $220,000 for married couples filing jointly, and between $95,000 and $110,000 for others—the law does not specify that contributions must be made by the beneficiary's parents. Other relatives or even friends who fall below the income cutoffs could presumably contribute. However, for 2025, no child can receive more than $2,000 in deposits to a Coverdell ESA in a given tax year from all contributors combined. But before you rush to fund one of these accounts, you should realize that the U.S. Department of Education currently views such accounts to be the asset of the student if the student is the owner of the account and also an independent student. In most cases, the parent will be the owner as long as the beneficiary is a minor, so this will not be a big problem. However, the situation gets tricky once the student reaches majority. Unless an election was made to keep the parent as owner after that point, the fund would then become student-owned, and could be assessed at the 20% federal financial aid assessment rate if the student is independent. Under the institutional methodology, any Coverdell owned by the student is considered a student asset.

Note: The current tax law permits tax-free withdrawals to cover certain qualified expenses from kindergarten through the senior year of high school including, but not limited to, private school tuition, certain computer equipment and software, as well as internet access. So if you are otherwise eligible for financial aid for college, you should consider withdrawing funds from Coverdells to cover these expenses as well as any qualified higher education expenses if ***a)*** *the ownership will soon revert to the student and* ***b)*** *the student is either applying for financial aid at a school that requires completion of the CSS Profile or is an independent student. (Check with the financial institution where you have the account if you are not sure who owns the account and when, if ever, the ownership changed or will change to the student in the future.) In this way, student assets in the aid formulas will be minimized.*

Sunrise . . . But No Sunset

Coverdell ESAs and Section 529s are wonderful ways to save money for college, but for years there had been a couple of important question marks about these programs. This was because some key provisions of the federal tax law pertaining to these programs had been scheduled to expire—or "sunset"—on Dec. 31, 2012. The good news is that these uncertainties have gone away as the American Taxpayer Relief Act, which became law in January 2013, made permanent some of the enhancements to Coverdells that were made in 2001. So for the time being, these enhancements will continue to be available:

- The annual contribution limits for Coverdells will continue to be $2,000 per beneficiary per year.

- Withdrawals from Coverdells for certain expenses other than college tuition and fees (i.e., elementary and secondary school tuition, certain computer-related expenses, internet access) will continue to be tax-free.

- In a given tax year, a child can continue to receive contributions to both a Coverdell and a 529 plan.

- Any tax-free distribution from a child's Coverdell will not automatically eliminate one's ability to claim certain Federal educational tax credits (i.e., the American Opportunity Credit, the Hope Credit, or the Lifetime Learning Credit) for that child in the same tax year. However, in order to be able to claim the full credit and have all the distributions from a Coverdell and/or 529 plan be tax-free, any funds paid for that child's tuition for purposes of claiming the credit cannot be coming from a Coverdell, a 529 plan, or other tax-advantaged funds used to pay for college. This is because federal tax law does not currently permit one to claim two or more educational tax benefits with the same funds used to pay for tuition. So to be able to claim the tax credit AND have the distributions from a Coverdell and/or a 529 plan be completely tax-free, some funds to pay for the student's tuition will have to come from your cash and/or your checking, savings, and/or money market account(s) and/or be paid with the proceeds of a loan.

It's anyone's guess what will happen in the future—which makes decisions down the road difficult. For example, if you think the law will change, and you're likely to qualify for the American Opportunity Credit (which allows you to reduce your taxes based on money you've spent on college tuition for your child), then it would not be a good idea to make any more contributions to a Coverdell. In addition, if you believe the laws will change and you want to plan ahead to reduce any existing funds in a Coverdell, you should then consider paying for other qualified educational expenses—such as private elementary or secondary school tuition, computer equipment, etc.—which are currently permitted.

Because of all the fine print in these plans, and the possibility that the tax law may change, we suggest you consult with a competent advisor before contributing any funds to these plans or making any withdrawals.

Look Before You Leap

Even though those provisions regarding 529 plans and Coverdells in the tax law did NOT sunset in December 2012, there are still a number of potential pitfalls that you should be aware of before you sign up for these plans—or have any well-intentioned relatives do the same. And unfortunately, while the brochures for these plans might make you think they are the best things to come along since sliced bread, the promotional materials are often light on specifics—especially the drawbacks.

The Financial Aid Impact of These Plans There are two possible impacts on financial aid involving 529 savings plans, 529 pre-paid plans and Coverdells. First there is the impact, if any, with the value of the particular plan being considered as an asset. For 529 savings plans and the Coverdells, the value is simply determined by the dollar amount in the plan. For 529 pre-paid plans, the value is the dollar value of the tuition credits. Secondly, the distributions or tuition credits redeemed from any 529 plan or Coverdell in a base income year can also potentially have an impact on financial aid.

What impact, if any, the value of the plan or any distribution from the plan will have on aid is primarily determined by who owns the plan, not by the beneficiary of the plan. For financial aid, there are three types of owners: the student, a parent or stepparent of the student required to report (step)parent financial information on the aid form, or "someone else" (for example, a grandparent, aunt or uncle, or potentially a parent or stepparent not required to report their information on the aid form). Each category of ownership can have a different potential impact on aid that we will discuss shortly. However, for distributions, the impact of aid can also be affected by whether a qualified or non-qualified distribution is made—as well as who owns the plan. Qualified distributions involve those assets withdrawn or tuition credits redeemed to pay qualified educational expenses. (IRS Publication 970 explains all the fine print.) Funds withdrawn for other purposes are considered non-qualified distributions, which will trigger tax consequences and reportable income that will raise one's gross income. On top of these considerations just mentioned, the federal methodology and the institutional methodology are similar in some ways, but different in others, in terms of how the asset value as well as any distributions are treated. Here's the scoop for different scenarios:

529 plans and Coverdells owned by the parent for the benefit of a child are the most common, so let's discuss them first. These plans normally have account titles that mention language with the NAME OF THE PARENT FBO THE NAME OF THE BENEFICIARY; the letters FBO are short for "For Benefit Of." In terms of the asset value of these plans, the Federal Methodology (FM) and the Institutional Methodology (IM) had both treated plans owned by a parent (or step-parent) of a dependent student who is required to report parent financial information on the aid forms the same way prior to FAFSA Simplification. Namely, the value of any plan owned by such a (step)parent was to be considered an asset regardless of the beneficiary. But with Simplification came confusion and disagreement as to how 529 plans and Coverdells would be treated in the 2024–2025 federal methodology. The FAFSA Simplification legislation itself basically kept the treatment of Coverdells and 529 plans to be the same as before, including a longstanding exception to the rules regarding certain accounts for the benefit of the student seeking aid. However, during the summer of 2023, the Department of Education announced in effect that the exception to the rule had become the rule. Therefore, accounts owned by an applicant's parent for the benefit of others (besides the student completing the FAFSA) were no longer required to be reported as part of the parent's assets on the 2024–2025 FAFSA. In effect, only accounts for the benefit of the applicant were to be reported. Since this policy did not follow the law, there was much disagreement in the aid community. Yet when the 2024–2025 FAFSA was released, the feds stuck to their previously announced guidance.

Preliminary statements by the USDOE that this policy would remain in effect for the 2027–2028 FAFSA raised comments by some influential aid organizations requesting that the FAFSA Simplification law be followed as originally written. Because of lingering uncertainty and the fact that the final version of the 2027–2028 FAFSA had not yet been released when we went to press, we recommend:

1. If you are completing the 2027–2028 FAFSA you should carefully read its accompanying instructions regarding how various 529 and Coverdells are to be reported (or excluded).

2. You should not assume that such accounts owned for the benefit of siblings or family members other than the applicant will not be considered reportable assets on the FAFSA for the 2027–2028 award year and beyond. As such, you should hold off switching accounts for the benefit of the applicant to other beneficiaries as a strategy to shelter assets from assessment. Better to wait and let the dust settle.

3. If you are completing the CSS Profile, be aware that the institutional methodology continues to treat Coverdells and 529 plans for the benefit of anyone as an asset of the owner of such accounts regardless of the beneficiary.

Now we'll cover how the value of any such plan "owned by the student" will be considered. We are not talking about who is the beneficiary of the plan. These plans are normally established when funds are transferred from a regular custodial account (UTMA or UGMA) and deposited into a 529 plan, which is why such student-owned plans for a minor are often referred to as "custodial 529 plans."

These 529s will have account titles such as NAME OF THE INDIVIDUAL ACF THE NAME OF THE MINOR CHILD with the letters ACF short for "As Custodian For." The account title will also usually mention UTMA or UGMA and the name of a state. As noted earlier, besides such student-owned custodial 529 plans, there can be Coverdells that become student-owned accounts if an election was never made to retain the person funding the account as the owner once the student reaches a certain age.

With these student-owned plans, the FM and IM differ in their treatment. Under the FM the asset is considered a student asset if the student is not required to report parental financial information on the FAFSA (i.e., the student is classified as an independent student). But if the student is a dependent student required to report parent information on the FAFSA, then such student-owned accounts will be considered a parent asset in the FM. However, the IM views such a student-owned account as a student asset. Being mindful that student assets are assessed at a higher rate than parent assets in the aid form, it is best to avoid such student-owned accounts.

And now we'll discuss accounts owned by someone else who is not required to report their information on the FAFSA (such as a grandparent). The values of these plans do not need to be reported on the FAFSA as an asset. However, depending on the college(s) involved, the CSS Profile or other institutional aid forms may ask questions about such plans. Besides the value of the plan, such plans owned by someone else can involve issues related to the distributions from such plans. For versions of the FAFSA covering the academic year 2023–2024 and earlier, the amount of the distributions from such plans made in a base income year prior to 2022 (i.e., a base income year prior to the 2022 base year for the 2024–2025 FAFSA) had been considered untaxed income to the student that could reduce aid by as much as 50 cents on the dollar in the FM. However, under a provision of the FAFSA Simplification legislation that took effect beginning with the 2024–2025 FAFSA, any distributions after December 31, 2021 from such plans owned by others will no longer be considered untaxed income for the base year to be reported on the FAFSA. (Note that the IM never considered such distributions from others as untaxed income to the student, even when the FM did.)

Don't jump for joy just yet. The jury is still out as to whether or not such distributions from such accounts owned by others will be considered a "resource" by a particular school. If a school views these funds coming from 529s owned by others as a resource, that could then reduce need-based aid eligibility dollar-for-dollar for the academic year when the distribution is made. The logic is that the student and others required to report their financial information on the aid forms will still be expected to contribute X amount based on their situation. Distributions from plans owned by someone else will be treated as a type of outside aid that will replace some or all of the aid initially offered. Since this can be complicated and there are strategies that can be employed based on one's own unique situation to avoid this potentially chilling effect on aid, it would be best to consult a professional prior to any such distribution being made. This is especially applicable if larger distribution amounts are involved and the student has been offered significant need-based grants or scholarships that do not need to be paid back.

Fortunately, situations involving distributions from such plans owned by the student or a (step) parent required to report their information on the aid forms are much more straightforward compared to distributions from accounts owned by someone else. Any qualified tax-free distribution from these plans is not considered untaxed income in the aid formulas and will never be considered a resource that could reduce aid dollar-for-dollar. For any distributions that do not cover such qualified expenses, the amount of any non-qualified distributions will be considered taxable income. Depending on who is considered the recipient of any such nonqualified distribution (including those unqualified distributions from accounts owned by others) as well as the amount of other types of income received by that individual, there could be an impact on their financial aid in future years if the student or the (step)parent of such dependent student must report this extra income on a tax return during any base income year.

Some of the biggest mistakes students and their parents make when completing the aid forms involve the incorrect characterization of these plans. Some applicants mistakenly include the value of all accounts for the benefit of the student as a student asset on the aid forms, failing to take into account who owns the plan. This will overstate the student's assets and can have a chilling effect on aid. Others double-count such accounts, including the value of any plan as both a student asset and a parent asset. This will also overstate the value of the reported assets. These mistakes are not surprising since the instructions on many aid forms are anything but clear.

Keep in mind that the aid system is only geared to prevent a student from receiving more aid than they are eligible to receive under the existing rules and regulations. So no one is going to notify you to correct your mistake if you improperly listed information on the aid forms that results in your being eligible for less aid than is legally possible. So in this respect, the aid system does not work in the same manner as the income tax system. That is, the IRS or your state will notify you and increase the size of your refund (or reduce the amount of tax you owe the government) if any mathematical or other errors in your favor are detected when your tax return is processed. But the financial aid system only has audit checks in place to avoid one getting more aid than they should. Here's a chart of possible scenarios to help you avoid costly errors.

HOW VALUES FOR 529s & COVERDELLS ARE TREATED	
For accounts owned by a (step)parent required to report financial information on the FAFSA	
If owned for benefit of (FBO) the student completing the FAFSA:	
FAFSA	Considered a parent asset
CSS Profile	Considered a parent asset
If owned for benefit of (FBO) a family member other than that student:	
FAFSA	See 2027–2028 FAFSA instructions
CSS Profile	Considered a parent asset
For accounts owned by the student applying for aid (e.g., custodial 529 plans)	
If the student must report parental information on the FAFSA:	
FAFSA	Considered a parent asset
CSS Profile	Considered a student asset
If the student is not required to report parental information on the FAFSA:	
FAFSA	Considered a student asset*
CSS Profile	Considered a student asset*
*If applicable, a plan owned by the student's spouse is considered a student asset	
For FBO accounts owned by others not required to report financial information on the FAFSA	
FAFSA	Not required to be reported
CSS Profile	Not required to be reported unless specific questions asked on form**
**Any biological/adoptive parent not required to report financial information on the FAFSA who must complete their own CSS Profile or any other aid form will include the value as a parent investment	

Tax Implications If the funds are not used for the child's education or are withdrawn prematurely, the portion of the distribution that represents investment earnings will be taxed at the contributor's (presumably higher) rate, plus a 10% penalty. So if junior decides not to go to school, you'd better hope you can find some other qualified family member who can use the funds for school and take the necessary steps to change the beneficiary on the account. Otherwise your Uncle Sam is going to get a nice windfall. (There are exceptions if the beneficiary dies or receives a scholarship for college.)

You should also realize that both types of 529 plans (as well as Coverdells) can impact your ability to take advantage of other higher education benefits that can sometimes be more advantageous to claim.

Even though Congress, a number of years ago, voted to permanently extend the ability to withdraw funds from 529s free of federal income taxes, there are still some thorny issues regarding state income taxes—especially if you invest in a 529 plan sponsored by a state other than the state in which you (or the student) live.

Note: A handful of states will now grant a state tax deduction for contributions made to out-of-state 529 plans. So if you're choosing between an in-state and an out-of-state plan, you should see what benefits, if any, you're giving up by choosing an out-of-state program over your home state program.

The federal tax law currently permits one to withdraw up to $20,000 annually for qualified K–12 expenses from a 529 plan. However, there are still some unanswered issues that could cause such distributions to reduce college aid eligibility with such K–12 distributions. Depending on where you live and which state's plan you have, there may be some state tax issues as well.

Limited Control Over the Funds As we have just mentioned, once you contribute funds to these state-sponsored plans, there can be sizable penalties if the funds are withdrawn prematurely. With the state savings plan, after you make your initial contribution, you can only move those funds to another state's plan or change your investment allocation plan once every 12 months to avoid any penalties.

If the plan uses an age-based asset allocation model, you may also find your assets being automatically transferred to fixed-income investments just after a significant short-term market correction. Any sane money manager would postpone such a transfer for a few months—but with many of these plans, the manager may not have that option: the transfer is automatically triggered on a certain date.

And because you're tying up your money for a number of years and giving up control, there are a number of questions you should be asking yourself before you contribute one penny to one of these plans.

1. Which type of plan are you investing in? Some states offer only the pre-paid option. Some offer only a tuition savings account. Others offer both.

2. Is the plan offered in your own state superior to plans available in other states? Many tuition savings plans will accept contributions from out-of-state residents and you may prefer another state's asset-allocation model to the one in your home state.

3. If you invest in an out-of-state plan, what additional benefits are you giving up? Funds invested in your home state's plan may not impact state-funded financial aid programs and the earnings may be free of state taxes. A state income tax deduction may be limited to contributions to your own state's plan. So, if you invest out-of-state, you won't necessarily get a state income tax deduction. The student may also owe some state income taxes to his home state when the funds are withdrawn. (He may even owe some state income taxes to the state whose program was used.) Funds invested in an out-of-state plan may also hurt your eligibility for state-based student aid.

4. If you invest in a plan sold to you by a financial advisor or offered by your employer, is it the best deal around? Your financial advisor may not even mention the benefits of your own state's plan or other more attractive out-of-state plans simply because she doesn't sell those plans. In addition, similar 529 plans sold by advisors may carry higher fees than if you contacted the plan administrators directly. A plan offered through your job may not be your home state's plan so be sure to read the fine print.

5. If you decide to transfer the funds to another state's plan, are there any penalties involved? While you may be okay from a federal tax standpoint, you should understand that many states have begun to implement their own penalties in response to the rather liberal federal transfer rules currently in effect. For example, New York residents who claimed a tax deduction on their state tax return by contributing to the New York Saves 529 plan will have to recapture (add back) the amount of that deduction to their state taxable income in the year they transfer those funds out of the Empire State.

6. Is the plan an approved Section 529 plan? Some states begin accepting contributions on newly announced plans before the IRS rules on the matter. You want to be sure that you qualify for the federal tax-deferred status before you lock up your funds.

7. What asset allocation model are you comfortable with? For example, in New Hampshire, the age-based plan allows for 94.99% in equities for a newborn, versus the New York State plan which permits you to allocate 62.5%, 87.5%, or even 100% in equities for a similarly aged child depending on your risk tolerance level. Some states, such as California, let you choose among a number of investment options, including a social choice equity option.

8. What fees are charged by the investment managers? While you won't be sent a bill, such charges can significantly reduce the return on your investment. Although traditional mutual funds are required by law to disclose such charges, tuition savings plans are not—and often bury this information in a thick prospectus (which you may not even see unless you specifically ask for it). Fees can vary tremendously from state to state, and are often much higher than ordinary mutual funds.

9. What happens if you are on the installment plan and can no longer contribute? For example, if you lost your job and can't keep up with the payments, some programs might automatically cancel the contract and/or impose other penalties as well.

10. What is the likelihood you will move out of the state before college begins? If you are in a state prepaid program and then move to another state, most programs will only provide for tuition credits at the resident rates. You'll have to come up with the additional funds to cover the extra tuition charged to out-of-state students.

11. If you are investing in a prepaid plan, how will the state determine the amount of funds you'll receive if the student attends a college out of state? Some plans will use the dollar value of the credits at the public university based on the tuition charges for each academic year. Others simply use the total dollar value of all the credits at the start of the first academic year and then allocate one quarter of the value for each of the four years. In the latter case, your funds for the sophomore, junior, and senior year will stop increasing in value once the student begins freshman year, no matter how much tuition inflation subsequently occurs.

Do You Have a Crystal Ball?

Unless you can predict the future, you should carefully think and rethink any decision that completely locks yourself and your loved ones into an investment that will mature so many years into the future. Obviously, these plans make sense for many people, especially since the "kiddie tax" rules make custodial accounts less attractive. But because of all the fine print in each state's plan, you should know exactly what you're getting into and carefully review the prospectus to make sure it is right for you. Because of the various tax consequences involved, it would also be a good idea to discuss the plan with an accountant or financial planner before you make your first contribution as well.

The following is a listing of states that offer prepaid programs and/or tuition savings accounts along with telephone numbers. The type of program offered is indicated by a "P" for prepaid plans and an "S" for savings plans.

State	Program Type	Telephone
Alabama	P*	1-800-252-7228
	S	1-334-242-7500
Alaska	S	1-888-425-2752
Arizona	S	1-602-542-7529
Arkansas	S	1-800-587-7301; 1-888-529-9552
California	S	1-800-343-3548; 1-800-544-5248
Colorado	S	1-800-997-4295; 1-800-448-2424
Connecticut	S	1-888-799-2438
Delaware	S	1-800-544-1655
Florida	P	1-800-552-4723
	S	1-800-552-4723

State	Program Type	Telephone
Georgia	S	1-877-424-4377
Hawaii	S	1-866-529-3343
Idaho	S	1-866-433-2533
Illinois	P*	1-877-877-3724
	S	1-877-432-7444
Indiana	S	1-866-485-9415
Iowa	S	1-888-672-9116
Kansas	S	1-800-579-2203; 1-888-903-3863
Kentucky	S	1-877-598-7878
	P*	1-502-696-7613
Louisiana	S	1-800-259-5626
Maine	S	1-877-463-9843
Maryland	P*	1-888-463-4723
	S	1-888-463-4723
Massachusetts	P (U. Plan)	1-800-449-6332
	S (U. Fund)	1-800-544-2776
Michigan	P	1-517-335-4767
	S	1-877-861-6377
Minnesota	S	1-877-338-4646
Mississippi	P	1-800-987-4450
	S	1-800-987-4450
Missouri	S	1-888-414-6678
Montana	S	1-800-888-2723
Nebraska	S	1-888-993-3746
Nevada	P	1-888-477-2667
	S	1-800-587-7305; 1-800-531-8722; 1-866-734-4530
New Hampshire	S	1-800-544-1914; 1-800-544-1722
New Jersey	S	1-877-465-2378
New Mexico	S	1-877-337-5268
New York	S	1-877-697-2837
N. Carolina	S	1-800-600-3453
N. Dakota	S	1-866-728-3529
Ohio	S	1-800-233-6734
Oklahoma	S	1-877-654-7284
Oregon	S	1-503-373-1903; 1-866-772-8464
Pennsylvania	S (guaranteed savings)	1-800-440-4000
	S	1-800-294-6195; 1-800-440-4000

State	Program Type	Telephone
Rhode Island	S	1-888-324-5057
S. Carolina	S	1-888-244-5674
	P*	1-888-772-4723
S. Dakota	S	1-866-529-7462
Tennessee	S	1-855-386-7827
Texas	P (Tuition Promise)	1-800-445-4723
	S	1-800-445-4723
Utah	S	1-800-418-2551
Vermont	S	1-800-637-5860
Virginia	P	1-888-567-0540
	S	1-888-567-0540
Washington	P	1-800-955-2318
West Virginia	P*	1-866-574-3542
	S	1-866-574-3542
Wisconsin	S	1-888-338-3789
	S	1-866-677-6933
Wyoming		No plan available
District of Columbia	S	1-800-987-4859; 1-800-368-2745
* Closed to new enrollment		

A Supplementary Form of College Fund

Owning Your Own Home

If you can swing it, owning your own home is a top priority in any plan for paying for college. Equally important, building equity in your home provides you with collateral you can use to help pay for college.

In addition, owning your home provides you with an investment for your own future, which you should never lose sight of. When the kids rush off to embark on their own lives, clutching their diplomas, will there be something left for you? What good is a college education for the child if it puts the parents in the poorhouse?

The Home as a Credit Line?

No matter how well prepared, many families end up at some point having to borrow money to pay part of the family contribution. Unfortunately, the financial aid formula doesn't recognize most types of debt; that is to say, they do not subtract these liabilities from your assets before they decide how much in assets you have available to pay for college.

We will be explaining this in great detail in the chapters on financial aid strategies, but here's a quick example. Suppose you had $25,000 in assets, but you also owed $6,000 on a consumer loan. If you asked any accountant in the world, she would say your total net assets were only $19,000; but as far as the colleges are concerned, you still have $25,000 available for them to assess. Many kinds of debt (such as consumer loans and outstanding credit card bills) don't make sense during the college years.

However, the more selective colleges that elect to use the institutional methodology (which looks at home equity) rather than the federal methodology (which does not) do recognize one kind of debt—mortgages, first and second, on your home. This means that your home can be a particularly valuable kind of college fund. Generally, the more equity you have in your home, the more you can borrow against it. And the best part is that if your child attends a school that assesses home equity, and you borrow against your home, you reduce your total assets in the eyes of the FAOs, which can reduce how much you have to pay for college.

Remember to Invest in Other Things Besides Your Child's College Education

Providing a college education for your child is probably not the only ambition you have in life. During the years you are saving for college you should not neglect your other goals, particularly in two important areas: owning your own home (which we have just spoken about) and planning for your retirement.

While the colleges assess your assets and income, they generally don't assess retirement provisions such as Individual Retirement Accounts (IRAs), 401(k) plans, Keoghs, tax-deferred annuities, etc. Any money you have managed to contribute to a retirement provision will be off-limits to the FAOs at most schools.

These contributions to retirement plans not only help provide for your future but also will shelter assets (and the income from those assets) from the FAOs. In addition, many employers will match contributions to 401(k) plans, in effect doubling your stake. And let's not forget that, depending on your income level, part or all of these contributions may be tax-deferred.

Now that you have an overview of some long-term investment strategies, let's talk about some specific plans for investing based on how many years away your child is from college.

If You Have 15 Years . . .

Because there is so much time, you can afford to choose aggressive investments of the types we've outlined above. We recommend that you invest about 75% of your fund in these higher-risk investments, and the remaining 25% in investments that lock in a reliable rate of return. There is little point in keeping this money in a bank account because the rate of return will probably not even keep up with inflation. However, as the college years get closer, start transferring out of stock funds and into something less subject to temporary setbacks.

If possible, try to invest large amounts in the early years to take advantage of compounding. When you get closer to the first year of college, take a hard look at your college fund. You may find that you have already accumulated enough money to pay for school, in which case you can start investing your money in other directions. On the other hand, you may find that you need to increase the amounts you are saving in order to get closer to your goal.

With this much time to plan, you should consider long-term ways to increase your earning power. Perhaps you might go back to school to pick up an advanced degree. Perhaps if one parent is not working at present you could begin thinking about a long-term plan for setting up a career for that parent to increase your family's earning power.

As you get closer to the college years, you will need to consider other points. In order not to repeat ourselves too much, we will cover these points below. Please keep on reading.

If You Have 10 Years . . .

With 10 years to go, you still have plenty of time to build a sizable college fund. To build your capital quickly, try to save as much as you can in the first several years when compounding will help you the most. Aggressive investments will also help to build your fund quickly. We recommend that with 10 years to go, you keep 70% of your money in aggressive investments of the type outlined above. The other 30% can be put into fixed-return investments with limited risk. As you get closer to the first year of college, you should gradually shift your fund into investments with more liquidity and no risk.

Because your child's academic ability will have an important effect not only on which colleges he can apply to but also on what kind of aid package the college will offer you, it is vital that you find a good elementary school that challenges his abilities.

In spite of taxes, braces, and saving for college, do not neglect your own future. If you have the means to purchase a home, consider making that investment (in a good school district). Contributions to retirement provisions should also be made regularly.

Now is also the first time you can realistically speculate about how much money you might be earning by the time your child is in college. If you believe you will be earning too much to qualify for aid, it becomes even more important to build your college fund. If you are 100% certain you are not going to qualify for aid, you might want to put assets into the child's name.

As you get closer to the college years, you will need to consider other points. In order not to repeat ourselves too much, we will cover these points below. Please keep on reading.

If You Have Five Years . . .

There is still plenty of time to build up a large college fund. Even if it entails a sacrifice, a large contribution in the first year will help build your investment faster through the miracle of compounding. In the first year or so, you can still afford to invest aggressively, although we recommend that you keep only about 50% of your money in aggressive investments, with 30% in limited-risk fixed rate of return financial instruments and 20% in liquid accounts that are completely insured.

With about four years to go, reconsider whether you are going to qualify for financial aid. You may have received promotions, raises, inheritances, or made investments that take you out of range of financial aid. In this case, consider moving assets into the child's name. On the other hand, you may discover that you are doing less well than you anticipated, in which case you will want to start thinking about the strategies that are outlined in the rest of this book.

Find a great high school for your child and try to encourage good study habits. Good grades will increase your child's options tremendously. It's probably too early to tell, but try to get a sense of what type of school your child will be applying to, and how much that school will cost.

As you get to the last three years before college, you will need to consider other points. In order not to repeat ourselves too much, we will cover these points below. Please keep on reading.

If You Have Three Years . . .

Parents find that with the specter of college tuition looming imminently, they are able to save substantial amounts in only two years. After all, many parents are at the height of their earning power at this time. However, because you will need the money relatively soon, it is probably better to stay away from high-risk investments that may suffer a temporary (or permanent) setback just as you need to write a check.

These next academic years are the most important for your child. Sit down with him and explain (in as unpressured and nonjudgmental a tone as you can manage) that because colleges give preferential packaging to good students, every tenth of a point he adds to his grade point average may save him thousands of dollars in loans he won't have to pay back later.

If your child did not score well on the PSAT, consider finding a good test preparation course for the SAT. Several recent studies have shown that coaching can raise a student's score by over 100 points. Again, every ten points your child raises her score may save your family thousands of dollars—and of course allow her to apply to more selective colleges. We, of course, are partial to The Princeton Review SAT course. The same applies to the ACT test.

If you have any interest in running a business on the side, this may be the ideal moment to start setting it up. Most businesses show losses during their first few years of operation. What better time to have losses than during the tax years that affect your aid eligibility? There are also many tax benefits to this strategy, but the business cannot exist just on paper. For tax purposes, it must be run with the intention of showing a profit in order not to run afoul of the "hobby loss" provisions of the tax code. If this seems like it might be for you, please read our financial aid strategies section, and the section on running your own business in the chapter "Special Topics."

Maneuvering

The most important thing to realize is that at this point, you are one year away from the all-important base income year. Colleges now use the tax year two years *before* college begins (from January 1 of the student's sophomore year of high school to December 31 of the student's junior year in high school) as their basis for deciding what you can afford to pay as a first-year student.

Thus you have one year to maneuver before the base income year begins. Read the financial aid strategies that we outline in the rest of this book extremely carefully. After you have read these chapters and consulted an accountant or financial aid consultant, you may want to move some assets around, take capital gains, take bonuses before the base income year begins, and so on. During the base income year itself, you may want to make some major expenditures, pay down your credit card balances, establish a line of credit on your home, and make the maximum contributions possible to certain retirement provisions.

Many times, parents come to consult us when their child is just about to fill out the need analysis forms in the senior year of high school. There is still a lot we can do to help them qualify for more aid, but we always feel bad for the family because if only they had come to us before the base income year started, there would have been so much more that we could have done.

You are in the fortunate position of having that extra time to maneuver. Read the rest of this book, and enjoy.

Chapter Three

Short-Term Strategies for Receiving More Financial Aid

In Chapter One, we introduced the concepts of aid eligibility being based on a "snapshot" of your financial situation as well as defining how the "base income year" of that snapshot is determined. You may find it helpful to reread that chapter before you proceed, as this chapter is going to be expanding on those basic concepts with much more detail.

Additionally, as we stated in the Introduction, there have been major changes regarding student aid as a result of the Consolidated Appropriations Act of 2021 (CAA), federal legislation that was signed into law in December 2020. Certain provisions of that legislation relating to FAFSA Simplification have resulted in the largest changes to federal student aid in 40 years with the last changes expected to be implemented for the 2027–2028 award year. There have also been many changes to the federal methodology (FM) relating to how one's base year income and one's assets will impact aid eligibility for such assistance.

As a reminder, the "snapshot" that the federal government (and most colleges as well as state aid agencies) takes for the base year income involves the calendar year two years prior to the academic year for which aid is sought. You may hear many aid professionals use the term "prior-prior year"—PPY for short—to describe the calendar year's income primarily used to determine aid eligibility. So for the 2027–2028 academic year, this means that your financial aid award will be based in part on your income from the 2025 calendar year.

Despite all these changes, the provisions of the CAA will still consider assets and additional other data reported on the FAFSA to be as of the date the FAFSA form is completed. So the PPY lookback period only involves the income and, if applicable, other tax return information reported on the FAFSA. Since it is easy to get confused by which calendar year's income is used as the base income year for a particular academic year's aid eligibility, here is an easy tip to get it right every time: to determine the PPY base income year for a given academic year (which spans portions of two calendar years), simply take the appropriate year when the academic year begins and subtract 2 from that year. Example: For the 2028–2029 academic year, subtract 2 from 2028 and so 2026 is the applicable PPY base income year.

The *intent* of the new federal methodology is to help families with low income by simplifying the FAFSA form and the student aid process as well as by increasing the predictability of Pell Grant eligibility. (The Pell is a need-based federal grant program for lower income students.) That all sounds great—but the *effect* of these changes has unfortunately been anything but simple given the number of moving parts involved with the aid delivery system.

Out With the Old...In With the New

We know from experience that our readers use the information in this book for differing reasons. There will be those with little or no knowledge of the financial aid system and no experience with the aid application process. For these readers, the following section may not make sense, as it involves the changes beginning with the 2024–2025 award year as the old rules and regulations that affected the FM prior to the 2024–2025 award year went by the wayside. For such readers, ignorance may be bliss as you will be learning the relatively new lay of the land that will apply to you. (That said, it's still useful to familiarize yourself with all the changes involved.)

However, there is also another group of readers of this 2027 edition, many of whom have purchased prior editions of this book. This includes families who have gone through the aid process for award years prior to 2027–2028, those who have college on the horizon in a few years and have done some research on the subject, high school guidance counselors, graduate students studying to become guidance counselors, accountants, and financial planners. Those in this group will of course need to know what they need to forget about any of the old rules they may have learned. It is for this group of readers that we are now going to deviate from our usual practice in most prior editions of this chapter and summarize the various changes that occurred because of FAFSA Simplification. Then we will continue with our usual approach of providing a detailed discussion of the various components of one's income, assets, and other factors that affect aid. This will include more specifics regarding the changes that appear below. We will also provide specific strategies on how to adjust those items so as to maximize aid eligibility in the new world of FAFSA Simplification. Some new concepts, strategies, and requirements will also be covered in Part Three's "Filling Out the 2027–2028 FAFSA Form."

The Old	FAFSA Simplification
Expected Family Contribution (EFC)	Student Aid Index (SAI)
IRS Data Retrieval Tool (DRT)	Future Act—Direct Data Exchange (FA–DDX)
Lowest possible EFC = 0 (zero)	Negative SAI concept introduced
Pell Grant eligibility tied to EFC	Some decoupling of Pell from SAI
Adjustment to parent component in EFC formula based on number of dependents in college	No multiple student adjustment in the SAI calculation, though schools can adjust for their own aid.
If two parents of student not living together, criteria for parent on FAFSA: physical presence test	If two parents of student not living together, criteria for parent on FAFSA: greater financial support test
Three possible criteria for alternate formula to exclude assets re: EFC	Two criteria for alternate formula to exclude assets re: SAI
Automatic-Zero EFC formula	Maximum Pell Grant concept

The Old	FAFSA Simplification
$50,000 AGI threshold for asset exclusion *if certain other criteria met*	$60,000 AGI threshold for asset exclusion *if new criteria met*
One criteria based on Schedule 1 of IRS 1040	One criteria based on lettered tax schedules
Dislocated Worker criteria for alternate EFC formulas	Dislocated Worker criteria eliminated
Untaxed income categories included seven categories not on the tax return	Fewer untaxed income categories (all appearing on the federal tax return)
Contributions to tax-deferred retirement plans such as 401(k)s, 403(b)s, and others deducted pre-tax of from W-2 income considered untaxed income	Such contributions no longer considered. (Only contributions to retirement plans that are adjustments to income on Schedule 1 of IRS 1040 will be considered untaxed income)
Foreign income exclusion reduces income	Foreign income exclusion added back to AGI
Net worth of "family businesses" and/or "family farms" excluded from assets	Such "family businesses" and "family farms" now considered assets
State and other tax allowance in EFC formula	Elimination of state and other tax allowance
Social Security Tax Allowance: separate calculation for each earner	Social Security Tax Allowance: based on combined earnings for a two-adult household
Income Protection Allowance based on number in household and number in college increased	Income Protection Allowance based solely on family size
No Employment Allowance for two-parent household if only one works	Employment Allowance granted even if only one parent in two-parent family works
Partnership income subject to self-employment taxes considered income earned from work	Such partnership income no longer considered income earned from work
Child support received considered untaxed income	Child support received considered an asset
Child support paid reduces income	Child support paid helps determine the parent of record required to complete the FAFSA

The FM vs. the IM

As stated earlier, colleges can use either their *own* methodology or the College Board's Institutional Methodology (IM) when they are awarding aid that doesn't come from the federal government. As we predicted in the 2024 edition of this book, the differences between the federal (FM) and institutional (IM) methodologies have become more pronounced as a result of FAFSA Simplification. And because many schools will not be happy with some of the provisions of the new law involving changes to what data elements are considered in the federal methodology and how aid eligibility will be determined under the new FM, we predict more schools that previously awarded their own institutional aid using only the FAFSA data will now require the College Board's CSS Profile application or their own extensive institutional aid form. Be aware that the College Board has not adjusted their IM formula as a result of FAFSA Simplification. To avoid confusion, however, they are following the new FM provisions so that if the student's two biological or adoptive parents are living apart, the same parent required to provide financial information on the FAFSA will be the same parent that completes the CSS Profile with parent and student financial information. So in that respect, the IM will mirror the change to the FM. (See Part Three for more details.)

For the 2023–2024 award year, the College Board had introduced a streamlined version of the CSS Profile (in addition to their regular CSS Profile form). This version provides an option for those colleges that will want to see certain additional information from an aid applicant that will no longer be asked on the FAFSA due to Simplification. But instead of requiring their aid applicants to complete the regular version of the CSS Profile to get the necessary information, a college can tell the College Board to have the applicant complete fewer questions. The CSS Profile skip-logic will do this automatically behind the scenes, so the applicant does not have an option to select the different version. Unless a student is also applying to other CSS Profile schools that require the regular version, the applicant will just be asked fewer questions when they complete the application. Those schools electing to use this streamlined form option will primarily be colleges that historically have required only the FAFSA (and possibly also their own rather simple institutional aid application) for use in awarding their own institutionally funded, need-based aid programs. Given the development of this streamlined alternative to the regular version, many institutions that used to require continuing students to file the regular CSS Profile (in addition, of course, to the FAFSA) each year will now only require the regular version of the CSS Profile from first-time applicants seeking institutional aid. Then for the renewal of aid for subsequent academic years, the institution will require only the streamlined version of the CSS Profile and the FAFSA for those continuing students currently receiving institutional aid.

Strategies that increase eligibility for federal aid might also result in no additional aid being offered at other levels. Whether schools use the College Board's Institutional Methodology (IM) or their own methodology to award gift aid (grants or scholarships that do not have to be paid back), any increase in federal and state grant aid often reduces the amount of institutional gift aid awarded on a dollar-for-dollar basis. This is because such schools—especially those that meet one's demonstrated need in full—first use the alternate institutional formula to determine the total amount of gift aid a student is eligible to receive. It is from that total amount of gift aid eligibility that the aid office then subtracts any federal or state gift aid eligibility (determined by those program's formulas) to figure out how much institutional gift aid will be awarded to help meet the student's need.

As a result of all these interrelated parts, FAFSA Simplification will necessitate parents and students employing different financial aid planning strategies that are much more customized to their own unique circumstances—and which may require more balancing of tax planning with such aid planning than ever before. So much for "simplification"!

Maximum Pell, Minimum Pell, and the SAI Disconnect

Given FAFSA Simplification's intent to help more students in lower income situations become Pell-eligible and have more of them qualify for the maximum amount, the law created two alternative criteria for Pell Grant eligibility that are not based on the student's calculated Student Aid Index (SAI). These two alternate ways, known as Maximum Pell and Minimum Pell (which we will sometimes refer to as "Max" and "Min"), add an additional wrinkle to such financial aid planning for those students and their families who can meet all the requirements for either the Max criterion or the Min criterion.

Prior to Simplification, the calculated bottom line number in the federal methodology, Expected Family Contribution (EFC), impacted not only the amount of need-based aid a student could receive but also the amount of the Pell Grant that a student could be awarded. With FAFSA Simplification, there is now a disconnect between the new calculated bottom line number in the federal methodology (the SAI) and Pell eligibility for many students.

> For the 2026–2027 academic year for a full-time student (normally defined as 12 credits or more per semester or the equivalent) the Maximum Pell Grant is $7,395. The Minimum Pell Grant award is 10% of the Maximum Pell Grant, so $740 for a full-time student given the rounding provisions.

Eligibility for the Max Pell criteria can be established via a scenario where no IRS 1040 was filed by the applicable person(s) due to low income. We'll refer to this as the "non-filer scenario." Eligibility for Max Pell or Min Pell may also be established by tax filers under what we'll refer to as the "poverty guidelines scenario." That is based on:

- the Adjusted Gross Income (AGI) on Line 11a of the IRS 1040 tax return plus (if applicable)
- the Foreign Earned Income Exclusion Amount (which we'll refer to as the FEIEA) on Line 8d of Schedule 1 of the IRS 1040 ["AGI + FEIEA"] for the applicable person(s) as well as their family size and composition
- one's state of residence
- the federal poverty guidelines of the U.S. Department of Health and Human Services (HHS) for the applicable base income year.

One can qualify for Max Pell even if the applicable person or persons do not live within the United States. Note that for the 2027–2028 award year, the sum of the AGI and the FEIEA for the 2025 tax year must be greater than zero to qualify for Max Pell. If the AGI is a negative number, then one must have an FEIEA that is greater than the negative AGI amount so that the sum of the AGI plus the FEIEA is a positive number. However, for the 2024–2025 and 2025–2026 award years that were prior to the implementation of the One Big Beautiful Bill Act, one could not qualify if the AGI was a negative number.

For federal student aid purposes, an aid applicant is classified as either an "independent student" or a "dependent student" (which has nothing to do with the applicant being claimed as a "dependent" on someone else's IRS 1040 tax return). We address the various ways a federal student aid applicant can be classified as an independent student in our tips for FAFSA questions 3, 5a-5i, 6a-6f, and 7 that appear in the section "Filling Out the 2026–2027 FAFSA" in Part Three as well as in the "Independents Students" section in Chapter Nine of this book. If an applicant does NOT meet at least one of the ways to be considered an independent student for the purposes of federal student aid eligibility, then by default they will be considered a "dependent student."

For an independent student, the "applicable person(s)" for purposes of the Max and Min Pell criteria is/are the student—as well as the student's spouse, provided the student is married at the time the FAFSA is filed. Only the financial information of an applicable person will be reported on an independent student's FAFSA.

> Note that prior to FAFSA Simplification a student who was married but separated from their spouse would be considered an independent student by virtue of that marital status alone. Under Simplification that is no longer the case!

So a student who may have formerly been considered an independent student for a prior academic year due to being married can revert to being classified as a dependent student if they subsequently are separated from their spouse at the time their FAFSA is filed for another academic year—unless of course, that student can meet at least one of the other ways to be classified as an independent student. This can happen even if the aid applicant filed a joint IRS 1040 tax return for the base income year.

For a dependent student, the "applicable person(s)" for the establishment of Pell eligibility via the Max or the Min criterion will be the "parent" who is required to report financial information on the FAFSA. According to federal guidelines, this could also include the current spouse or partner (provided that partner is the other parent of the student) of that parent. The dependent student's tax return status or other financial information never impacts such dependent student's eligibility for the alternate Max Pell criteria, regardless of what financial information is provided in the "Student" section of the FAFSA. However, the dependent student's financial information on the FAFSA can impact the student contribution from income and the student contribution for assets components used to determine the calculated SAI in the FM. In some but not all cases the student's financial information can also impact Min Pell eligibility, as we'll explain shortly.

If both biological or adoptive parents of a dependent student are married and living together, things are much more straightforward. Both parents are the "applicable person(s)." However....

...if a dependent student's biological or adoptive parents are NOT currently both living together AND married to each other, things get much more complicated given all the federal regulations under FAFSA Simplification. Please refer to the section "Which Parent(s) Must Report Information on the 2027–2028 FAFSA and CSS Profile" in Part Three for more details as to who is considered the dependent student's "Parent"—and if applicable, the "Parent's Spouse" or the "Parent's Partner" for federal student aid purposes. The same regulations will define the "applicable person(s)" for the purposes of the Max and Min Pell criteria as well as (if applicable) the parent contribution portion of the bottom-line number determined under the calculated SAI formula.

Two Qualifying Scenarios for the Maximum Pell

The Maximum Pell criterion can be met if either of the following two scenarios apply to your situation for the base income year:

1. **The Non-Filer Scenario:** *The applicable person(s) did not AND will not file an IRS Form 1040 federal income tax return for the base income year because their income was too low to be required by the IRS to file such a return.* Any reason for the applicable person(s) not filing an IRS 1040 other than the income being below any of the IRS filing thresholds is not relevant. Note: If the student's marital status is "Married (not separated)" or "Remarried" at the time the FAFSA is filed, then both that independent student <u>and</u> their current spouse must not have filed any tax return. For a dependent student, if applicable, any "Parent Spouse / Partner" required to report their own information on the FAFSA must also not have filed any tax return in addition to the "Parent" on the FAFSA being a non-filer. If the applicable person(s) meet(s) all the requirements for this Max Pell non-filer scenario, the student will automatically be assigned an SAI of –1500 (negative 1500). The student's SAI cannot be lower than –1500.

2. **The Poverty Guidelines Scenario (for tax filers):** *The base income year's AGI + FEIEA dollar amount for applicable individual(s)—or the sum of the AGIs + FEIEAs, if the applicable persons filed separate tax returns—is greater than zero but equal to or less than a percentage of federal poverty guidelines for that same calendar year.* There are different HHS federal poverty guidelines for residents of Hawaii, for residents or Alaska, and for residents of the other 48 contiguous states (a category that includes the District of Columbia or U.S territories and applies to those residing in a foreign country). In addition to residency, the AGI + FEIEA poverty guidelines amount is also based on the "family size" as well as whether the applicable person is considered a "single parent" or "not a single parent" as defined in the FAFSA Simplification legislation.

The Fine Print: Determining Conditions

Since this poverty guidelines scenario has a great deal of fine print, we'll first clarify how one's "family size" is determined. Then we will review the various requirements under this scenario that must be met if one is to be considered a "single parent." After that, we will explain how you can determine the applicable HHS poverty guideline amount for the applicable base income year.

Family Size

The "family size" determination applicable to Max and Min under the poverty guidelines scenario, defined in the Simplification legislation, appears as part of USDOE's instructions for certain questions on the FAFSA form. Specifically, FAFSA question 34 defines family size for a dependent student while FAFSA question 9 pertains to an independent student. Such instructions for each of these two FAFSA questions can be found on the reprint of the draft version of the 2027–2028 FAFSA that appears in Part Five of this book.

Who Is Considered a "Single Parent"?

The "single parent" definition in the FAFSA Simplification legislation is more complicated. Be aware that for an applicable person to be considered a "single parent" for purposes of the poverty guidelines scenario under both the Max Pell and Min Pell criteria, such determination is related to the applicable person's tax return information. So this "single parent" concept involves different rules than the USDOE's policy guidelines affecting whose financial information is required on the FAFSA.

For the parent of a dependent student to be considered a "single parent" under the poverty guidelines scenario: on page 1 of their base year IRS Form 1040 tax return, that parent must have claimed either "Head of Household" or "Qualifying Surviving Spouse" for their tax return's Filing Status OR they must have been eligible for the Earned Income Credit (reflected as a positive dollar amount on line 27 on page 2 of the 1040). Additionally, this parent must not be considered "Married" according to USDOE policy as of the date the original FAFSA is submitted. For the purposes of Max and Min Pell eligibility (as well as for the calculated SAI), USDOE policy considers the "Parent" required to report information on a dependent student's FAFSA as being "Married" if the Parent Current Marital Status reported on FAFSA question 32 is "Married," "Remarried," or even "Unmarried and both legal parents living together" (despite the fact the Parent listed on the FAFSA is not legally married to the student's other biological or adoptive parent who will be considered the Parent's Partner, not the Parent's Spouse).

If all the requirements mentioned above are not met, the parent of a dependent student required to report their financial information on the FAFSA will NOT be considered a "single parent" for the purposes of the Max or Min Pell criteria. Note that if a parent of a dependent student filed a joint tax return with their estranged spouse but could be considered (legally or informally) separated for purposes of the FAFSA, that situation will be considered a "one parent" household in the calculated SAI formula, but that parent will NOT be considered a "single parent" for either the Max or Min Pell criterion under the poverty guidelines scenario.

Qualifying for the Max Pell as a "Single Parent"

If the Parent (required to report information on the FAFSA) for a dependent student is considered a "single parent" by meeting all the requirements discussed above: to qualify for Max Pell under the poverty guidelines scenario, the parent's AGI + FEIEA on the corresponding base income year's IRS Form 1040 return must be a greater than zero but less than or equal to 225% of the poverty line guidelines for the applicable family size and state of residence.

Qualifying for the Max Pell *not* as a "Single Parent"

If the parent cannot be considered a "single parent," then 175% of the appropriate poverty guideline amount will be compared to the positive parental AGI + FEIEA amount, instead of 225%. (If this is a "two-parent" household for FAFSA purposes with separate base year tax returns being filed by the "Parent" of record and the "Parent's Spouse or Partner" on the FAFSA, then the sum of the AGIs + FEIEAs on both returns will be compared to 175% of the poverty guideline amount for this method.)

Qualifying for the Max Pell as an Independent Student

The same definition of "single parent" will apply in most cases to an independent student. Also, the same percentages basically apply for Max Pell for an independent student as they do for the applicable person(s) with a dependent student. Namely:

- a positive sum of the AGI + FEIEA amount equal to or less than 225% of the poverty guidelines for an independent student is considered a "single parent"

- a positive sum of the AGI + FEIEA equal to or less than 175% of the poverty guidelines for an independent student does not meet the definition of "single parent" (regardless of whether or not the student is married). However if the student and the student's spouse are considered married when the FAFSA is completed but filed separate tax returns for the base income year, then *the sum of the AGIs + FEIEAs amounts for the student and their spouse will be compared to the 175% poverty guidelines amount.*

Poverty Guidelines

Appropriate dollar amounts based on the poverty guideline percentages for the 2025 base income year (used for the 2027–2028 aid year) and 2026 base income year (used for the 2028–2029 award year) can be found online in your student tools.

Note that the residency of the parent(s) will determine whether to use the poverty guidelines for Alaska, Hawaii, or the other 48 contiguous states. For future years, the guidelines are normally published by the federal government by the end of January (e.g., by the end of January 2027 for 2027 HHS poverty guidelines, which would apply for the 2029–2030 award year) and the most recently published guidelines should be accessible at https://aspe.hhs.gov/topics/poverty-economic-mobility/poverty-guidelines. To determine a specific amount, you'll need to first find the poverty guideline for the year in question, your family size, and your state of residence, and then multiply by the applicable percentage in decimal form. For example, to find the 225% poverty guideline amount, you'll need to multiply the guideline dollar amount by 2.25. This can then be compared to the base income year AGI of the applicable person under the Max Pell criteria for a "single parent."

Qualifying Under the Second Max Pell Scenario

If you qualify under the second Max Pell poverty guidelines scenario, then the student will be temporarily assigned an SAI of 0 (zero) by the processor. The SAI will be also calculated under the federal methodology that takes into account the financial information of all contributors required to provide information on the FAFSA.

For a dependent student, this is the "Student," the "Parent," and, if applicable, the "Parent's Spouse /Partner."

For an independent student, this is the "Student" and, if applicable, the "Student's Spouse."

The lesser of the calculated SAI or the assigned zero SAI will then become the SAI used to indicate both Maximum Pell Grant eligibility as well as eligibility for other federal student aid programs (such as federal work-study and subsidized federal student loans, which we discuss in Part Four). This will occur once the FAFSA is processed. That lesser SAI can also determine eligibility for institutional need-based aid funded by the school itself and/or state aid, provided the school and/or your state uses the SAI to award such aid. So with this second Max Pell scenario, the calculated SAI will only eventually become the student's SAI number if such calculated SAI is less than zero.

Note that if the AGI + FEIEA of the applicable person(s)—or the sum of the AGIs + FEIEAs, if the applicable persons filed separate tax returns—is either zero or less than zero (a negative number), then the student does not qualify under the second poverty guidelines scenario for Max Pell. However, it may still be possible for the student to receive the maximum amount for the Pell Grant if their calculated SAI is 0 (zero) or a negative number. And if there are two applicable persons, and one filed a tax return and the other did not file a return for the base income year due to low income, the AGI + FEIEA of the tax filer is all that matters regarding the poverty guidelines scenario under Max or Min, with the "not a single parent" percentage being applicable.

Having a calculated SAI below 0 (zero) does not get one a larger Pell Grant, nor does it result in one being able get more aid than the Cost of Attendance. The negative SAI concept was just introduced as a diagnostic tool for aid offices to determine which students that qualify for the Maximum Pell Grant have the fewest resources to pay for college. After all, an applicant with an assigned SAI of 0 (zero) because of the applicable AGI being below the poverty guidelines could still have a calculated SAI that is greater than the Cost of Attendance: for example, as a result of significant assets and/or a large amount of untaxed income, neither of which have any impact under this second Maximum Pell Grant scenario based on the AGI + FEIEA. Later in this chapter we will discuss in detail the various data elements that impact the calculated SAI.

The Minimum Pell Grant

If neither of the two Maximum Pell scenarios mentioned above are applicable, then the calculated SAI will be used. As the calculated SAI number rises above zero, Pell Grant eligibility will be reduced until such point that the calculated SAI for a given academic year exceeds the difference between the Max Pell and the Min Pell dollar amounts for that award year. At that point, the student is not Pell-eligible according to the calculated SAI formula. However given FAFSA Simplification's goal to have more students qualify for Pell, a Minimum Pell Grant criterion was introduced as an alternate way to get a Pell Grant for certain lower-income applicants with a calculated SAI too high to otherwise qualify. Note though that the calculated SAI will still be the key determinant for other federal need-based student aid programs such as federal work-study or subsidized student loans—and if applicable, for other types of aid (e.g., state grants or institutional gift aid) where the SAI is used to determine eligibility.

Criteria for the Minimum Pell Grant

The Minimum Pell Grant criterion is similar to the second Maximum Pell Grant scenario based on poverty guidelines, but with some key differences. First, the percentages for the poverty guidelines are higher for Min Pell. Second, instead of there being two percentages (for Max Pell), there are three different percentages for Min Pell for an independent student:

- the student is a parent
- the student is a *single* parent
- the student is not a parent

A third difference between Max and Min Pell is that with Min Pell the sum of the AGI + FEIEA can be a negative number and still qualify.

Here now are the relevant Min Pell percentages for each applicant category. *For the parent of a dependent student:* the applicable AGI + FEIEA amount must be equal to or below 325% of the poverty guidelines if considered a "single parent" as defined above; otherwise 275% if not a "single parent." *For an independent student:* The threshold percentages are 400% of the applicable AGI + FEIEA amount of a "single parent"; 350% if the student is a parent but not a "single parent"; and 275% if student is not a parent (regardless of whether the student is married).

"Pellionaires" and a New Requirement for Min Pell

With the passage of the One Big Beautiful Bill Act (OBBBA), there is also now one additional requirement to qualify for Min Pell (which is a fourth difference when compared to Max Pell). But first the backstory.

While the goals of FAFSA Simplification may have been well-intentioned, it had some unintended consequences. For one, it created "Pellionaires," a new word coined to describe those students and their families who have significant reported assets on the FAFSA yet low AGI + FEIEA dollar amounts, thereby allowing them to qualify for Pell Grants under either the Max or Min criteria. These students' calculated SAIs would be so high that they would be ineligible for any Pell Grant funds (and oftentimes ineligible for any other types of need-based aid), but because of the alternate criteria for Max or Min poverty guidelines this occurred in the 2024–2025 and 2025–2026 award years. Truth be told, we were not at all surprised by this outcome and even raised this issue with national media prior to the enactment of FAFSA Simplification. At any rate, members of Congress received many complaints about the "Pellionaires" from their constituents, who rightly wondered why they or their children did not qualify for a Pell Grant when wealthier folks did under Simplification.

To resolve this, a new requirement was included in the OBBBA to stipulate that a student could only qualify for a Pell Grant if their official SAI was less than twice the maximum Pell Grant dollar amount for the award year. So for example, a student's SAI would have to be less than $14,790 to get a Pell Grant (Formula: maximum Pell Grant award times 2: $7,395 × 2 = $14,790.) If the maximum Pell grant award is increased for the 2027–2028 award year, then the less than two times SAI threshold will increase as well.

While most folks in the aid community keep stating that there are no more Pellionaires due to this provision in the law, here's why that's not true. With Min Pell, the calculated SAI is generated by the processor and listed on the output document made available to the student after all the required FAFSA information has been submitted and been processed. That document is known as the FAFSA Submission Summary or FSS, which is pronounced by sounding each letter individually. The colleges listed on the student's FAFSA receive an applicant's processed FAFSA data on a different output document that also contains the SAI number. That document is known as the Institutional Student Information Record (ISIR, pronounced I-ser by aid professionals). So unless the SAI listed on the ISIR is less than the twice the maximum Pell Grant award threshold for that award year, the student no longer meets the Min Pell poverty guideline scenario. Therefore, no college will not certify the student's eligibility for a Pell Grant based on that SAI. As a result of this change due to the OBBBA, a dependent student's income and asset information can now potentially impact Min Pell eligibility. This would occur if the dependent student's financial information leads to a marginal increase to the calculated SAI that then results in that calculated SAI now equaling or exceeding the threshold for an applicant whose parent SAI component alone in the FM would have been less than the threshold.

However, if the applicable person(s)'s AGI + FEIEA dollar amount is a positive number that is low enough to qualify for Max Pell under the poverty guidelines scenario, then under the current regulations the applicant's official SAI on the FSS and the ISIR is the lesser of zero or the calculated SAI, which can be no lower than –1500. (For those applicants who qualify under the Max Pell poverty guideline scenario, the calculated SAI never appears on the FSS or the ISIR, unless it is a negative number between –1500 and –1.) A dependent's student's financial information will only possibly impact how low the negative SAI would be, but will never impact Max Pell eligibility.

Additionally, the current regulations further stipulate that if one meets the criteria for Max Pell (via either scenario), then any assets reported on the student's FAFSA will not be considered when the processor calculates the SAI. So even if the calculated SAI is very high due to a large amount of untaxed income that is assessed along with the AGI in the FM, that calculated high positive SAI number never becomes the SAI listed on the FSS or ISIR, which would be zero for such a Pellionaire with Max Pell eligibility. So this is now another way that the Max Pell poverty line scenario differs from Min Pell.

As such, former Pellionaires prior to OBBBA via Min Pell who cannot now meet the added SAI-related requirement will likely be the only ones to no longer be part of the Pellionaire class. We say likely, because due to other student aid provisions in OBBBA (which we'll discuss later in the chapter) some applicants will no longer be required to report certain assets on the FAFSA. So to repeat, this new OBBBA "having an SAI less than two times the maximum Pell grant dollar amount for the award year" provision only impacts those who would otherwise have met all the Min Pell criteria yet have an AGI + FEIEA amount that is too high to qualify for Max Pell.

Moving Right Along

We will now provide a detailed discussion of the various data elements that can influence the calculated SAI in the federal methodology as well as those items that affect the institutional methodology under the current rules and regulations in place. Strategies to lower the calculated SAI and/or to boost aid eligibility are included as well. We realize that most of our readers over the years are tax filers and have situations in which their AGI is too high to meet the criteria for the Maximum Pell Grant and/or they are interested in schools that use an institutional methodology (and so require additional aid forms besides the FAFSA) to determine the total amount of gift aid offered to the student as described earlier.

However if you have a situation where the applicant's applicable percentage of AGI is close to a poverty line threshold that would meet the Maximum Pell Grant criteria mentioned above AND all the colleges under consideration only ever require the FAFSA to apply for need-based aid (or you will only be eligible for federal aid but not any institutional need-based gift aid at any school that requires additional aid forms for institutional aid consideration) THEN the only strategies that matter will involve those that either a) reduce the applicable AGI so that it is low enough to meet the second Maximum Pell criteria mentioned above or b) lower the applicable person(s)'s gross income enough such that no tax return is required to be filed according to IRS tax code nor is ever actually filed.

As you begin to learn more about the counterintuitive world of financial aid, it is easy to lose your perspective. In the first flush of learning how to maximize aid by minimizing income from the base income year, it might seem like more money is actually bad. Let's look at an example of why that's not actually the case.

I'm About to Get a Raise. Should I Say No?

It's easy to get carried away with the concept of reducing income, and it may appear at first that you would be better off turning down a raise. However, the short answer to this question is, "Are you crazy?"

More money is almost always good. Our discussion here is limited to minimizing the *appearance* of more money. Let's say you get a raise of $3,000 per year. This will certainly reduce your eligibility for college aid, but will it negate the entire effect of the raise? Not likely (unless the raise eliminates you from qualifying for Max Pell). Let's say you're in the 22% federal tax bracket, your raise is still subject to social security taxes of 7.65%, and your income is being assessed at the maximum rate possible under the aid formulas. Looking at the chart that follows, you'll see that even after taxes and reduced aid eligibility are taken into account, you will still be $1,119 ahead, though state and local taxes might reduce this somewhat.

raise of:			**$3,000**
minus:	federal tax	$660	
	FICA taxes	$230	
	reduced aid	$991	
what you keep:			**$1,119**

My Spouse Works. Should He or She Quit?

The same principle applies here. More money is good. Not only are you getting the advantage of extra income but also, under the federal financial aid formula, for a two-parent family with both parents working the deduction in the FM for Social Security and Medicare taxes can be greater. Even if this increased income decreases your aid eligibility, you will still be ahead on the income. In addition, you will be creating the impression of a family with a work ethic, which can be very helpful in negotiating with FAOs later. They are more likely to give additional aid to families who have demonstrated their willingness to make sacrifices.

Income vs. Assets

Some parents get confused by the differences between what is considered income and what are considered assets. Assets are the money, property, and other financial instruments you've been able to accumulate over time. Income, on the other hand, is the money you actually earned or otherwise received during the past year, including interest and dividends from your assets.

The IRS never asks you to report your assets on your 1040—only the income you received from these assets. Colleges, on the other hand, are very interested in your income and your assets. Later in this chapter, there will be an entire section devoted to strategies for reducing *the appearance* of your assets. For now, let's focus on income.

The colleges and the U.S. Department of Education decided long ago that income should be assessed much more heavily than assets. The intention is that when a family is finished paying for college, there should be something left in the bank. (Don't start feeling grateful just yet. This works only as long as the colleges meet a family's need in full.)

Income

When considering their chances for financial aid, many families believe that the colleges are interested only in how much income you make from work. If this were the case, the colleges would just be able to look at your W-2 form to see if you qualified for aid. Unfortunately, life is not so simple. The colleges' and the federal government's complicated formulas make the IRS tax code look like child's play.

For financial aid purposes, the colleges and the federal government will be looking at the same income the IRS does. For most of us, that boils down to Line 11a of the 1040 IRS form: the Adjusted Gross Income (AGI).

For those who file a tax return, the feds will usually look at certain other types of income that are not subject to tax, for example, tax-exempt interest and voluntary contributions to a traditional IRA or other retirement plan claimed as a deduction on Schedule 1 of the IRS Form 1040 as an adjustment to income (unless you meet the Max Pell criteria).

And for those who don't file any tax return, the colleges may still look at income earned from work plus other untaxed income when awarding their own aid.

The Criteria to Exclude Assets in the 2027–2028 FM

Before we begin discussing the components of taxable and untaxed income, it is important to understand that by meeting certain requirements, you may be able to have parent and student assets excluded from the federal financial aid formula. In the pre-Simplification world, this special carve-out in the FM was known as the "Simplified Needs Test" (SNT). Under Simplification, this alternative to the regular FM formula just refers to situations where "applicants are exempt from asset reporting." There are three scenarios in which assets are excluded from the SAI calculations, specifically:

1. For at least one day in either 2025 or 2026, a family member—as defined by the 2027–2028 SAI formula—received at least one of the following federal means-tested benefits (MTBs):

    - the Earned Income Credit
    - federal housing assistance
    - Medicaid
    - the Supplemental Nutrition Assistance Program (SNAP)
    - Supplemental Security Income (SSI, *not social security benefits*)
    - Temporary Assistance for Need Families (TANF)
    - Special Supplemental Nutrition Program for Women, Infants and Children (WIC)
    - lower premiums for a plan purchased through the health insurance marketplace
    - the free or reduced-price school lunch program (based on income)

        i. *Note that this last MTB refers to the federal program based on certain financial criteria. If all students in a school or school district automatically receive free lunch (e.g., at New York City Public Schools), such a universal free lunch program does NOT necessarily count as an MTB. One must apply, meet the financial criteria, and be certified as eligible for the federal means-tested free or reduced-price lunch program to be considered a recipient of this MTB.*

Key point: This first criteria to have assets excluded based on MTB eligibility does NOT have any income cutoff (as it did prior to FAFSA Simplification).

2. The applicant meets the criteria for Maximum Pell Grant Eligibility mentioned earlier in this chapter.

3. The parent(s) [or if applicable, the parent and stepparent] required to report their information on the FAFSA for a dependent student had:

   An Adjusted Gross Income (AGI) less than $60,000 *(Note: If two adults are required to report their income information on the FAFSA, the combined AGI will be considered.)*

   AND

   Did not file at least one of the lettered schedules A, B, D, E, F or H with their IRS 1040 tax return **AND**

   a. They also did not file Schedule C **OR**

   b. They did file Schedule C, but the net profit (on line 31 of Sch. C) was not more than $10,000 nor was a net loss reported on line 31 that was greater than negative $10,000.

These "lettered schedules" involve certain types of income, losses, and gains, etc., which we explain on the following page.

Exception: A dependent student whose parents (required to report information on the FAFSA) 1) live outside of the United States OR 2) do not file taxes in the U.S. or a U.S. territory will not be eligible to have their assets excluded unless their non-filing is due to having income below the filing threshold.

Schedule A—Itemized deductions (for those whose deductions exceed the standard deduction).

Schedule B—Interest and Dividend Income (for those who received interest or dividend income exceeding a certain amount defined by the IRS).

Schedule C—Net profit or loss from a sole proprietorship or another business entity that is not a partnership or a corporation. We cover the various types of business entities in more detail in Chapter 9.

Schedule D—Capital gains or losses including carryover losses (other than capital gains distributions). One is not required to file Schedule D if *capital gains distributions* are the only type of capital gain and there is no capital loss applicable to that tax year. (For example, a gain during the year from a mutual fund that is not sold, but that generates a gain due to the fund manager selling some assets in the mutual fund's investment portfolio is a *capital gains distribution.*) Note that any increase or decline in the value of any asset is not reported on Schedule D for a given tax year unless the applicable asset is considered sold by the IRS during that tax year (i.e., it is a "realized gain or loss"). If an asset appreciates or declines in value during the year as a result of market fluctuations and no part of that asset is sold during the year, such increase or decline in value of that asset is considered an "unrealized gain or loss." A gain or loss from the sale of any asset in a qualified retirement account [i.e., 401(k), 403(b), Keoghs, any IRAs other than an Educational IRA, or any other tax-deferred retirement account] also isn't reported on Schedule D.

Virtually all capital gains or losses required to be reported on Schedule D involve realized gains or losses as the result of a sale of certain assets during the applicable tax year that are not in a qualified retirement account. Such sale transactions will normally generate an IRS Form 1099 or a summary document with 1099 information issued to the former owner of the asset by the financial institution that held that asset—with such 1099 being generated a few weeks after the end of the tax year. (Both realized and unrealized gains may appear on such a document.) Carryover losses are also listed on Schedule D.

Schedule E—Income or a loss from rental real estate, royalties, estates, partnerships, Subchapter S corporations, trusts, and/or residual interests in real estate mortgage investment conduits (aka REMICs).

Schedule F—Farm income and expenses.

Schedule H—Household employment taxes, i.e., wages paid to a household employee that were subject to payroll taxes and/or had federal income taxes withheld. It is required to be filed with the IRS 1040 if one is otherwise required to file a U.S. income tax return. If one is not required to file a U.S. tax return, Schedule H can be filed by itself without the IRS 1040 needing to be filed with the IRS.

More detailed information regarding these IRS 1040 schedules can be found at www.irs.gov.

Strategies for Meeting the Lettered Schedule Criteria

Here's the nitty-gritty. If you meet either the MTB criteria or the Maximum Pell Grant criteria, you're in the clear and your assets will be excluded in the federal methodology. If not, then the only way to have your assets excluded from consideration will be to be sure that you do not have to file Schedule A, B, D, E, F or H and that if you do need to file Schedule C, the amount reported on Line 31 on page 1 of Schedule is between –$10,000 and $10,000. Prior to FAFSA Simplification, the reporting of any amount of profit or loss on Schedule C would have required you to have assets assessed unless you met one of the other criteria for asset exclusion under the old FM. So now it is possible to still have assets excluded if no other lettered schedules are filed, provided your Schedule C net profit or loss falls within the stipulated range.

When *Not* to File Schedules

Because some lettered schedules may now disqualify you from having assets excluded, make sure you avoid unnecessary filings. This is especially true because the new method for transferring IRS data onto the FAFSA is not sophisticated enough to distinguish between required and non-required schedules. Don't let this mistake be the reason you have to report your assets on the FAFSA.

Schedule A Issues The reason to fill out Schedule A is because it would provide you with a larger deduction than the standard deduction. Therefore, if you choose to take the standard deduction, make sure you do not submit Schedule A. Likewise, if your itemized deduction would exceed the standard deduction but would *not* reduce your tax liability (i.e., provide you with a larger refund or a smaller tax bill to pay), then there's no benefit in filing Schedule A. Finally, if your result by itemizing would only be marginal, you'll want to balance your tax planning with your aid planning to see if you'd be eligible for more money in aid than you would pay in tax.

Schedule B Issues You are usually only *required* to file this schedule if the amount of taxable interest income and/or the amount of dividend income received during the year exceeded the threshold amount sent by the IRS. (For the 2025 tax year, this was $1,500 for taxable interest and $1,500 for ordinary dividends.) If not, in most cases, you can simply report such income on your main IRS Form 1040.

Schedule E Issues Many tax preparation computer software programs will automatically continue to list partnerships and S-corporations that you had a stake in. If they no longer generate K-1s because they have been closed or dormant for some time, and/or you have not had ownership since before the beginning of the tax year, you may not have to file this.

The strategy for Schedule C *If you otherwise will qualify to have assets excluded,* except your Schedule C business loss of slightly more than $10,000 will knock you out of the box, consider not claiming all your deductible expenses on Schedule C. There is nothing in the federal tax code that prohibits you from doing so; you just can't claim ineligible expenses. If your assets are significant and therefore to your advantage to *not* have to report them on the FAFSA, it might be worth the increased income tax you'd wind up paying as a result of not claiming those deductions. Also remember that any reduction in a loss claimed on Schedule C will likely result in a dollar-for-dollar increase in the Adjusted Gross Income—which still needs to be below $60,000 to qualify to have assets excluded under the new law.

Similarly, if your *profit* from your Schedule C business looks like it might be *more* than $10,000 before the end of any base income year and such profit will be the sole reason disqualifying you from having assets excluded, consider taking steps to reduce that profit for that year. By postponing invoices or accelerating allowable expenses, you might be able to keep your Schedule C net profit under the $10,001 threshold, allowing you to not have to report your assets on the FAFSA.

The strategy to meet the income threshold criteria If you are close to the $60,000 ceiling (and you do not meet at least one of the two other qualifying criteria to be exempt from reporting assets on the FAFSA), there may be some actions you can take to lower your AGI before the end of the base income year. For instance, if your employer allows it, you could boost your contributions to tax-deferred contributions retirement plans towards the end of the base income year. This would reduce your taxable wages reported on your W-2 form and therefore your AGI. It may even be possible to reduce your AGI after the base income year is over if you are permitted to contribute to a traditional IRA or other qualified retirement plan, as these allow you to contribute and claim a deduction up to the time your Form 1040 is required to be filed with the IRS. But again, you will want to balance your aid planning with your overall financial planning and—as always—keep in mind that at those schools that use an alternate formula to award their own aid, any increase in federal gift aid may only result in a dollar-for-dollar reduction in institutional aid, which will not reduce what you are expected to pay for college by one penny.

TIP 1:
There may be some financial aid advantages to completing your tax return in a certain manner provided the IRS permits you to do so. There can also be some advantages if you are not required to file a personal tax return.

A Parents' Step-by-Step Guide to the Federal Income Tax Form

By reducing your total income reported on your tax return, you can increase your financial aid, which, you should remember, is largely funded by your tax dollars anyway. Let's examine how various items on your tax return can be adjusted to influence your aid eligibility. The IRS line numbers below refer to the line items on Pages 1 and 2 of the 2025 IRS 1040, while the Schedule 1 line items involve the different items that appear on that schedule. For your benefit, sample copies of Pages 1 and 2 of the 2025 IRS 1040 as well as Schedule 1 appear toward the end of this book in the Sample Forms section.

Line 1a—Wages, Salaries, Tips, etc.

For most parents, there is not much to be done about Line 1a. Your employers will send you W-2 forms, and you simply report this income. However, there are a few points to be made.

Defer Your Bonus

If you receive a bonus, you might discuss with your boss the possibility of moving your bonus into a non-base income year. For example:

If your child is in the beginning of her sophomore year of high school (in other words, if the first base income year has not yet begun) and you are due a year-end bonus, make sure that you collect and deposit the bonus *before* January 1 of the new year (when the base income year begins). As long as the bonus is included on your W-2 for the previous year, it will not be considered income on your aid application.

The money will still appear as part of your *assets* (provided you haven't already spent it). But by shifting the bonus into a non-base income year, you will avoid having the colleges count your bonus twice—as both asset and income.

If you are due a year-end bonus and your child is starting his junior year of high school, see if you can arrange to get the bonus held off until *after* January 1. Yes, it will show up on next year's financial aid form, but in the meantime you've had the benefit of financial aid for this year.

Just as important, FAOs make four-year projections based on your first base income year. Your FAO will have set aside money for you for the next three years based on the aid your child receives as a first-year in college. Who knows what might happen next year? You might need that money. If the FAO hasn't already set it aside for you, it might not be there when you need it.

TIP 2:
Move your bonus into a non-base income year.

If You've Had an Unusually Good Year

Maybe you won a retroactive pay increase during the base income year. Or perhaps you just worked a lot of overtime. If you can arrange to receive payment during a non-base income year that would, of course, be better, but there are sometimes compelling reasons for taking the money when it is offered (for example, you are afraid you might not get it later).

However, unless you explain the details of this windfall to the colleges, they will be under the impression that this sort of thing happens to you all the time.

If the base income year's income is really not representative, write to the financial aid office of each of the colleges your child is applying to, and explain that this was a once-in-a-lifetime payment, never to be repeated. Include a copy of your tax return from the year *before* the base income year, or from the year *after*, which more closely reflects your true average income. If helpful to your cause, you may wish to include a projection of your income for the "current year"—the calendar year that will end on December 31 in the middle of the academic year for which you are seeking aid.

Don't bother sending documentation like this to the processors of the standardized analysis forms. They are only interested in crunching the numbers on the form, and anyway have no power to make decisions about your aid at specific schools. Documentation regarding a change in circumstances should never be sent to the processors of the forms. Send it directly to the schools.

TIP 3:
If you've had an unusually good year, explain to the colleges that your average salary is much lower.

Become an Independent Contractor

If you are a full-time employee receiving a W-2 form at the end of the year, you have significant unreimbursed business expenses, and you are otherwise ineligible to have assets excluded or be eligible for the Maximum Pell Grant, you might discuss with your employer the viability of becoming an independent contractor. The advantage to this is that you can file your income under Schedule C of the tax form ("profit or loss from business"), enabling you to deduct huge amounts of business-related expenses *before* Line 11a of the 1040 Form, where it will do you some good. Note: if you are otherwise eligible to have assets excluded, filing Schedule C may disqualify you from receiving such favorable aid treatment under the federal methodology, unless you are not required to file a tax return (which is very difficult due to the gross income test based on Schedule C's total revenue and not the net profit) or you are eligible by meeting by meeting the MTB or Maximum Pell criteria explained earlier.

An independent contractor can deduct telephone bills, business use of the home, dues, business travel, and entertainment—basically anything that falls under the cost of doing business—and thus lower the adjusted gross income.

You would have to consult with your accountant to see if the disadvantages (increased likelihood of an IRS audit, difficulties in rearranging health insurance and pension plans, possible loss of unemployment benefits, increased social security tax, etc.) outweigh the advantages. In addition, the IRS has been known to crack down on employers who classify their workers as independent contractors when they are really salaried employees. Like all fuzzy areas of the tax law, this represents an opportunity to be exploited, but requires careful planning.

TIP 4a:
If you have significant unreimbursed employee expenses, consider becoming an independent contractor so that you can deduct expenses on Schedule C of the 1040. However, be careful if you are otherwise eligible to have assets excluded.

Even better, you might suggest to your boss that she cut your pay. No, we haven't gone insane. By convincing your employer to reduce your pay by the amount of your business expenses, and then having her reimburse you directly for those expenses, you should end up with the same amount of money in your pocket, but you'll show a lower AGI and therefore increase your aid eligibility.

TIP 4b:
If you have significant unreimbursed employee expenses, try to get your employer to reimburse these business expenses directly to you—even if it means taking a corresponding cut in pay.

If your employer won't let you pursue either of these options, you should be sure to explain your unreimbursed employee expenses in a separate letter to the FAOs.

Lines 2b and 3b—Taxable Interest and Dividend Income

If you have interest or dividend income, you have assets. Nothing prompts a "validation" (financial aid jargon for an audit) faster than listing interest and dividend income without listing the assets it came from.

For the most part, there is little you can do, or would want to do, to reduce this income, though we will have a lot to say in later chapters about reducing *the appearance* of your assets.

Some parents have suggested taking all their assets and hiding them in a mattress or dumping them into a checking account that doesn't earn interest. The first option is illegal and not so smart. The second is just not so smart. In both cases, this would be a bit like turning down a raise. More interest is *good*. The FAOs won't take all of it, and you will need it if you want to have any chance of staying even with inflation.

The one type of interest income you might want to control comes from Series E and EE U.S. Savings Bonds. When you buy a U.S. Savings Bond, you don't pay the face value of the bond; you buy it for much less. When the bond matures (in five years, 10 years, or whatever) it is then worth the face value of the bond. The money you receive from the bond in excess of what you paid for it is called interest. With Series E and EE Savings Bonds, you have two tax options: you can report the interest on the bond as it is earned each year on that year's tax return, or you can report all the interest in one lump sum the year you cash in the bond.

By taking the second option, you can, in effect, hold savings bonds for years without paying any tax on the interest because you haven't cashed them in yet. However, when you finally do cash them in, you suddenly have to report all the interest earned over the years to the IRS. If the year that you report that interest happens to be a base income year, all of the interest will have to be reported on the aid forms as well. This will almost certainly raise your SAI.

The only exception to this might be Series EE bonds bought after 1989. The U.S. government decided to give parents who pay for their children's college education a tax break: low- or middle-income parents who bought Series EE bonds after 1989 with the intention of using the bonds to help pay for college may not have to pay any tax on the interest income at all. The interest earned is completely tax-free for a single parent making up to $101,800 or a married couple filing jointly earning up to $152,650. Once you hit these income levels, the benefits are slowly phased out. A single parent earning above $116,800 or a married couple earning above $182,650 becomes ineligible for any tax break. All of these numbers are based on 2026 tax rates and are subject to an annual adjustment for inflation.

However, we still recommend that parents who bought these bonds with the intention of paying for college cash them in *after* the end of the last base income year (after January 1 of the student's sophomore year in college). Whether the interest from these bonds is taxed or untaxed, the FAOs still consider it income and assess it just as harshly as your wages.

Thus, if at all possible, try to avoid cashing in any and all U.S. Savings Bonds during any base income year. With Series E or EE bonds, you may be able to roll over your money into Series H or HH bonds and defer reporting interest until the college years are over. There is also no law that says you have to cash in a savings bond when it matures. You can continue to hold the bond, and in some instances it will continue to earn interest above its face value.

TIP 5:
If possible, avoid cashing in U.S. Savings Bonds during a base income year, unless you've been paying taxes on the interest each year as it accrued. And if you otherwise qualify to have assets excluded, do not file Schedule B with your tax return if your interest and dividend income are both below the $1,500 Schedule B filing threshold.

If You Have Already Put Assets in Your Other Children's Names

Parents are often told by accountants to transfer their assets into their children's name so that the assets will be taxed at the children's lower rate. While this is a good tax reduction strategy, it stinks as a financial aid strategy, as you will find out later in this chapter. However, if this is your situation and you have *already* put assets under the student's *younger siblings'* names, there is one small silver lining in this cloud: the tax laws give most parents with children under age 18 (or under age 24 if the child is a full-time student for at least 5 months during the tax year) the option of reporting their child's investment income on a separate tax return or on the parents' own tax return.

Either way, the family enjoys the benefit of reduced taxes due to the child's lower bracket. The principal advantage of reporting the child's income on the parents' return is to save the expense of paying an accountant to do a separate return.

However, if you are completing your tax returns for a base income year, we recommend that you do not report any of the student's or student's siblings' investment income (i.e., interest, dividends, and capital gains) on your tax return. By filing a separate return for those children, you remove that income from your AGI and lower your Student Aid Index. (We'll discuss reporting of the student's income later in this chapter.)

TIP 6:
During base income years, do not report children's investment income on the parents' tax return. File a separate return for each child.

Leveraged Investments

An important way in which the financial aid formulas differ from the tax code is in the handling of the income from leveraged investments. You leverage your investments by borrowing against them. The most common example of leverage is margin debt. Margin is a loan against the value of your investment portfolio, usually made by a brokerage house, so that you can buy more of whatever it is selling—for example, stock.

Let's say you had $5,000 in interest and dividend income, but you also had to pay $2,000 in tax-deductible investment interest on a margin loan. The IRS may allow you to deduct your investment interest expenses from your investment income on Schedule A. For *tax* purposes, you may have only $3,000 in net investment income.

Unfortunately, for *financial aid* purposes, interest expenses from Schedule A are not taken into account. As far as the colleges are concerned, you had $5,000 in income.

Of course you will be able to subtract the value of your margin debt from the value of your *total assets*. However, under the aid formulas, you cannot deduct the *interest* on your margin debt from your investment *income*.

During base income years, you should avoid—or at least minimize—margin debt because it will inflate your income in the eyes of the FAOs. If there is no way to avoid leveraging your investments during the college years, you should at least call the FAO's attention to the tax-deductible investment interest you are paying. Be prepared to be surprised at how financially unsavvy your FAO may turn out to be. He may not understand the concept of margin debt at all, in which case you will have to educate him. In our experience, we have found that if the situation is explained, many FAOs will make some allowance for a tax-deductible investment interest expense.

TIP 7:
During base income years, avoid large amounts of margin debt.

Schedule 1, Line 1—Taxable Refund of State and Local Income Taxes

Many people see their tax refunds as a kind of Christmas club—a way to save some money that they would otherwise spend—so they arrange to have far too much deducted from their paychecks. Any accountant knows that this is actually incredibly silly. In effect, you are giving the government the use of your money, interest-free. If you were to put this money aside during the year in an interest-bearing account, you could make yourself a nice piece of change.

So Why Does Your Accountant Encourage a Refund?

Even so, many accountants go along with the practice for a couple of reasons. First, they know that their clients are unlikely to go to the bother of setting up an automatic payroll savings plan at work. Second, they know that clients feel infinitely better when they walk out of their accountant's office with money in their pockets. It tends to offset the fee the accountant has just charged for his or her services. Third, a large refund doesn't affect how much tax you ultimately pay. Whether you have your company withhold just the right amount, or way too much, over the years you still end up paying exactly the same amount in taxes.

So accountants have gotten used to the practice, and yours probably won't tell you (or maybe doesn't know) that a large refund is the very last thing you want during base income years. Unfortunately, a large refund can seriously undermine your efforts to get financial aid.

Here's why:

If you itemize deductions and get a refund from state and local taxes, the following year you may have to report the refund as part of your federal adjusted gross income. Over the years, of course, this will have little or no effect on how much you pay in taxes, but for aid purposes, you may have just raised your Line 11a on the 1040 Form. This might not seem like it could make a big difference, but if you collect an average state and local refund of $1,600 each year over the four college years, you may have cost yourself as much as $3,000 in grant money. During college years, it is very important to keep your withholding as close as possible to the amount you will actually owe in taxes at the end of the year.

TIP 8:
If you itemize deductions, adjust your withholding to minimize state and local tax refunds.

Schedule 1, Line 2a—Taxable Alimony Received

Even though this may seem like an obvious point, we have found it important to remind people that the amount you enter on this line is not what you were *supposed* to receive in alimony, but the amount you actually got. Please don't list alimony payments your ex never made.

In fact, if your ex fell behind in alimony payments, it's important that you notify the college financial aid offices that you have received less income this year than a court of law thought you needed in order to make ends meet.

By the same token, if you received retroactive alimony payments, you would also want to contact the colleges to let them know that the amount you listed on this line is larger this year than the amount you normally receive. In a situation like this, you might be tempted to put down on the financial aid form only the amount of alimony you were supposed to receive. Please don't even think about it. Your need analysis information will be checked against your tax return. By the time they've finished their audit, and you've finished explaining that this was a retroactive payment, all the college's aid money might be gone.

Under the IRS tax code law (*but only for those with divorce agreements or who had the latest amendment to such an agreement entered into after December 31, 2018*), any alimony received will no longer be taxable. For agreements or the most recent amendment entered into prior to January 1, 2019, any alimony received will still be taxable income reportable on Schedule 1. Since untaxed alimony does not appear on the tax return, it will not be considered untaxed income for the 2027–2028 FM since the thrust of FAFSA Simplification is only to include types of untaxed income that appear on the tax return, such as tax-exempt interest. However, the College Board will consider any untaxed alimony as part of untaxed income in the IM.

Schedule 1, Line 3—Business Income

As we mentioned earlier, it can be to your advantage to become an independent contractor if you have large unreimbursed business expenses. A self-employed person is allowed to deduct business expenses from gross receipts on Schedule C. This now much smaller number (called net profit or loss) is written down on Line 3 of Schedule 1 of the 1040 form, thus reducing both taxable income and the family contribution to college tuition. We will discuss running your own business in greater detail in the "Special Topics" chapter of this book; however, a few general points should be made now.

Many salaried people run their own businesses on the side, which enables them to earn extra money while deducting a good part of this income as business expenses. However, before you run out and decide that your stamp-collecting hobby has suddenly become a business, you should be aware that the IRS auditors are old hands at spotting "dummy" businesses, and the colleges' FAOs aren't far behind.

On the other hand, if you have been planning to start a legitimate business, then by all means, the time to do it is NOW (provided this entity will not result in a great loss of aid due to you no longer being eligible for the exclusion of assets).

TIP 9:
Setting up a legitimate business on the side will enable you to deduct legitimate business expenses and may reduce your AGI.

Just bear in mind that a business must be run with the intention of showing a profit to avoid running afoul of the IRS "hobby loss" provision. The institutional methodology currently adds back business losses to your AGI.

Line 7—Capital Gains or Losses; Schedule 1, Line 4—Other Gains or Losses

When you buy a stock, bond, or any other financial instrument at one price and then sell it for more than you paid in the first place, the difference between the two prices is considered a capital gain. If you sold it for less than you paid in the first place, the difference may be considered a capital loss. We say "may be" because while you are required to report gains on all transactions, the IRS does not necessarily recognize *losses* on all types of investments.

When you sell an asset, your net worth really stays the same; you are merely converting the asset into the cash it's worth at that particular instant. However, for tax and financial aid purposes, a capital gain on the asset is considered additional *income* in the year that you sold your asset.

During base income years, you want to avoid capital gains if you can because they inflate your income. When you sell a stock, not only does the FAO assess the cash value from the sale of the stock (which is considered an asset) but she also assesses the capital gain (which is considered income).

If you need cash it is usually better to borrow against your assets rather than to sell them. Using your stock or the equity in your house as collateral, you can take out a loan. This helps you in three ways: you don't have to report any capital gains on the financial aid form, your net assets are reduced in the eyes of the FAO since you now have a debt against that asset, and in some cases, you get a tax deduction for part of the interest on the loan.

TIP 10:
If possible, avoid large capital gains during base income years.

However, there may be times when it is necessary to take capital gains. Below you will find some strategies to avoid losing aid because of capital gains. The following are somewhat aggressive strategies, and each would require you to consult your accountant and/or stockbroker:

- If you have to take capital gains, at least try to offset them with losses. Examine your portfolio. If you have been carrying a stock that's been a loser for several years, it might be time to admit that it is never going to be worth what you paid for it and take the loss. This will help to cancel your gain.

- You can elect to spread your stock losses and gains over several years. One example: the IRS allows you to deduct capital losses directly from capital gains. If your losses exceed your gains, you can deduct up to $3,000 of the excess from other income—in the year the loss occurred. However, net losses over $3,000 *are carried over to future years.* It might be possible to show net losses during several of the base income years and hold off on taking net gains until after your kids are done with college.

- The institutional methodology does not recognize capital losses that exceed gains. However, certain kinds of government aid are awarded without reference to the schools—for example, the Pell Grant and some state-funded aid programs. Because this aid is awarded strictly by the numbers, a capital loss can make a big difference. (Consult your state aid authorities and the individual schools to see how capital losses will be treated.)

- If you are worried about falling stock prices but don't want to report a capital gain, you should consult your stockbroker. There may be ways to lock in a particular price *without* selling the stock.

- If you have any atypically large capital gain in a base income year that you must report on an aid form, you should write to the colleges explaining that your income is not normally so high.

The Sale of Your Home

Under the current tax law, you are permitted to exclude up to $250,000 in capital gains every two years on the sale of your home (up to $500,000 for a married couple filing jointly). To qualify, the home must have been your primary residence that you owned and occupied for at least two of the last five years prior to the sale. Any gains in excess of the exclusion limits would, of course, be subject to income taxes.

Representatives at the Department of Education and the College Board have stated that only gains above the excludable amounts need to be reported on the aid forms, since they are then part of your Adjusted Gross Income. If you sold your home and must complete the aid forms before you purchase another property, you'll need to report the money you have from the sale as part of your assets on the aid forms. However, you should be sure to write a letter to the FAOs explaining that you will no longer have those assets once you purchase another property, if that is the case.

Lines 4a–5b—IRAs, Pensions, and Annuities

These lines on the 1040 form cover any withdrawals (called "distributions" by the IRS) made during the year from Individual Retirement Accounts (IRAs) as well as pension and annuity distributions. Most financial planning experts advise against early withdrawals before retirement since one of the biggest benefits of a qualified retirement plan is the tax-deferred compounding of investment income while the funds are in the account. In many cases, early withdrawals will trigger a 10% penalty (if you took out the funds before age 59 1/2) and you'll have to pay income taxes on part or all of the money withdrawn. (Which part of the withdrawal will be subject to income taxes will depend on whether your prior contributions were deductible or not.)

If that is not enough bad news to discourage you, consider the financial aid implications. Any IRA withdrawal during a base income year will raise your income in the financial aid formulas, thereby reducing aid eligibility. The part of the withdrawal that is taxable will raise that all-important Line 11a on your tax return; the portion that is tax-free will also likely affect your SAI, since the aid formulas assess untaxed income as well unless you qualify for the Maximum Pell Grant.

To demonstrate the negative impact of an early IRA withdrawal, let's look at an example of a parent, age 55, who took funds out of an IRA during the first base income year. The family is in the 22% federal tax bracket and since all prior IRA contributions were tax deductible, the withdrawal will be fully taxable. After subtracting the early withdrawal penalties, income taxes, and reduced aid eligibility, there will be only about 32 cents on the dollar left. Get the point? Early withdrawals from IRAs should be avoided at all costs.

A legitimate rollover of an IRA (when you move your money from one type of IRA investment into another within 60 days) is not considered a withdrawal. You do have to report a rollover to the IRS on the 1040 form, but it is not subject to penalties (so long as you stick to the IRS guidelines) and it is not considered income for financial aid purposes.

TIP 11:
Try to avoid distributions from IRAs and other qualified retirement plans during base income years.

Parents sometimes ask whether it is possible to borrow against the money in their IRAs. You are not allowed to borrow against the assets you have in an IRA. The IRS calls this a "prohibited transaction."

Note: The current tax law provides for penalty-free distributions from IRAs if the funds are used to pay for qualified educational expenses (tuition, fees, books, supplies, room and board for the undergraduate or graduate studies of the taxpayer, taxpayer's spouse, or taxpayer's child or grandchild). The words "penalty-free" only apply to the 10% early withdrawal penalty. As such, you should not assume that you will not be penalized in the financial aid process or that you will not owe any income taxes if you withdraw funds for qualified education expenses.

The law also provides taxpayers the opportunity to convert an existing IRA into a Roth IRA, provided certain criteria are met. The major benefit of this type of IRA is the fact that almost all withdrawals from a Roth IRA after age 59 1/2 will be totally tax-free. While the 10% early withdrawal penalty will not apply to this conversion, income taxes must be paid on the entire amount converted unless part of the account represents prior contributions to a non-deductible IRA. If you converted your IRA into a Roth IRA in a given year, you must report this conversion as part of Line 4b on that year's IRS 1040, thereby raising your income and your SAI in the aid formulas. However, it is important to notify the financial aid offices about any such conversion since the U.S. Department of Education has granted colleges the ability to adjust the SAI for this unusual transaction. (We'll discuss the IRAs and Roth IRAs in more detail in Chapter Ten.)

If You've Just Retired

As people wait until later in life to have children, it is becoming more commonplace to see retirees with children still in college. If you have recently retired and are being forced to take distributions from traditional IRAs, we suggest that you pull out the minimum amount possible. The government computes what this minimum amount should be based on your life expectancy (the longer you're expected to live, the longer they are willing to spread out the payments).

Because it turns out that the average American's life expectancy is higher at 66 than it is at 65, it pays to get them to recalculate your minimum distribution for each year your child is in college. Obviously, if you need the money now, then you should take it. But try to withdraw as little as possible, since IRA distributions increase your income and thus reduce financial aid.

Note: You are not required to take distributions from Roth IRAs regardless of your age.

Regarding aid, the same is true of pension distributions, as well as any distributions from annuities. The same is true with inherited IRAs. Sometimes it is possible to postpone retirement pensions or roll them over into an IRA. If you can afford to wait until your child is through college, you will increase your aid eligibility. The money isn't going anywhere, and it's earning interest.

Note: Any unusually large or early distributions from IRAs or pensions should be explained to the college financial aid offices. Any "rollovers" should also be explained when you submit a copy of your taxes to the school. Since you must include "rollovers" as part of the amount you list on Line 4a and/or 5a of the IRS 1040, some FAOs have been known to incorrectly assume that the family received the funds but failed to report this untaxed income on the aid forms. If they make this error, the SAI they determine will be much higher than it should be.

Schedule 1, Line 5—Rents, Royalties, Estates, Partnerships, Trusts, and Schedule 1, Line 6—Farm Income

Like Schedule C income, items coming under these categories are computed by adding up your gross receipts and then subtracting expenses, repairs, and depreciation. Be especially thorough about listing all expenses during base income years.

If you have a summer house or other property, you may have been frustrated in the past because, costly as it is to operate a second home, you haven't been able to deduct any of these expenses. You could consider renting it out while your son or daughter is in college. The extra income might be offset (perhaps significantly) by the expenses that you'll now be legitimately able to subtract from it. By changing how interest expense and real estate taxes are reflected on your tax return (from an itemized deduction on Schedule A to a reduction of rental income on Line 5 on Schedule 1) you reduce the magical AGI. There are special tax considerations for "passive loss" activities and recapture of depreciation, so be sure to consult your advisor before proceeding with this strategy and remember that many private colleges and a few state schools will not recognize losses of this type when awarding institutional funds since the institutional methodology adds back losses to income.

Schedule 1, Line 7—Unemployment Compensation

If you are unemployed, benefits received during the base income year are considered income under the aid formula. However, some special consideration may be granted to you. We will discuss this in more detail under the "Recently Unemployed Worker" heading in Chapter 9.

Lines 6a and 6b—Social Security Benefits

Total social security benefits are listed on Line 6a. The taxable portion of those benefits is listed on Line 6b. Whether you have to pay tax on social security benefits depends on your circumstances. Consult the instructions that come with your tax return. For some parents who have other income, part of the social security benefits received may be taxable.

Schedule 1, Line 9—Other Income

Any miscellaneous income that did not fit into any of the other lines goes here. Some examples: money received from jury duty or from proctoring SAT exams, extra insurance premiums paid by your employer, gambling income. On Schedule 1, Line 9 is the sum of Lines 8a to 8z.

Gambling income presents its own problem. The IRS allows you to deduct gambling losses against winnings. However, the deduction can, once again, only be taken as part of your itemized deductions on Schedule A. Since this happens *after* Line 11a, it is not a deduction as far as the aid formulas are concerned.

Since gambling losses are not likely to provoke much sympathy in the FAOs, we don't think there would be any point to writing them a letter about this one. During the college years, you might just want to curtail gambling.

This is the last type of taxable income on the 1040, but don't start jumping for joy yet. The colleges are interested in more than just your taxable income.

Untaxed Income

We've just looked at all the types of income that the IRS taxes and discussed how the financial aid process impacts it. There are several other types of income that the IRS doesn't bother to tax. Unfortunately, the colleges and the U.S. Department of Education do not feel so benevolent. While the IRS allows you to shelter certain types of income, the colleges and the U.S. Department of Education will assess this income as well in deciding whether you receive financial aid, and if so, how much.

Here are the other types of income the need analysis forms will ask you to report, and some strategies.

Untaxed Social Security Benefits

Any social security benefits that are not taxable are defined as "untaxed social security benefits" in the financial aid regulations. Untaxed social security benefits (as well as certain other untaxed income items that years ago were previously assessed as income in the Federal Methodology) do not need to be reported as untaxed income on the FAFSA. Such excluded untaxed social security benefits could include any untaxed benefits paid for the student (whether such benefits are paid to the student directly or paid to the parent for the benefit of the student), untaxed benefits paid to a parent for other children, or the untaxed portion of any social security benefits paid for the benefit of the parent(s) themselves. Depending on other income received by the parents during the year, a parent's own social security benefits may be fully tax-free or partially tax-free. Since any taxable social security benefits are part of the Adjusted Gross Income, they will continue to be assessed in the federal formula and the institutional formula.

Since the social security benefits for most students normally end before the student starts college (and are normally tax-free), the Institutional Methodology has excluded any untaxed social security benefits received for the student from untaxed income for a number of years. However, untaxed benefits paid to a parent for children other than the student (unless the sibling will attend college in 2027–2028) and/or the untaxed portion of any social security benefits received by the parent(s) themselves will continue to be assessed in the IM.

We'll discuss social security benefits in greater detail in Part Three, "Filling Out the Standardized Forms."

Payments Made into IRAs, Keoghs, 401(k)s, 403(b)s, and TDAs

IRAs (Individual Retirement Accounts), Keoghs, 401(k)s, 403(b)s, and TDAs (short for Tax Deferred Annuities) are all retirement provisions designed to supplement or take the place of pensions and social security benefits. The tax benefit of these plans is that in most cases they allow you to defer paying income tax on contributions until you retire, when presumably your tax bracket will be lower. The investment income on the funds is also allowed to accumulate tax-deferred until you start withdrawing the funds.

The 401(k) and 403(b) plans are supplemental retirement provisions set up by your employer in which part of your salary is deducted (at your request) from your paycheck and placed in a trust account for your benefit when you retire. Some companies choose to match part of your contributions to the plans. TDAs fulfill much the same purpose for employees of tax-exempt religious, charitable, or educational organizations.

Contributions to 401(k)s, 403(b) and other qualified retirement plans set up by your employer in which contributions to such plans reduce the amount eventually reported in Box 1 of your W-2 form—i.e., contribution to such plans listed in Box 12 for the W-2 form with codes D, E, F, G, H and S—are NOT considered untaxed in the FM, but ARE considered untaxed income in the IM.

IRAs are supplemental retirement provisions for everyone. Contributions to these plans are tax-deductible in many cases. For example, if an unmarried individual is not covered by a retirement plan at work or a self-employed retirement plan, she can make tax-deductible contributions to an IRA of up to $7,500 (up to $8,600 if age 50 or older) for 2026 regardless of her income level. If a person is covered by a retirement plan, his contribution to an IRA may or may not be tax-deductible, depending on his income level. Self-employed, SEP, Keogh, SIMPLE, and other qualified plans have restrictions as to who can contribute. Such contributions in 2025 to a plan in which the contributions will be claimed as a deduction on either Line 16 or Line 20 of Schedule 1 of the IRS 1040 return will be considered untaxed income in both the FM and the IM. Be aware that contributions to Roth IRAs or other non-deductible IRAs are not reported on Line 20 and so are not considered untaxed income in the aid formulas.

Note: The new SECURE 2.0 Act involves many changes to the IRA rules, especially regarding inherited IRAs. Before making any new contributions, withdrawals, or changes to an IRA, you should be sure to consult IRS Publication 590 for the corresponding tax year (it covers the IRA regulations and is free from Uncle Sam) or seek the advice of a qualified professional who is familiar with the tax laws as well as the financial aid regulations.

Strategies for Handling Retirement Assets

Retirement assets have long been excluded from the federal methodology (allowing parents to keep their retirement funds intact). However, as explained earlier in this chapter, contributions you make to tax-deferred retirement provisions during any base income year and during the college years had always been considered as *untaxed income in the federal formula affecting aid eligibility prior to FAFSA Simplification.* The great news is that now 401(k), 403(b), and 457(b) contributions that are deducted pre-tax by your employer from your paycheck are no longer considered untaxed income. However, contributions to traditional IRAs and other retirement plans that reduce your AGI as a result of your claiming such contributions on Schedule 1 of the IRS 1040 will still be considered as untaxed income in the FM. This is because the FAFSA Simplification provisions of the CAA only consider untaxed income items that are reported on the IRS 1040 tax return.

The strategy It will now make sense to contribute as much as possible to your 401(k), 403(b), or similar plan not just during the tax years *before* the first base income year but during any base income year used to determine aid eligibility under the new federal methodology. If you or your spouse have a choice between contributing to:

(A) a retirement plan such as a 401(k) or 403(b) that reduces the amount of your taxable wages reported on Box 1 of your W-2 form

or

(B) an IRA or other retirement plan where such a contribution is claimed on Schedule 1 of the IRS 1040 as an adjustment to income

then choose (A).

Tax-Exempt Interest Income

Even though the government is not interested in a piece of your tax-free investments, the colleges are. Some parents question whether there is any need to tell the colleges about tax-free income if it does not appear on their federal income tax return.

In fact, tax-free interest income is supposed to be entered on Line 2a of the 1040. This is not an item the IRS tends to flag, but there are excellent reasons why you should never hide these items. For one thing, tax law changes constantly. If your particular tax-free investment becomes taxable or reportable next year, how will you explain the sudden appearance of substantial taxable interest income? Or what if you need to sell your tax-free investment? You will then have to report a capital gain, and the FAO will want to know where all the money came from.

More Untaxed Income

Other untaxed income for the purposes of the federal methodology will be limited to types of untaxed income that appear on the IRS 1040 tax return, namely: the tax-free portion of any pensions or annuities received (excluding rollovers), the tax-free portion of IRA distributions (excluding rollovers) and the foreign income exclusion. These will be considered untaxed in the IM as well. Child support received will be considered as an asset, but not as income in the FM under FAFSA Simplification. It will, however, still be considered untaxed income in the IM. Workers' compensation, veterans noneducation benefits, the Health Savings Account (HSA) deduction (Schedule 1, IRS 1040 Line 13), and living allowances paid to members of the military and clergy will only be considered untaxed income in the IM. Some other categories of untaxed income (for example, untaxed disability benefits) will need to be reported on CSS Profile, but not on the FAFSA. There is little to do about this kind of income except write it down if asked about it. As with alimony, child support reported should include only the amount you actually received, not what you were supposed to receive.

Note: The federal methodology excludes contributions to, or payments from, flexible spending arrangements. As of the 2024–2025 CSS Profile, the institutional methodology excludes pre-tax contributions withheld from wages for FSA dependent care and FSA medical spending accounts, but still considers contributions to HSA accounts as part of untaxed income for the 2027–2028 award year. Along with the HSA deduction, schools will have the opportunity to exclude such HSA contributions. In addition, the following types of untaxed income not considered in the FM are considered part of untaxed income in the IM: welfare benefits, untaxed alimony received, and the credit for federal tax on special fuels.

Good News About Untaxed Income in the FM

With FAFSA Simplification, monies received or bills paid on the student's behalf—for example, distributions for a 529 plan or a Coverdell plan owned by someone other than the student or their (step)parent required to report their information on the FAFSA—will no longer be considered untaxed income to the student under the federal formula as they did in the past. (The IM did not and will continue to not consider such distributions as untaxed income.) Of course, we don't know if individual schools will feel the same way. There is the possibility such distributions could now reduce your aid package by the amount of any such distribution. This is because some schools will consider these as "resources" similar to an outside scholarship, which reduce one's demonstrated need, and the school will still expect the calculated contribution from the student (and if applicable the student's spouse and parents). It is important to remember that if such distributions are considered a "resource," the reduction in aid will be immediate and occur during that award year—and so the timing of such a distribution outside a base income year will be irrelevant.

The strategy If you think you can qualify for aid, you still might want to advise well-meaning relatives to avoid setting up these plans with themselves as the owner. But if they have already done so, it may make sense to have the ownership changed to a custodial (step)parent for some or all of the funds in the plan, if permitted, prior to such a qualified distribution being made.

Here's a small silver lining for separated/divorced parents: under the new federal methodology, child support will now be considered an asset, but not untaxed income. (And if you meet the criteria to have assets excluded, it will no longer be considered at all since assets are not required to be reported.) This is good news since, as explained earlier in the chapter, the next dollar of available income for the parent of a dependent student is assessed up to 47 cents on the dollar, while the next dollar of reportable assets for such a parent is assessed at most 5.65% in the federal formula. (The IM will continue to treat child support as income.)

The strategy Try to meet the criteria to have assets excluded if possible. But bear in mind that while child support will now be treated more favorably in the new federal methodology, many schools are probably going have their own ideas about this more benign treatment and may still consider such support as untaxed income.

There's good news for parents or children who receive untaxed allowances for housing, food, and certain other expenses: these living allowances paid to members of the military, clergy, or others will no longer be considered untaxed income in the new federal methodology. Other types of untaxed income such as veteran's non-education benefits, worker's compensation, and disability benefits will not be considered in the FM either. As stated above in the section regarding 401(k) contributions, this is in keeping with the spirit of FAFSA Simplification to only consider as untaxed income those types of income that are reported on the IRS 1040: contributions to SEPs, Keoghs, Traditional IRAs, SIMPLE plans and other qualified retirement plans; tax-exempt interest income; and untaxed portions of distributions from IRAs, pensions and annuities—all of which were considered untaxed income under the old FM as well.

Expenses

After adding up all your income, the need analysis formulas provide a deduction for some types of expenses. A few of these expenses mirror the adjustments to income section of the 1040 income tax form. Many parents assume that all the adjustments to income from the IRS form can be counted on the standardized financial aid forms. Unfortunately, this is not the case. Likewise, many parents assume that all of the itemized tax deductions they take on Schedule A will count on the financial aid forms as well. Almost none of these are included in the financial aid formula. Let's look at adjustments to income first.

Expenses According to the IRS: Adjustments to Income

Schedule 1, Line 11—Educator expenses

This adjustment to income involves educators in both public and private elementary and secondary schools who work at least 900 hours during a school year as a teacher, instructor, counselor, principal, or aide and who have certain qualifying out-of-pocket expenses. The maximum deduction for this item was $300 per taxpayer in 2025, and there are other criteria you need to meet. If allowable, it is to your advantage to take the deduction as an adjustment to income.

Schedule 1, Line 14—Moving Expenses

Job-related moving expenses are deductible as an adjustment to income for members of the Armed Forces. Years ago, these expenses could be taken only as part of your itemized deductions and did not affect your aid eligibility. Since this item will both reduce your tax liability and potentially increase your aid eligibility, you should be sure to include all allowable moving expenses. There is a great deal of fine print in the tax law regarding what constitutes a moving expense, so be sure to read the IRS instructions or consult a competent advisor.

Schedule 1, Line 15—Deductible Part of Self-Employment Tax

Self-employed individuals can deduct one half of the self-employment taxes they pay. The federal and institutional formulas take this deduction into account.

Schedule 1, Lines 16 and 20—IRA Deductions and Self-Employed SEP, SIMPLE, and Qualified Plans Deductions

As we explained above, while these constitute legitimate tax deductions, contributions to deductible IRAs, SEPs, KEOGHs, and other plans that can be deducted on Line 16 or Line 20 of Schedule 1 will not reduce your income under the FM or IM aid formulas.

However, some forms of state aid (which do not use the federal methodology employed by the colleges themselves) may be boosted by contributions to retirement plans that reduce your AGI, as some state programs are based solely on taxable income. We'll discuss this in detail in Chapter Six, "State Aid." Contributions to an IRA could lower your AGI below the $60,000 cap to have assets excluded in the FM, provided you meet the other criteria. Individuals who make contributions to plans that are deducted on Line 16 of Schedule 1 are either self-employed or a partner and therefore generally cannot meet the criteria to have assets excluded unless someone in the household received a federal means-tested benefit in the PPY or PY years or the student meets the Maximum Pell criteria.

Schedule 1, Line 17—Self-Employed Health Insurance Deduction

This is another adjustment to income recognized by the FAO. If you are self-employed or own more than 2% of the shares of an S corporation, it is to your advantage to deduct qualifying premiums on Line 17 of Schedule 1 instead of lumping qualified health insurance premiums together with all your other medical expenses on Schedule A. First, this will reduce your AGI, and second, because it is a sure deduction here. If your total medical expenses do not exceed a certain percentage of your AGI, you won't get a deduction for medical expenses at all on your taxes. In addition, high medical expenses (other than those included here on Line 17) are no longer an automatic deduction in the federal aid formula. We'll describe this in detail, under "Medical Deduction" later in this chapter.

Schedule 1, Line 18—Penalty on Early Withdrawal of Savings, and Line 19a—Deductible Alimony Paid

If you took an early withdrawal of savings before maturity, which incurred a penalty, and/or you paid out alimony, these amounts will be claimed here. The FM and IM aid formulas grant you a deduction for these two adjustments to income as well. Alimony paid that is not deductible on Schedule 1 will also be a deduction in the IM, though not in the FM.

Schedule 1, Line 21—Student Loan Interest Deduction

This deduction can involve loans used to cover your own post-secondary educational expenses as well as those of your spouse or any other dependent at the time the loan was taken out. We'll discuss more of the fine print in Chapter Ten. You should realize that any deduction claimed here will reduce your income under both the federal and the institutional formulas.

Schedule 1, Line 12—Certain Business Expenses of Reservists, Performing Artists, and Fee-Basis Government Officials; Other Adjustments included as Part of Schedule 1, Line 26

While each of these adjustments to income will lower your AGI—and therefore your SAI—they are not applicable for the vast majority of tax filers.

Other Expenses According to the Financial Aid Formula

You've just seen all the adjustments to income that the IRS allows. The colleges allow you a deduction for several other types of expenses for financial aid purposes as well.

Federal Income Tax Paid

The advice we are about to offer may give your accountant a heart attack. Obviously, you want to pay the lowest taxes possible, but timing can come into play during the college years. The higher the taxes you pay during a base income year, the lower your family contribution will be. This is because the federal income taxes you pay count as an expense item in the aid formula. There are certain sets of circumstances when it is possible to save money by paying higher taxes. The principle here is to end up having paid the same amount of taxes over the long run, but to concentrate the taxes into the years the colleges are scrutinizing, thus increasing your aid eligibility.

Let's look at a hypothetical example. Suppose you make exactly the same amount of money in two separate years. You are in the 22% income tax bracket, and the tax tables don't change over these two years. Your federal tax turns out to be $6,000 the first year and $6,000 the second year, for a total tax bill of $12,000 for the two years.

Let's also suppose you decide to make an IRA contribution during only one of the two years, but you aren't sure in which year to make the contribution. You're married, 52 years old, and neither of you is covered by a pension plan at work, and you decide to make a tax-deductible IRA contribution of $6,500. This turns out to reduce your federal taxes by $1,430 for the year in which you make the contribution. Since, in this case, your tax situation is precisely the same for both years, it doesn't make much difference in which year you take the deduction.

$12,000	total taxes over 2 years (if no IRA contribution made)
– $ 1,430	tax savings for IRA contribution
$10,570	total taxes for the 2 years

Over the two years, either way, you end up paying a total of about $10,570 in federal taxes.

It's All a Matter of Timing

Here's where timing comes in. What if the second of the two years also happens to be your first base income year? In this case, you're much better off making the contribution during the previous year. By doing so, as we've already explained, you shelter the $6,500 asset from the need analysis formula and get a $1,430 tax break in the first year.

But much more important, by making the contribution during the first year, you choose to pay the higher tax bill in the second year—the base income year—which in turn lowers your Student Aid Index. Over the two years, you're still paying close to the same amount in taxes, but you've concentrated the taxes into the base income year where it will do you some good.

TIP 12:
Concentrate your federal income taxes into base income years to lower your Student Aid Index.

Obviously, if you can afford to make IRA contributions every year, you should do so; building a retirement fund is a vital part of any family's long-term planning. However, if like many families, you find that you can't afford to contribute every year during college years, you can at least use timing to increase your expenses in the eyes of the FAOs. By loading up on retirement provision contributions during non-base income years, avoiding tax-deductible retirement contributions to plans where the contribution is deducted on Schedule 1 of the IRS 1040, and making other tax-saving measures during base income years, you can substantially increase your aid eligibility.

The above example assumed that tax rates would be the same from year to year. Should tax rates change from one year to the next, you will need to balance your tax planning with your financial aid planning to determine the best course of action.

Charitable Contributions

Large donations to charity are a wonderful thing, both from a moral standpoint and a tax standpoint—but not during a base income year. When you lower your taxes, you raise your family contribution significantly. We aren't saying you should stop giving to charity, but we do recommend holding off on large gifts until after the base income years.

Extra Credits

When you are asked questions on the FAFSA about U.S. income taxes paid, the government and the colleges are not interested in how much tax you had withheld during the year or whether you are entitled to a refund. Instead, they are interested in your federal income tax liability after certain tax credits are deducted, which happens to be the amount of Line 24 on the 2025 IRS 1040 for the FM and Line 22 for the IM. While most tax credits that you claim will eventually reduce your aid eligibility (since lower taxes mean lower expenses against income in the formulas), the tax benefits from these credits will be much greater than the amount of aid that is lost. As such, you should be sure to deduct any and all tax credits that you are entitled to claim on your tax return.

Be aware that under the federal formula, any education tax credits claimed (such as the American Opportunity Credit (AOC) and the Lifetime Learning Credit) will not reduce aid eligibility. While any nonrefundable education credits claimed—for 2025, these would be claimed on Line 3 of Schedule 3 of the IRS Form 1040—will reduce the amount of U.S. income taxes paid, they will also be considered an "exclusion from income," which in aid speak means a deduction against income. So in effect, any education credits claimed will reduce expenses and income by an equal amount, thereby allowing families and students the full benefit of the American Opportunity Credit or the Lifetime Learning Credit. (Later in Chapter Ten, we'll discuss some strategies to ensure you get the maximum credits allowed by law; for now, we just want to focus on their aid impact.)

Unfortunately, the institutional formula has not been as benevolent. Since the nonrefundable education credits are not considered an exclusion against income, any nonrefundable credits claimed will partially reduce aid eligibility. However, the College Board will give colleges the option of having any refundable education credits added back to the amount of U.S. income taxes paid, so that any impact on aid will be negligible.

Both the FM and IM do not consider any refundable portion of the American Opportunity Credit to be untaxed income. This would be claimed on Line 29 of the 2025 IRS 1040, using Form 8863 to calculate the amount of the refundable amount as well as the nonrefundable amount, if any, for the AOC or LLC. A nonrefundable credit can only be claimed if a taxpayer has income tax liability, while a refundable credit can be claimed even if the taxable income is so low that there is no resulting income tax liability.

The FM currently considers the refundable portion of the American Opportunity Credit claimed on Line 29 of the IRS 1040 to also be an exclusion from income. However, the IM does not.

The Alternative Minimum Tax

Until recently, those families who were subject to the Alternative Minimum Tax were actually penalized in the aid formulas—for while they had to pay the tax, the formulas did not take this additional tax into account. The Alternative Minimum Tax (AMT) is an additional tax that is incurred if certain deductions or tax credits reduce the amount of U.S. income taxes paid below a certain level. Many of our readers don't have to worry about the AMT since it usually impacts more individuals in the top income tax brackets.

But we have good news for those few readers who must pay the AMT. Federal income taxes paid in the financial aid formulas currently include any Alternative Minimum Tax liability. This will generally reduce the SAI in both the federal and institutional methodologies for those subject to the AMT, since the amount of federal income taxes paid is a deduction against income in the formulas.

Deduction for Social Security and Medicare Taxes

The financial aid formulas give you a deduction for the Medicare and social security taxes (otherwise known as FICA) that you pay. Parents often ask how the colleges do this since there doesn't seem to be a question about social security taxes on the financial aid forms. The deduction is actually made automatically by computer. On the FAFSA it will be based on the Income Earned from Work question, calculated jointly in a special formula for joint return filers.

On the CSS Profile, the two relevant questions are "father's income earned from work," and "mother's income earned from work." At first glance these questions on both forms appear to be about income. In fact, for tax filers, these are expense questions. If you minimize the amounts you put down here, you may cost yourself aid.

Therefore, you should be sure to include all sources of income from work on which you've paid FICA or Medicare taxes: wages (box 1 of your W-2) and income from self-employment (Line 3 on Schedule 1 of the 1040). As we went to press, it still seems that income from partnerships subject to self-employment taxes (not including income from limited partnerships) would not be considered in the FM. However, such partnership income should be included as part of any CSS Profile questions pertaining to income earned from work.

State and Local Tax Allowance

Under FAFSA Simplification, this allowance was eliminated in the FM, given the significant increase in the Income Protection Allowance which we will discuss shortly.

However, this is another calculation that is done automatically by the CSS Profile processor. The computer determines your deduction by taking the sum of your taxable and untaxable income and multiplying it by a certain percentage based on the state in which you live. The formula for each state is slightly different.

This works very well for people who live and work in the same state but presents real problems for everyone else. If you live in one state but work in another where the taxes are higher, you may be paying more in taxes than the formula indicates. The financial need computer isn't programmed to deal with situations like this, and people who don't fit the program get penalized.

The only way to deal with this is to write to the individual colleges' aid offices at schools that require the CSS Profile to let them know about your special situation.

Employment Allowance

Under the federal methodology, whether you are a single parent who works or you are in a two parent-family situation where at least one parent works, then you qualify for the employment allowance. For the 2027–2028 SAI formula, two-parent households get a deduction of 35% of the combined wage earners' income from work up to a maximum deduction of $5,200. Single parents (i.e., separated, divorced, widowed, or never married) get a deduction of 35% of their income earned from work up to a maximum deduction of $5,200. The employment allowance is figured out for you automatically by the need analysis computer.

The Income Protection Allowance

The Income Protection Allowance amounts will be getting a significant boost under FAFSA Simplification, though this is being offset by the elimination of the State and Other Tax Allowance. This is the federal financial aid formula's idea of how much money your family needs to house, feed, and clothe itself during one year. According to the formula for the 2027–2028 award year:

- a family of 6 can live on $64,290
- a family of 5 can live on $54,970
- a family of 4 can live on $46,590
- a family of 3 can live on $37,720
- a family of 2 can live on $30,300

For each additional family member add $7,260.

The Income Protection Allowance is based solely on the number of family members currently living in the household. Under Simplification, the number of dependent children in college will no longer impact this allowance. It is determined by the U.S. government figures for the poverty line and does not take into account the cost of living in your part of the country.

Many parents assume that a portion of their monthly mortgage payments will be deducted from their income on the aid formulas in much the same way as it is on their taxes. Unfortunately, this is not the case. The Income Protection Allowance is supposed to include all housing expenses.

We strongly recommend that you sit down and write out a budget of how much it actually takes to keep your family going and send it to the individual colleges. Include everything. In many parts of the country, the Income Protection Allowance is fairly ludicrous, but it is up to you to show the FAO just how ludicrous it is in your case.

The institutional methodology uses current consumer expense survey data to determine this allowance in the formula. While the formula is not available, in the past the numbers have been somewhat higher than in the federal formula.

Annual Education Savings Allowance

Recognizing the fact that parents should be saving for any younger siblings' college expenses while simultaneously financing the older child's college expenses, the College Board's IM includes a deduction against income called the Annual Education Savings Allowance. The CSS Profile processor will automatically calculate the amount of this allowance, which was 1.52% of the parents' total income (up to a maximum of $2,770 for the 2010–2011 formula, which was the last year the IM was published) multiplied by the number of pre-college children, excluding the student applicant.

Optional Expenses

Under the federal methodology, high unreimbursed medical and dental expenses as well as elementary/secondary school tuition for the student's siblings are no longer automatically deducted from income. However, you may well have to answer questions about these categories anyway on both the CSS Profile form and the school's own aid forms—the reason being that under the institutional methodology or the schools' own aid policies, these items may be considered as deductions against income.

Even if you are only completing the FAFSA (which does not ask about these items) it still makes sense to let the FAOs know about any high expenses they would not otherwise find out about. As we have already mentioned, information like this should be sent directly to the schools under separate cover.

Here are some tips on how to answer questions about medical and tuition expenses.

Medical Deduction

To be able to deduct medical expenses on your federal tax return, you must have expenses in excess of 7.5% of your AGI. However, college financial aid guidelines are not necessarily as strict. Some families who don't qualify under federal tax law just assume they won't qualify under the financial aid rules either, so they enter "0" for their medical expenses on the aid forms. This can be a costly mistake.

Here's a quick example. Let's say your family's adjusted gross income is $50,000, and you had medical expenses of $3,000. As far as the IRS is concerned, you won't get a medical deduction this year. Your $3,000 medical bills fall well short of 7.5% of $50,000 ($3,750). However, under the financial aid formulas, you may indeed receive a deduction against income. Under the federal methodology, the FAOs can use their discretion for this item. Under the institutional methodology, the rules for this expense category are more defined.

Therefore, even if you don't have enough medical and dental expenses to qualify under the federal tax law, don't assume that it would be a waste of time to disclose these figures. Many colleges are using the institutional methodology, which will grant an allowance for unreimbursed medical expenses in excess of 3% or 4% of your income. If you are filling out the CSS Profile form, there is a place on the form to report this information. Many of the schools' separate financial aid forms ask for this information as well.

What Constitutes a Medical Expense?

There are more than 100 legitimate medical deductions. Here are just a few: doctors, dentists, prescription eyeglasses, therapists, after-tax health insurance premiums that were deducted from your paycheck or that you paid personally, medical transportation and lodging.

Note: Self-employed individuals and owners of more than 2% of the shares of a subchapter S corporation are better off deducting their health insurance premiums on Line 17 of Schedule 1 of the 2025 IRS 1040 form.

Whose Medical Expenses Can Be Included?

You should include medical expenses for every single member of your household, not just the student who is going to college. When families come in to see us, they inevitably start out by saying that they do not have much in the way of unreimbursed medical expenses.

However, when we get them to write it all down, it often turns out to be a hefty sum. Keep careful records and include EVERYTHING. Did you take a cab to and from the doctor's office? Did anyone get braces? Did anyone get contact lenses?

And If We Have Very Low Medical Expenses?

Congratulations, but keep records anyway. The CSS Profile form now will advise you to list 0 (zero) for an applicable year when the total is less than a certain percentage of your income. But you may have to answer questions about these items on the schools' own aid forms. You might as well give the FAOs a realistic sense of what your monthly bills look like.

Last Medical Point

We recommend that if you don't have medical expenses in excess of 3.0% of your total taxable and untaxable income each year, you might consider postponing some discretionary medical procedures and advancing others in order to bunch your deductions together and pass the 3.0% mark during one particular year. This might seem at first to fly in the face of conventional wisdom. Facing the burden of college, many parents' first thought would be to put off braces for a younger child, for example. In fact, if you are in a base income year, it makes much more sense to get them now. Once you reach the 3.0% threshold, each dollar in excess may increase your aid eligibility by 47 cents.

Finally, if you anticipate large medical bills in the near future, you should certainly let the colleges know what's coming up.

Elementary and Secondary School Tuition

If the child going to college will have a younger brother or sister concurrently attending a private elementary or secondary school, you may be able to get a deduction for part of the tuition you pay for the private school during the academic year. Neither the federal nor the institutional methodologies provide an automatic deduction, but the CSS Profile form and many of the individual college aid forms do ask questions about this category. The FAOs are supposed to use their judgment in deciding whether to make any deduction for younger children's tuition.

Obviously, you can't include the private high school tuition of the child who is now applying to college because next year the student won't be there anymore. You are also not allowed to include the cost of pre-school (unless specified on the school's aid form). Nor can you include college tuition of other siblings. (Don't worry. If you have more than one child in college at the same time, this will be taken into account elsewhere.) When you write down the amount you pay in elementary and secondary school tuition, remember to subtract any scholarship money you receive.

Keeping Track of Information

What makes all this complicated is that some of the schools you will be applying to will require just the FAFSA (which does not ask about medical expenses and siblings' tuition), others will also require the CSS Profile form (which asks about medical expenses and siblings' tuition), and others will have their own forms as well. It's easy to forget which schools know what information.

If you apply to a school that requires only the FAFSA, they will not see any of the information you filled out on your CSS Profile form. If that school does not ask questions about items such as unreimbursed medical expenses on their own aid form and you consider this information important, you should send it to the school under separate cover.

In addition, some state grant aid programs will increase award amounts if you send them proof of high medical expenses.

Good News for a Few Parents

The institutional methodology will still allow a deduction for the payment of child support (excluding support paid for children in the household). Under Simplification, this offset against income was eliminated in the FM.

So Far So Good

Now that you've given the need analysis people all this information, they will add up all your taxable and untaxable income and then subtract all the expenses and adjustments they have decided to allow. What's left is your available income.

Available income will be assessed on a sliding scale. If your available income is zero (or less), the parents' contribution from income will be zero. If your available income is greater, the contribution will be greater. The parents' contribution from income can go only as high as 47% of available income under the federal formula and as high as 46% under the institutional methodology.

If you are applying to colleges that require the CSS Profile form (and thus use the institutional methodology), the parents' contribution from income may be higher or lower than it would be under the federal methodology.

Income and Expenses: How the Methodologies Differ

Federal Methodology

- Excludes medical/dental expenses
- Income Protection Allowance based on poverty line figures, adjusted for inflation
- Excludes all untaxed social security benefits. With the exception of child support, which will be considered an asset, the FM will only consider untaxed income items that appear on the IRS 1040 tax return including the foreign income exclusion that appears on the IRS 1040 tax return.

Institutional Methodology

- Provides an allowance for unreimbursed medical and dental expenses in excess of 4% of income (though some schools may use a lower %)
- Excludes any untaxed social security benefits received for the student
- Income Protection Allowance based on current consumer expenditure survey data
- No Employment Allowance
- Provides a set-aside for younger siblings' educational costs
- Adds back losses that appear on Line 7 of the IRS 1040 as well as on Lines 3, 4, 5, 6, and any part of Line 8 on Schedule 1 of the 2025 IRS 1040
- Considers deductible contributions to Health Savings Accounts (Line 13 on Schedule 1 of the 2025 IRS 1040) as well as HSA contributions deducted by the employer
- Gives colleges the option of making an allowance for elementary/secondary tuition paid for the student's siblings
- No criteria for the exclusion of assets
- Nonrefundable education tax credits reduce aid eligibility, unless the school chooses to have them added back to U.S. income taxes paid

Assets and Liabilities

Now that the need analysis companies know about your available income, they want to know about your assets and liabilities. On the standardized financial aid forms, these two items are joined at the hip. Liabilities are subtracted from assets to determine your net assets. In a nutshell, the strategies you will find in this section are designed to make the value of your assets look as small as possible, and the debts against your assets as large as possible. Note that information about businesses and farms may yet change.

What Counts as an Asset?

Cash, checking and savings accounts, money market accounts, CDs, U.S. Savings Bonds, Educational IRAs, stocks, other bonds, mutual funds, trusts, ownership interests in certain businesses and farms, and the current market value of real estate holdings other than your home.

None of these items appear directly on your tax return. However, your tax return will still provide the colleges with an excellent way to verify these assets. How? Most assets create income and/or tax deductions, both of which do appear on your tax return in the form of capital gains, capital losses, interest, dividends, and/or itemized deductions on Schedule A.

Assets in insurance policies and retirement provisions such as IRAs, Keoghs, annuities, and 401(k)s are generally not assessed in the aid formulas (though as we have already said, voluntary tax-deductible contributions to retirement provisions made during base income years must be listed as part of untaxed income). Cars are also excluded from the formula and don't have to be listed on the form. Coverdell ESAs (formerly known as Education IRAs) and Section 529 plans have some interesting quirks which we'll explain shortly.

What About My Home?

Under the federal methodology, the value of your home is not considered part of your assets. This is great news and will help many families who own their own home to qualify for a Pell Grant and other federal aid programs. However, many colleges are using the more stringent institutional methodology to award their own funds. Under this formula, the value of your home will not be excluded from your assets.

Which schools will exclude the value of your home? It's safe to say that most state schools will do so. If a school asks you to complete the CSS Profile form and/or asks you for the value of your home on their own aid form, then most likely the value of the home is going to be treated like other assets. You can bet that the highly selective private colleges that meet a high percentage of their financial aid students' need will be looking closely at home equity. Other private colleges may or may not.

However, even if you're considering colleges that have decided to look at home value, the news is not all bad. Starting with the 2003–2004 award year, 28 highly selective private colleges and universities agreed to cap home value at 2.4 times the parents' total yearly income. In other words, if you earn $50,000 for the year, at these schools the value of your home (for assessment purposes) will be considered to be no more than $120,000 ($50,000 × 2.4)—even if you own a home worth $200,000.

It appears that the actions by these schools has had a "trickle down" effect as more and more schools that used to look at the full value of the home have ceased taking the total home equity into account when awarding their own aid funds. Some schools, including a number of those 28 schools, have more recently decided to cap the amount of home equity at two times income, while others will no longer assess home equity at all or will not assess it if the family's income is below a certain level.

One of the questions you may want to ask the FAO at any school you are considering is the way(s) they will treat home value—not at all, only if the income exceeds a certain amount, with the value capped at a certain percentage of income, with the equity capped at a particular percentage of income, or at full value.

Under the federal methodology, the definition of "home" is the primary residence. If you own a vacation home in addition to your primary residence, the vacation home will not be excluded from your assets. If you own a vacation home, and you rent your primary residence, the value of the vacation home will still not be excluded under the federal formula—as it is considered "other real estate."

What About My Farm?

Prior to Simplification, the net worth of a family farm was exempted as an asset for decades in the FM. Simplification then rescinded this exemption. So beginning with the 2024–2025 FAFSA, the net worth of such a family farm (excluding the value of the farmhouse that served as the family's primary residence) was required to be reported (unless the applicant was otherwise exempt from reporting all assets). However with the passage of the One Big Beautiful Bill Act (OBBBA), the family farm exemption was restored. So only the net worth of investment farms (that are not incorporated or part of a partnership) are now required to be reported. Under the IM, the value of any farm property needs to be reported.

How Much Are My Assets Worth?

To repeat, the need analysis form is a snapshot of your financial situation. The value of most assets (with the exception of money in the bank) changes constantly, as financial markets rise and fall. The colleges want to know the value of your assets *on the day* you fill out the form.

Remember, This is One Snapshot for Which You Don't Want to Look Your Best

When people sit down to fill out financial statements, they tend to want to put their best foot forward. After all, most of the time when you fill out one of these forms it is because you are applying for a credit card, or a bank loan, or hoping to be accepted by a country club or an exclusive condominium. Trying to look as fiscally healthy as possible has become almost automatic. However, you must remember that in this case you are applying for financial aid. They aren't going to give it to you if you don't let them see the whole picture, warts and all. On the financial aid form, you don't want to gloss over your debts.

What Counts as a Debt?

The only debts that are considered under the financial aid formulas are debts against the specific assets listed on the aid forms.

For example, you do NOT get credit for: unsecured loans, personal loans, educational loans like Stafford or PLUS loans for college, consumer debt such as outstanding credit card balances, or auto loans. If you have any debt of these types, you should realize that it will NOT be subtracted from your assets under the financial aid formulas.

It will be to your advantage to minimize these types of debt during the college years. In fact, you may want to convert these loans into debts that do get credit under the financial aid formulas.

You DO get credit for: margin loans, passbook loans, home equity loans, first mortgages, and second mortgages on "other real estate." Of course, you will only get credit for debts on your *primary* residence if the college has decided to look at your home value.

TIP 13:
Convert debts that are not counted by the aid formulas into types of debt that do count.

Let's go through the different types of assets you have to report and discuss strategies for minimizing the appearance of those assets.

Cash, Checking Accounts, Savings Accounts

The need analysis forms ask you to list any money in your accounts on the day you fill out the forms. However, you can't list this money if it isn't there.

We are not counseling you to go on a spending spree, but if you were planning to make a major purchase in the near future, you might as well make it now. If roof repairs are looming, if you can prepay your summer vacation, if you were going to buy a new car sometime in the next year, do it now, and pay cash. You were going to make these purchases anyway. By speeding up the purchase, you reduce the appearance of your cash assets.

TIP 14:
If you were going to buy soon, buy now and use cash.

Another way to reduce assets in the bank is to use the cash to pay off a liability that the colleges refuse to look at.

Plastic Debt

If you have credit card debt, your need analysis form won't give a realistic picture of your net worth, because as far as the colleges are concerned, plastic debt doesn't exist. You could owe thousands of dollars on your VISA card, but the aid formula does not allow you to subtract this debt from your assets, or to subtract the interest on the debt from your income.

Any financial advisor will tell you that if you have any money in the bank at all, it is crazy not to pay off your credit card debt. Recently we had one parent say to us, "But it makes me feel secure to have $7,000 in the bank. I know I could pay my $2,000 MasterCard bill, but then I would have only $5,000 left."

There are three reasons why this is wrong-headed thinking.

First, any way you look at it, that parent really did have only $5,000. It is a complete illusion to think that you have more money just because you can see it in your bank account at the moment.

Second, this guy's $2,000 credit card debt was costing him a lot of money—around 20% each year. This was 20% that could not be deducted from income on his taxes or on his financial aid form. Meanwhile, the $2,000 he was keeping in the bank because it made him feel better was earning all of 0.1% after taxes. He was being taken to the cleaners.

Third, and most important, by paying off his credit card debt he could reduce his net assets on the need analysis form and pick up some more aid.

TIP 15:
Use cash in the bank to pay off credit card balances. This will reduce your assets and thus increase your eligibility for aid.

Your Tax Bill

If you did not have enough tax withheld from your wages this year, and you will end up owing the IRS money, consider speeding up the completion of your taxes so that you can send in your return—with a check—before you complete the need analysis form.

If you are self-employed, you might consider prepaying your next quarterly estimate. The IRS is always pleased to receive the money early. You will lose out on the interest the money would have earned if it had stayed in your account a little longer, but this will probably be more than offset by your increased aid eligibility.

TIP 16:
Use cash in the bank to pay off tax bills to reduce your assets and increase your eligibility for aid.

You will notice on the FAFSA that next to the item "cash, savings, and checking accounts," there is no mention of debts as there is for the other asset categories on the form. For the most part, you can't have debts on these kinds of assets. However, there is one exception.

Passbook Loans

With a passbook loan, you use your savings account as collateral for a loan. This is a legitimate debt against your asset. To get credit for the debt, you should include your savings account and the debt against it under "investments" (on the FAFSA) and under "investments" (on the CSS Profile form).

IRAs, Keoghs, 401(k)s, 403(b)s and other qualified retirement accounts

In most cases, money that you contribute to a retirement provision—such as an IRA, Keogh, 401(k), or 403(b)—*before* the base income years begin is completely sheltered from the FAOs. That money isn't part of the snapshot; they can't touch it.

However, as we stated in our section on income, contributions to those qualified retirement plans that reduce your Adjusted Gross Income (AGI) made *during* base income years are a different story, depending on the type of account. So contributions to 401(k)s, 403(b)s, 457(b)s, and other qualified retirement plans in which the contributions reduce your wages reported in Box 1 of your W-2 form will no longer be considered untaxed income in the FM but will be considered untaxed income in the IM. (The amount of such contributions withheld from your pay by your employer will appear in Box 12 of your W-2. It is this amount that will affect your family contribution in the institutional methodology.) However, any deduction claimed for any contributions to a retirement account on Schedule 1 of your IRS Form 1040 personal income tax return will still be considered untaxed income in the FM and will continue to be considered untaxed income in the IM.

Prying Colleges

Although the FAFSA doesn't ask questions about the money in parents' retirement provisions or insurance policies, a few private colleges ask for this information on their own forms. Short of refusing to apply to these colleges, there is nothing you can do but supply the information gracefully. Unless you have several hundreds of thousands of dollars of these assets, however, there should be little effect on your family contribution. While the CSS Profile does ask separate questions regarding the value of your qualified retirement accounts, such assets are not assessed in the IM.

They Won't Give Aid to *Us*—We Own Our Own Home

One of the biggest myths about financial aid is that parents who own their own home will not qualify for aid. This is not the case at all. As we have already mentioned, the federal methodology (used to award Pell Grants and other federal aid programs) no longer looks at home equity. While many private colleges and some state universities continue to use home equity in determining eligibility for their own aid programs, it has been our experience that most homeowners—even in this situation—do get aid. In some cases, this will be true even if they have several properties, if they apply for it in the right way.

Real Estate Strategies

Because we know that many of our readers will be applying to schools that assess home equity in awarding the funds under their own control, the next few sections of this chapter will suggest strategies that focus on both your primary residence and any other real estate you may own.

If none of the schools you are considering assess home equity, then the following strategies will apply only to your other real estate holdings.

Valuing the Property—Be Realistic

Figuring out the value of your home can be difficult. Is it worth what your neighbors down the street sold theirs for last week? Is it worth what someone offered you three years ago? Is it worth the appraised value on your insurance policy? Figuring out the value of other properties can be even more difficult, especially if you rarely see them.

You want to try to be as accurate as possible. The temptation to over-represent the value of your real estate should be firmly controlled. The forms are asking for the value of the property if you had to sell it right this minute, today—not what you would get for it if you had a leisurely six months to find a buyer. If you had to sell it in a hurry—at fire-sale prices—how much is it worth? Remember also that there are always attendant costs when you sell a property: painting and remodeling, possible early payment penalties for liquidating your mortgage, real estate agent's commission. If the colleges want to know what your real estate is worth, these costs should be taken into account. Be realistic. Inflating the price of your property beyond what it is really worth will reduce your aid eligibility.

At the same time, you don't want to under-represent the value either. The colleges have verification procedures to prevent parents from lowballing. One of the procedures: the CSS Profile form asks when you purchased your home and how much you paid for it. The analysis computer will then feed these numbers into the Federal Housing Index Multiplier to see whether your current valuation is within reasonable norms. Some schools have also started to use zillow.com to value properties.

Equity

Ultimately, what your real estate is worth is much less important than how much equity you've built up in it. Your equity is the current market value of your real estate minus what you owe on it (mortgages, home equity loan balances, debts secured by the home). Let's assume for a moment that two families are looking at a private college that considers home equity as an asset. All other things being equal, the family with a $100,000 house fully paid up would probably pay a higher family contribution to that college than the family with a $300,000 house with a $250,000 mortgage. Sounds crazy? Not really. The first family has built up equity of $100,000; the second family has equity of only $50,000.

Parents often don't remember when they are filling out the need analysis forms that their first mortgage need not be their only debt against their property. Did you, for example, borrow money from your parents to make a down payment? Have you taken out a home improvement loan? Have you borrowed against a home equity loan line of credit? Is there a sewer assessment? All of these are also legitimate debts against the value of your real estate.

If you are a part-owner in any property, obviously you should list only your share of the equity in that property.

The Home Equity Loan: A Possible Double Play

One of the smarter ways to pay for college is the home equity loan. A home equity loan is a line of credit, secured, most likely, by the equity in your home. Of course, it is also possible to get a home equity loan using one of your other properties as collateral. You draw checks against this line of credit, up to the full value of the loan, but you pay no interest until you write a check, and you pay interest only on the amount that you actually borrow.

There are two possible benefits to a home equity loan. First, you temporarily reduce the equity in your property, which, in turn, lowers your net assets, which lowers your family contribution—provided, of course, that the loan is taken against a property that is being considered an asset by the college. Second, because it is a secured loan, the interest rates are fairly low. As always, you should consult with your accountant or financial planner on this.

If you have any outstanding loans that cannot be used as a deduction under the financial aid formulas (personal loans, car loans, large credit card balances, etc.), it might make sense to use a home equity line of credit to pay off these other obligations. The interest rate will probably be lower and the value of one of your prime assets may look smaller to the FAOs.

Which Property Should I Borrow Against?

If you have only one property, the decision is easy. Borrow against your one property. You'll almost certainly get a low interest rate. Whether you will reduce your equity in the eyes of the FAOs depends on whether they have decided to assess the value of the primary residence—and if so whether they are choosing to assess it at full market value or at a lower rate.

If your college is actually going to follow the federal methodology, a home equity loan on a primary residence would no longer help you to qualify for more aid (although it still may be a good idea). If you own two homes, take out the loan on the second residence instead.

If your prospective colleges are using the institutional methodology *and* electing to cap home value at 2.4 times income (and a number of private colleges will be), the effectiveness of our strategy will depend on how much equity you have in your home. Let's take a family with income of $60,000 and a home valued at $200,000 with a $100,000 mortgage. At schools that choose to cap the home value at 2.4 times income, the maximum value of this family's home would be 2.4 times $60,000, or $144,000. The colleges will subtract the $100,000 debt from the $144,000 asset and decree that the family has equity of $44,000—which the colleges feel is available to help pay for college—and will assess at a rate of up to 5% per year. In this case, it would still make sense to take out a home equity loan of up to $44,000 to reduce the appearance of equity in the house.

However, let's take a family with a combined income of $60,000, a home valued at $300,000, and a mortgage of $200,000. If the schools choose to cap home value at 2.4 times income, the maximum value for the house (for assessment purposes) is $144,000. The colleges then subtract the mortgage of $200,000. In this case, there is, in fact, no equity at all in the home, as far as those colleges are concerned. Thus, if this family took out a home equity loan on their primary residence, their assets would not be reduced in the eyes of the colleges (since as far as the colleges are concerned, the family has no equity in the house in the first place). To reduce the appearance of their assets, this family could borrow instead against a second home, other real estate, or their stock portfolio.

If the schools you are considering either use a cap on home value or a cap on home equity, our tips #2 through #11 (which describe ways to lower the appearance of your Adjusted Gross Income) become even more important. Lowering your AGI and untaxed income will keep your capped home value or capped home equity down, and may thus protect more of the value of your home from the FAOs.

TIP 17a:
Take out a home equity loan to pay for college and/or to consolidate debt not taken into account in the aid formulas.

A home equity loan is not something to be done lightly. Unlike unsecured loans and credit card balances, a home equity loan uses your real estate as collateral. If you default, the bank can foreclose. Nonetheless, if you have a low mortgage to begin with and your income seems stable, this is an excellent alternative.

A Home Equity Loan vs. a Second Mortgage

When you take out a second mortgage, the bank writes you a check for a fixed amount, and you begin paying it back immediately with interest. Parents sometimes ask, "Isn't a second mortgage just as good as a home equity loan?" It depends on what you're going to do with the money you get from the loan. If you put it in the bank to pay for college bills as they come due, then a second mortgage is not as good at all. Consider: you are paying interest on the entire amount of the loan, but you aren't really using it yet. The money will earn interest, but it will not earn nearly as much interest as you are paying out. For financial aid purposes, the interest you earn will be considered income, yet the interest you are paying on the second mortgage will not be taken into account as an expense.

Even worse, if the money you received from your second mortgage is just sitting in the bank, the debt does not reduce your net assets either. The reduced equity in your house will be offset by the increased money in your bank account. Under these circumstances, a home equity line of credit loan is a much better deal. You pay interest only when you withdraw money, and you withdraw only what you need.

And if the school you select has opted not to look at home equity, then a second mortgage becomes the worst deal in the world. You will have taken an asset that the college could not touch and converted it into an asset with no protection at all. This could actually raise your SAI by several thousand dollars.

Should We Buy a House Now?

We're all for it if you want to buy a house, but don't think of it as an automatic strategy for reducing your assets in the eyes of the FAOs. If the school assesses home equity, then exchanging the money in your bank account for a down payment on a house just shifts your assets around, rather than making them disappear. Your net assets will be exactly the same with or without the house (at least until the house starts appreciating in value). On top of that, your monthly housing costs will probably increase. As you may remember from the "Expenses" section of this chapter, you don't get credit in the aid formulas for mortgage payments.

However, if the school uses only the federal methodology or excludes home equity, then a first-time home purchase could make a lot of sense. You would be exchanging an unprotected asset for an asset that could not be touched.

By the same token, it might also make sense to prepay or pay down the mortgage on your primary residence since this will reduce your net assets in the federal formula. You will need to consider any prepayment penalties you may incur before you pursue this course of action.

TIP 17b:
If the college your child will attend does not look at home equity, consider buying a primary residence if you currently rent. If you already own your primary residence, consider liquidating unprotected assets to prepay your home mortgage.

The Perils of Inheritance and Gifts from Grandparents

Many accountants suggest that elderly parents put assets in their children's name. In this way, the elderly parents more readily qualify for government benefits such as Medicaid; they avoid having their investments eaten up by catastrophic illness; and, if they are wealthy, their heirs avoid having their inheritance eaten up by estate taxes.

If a grandparent is contemplating putting assets in the parents' name, the parents should at least consider the possible financial aid consequences before accepting. Obviously, such a transfer will inflate your assets and possibly your income as well (the interest on monetary assets could be considerable). In many cases, while the grandparents may have transferred their assets to the parents, the parents do not feel that this money really belongs to them yet. When grandparents decide to move to a nursing home, or need health care not provided by insurance, the parents often pay the expenses. Since the money is not really yours to spend, you may feel dismayed when the colleges ask you to pony it up for tuition.

If it is possible to delay the transfer of assets until you no longer have to complete aid forms, you might wish to do so. Or perhaps the assets could be put in the name of another relative who does not have college-age children. If that is impossible, you should explain to the FAOs that this money really does not yet belong to you.

An even worse situation arises when grandparents transfer assets to the grandchild's name. These assets will be assessed at a much higher rate than those of the parents (20% versus a maximum of 5.65%). If the only possible choice left to you is to put the grandparents' gift in the name of the parent or the child, it is better to put it in the parents' name.

Trusts

While there's much to recommend about trusts, their effect on the financial aid formulas can be disastrous. We are not speaking of the general feeling among FAOs that "trust fund babies don't need aid" (although this is a pervasive feeling).

The real problem is that the FAOs assume the entire amount in the trust is available to be tapped even if the trust has been set up so that the principal can't be touched. Let's see how this works:

Suppose your child Johnny has a $10,000 trust that has been prudently set up so that he can't touch the principal, a common practice. He gets a payment from the trust every year until he reaches age 25, at which time he gets the remaining balance in the trust. Parents often set up trusts this way under the mistaken impression that the colleges will thus never be able to get at the principal.

However, because the money is in his name, it is assessed for his freshman year at 20% in the federal formula, or $2,000. Never mind that Johnny can't get $2,000 out of the trust. He, or more likely you, will have to come up with the money from somewhere else.

Next year, the need analysis company looks at the trust again, and sees that it still contains $10,000. So it gets assessed at 20% again, and again Johnny gets up to $2,000 less in aid.

If this continues for the four years of college, and it will, Johnny's $10,000 asset may have cost you $8,000 in aid. The trust may have prevented you from getting aid entirely, but couldn't actually be used to pay for college.

Don't Put Your Trust in Trusts

If you are counting on any kind of financial aid and you have any control over a trust that is being set up for your child, prevent it from happening. If a grandparent wants to help pay for schooling, the best way to do this is to wait until the child has finished college. Then the grandparent can help pay back the student loans when they become due.

If a trust has to be set up, make sure that it is set up so that the principal money can be withdrawn if necessary. You might also consider setting the trust up in *your own* name. Parents' assets are assessed at the much lower rate of 5.65% each year.

Setting up a trust that matures just as your child is entering college would at least ensure that the money could be used to pay for tuition. However, if the trust is sizable, you may be jeopardizing any chance to receive financial aid.

If Grandmother wants to provide for Johnny's *entire* education, but doesn't want to wait until after graduation, perhaps a better idea would be for her to take advantage of one of the prepayment plans being offered by a growing number of colleges. We generally don't think a prepayment plan makes economic sense (see Chapter Seven), but in this one case, it would be infinitely better than a restrictive trust.

Direct Payments to the School

If you are in the happy position of having a rich uncle who wants to pay for part of your child's college education, he can avoid paying gift tax on the money (even if it is above the $19,000 annual limit) by writing the check directly to the school. However, he and you should realize that if your uncle is paying less than the entire amount of the tuition, this won't necessarily save you any money.

If you are eligible for aid and you receive any money from a third party toward college, the FAOs will treat this money like a scholarship. They will simply reduce the amount of aid they were going to give you by the size of your uncle's payment. Your family contribution will probably remain exactly the same.

If your uncle wants to be of maximum help, he could wait until your child is finished with college and then give you the money. If you were going to qualify for aid, this would ensure that you actually got it. You can then use your uncle's money to pay off any loans you've taken out along the way.

Stocks, Bonds, Money Market Accounts, and CDs

The need analysis forms ask for the value of your assets on the day you fill out the forms. For stocks and bonds, you can find the prices online or by consulting your broker. Remember that bonds are not worth their face value until they mature. Until that time, they are worth only what someone is willing to pay for them at a given moment.

In the aid formulas, debts against these assets reduce your net assets. However, the only real debt you can have against these types of assets is a margin debt.

Many parents shudder when they hear the word *margin*. "Oh, that's just for people who really play the market," they say. In fact, this is not true at all, and margin debt may be one of the more sensible approaches to paying for college if you run out of liquid assets. Here's how it works:

In most cases, you set up a margin account with a brokerage firm. Using stock that you own as collateral, they will lend you a certain amount of money. Traditionally, you would then use this money to buy more stock. However, there are no rules that say you have to buy stock—these days, the brokerage firms are just as happy to cut you a check for the full amount of the loan.

Because this is a secured loan based on the value of your stock portfolio, the interest rates are far superior to unsecured personal loans. You still own the stock, and it continues to do whatever it was going to do. (Out of all the long-term investment possibilities, the stock market has been the single best way to build principal over the past 50 years.) In most cases, you get to deduct the interest expense against your income on your tax return. And—here's the best part—you get to deduct the entire loan from your assets on the need analysis forms.

Margin Can Pay for College

If you own stocks or bonds and you need the money to pay for college, it may make sense to borrow against these assets rather than to sell them. If you sell the investment and write the college a check, the money is gone forever. By borrowing on margin, you can avoid capital gains (which will raise your AGI) and still retain your assets.

A margin loan is a bet that the value of your stock will increase faster than the interest you are paying on the loan (and based on long-term past performance, this is a reasonable bet). Even if you don't make money on the deal, it will likely cost far less than an unsecured personal loan, and your assets will still be there when your child walks back from the podium with his diploma and tells you he wants to go to graduate school.

Margin allows you to avoid paying taxes on capital gains, keep your investment working for you, and reduce your assets in the eyes of the FAOs.

TIP 18:
Use a margin loan to pay for college and reduce the appearance of your assets.

A major drawback to this type of loan is that if the stock market declines drastically, you may be asked to put up additional stock as collateral, or even (it would have to be a very drastic decline) pay back part of the money you borrowed. If you were unable to put up additional stock or money—or if you couldn't make the loan payments—you could lose the stock you put up as collateral. This is the kind of calculated risk you should discuss with your broker or accountant before you jump in.

Doesn't This Margin Strategy Conflict with What You Said Earlier?

In the "Income" section of this chapter we suggested that you avoid margin debt as an investment strategy. How then can we turn around now and say it's a good strategy for paying for college? Whether margin makes sense for you depends on what you're using it for. If you are using it to purchase more stock, this should be avoided as it will overstate your investment income and, therefore, your AGI.

On the other hand, if you do not have sufficient income or liquid assets (such as savings, checking, or money market accounts) to pay the college bills, margin debt is infinitely preferable to:

a. borrowing at high rates from loan sources that are not considered debts under the aid formulas and/or

b. selling off assets that will generate capital gains during a base income year.

Mortgages Held

This category has nothing to do with the mortgage you have on your house. It refers to a situation in which you are acting as a bank and someone else is making monthly payments to you. This situation might have come up if you sold your house to a person who could not get a mortgage from a bank. If you were anxious to make the sale, you might agree to act as the banker. You receive an initial down payment, and then monthly installments until the buyer has paid off the agreed price of the house plus interest. The exact terminology for this is an installment or land-sale contract.

If you are the holder of a mortgage, the amount owed to you is considered a part of your assets. However, you should not write down the entire amount that is owed to you. A mortgage, installment contract, or land-sale contract is worth only what the market will pay for it at any particular moment. If you had to sell that mortgage right now, it might not be worth its face value. You should consult a real estate professional or a banker who is familiar with second mortgage markets (yes, there actually is a market in second mortgages) to find out the current market value of your investment.

529 Plans (Prepaid Tuition Programs & Tuition Savings Accounts) and Coverdell ESAs

Since these are generally long-term planning options, see Chapter 2 for more details on how these plans are treated under the federal and institutional methodologies. Also, please consult the Student Tools as there were some unanswered questions when we went to press as to how the value for some of these accounts would be treated in the federal methodology for 2027–2028.

As with the prepaid plans, the tax-free earnings portion of any withdrawal from a 529 savings plan or a Coverdell ESA used to pay qualified post-secondary educational expenses will not be considered income to the student for the purposes of the 2027–2028 aid forms.

What About Contributions from Grandma or Uncle Joe?

If someone other than a custodial parent or student is the owner of a 529 plan or Coverdell, then it appears that the account would be completely sheltered as an asset from the federal formula for the 2027–2028 academic year. Under the institutional methodology, these accounts owned by others will be treated the same way as they are in the federal formula. However, colleges will have the option of asking additional questions regarding 529 plans or Coverdells that were funded by individuals other than the student or the parents. These optional questions will appear in the Supplemental Questions section of the CSS Profile. As we went to press, it was impossible to determine how many colleges would be exercising this option.

Warning: with each successive year, more and more colleges are asking questions about these plans. Who set them up? Who owns them? How much will be withdrawn or redeemed in a given year? What's the total value? Because of this increased scrutiny... because the colleges know these funds are specifically set up for the student beneficiary's education... and because the FAOs can choose to ignore the federal and institutional formulas when awarding the school's own money, placing funds in these accounts is increasingly risky if the student is otherwise eligible for aid—especially for grants awarded by the colleges themselves. Well-intentioned relatives should be alerted to the possible problems with these programs as well.

Ownership of a Business

For the federal methodology prior to 2024–2025, if you owned and controlled a business with fewer than 101 full-time (or full-time equivalent) employees, you did not have to report the net worth of such a business on the FAFSA form. Note that "owned and controlled" is defined as owning more than 50% of the business yourself or together with other members of your family by blood or marriage. The U.S. Department of Education classifies such entities as "family businesses."

Similar to the treatment of a family farm, this exemption was rescinded under Simplification only to be restored via the OBBBA, but with an additional carve out for commercial fishing businesses.

Whether it's a "family business" or not, you will still be required to list ALL of your business assets and business debts on the CSS Profile form. This could have a chilling effect on your eligibility for aid from the schools themselves.

Remember, though, if you need to report the equity of your business on any aid form, net worth is NOT the same thing as what you would get if you sold the business. It does not include goodwill; it has nothing to do with gross receipts.

The net worth of a business consists of the cash on hand, receivables, machinery and equipment, property, and inventory held, minus accounts payable, debts, and mortgages. In most cases, you can find the figures you will need from the company's year-end balance sheet or a partnership or corporate income tax return (IRS forms 1065, 1120, or 1120S). The main thing to realize here is that just like when you are assessing the value of your real estate, there is no point getting carried away with your valuation of your company. Business owners are rightfully proud of what they have accomplished, but this is not the time to brag.

The higher your net assets, the worse your chances of receiving aid. The FAOs are interested in only selected portions of your balance sheet. Don't look any further than they do.

For example, if your company is part of the service industry, it may have a very small net worth, even if it is extremely successful. Let's assume for a moment that you own a small advertising agency. Like most service industry companies, you would have no real inventory to speak of, little in the way of property, and, because you're putting your profits back into the company, not much money in the bank. The net worth of this company—even if you were required to report its equity on an aid form—would be almost nil. This would be true even if it were one of the most well-respected agencies on Madison Avenue.

Business Assets Are Much Better Than Personal Assets

Because the FAOs acknowledge that a parent's business needs working capital to operate, the net worth of the entity reported on the FAFSA or CSS Profile is assessed much less harshly than the parent's personal assets. For example, of the first $180,000 in net worth, the colleges count only 40 cents on the dollar.

So even if you must report the value of the business on the FAFSA, all is not lost. As long as you own at least 5% of the stock in a small corporation, it may be possible to call yourself a part-owner and list the value of your stock as a business asset on the aid form instead of as a personal investment. How much difference would this make? If you had $40,000 in stock in a small, privately held corporation, you could find yourself eligible for up to $1,300 per year in increased aid simply by listing this stock as a business asset rather than as a personal asset.

Real Estate as Business

Can you turn your various real estate properties into a business? It depends. If you own several properties, receive a significant portion of your income from your properties, and spend a significant proportion of your time managing the real estate, then you probably can.

If you own your own business and the building in which you conduct business, then you certainly can. If you rent out one or more properties and file business tax returns, then you perhaps can. Some schools will want to see extensive documentation before they will buy this strategy. The benefits, of course, are enormous. Business assets reported on the aid form are assessed much less severely in both the federal and institutional aid formulas. Listing your real estate holdings as a business could reduce your Student Aid Index by thousands of dollars—if the FAOs buy it.

Limited Partnerships

Under the aid formulas, a limited partner's stake in the entity is considered an investment, not a business asset. Determining a value for limited partnerships can be difficult. If you can't sell your interest in the partnership, and the general partners are unable or unwilling to buy back your shares, then it isn't worth anything at the moment, and you should list this worth as "zero." Again, the FAOs may not buy this strategy, but let them tell you that you can't do it.

The Business/Farm Supplement

Some schools ask the owners of businesses and farms to fill out a standardized form that asks about your business or farm net worth and income in greater detail. We will discuss this, as well as some more complicated strategies, in the "Special Topics" chapter of this book.

Asset Protection Allowance

After the FAFSA processor has determined your net assets, there is one final subtraction, called the Asset Protection Allowance.

This number, based on the age of the older custodial parent (or custodial stepparent), is how much of your net assets can be exempted from the federal financial aid assessment. The older you are, the more assets are sheltered. Below is a chart that will give you a rough idea of the asset protection allowance permitted at various ages under the federal methodology. According to the Department of Education, this allowance is calculated to yield the same amount of money as "the present cost of an annuity which, when combined with social security benefits, would provide at age 65 a moderate level of living for a retired couple or single person." Of course, their idea of "a moderate level of living" probably means a more spartan existence than you had in mind. *For the 2027–2028 FM, the Asset Protection Allowance is 0 (zero) but it may change in future years.*

Asset Protection Allowance		
Age	**Two-Parent Family**	**One-Parent Family**
34 or less	0	0
35–39	0	0
40–44	0	0

Asset Protection Allowance		
Age	**Two-Parent Family**	**One-Parent Family**
45–49	0	0
50–54	0	0
55–59	0	0
60–64	0	0
65 or more	0	0

After subtracting the asset protection allowance, the remaining assets are assessed on a sliding scale (depending on income). The maximum assessment on parents' assets is 5.65%. In other words, the most you will have to contribute is slightly more than five and a half cents for each additional dollar of assets.

Parents with few assets worry that the colleges will take what little they have. In fact, a family with low income and, say, $5,000 in assets would almost certainly not have to make any contribution from assets at all. If your total net assets are less than your protection allowance, then your assets will not be touched by the FAOs. In the federal methodology, the assessment of assets is related to the parents' available income. After the asset protection allowance is subtracted, any remaining assets are then assessed at 12%. The result is then added to the available income to come up with what is called the adjusted available income (AAI). Since the maximum assessment rate on the AAI is 47%, the maximum contribution from assets is therefore approximately 5.65%

$$(0.12 \times 0.47 \approx 0.0565 \text{ or } 5.65\%).$$

College Board Asset Allowances

The institutional methodology no longer contains an asset protection allowance similar to the federal formula. Since the aid formulas do not assess assets in retirement accounts, the College Board feels that it is redundant to also protect some non-sheltered assets for retirement. Instead, the institutional formula contains three other asset allowances: The Emergency Reserve Allowance, The Cumulative Education Savings Allowance, and The Low Income Asset Allowance.

The Emergency Reserve Allowance (ERA) recognizes that every family should have some assets available in the case of sudden, unexpected costs brought about by things like illness or unemployment. The specific amount awarded varies based on the size of the family. The College Board has not released specific figures since 2010. This is our best estimate of the minimum ERA that will be granted:

Emergency Reserve Allowance (ERA)	
Family Size	**Estimated Allowance**
2	$35,000
3	$39,000
4	$44,000
5	$47,000
6	$50,000

Approximately $3,000 will be granted for each additional person.

The Cumulative Education Savings Allowance is granted to shelter those assets that the family has presumably set aside each year to meet their annual goal for the educational savings allowance (see Chapter 3, "Annual Education Savings Allowance"). For the student applicant and any other siblings also enrolled in college during the same academic year, the institutional formula assumes that the savings goal was met for each child for 18 years and that the accumulated savings are then used up during the student's college career. For younger siblings, the allowance will be based on the number of children and their ages. All families received a minimum allowance of $23,130 in the 2010–2011 version of the institutional formula. Because this allowance protects assets for each dependent child in the household, any parental assets held in the names of the student's siblings will be considered as part of the parents' assets.

Lower income families who have negative available income in the institutional formula will be given a third asset allowance equal to the amount of the negative available income. This low income asset allowance is granted because such families generally need to use up some of their assets to cover those basic expenses in excess of their income.

The Emergency Reserve Allowance, the Cumulative Education Savings Allowance, and the Low Income Asset Allowance (if applicable) will automatically be calculated by the CSS Profile processor. These allowances are then subtracted from the parents' net assets (the value of the assets less any debts secured by those assets) to determine the parents' discretionary net worth. This net worth is then assessed to calculate the parents' contribution from assets. Previously, the asset assessment rate was based in part upon the family's available income, with higher income families having their assets assessed at a higher rate. Under the institutional formula, there is no linkage between income and the rate of asset assessment. For the 2010–2011 academic year, the first $34,450 of the parents' discretionary net assets was assessed at 3%. The next $34,450 was assessed at 4%. Any assets in excess of $68,900 were assessed at the rate of 5%. We expect these brackets to widen only marginally in future years. In addition, families with negative discretionary net worth will not have their available income reduced in the institutional methodology.

Multiple College Students

Prior to FAFSA Simplification for both the FM and IM, the parents' contribution was calculated and then adjusted based on the number of family members in college on at least a half-time basis, excluding the parents of the student. (If a parent plans to attend graduate school during the same academic year as the student seeking aid, it would be a good idea to explain this situation to the FAO directly, since some may take the parent's educational expenses into account on a case-by-case basis.)

While the federal formula simply divided the parents' contribution by the number in college to arrive at the parents' contribution per student, the College Board used a different formula for multiple students. If there were two in college, the parents' contribution for each student was 60% of the total parents' contribution. If there were three in college, 45% was likely to be the applicable rate. If there were four or more in college, 35% of the total parents' contribution was likely apply to each student.

Multiple Student Adjustment Eliminated in FAFSA Simplification

Hands down the worst aspect of the new federal methodology is that there will no longer be any adjustment to the parent's component in the federal aid formula based on the number of household members—excluding the student's custodial (step)parents—enrolled in college on at least a half-time basis. The impact of this change on the federal formula cannot be underestimated. With the exception of those who met the criteria for the Automatic Zero-EFC or would have otherwise had a zero EFC with only one student in college under the old FM before Simplification, the number of family members in college was the single most important data element affecting eligibility for need-based aid.

Be aware that even with the new rules, the FAFSA will still continue to ask how many members of the family are enrolled in college, but only for the purpose of institutional aid being awarded by the school itself. So when you see this question on the FAFSA, do not mistakenly conclude that the new law's provision to eliminate this adjustment has not yet been implemented for that award year. Fortunately, the College Board has confirmed that they will still provide for the multiple student adjustment in the institutional methodology. As a result, the contribution in the IM will likely be considerably less in the IM compared to the FM if there are multiple students concurrently enrolled in college during the same award year.

Assets and Liabilities: How the Methodologies Differ

Please check your free online student tools (see page vi), as there may be updates on this topic as a result of late-breaking developments.

The Federal Methodology

- Does not assess home value
- Asset protection table based on present cost of an annuity
- Provides for exclusion of various assets if you meet certain criteria
- Asset assessment on a sliding scale based, in part, on income

The Institutional Methodology

- Assesses home value, but some colleges will choose to ignore home equity (though sometimes only if family income is below a certain threshold), cap home value at 2.4 times income, or cap home equity at 2 times income
- Multiple student adjustment made to parent contribution
- All assets are assessed; no asset exclusion criteria
- Asset assessment is unrelated to income, except for those with negative available income
- Parental assets held in names of siblings considered as parental assets
- Asset allowances based on emergency reserves, educational savings, and low-income supplements

Student Resources

Need analysis companies ask precisely the same questions about students' income and assets that they do about the parents' income and assets, but there is one major difference in the way students' money is treated.

Colleges take a much larger cut of students' money. In the federal formula (FM), a student's assets are assessed at a whopping rate of 20% each year (versus a ceiling of 5.65% on parents' assets). In the institutional formula (IM) for the past few years, the assessment rate has been 25%. A student's income under the FM is assessed at up to 50% (versus a ceiling of 47% on parents' income). For the IM, we'll soon discuss how student income is assessed.

Student Income

Under the federal formula, there is no minimum contribution from student income, and the first $12,220 (after tax) dollars earned by a dependent student are excluded. However, if a dependent student meets the criteria for Maximum Pell Eligibility (which is based on the parent's financial information as explained earlier in the chapter), the student in most cases can have an unlimited amount of base year income, since the SAI will be 0 (zero) or less. Most students not required to file a base year tax return due to low enough income per IRS regulations (which we will cover shortly) can also have higher income up to the amount of their standard deduction.

In short, an incoming first-year student can earn about $13,232 before he will be assessed one penny. Once he crosses the $13,232 threshold, his additional income will most likely be assessed at a rate of 50%. If he then saves his money, it will also be assessed as an asset at a rate of 20%. Thus, if he banks his $13,233rd dollar, 50 cents of it will be assessed as income and 20 cents of it will be assessed as an asset. The extra dollar he earned could cost him 70 cents in reduced aid. While this is much better than the old ridiculous rule under which the same child would have been assessed $1.05 for each dollar earned over a certain amount, most students will still be better off devoting their extra time to their studies once they have hit the $13,233 mark.

And that's only if the college is using the federal formula. If your child attends a private college that uses the institutional methodology, she may be responsible for a minimum first-year contribution as high as $2,650 ($3,650 as an upper-level student) and there is no Income Protection Allowance. A student considering a private college will owe no more than the minimum contribution as long as she keeps her income below $6,235 for the base income year used to calculate a first-year's aid and $8,590 afterward. Over $6,255, she may be losing 71 cents in aid eligibility on each additional dollar she earns and saves. Recognizing that a student from a lower income family may be using their earnings to supplement the parent's income, the institutional methodology now uses a complicated formula for calculating a student's contribution from income.

TIP 19a:
For a student who hopes to receive aid from a school using only the federal methodology, it doesn't make sense to have prior-prior year (PPY) income higher than $13,232 (unless eligible for Max Pell, or the student is not required to file a federal tax return).

TIP 19b:
For a student who hopes to receive aid from a school using the institutional methodology, it doesn't make sense to have PPY income higher than $6,235 as an incoming first-year, or $8,590 as an upper-level student.

The current assessment rates have set up a bizarre situation in which the best way a student receiving financial aid can help his parents pay for college is by not working very much. If your family has no chance of receiving aid, then by all means encourage your child to make as much money as possible. However, any student who might qualify for aid will find that most of the money he earns will just be canceled out by the money he loses from his aid package.

Under current rules, it makes more sense for students receiving financial aid to earn the minimum amount of money the college will allow, and concentrate on doing as well as possible in school. Most aid is dependent at least in part on the student's grades. A high GPA ensures that the same or better aid package will be available next year; a good GPA also helps students to find better-paying jobs when they graduate so they can pay back their student loans.

It's Too Late. My Daughter Already Earned $14,000 Last Year!

Earning extra money is not the end of the world. Just remind her that as much as $892 of that $14,000 will have to go to the college. If she buys a car with it, she—or you—will have to come up with the money from some other source. You might also want to remind the colleges that while your daughter managed to earn $14,000 as a senior in high school, she is unlikely to earn that much again now that she is in college and has a tough work load. They might bear this in mind when they are allocating aid for the coming year. Some schools (Cornell is one) specifically ask you if your child will be earning less money in future years.

Student Income and Taxes: Not Necessarily Joined at the Hip

When does a student have to file a tax return? Generally, an individual who is being claimed as an exemption on his parents' tax return has to file if he has gross income of over $1,350 AND at least $450 of that income is unearned income (i.e., interest or dividends). If the student has NO unearned income at all, he can earn up to $15,750 in wages reported on a W-2 form before he is required to file a federal return. If the student is working as an independent contractor (with earnings reported to the IRS on a 1099), there are special rules to follow. Ask your accountant if the student has to file and/or review the IRS instructions for the 1040 return, particularly the "Filing Requirements" section near the beginning.

The rules used to be more lenient. The IRS is cracking down on parents who are sheltering assets by putting them in the child's name. If your child has any investment income at all, his standard deduction can drop from $15,750 to as low as $1,350.

A student who cannot be claimed as a dependent on her parents' taxes can have income up to $15,750 without needing to file a federal tax return, provided she gets no more than $400 net earnings from self-employment.

As long as your children are under 24 years old and are full-time students, they can be claimed as dependents on the parents' tax return, whether they filed income taxes or not, and regardless of how much money they earned.

You should also realize that the colleges' criteria for who can be considered an independent student are much tougher than the IRS's. A student could have been filing a separate tax return for years without being claimed as a dependent by someone else, but that does not necessarily mean that she will qualify as an independent under the financial aid formula.

Can My Child Go the Independent Route?

If the colleges decide that a student is no longer a dependent of his parents, then the colleges won't assess the parents' income and assets at all. Since independent students are often young and don't earn much money, they get large amounts of financial aid. The key point to grasp here is that it is the federal government and the colleges themselves who get to decide who is dependent and who is independent, and it is obviously in their best interest to decide that the student is still dependent.

We will discuss the criteria for becoming an independent student in Part Three, "Filling Out the Standardized Forms," and in Chapter Nine, "Special Topics," but don't get your hopes up. The rules are tough and getting tougher all the time.

Student Assets

Accountants and other financial counselors love to advise parents to "put some of their assets in the kid's name."

As a tax reduction strategy, this may be pretty good advice, since some of the income generated by the money in your child's name will almost certainly be taxed in a lower bracket than yours. Unfortunately, as many parents learn the hard way, following this advice during college years could be disastrous.

Parental assets are assessed by the colleges at a top rate of 5.65% each year, after subtracting your protection allowance. Your child's assets, on the other hand, will be hit up for 20% in the federal formula (25% in the institutional formula) each year, *and your child has no protection allowance at all.* Any potential tax benefits of putting assets in the child's name can be completely wiped out by the huge reduction you will see in your aid package.

TIP 20:
If you think you will qualify for financial aid, do not put assets in the child's name.

Even worse, some of the assets in the child's name can be hit twice each year: first, colleges take 20% off the top of the entire amount of the asset; second, the colleges take up to 50 cents out of every dollar in income generated by the asset.

Let's say a parent puts $10,000 in the child's name and invests it in a bond fund that pays 6%. When he fills out the FAFSA form, he enters the $600 interest the fund earned that year as part of the student's income; because the $600 was reinvested in the bond fund, the fund now has $10,600 in it, so he enters $10,600 under the student's assets. The federal processor assesses the $10,600 asset at 20% (in this case $2,120). The federal processor also assesses the $600 income at a rate of up to 50% (in this case, $300). Note that the $600 income got assessed twice—20% as an asset, and 50% as income, for a total of 70%. That $600 in income may have cost the family $420 in lost aid.

It's Too Late. I Put Assets in My Child's Name!

If you have already transferred assets to your child in the form of a custodial account (such as an UGMA or UTMA) or a trust, you should pause and consider three things before you fire your accountant.

1. You may not have been eligible for need-based aid in the first place. If you weren't going to qualify for aid anyway, those assets may be in just the right place, and your accountant is a genius. However, you should probably contact her to discuss the "kiddie tax" provisions (See Chapter 2, "Should Money Be Put in the Child's Name?").

2. You may have been offered only a subsidized Direct loan. If you were going to qualify only for minimal need-based aid in the form of student loans, the tax benefits of keeping assets in the child's name may well exceed the aid benefits, and you did just the right thing.

3. Even if it turns out that putting assets in your child's name was a bad mistake, you can't simply undo the error by pulling the money out of your child's account now. When you liquidate a custodial account, the IRS can disallow the gift, come after you for back taxes and back interest, and tax the money at the *parents'* tax rate from the time the funds were first transferred to the child.

Is There Anything We Can Do to Get Assets Back in Our Name?

There may be, but this situation is much too complicated for us to give general advice. You should consult with a competent financial advisor who has a sound understanding of both the tax code and the ins and outs of financial aid.

Student Income and Assets: How the Methodologies Differ

The Federal Methodology

- First $12,220 in student's after-tax income is sheltered for a dependent student
- No minimum contribution from income
- Asset assessment rate of 20% (unless eligible for Max Pell)

The Institutional Methodology

- No Income Protection Allowance
- Minimum contribution from income as high as: $2,650 for incoming first-years, $3,650 for upper-level students
- Asset assessment rate of 25%

Putting It All Together

Making an Estimate of How Much You Will Be Expected to Pay

After receiving all your financial data, the need analysis service crunches the numbers to arrive at your family contribution:

Parent's income –expenses available income (x assessment rate)	+	Parent's assets –debts –protection allowance net assets (x assessment rate)	=	Parent Component
Student's income –expenses available income (x assessment rate)	+	Student's assets –debts net assets (x assessment rate)	=	Student Component
Parent Component	+	Student Component	=	SAI in FM; Family Contribution in IM

If you have read this book carefully up to now, you know that behind the apparent simplicity of the chart above lies a wealth of hidden options that can save—or cost—you money.

By using the information in Part 5, you can get a rough approximation of what your Student Aid Index will be under the federal methodology. Bear in mind that it will be just that—an approximation. Our worksheet uses basically the same formula(s) used by the FAFSA processor, but because you will be estimating many of the numbers there is little likelihood that it will be exact.

Parents always want the bottom line. "How much will I have to pay?" they ask, as if there were one number fixed in stone for their family. In fact, you will see as you begin to play with your numbers that there are numerous ways to present yourselves to the colleges. By using the strategies we have outlined in Part Two of this book, you can radically change the financial snapshot that will determine your Student Aid Index.

Your bottom line will also be determined in part by whether you choose schools that use the federal or the institutional methodology to award institutional aid. We'll discuss this in more detail in our chapters on "How to Pick Colleges" and "The Offer."

Filling out our worksheet will be a quite different experience from filling out the need analysis form. The need analysis form asks you for your raw data, but does not allow you to do the calculations to determine the SAI before you submit the raw data.

The FAOs Tinker with the Numbers

You should also bear in mind that the college financial aid officers have a wide latitude to change the figures the need analysis companies send to them. If a school wants a particular student badly, the FAO can sweeten the pot. If a school has a strict policy on business losses, the amount you will be expected to finance at that school may be higher than the federal formula said it would be.

It's as if you submitted your tax return to five different countries. Each of them will look at you a little differently. One country may allow you to have capital losses that exceed capital gains. Another country may disallow your losses.

We know of one parent with unusual circumstances whose need analysis form generated a contribution of $46,000 but who still ended up getting $7,000 in financial aid for his son's freshman year at a $27,000-per-year school. We know of another couple whose contribution was calculated to be $10,000, but who ended up having to pay $22,000 because there was not much aid money left.

Even if your numbers look high, you should not assume that you won't qualify for aid.

Chapter Four

How to Pick Colleges

How to Pick Colleges—with Financial Aid in Mind

Richard Freedman, a former guidance counselor at prestigious Hunter College High School in New York City, used to keep a copy of *Who's Who* handy in his office. When parents came in with visions of Ivy dancing in their eyes, he invited them to look up famous people they admired in *Who's Who.* It turned out that their heroes almost never attended Ivy League schools.

We aren't suggesting that Ivy League schools are no good, or that your child should not apply to one of them, but it is worth noting (even as you look at the more than $90,000 price tag) that many important, interesting people managed, and are still managing, to get good educations elsewhere—and for less money.

There are many factors that go into a decision to apply to a particular college, and one factor that cannot be ignored is money. You and your child are about to make a business decision, and it's vital that you keep a clear head. How much are you willing to pay for what level of quality of education under what circumstances? It is possible to pay $60,000 per year for a worthless education, and possible to pay $5,000 per year for an outstanding education. Price is not always synonymous with quality. The real determining factor in the kind of education a student comes away with is how seriously the student took the experience.

This Is a Joint Decision . . .

Many parents feel that it is somehow their duty to shield their children from the harsh economic realities of higher education. It is a form of need-blind application, in which parents do their level best to remain blind to their own needs. They allow their children to apply to any school they like, without thinking through the consequences of what an acceptance at that school would mean. Taking on large amounts of debt should be a rational rather than an emotional decision, and any important decision like this should involve the student as well. Especially if money is a concern, your child should be included in every step of the decision-making, from computing a rough estimate of the Student Aid Index to picking colleges with a view toward financial aid.

. . . That You Must Make in the Dark

One of the frustrating parts about applying to college is that you have to apply without really knowing what it is going to cost. Well, of course you do know the sticker price, but as we've already said, the vast majority of families don't actually pay the sticker price. The $64,000 question is what kind of aid package the different schools will give you to reduce that sticker price.

The process has been made even more difficult by a Justice Department investigation years ago into possible violations of anti-trust law by many of the highly selective colleges, including the Ivies. Prior to the investigation, the FAOs from these schools would get together at an annual "overlap" meeting to compare notes on students who were going to be accepted by more than one of these colleges. After these meetings, there was usually an amazing similarity between the financial aid packages offered to an individual student by the competing colleges. While the Justice Department eventually worked out an agreement with the colleges on this matter, it remains to be seen to what extent colleges will be sharing information with each other after this experience.

Therefore, financial aid offers are still likely to differ by many thousands of dollars. Any counselor who says he can predict the precise amount and type of aid you will receive at one of these selective schools is lying. Thus applying for college is something of a financial crapshoot.

Applying to More Schools

Many counselors feel that it is now necessary to apply to more schools than before, to ensure that one of them will give you a good deal.

One good offer can frequently lead to others. If you have received a nice package from school A, you can go to a comparable school B that your child is more interested in, and negotiate an improved package. For the same reason, even if your child has been accepted "early action" or "early notification" by her first-choice school, you might want to apply to several other schools as well.

An early action or early notification acceptance (unlike a "restrictive early decision" acceptance) does not bind the student to go to that school. The college is just letting you know early on that you have a spot if you want it. Your child has just been accepted by her first-choice school, which is great news, but you may not receive an aid package for several months. If the college knows that you applied only to one school, they will be under no pressure to come up with a good aid package. However, if you have received several offers, you may find that the first choice will be willing to match a rival school's package or at least sweeten the pot.

Students who need financial aid should always apply to a variety of colleges. Perhaps one or two of these should be "reach" schools at which the student is less certain of admission; the student should also apply to several schools that not only fit his academic profile but also have good reputations for meeting students' "remaining need"; finally, the student should apply to what we call a "financial safety school."

The Financial Safety School

Now it may well be that your child will ultimately get into his or her first choice. (According to a 2023 survey conducted by the Higher Education Research Institute at UCLA, 70% of applicants to colleges in the United States *were* accepted by their first-choice school.) Just as important, your child's first choice may even give you a financial aid package that is acceptable to you. However, part of picking colleges entails selecting second, third, fourth, and fifth choices as well.

This is an opportunity for your child to get to know several schools better. Students sometimes seem to pick their first-choice schools out of thin air. We have often seen students change their minds as they actually go to visit the schools and read the literature. If money is a consideration, discuss this openly with your child. Look at the relative merits of the schools as compared to their price tags, and discuss what sacrifices both the parent and the student would have to make in order to send the student to one of the more expensive schools if the aid package you get is low.

At least one of the schools you apply to should be a "financial safety school." There are three factors to take into account when picking a financial safety school. You want to pick a school that . . .

(A) . . . the student is pretty much guaranteed to get into. What is an admissions safety school for one student may be a reach for another. Force yourself to be dispassionate. A good way to figure out a student's chances for admission is to look up the median SAT scores and class ranking of last year's freshman class (available in most college guides). A particular college qualifies as a safety school if the student who is applying is in the top 25% of the students who were admitted to the college last year.

(B) . . . you can afford even if you receive no aid at all. For most families, of course, this means some sort of state or community college. There are some extremely fine public colleges, whose educational opportunities rival those of many of the best private colleges.

(C) . . . the student is willing to attend. We've met some students who freely admit they wouldn't be caught dead going to their safety school. As far as we are concerned, these students either haven't looked hard enough to find a safety school they would enjoy, or they have unreasonable expectations about what the experience of college is supposed to be.

Let's examine what you might be looking for in a financial safety school based on a rough approximation of your Student Aid Index (SAI).

Federal vs. Institutional Formulas

In the previous chapters we have constantly referred to the differences between the federal and the institutional methodologies. By now you have probably figured out that in some cases, the federal methodology is kinder on a parent's pocketbook than the institutional methodology. However, before you start looking only at schools that use the federal methodology, there are a number of points to be made:

First, a college that uses the institutional methodology must still award federal money such as the Pell Grant and the subsidized Direct Loan using the federal criteria. Thus, the institutional methodology will only affect funds under the institution's direct control—principally, the school's private grant money.

Second, families may find that the difference in aid packages from two schools using the different methodologies is actually not very significant. Families who don't have a lot of equity built up in their primary residence, who don't show business or capital losses, or losses on property rental may not notice much difference at all.

Third, most of the competitive schools will be using the institutional methodology this year to award the funds under their control. It would severely limit your choice of colleges to apply only to schools that use the federal methodology.

Fourth, the institutional methodology will continue to recognize its multiple student adjustment to the parent contribution. However, with FAFSA Simplification, the federal methodology no longer takes multiple dependent children attending college in the same academic year into account to determine federal aid eligibility. This change to the FM cannot be underestimated for most families who will have more than one child in college on at least a half-time basis for at least one term during the same award year. This difference in the methodologies will have an increasing impact as the number of academic years of "overlapping" college attendance increases for those eligible for need-based aid.

The best way to find out which methodology is being used at a particular school is to ask an FAO at that school. However, as a rough guide, if the school wants you to fill out the CSS Profile form, then it will most likely be using the institutional methodology.

Should We Apply Only to Schools that Use the Federal Methodology?

No. There are so many other factors that determine an aid package—demographics, special talents, academic performance, just to name a few. Any of these factors could make an FAO decide to award merit-based aid or to be more generous in awarding need-based funds. However, if money is a concern, then it makes sense to apply to a financial safety school.

If You Have Extremely High Need

If your Student Aid Index is in the –1,500 to 5,000 range, a good safety school would be a public university or community college located in your own state. This type of school has two advantages. First, the likelihood that you will be eligible for state aid is extremely good. Second, your child may be able to live at home and commute, thus saving many of the expenses of room and board.

However, a student with high need should not neglect to apply to private colleges as well, preferably colleges where that student will be in demand. If the student has good grades, or some other desirable attribute, the student may receive an aid package that makes an expensive private school cheaper to attend than the local community college. Remember, by good grades we are not necessarily talking straight As. At many colleges, there are scholarships available for students with a B average and combined SAT scores of over 1,000 (or the equivalent on the ACT). We've sometimes even seen students with C averages and high need get generous aid packages at some private colleges.

If You Have High Need

We are frequently amazed at how often families with high need choose an out-of-state public university as their safety school. For most families with an SAI of between 5,000 and 25,000, an out-of-state public university is the most expensive option they could possibly choose. Why? First, students from out-of-state are charged a lot more. Second, much of the financial aid at these schools is earmarked for in-state students. Third, you will most likely not be able to take aid from your own state across state lines. Fourth, if the student is likely to fit into the top half of the entering class, he will probably get a better deal from a private college.

Families with limited means have difficulty imagining that they could get an aid package of $75,000 per year or more at a selective private college, but in fact, this is not out of the bounds of reality at all. Choose schools with high endowments where the child will be in the top quarter of the entering class.

Naturally, you can't depend on a huge package from a private college, so again, a financial safety school is a must. For families with high need, the best financial safety school is probably still an in-state public university or community college.

If You Have Moderate Need

A family with a Student Aid Index of 25,000 to 50,000 is in a tough position. This is a lot of money to have to come up with every year, perhaps more than you feel you can afford. As Jayme Stewart, a counselor at York Preparatory in New York City, once quipped, "A four-year private school education is not an inalienable right guaranteed by the Constitution."

A family with moderate need might want to choose two financial safety schools consisting of in-state public universities. Depending on your circumstances, either choice may actually cost you *less* than your SAI.

Financial planning is particularly vital to moderate-need families. The strategies we have outlined in the previous chapters can make a much bigger difference in the size of your aid package than you probably think and may make it possible for your child to attend a private college. For private colleges, you should again be looking at several schools where the student will be considered desirable and stands a good chance of getting institutional grants and scholarships.

Preferential packaging is particularly important to moderate-need families, as is the practice of applying to a wide variety of schools. By applying to more schools, you increase the likelihood that one of the schools will give you a particularly good package. You can then either accept the offer or use it to try to get a better deal at another college.

If You Have Low Need

A family with an SAI of between 50,000 and 70,000 (or more) must decide how much it is willing to pay for what kind of education and how much debt it is willing to take on. If you are willing to go into debt, then your financial safety school becomes merely a regular safety school.

If you are unlikely to get aid, some of the advice we have given in this book to people who want aid does not apply to you; for example, you might be well advised to put some assets into the child's name, you might want to set up a trust for the child, and the child should be earning as much money as possible in the years before and during college.

However, even families with low need should apply for aid. For one thing, with the cost of college being what it is, you may still qualify for some. You also have to look ahead four years. Perhaps your situation will change; for example, you might have only one child in college now, but next year you might have two, which is important at schools using the institutional methodology.

Finally, with their high sticker prices, some private colleges are having trouble filling their classrooms. The FAOs at many of these schools seem to be more and more willing to play "let's make a deal." As a result, a family's final family contribution may end up being several thousand dollars less than was calculated in the aid formulas. If you have used our worksheets in Part 5 to determine your Student Aid Index, you should bear this in mind before you decide that your SAI is too high to bother applying for aid.

The Public Ivies

Over the past few years, the cost of some of the best public universities has skyrocketed to the point at which an out-of-state resident can pay more to attend a public university than a private college. At the University of Michigan and the University of California—Berkeley, for example, the cost to an out-of-state student is more than $75,000 per year—hardly a bargain, even if the quality of education is high. However, these and other "public Ivies" remain good deals for in-state residents.

In the past, it was relatively easy to change your state of residence and qualify for lower tuition and state aid. However, in recent years, it has become almost impossible for an undergraduate student to pull this off unless the entire family moves to that state.

Nevertheless, some of the "public Ivies" remain bargains for everyone—for example, Georgia Tech and SUNY Binghamton are two first-class schools with undervalued price tags, even for out-of-staters.

What to Look for in a Private College

If you are selecting a private college with financial aid in mind, there are some criteria you should bear in mind as you look at the colleges:

- What is the average percentage of need met? You can find this statistic in most college guides. A high percentage is a sign that the school is committed to meeting as much of a student's "need" as possible. This statistic should not be misunderstood, however, for it is based on an average. A school that normally meets only a low percentage of need may come through with a spectacular offer for a student the school really wants. Another school that normally meets a very high percentage of need may make a very poor offer to a student the school considers marginal.

- Does the student have something this particular school wants? Is the student a legacy? Is he a track star applying to a school known for its track stars? Is she a physics genius applying to a school known for its physics department?

- How does the student compare academically to last year's incoming class? If this is a reach school for the student, the aid package may not be outstanding.

- Some colleges are very open about their academic wants; they mention right up front in their promotional literature that a student with SAT scores above *x* and a GPA of above *y* will receive a full scholarship.

- What percentage of gift aid is NOT based on need? If a student has an excellent academic record, this statistic might give some indication of whether she will be eligible to receive non-need scholarships. Of course, this statistic might be misleading for the same reasons we mentioned above.

- What is the school's endowment per student? If the school is on its last legs financially, then it may not be able to offer a great aid package—to say nothing of whether it will remain open long enough for the student to graduate. Don't necessarily be scared if a small school has a small endowment—take a closer look at what that actually means.

- Will the school use the institutional methodology in awarding aid under the school's direct control?

A General Note of Caution

Take the statistics in the college guides with a grain of salt. These statistics may show general trends, but (like all statistics) they are subject to interpretation. First of all, the information presented in these books usually comes from the colleges themselves, and as far as we know, is never checked.

Second, a particularly affluent (or poor) pool of applicants could skew the statistics. It would be easier for a school to meet a high percentage of need if the applicants to that school tend to be well off.

Chapter Five

What the Student Can Do

What the *Student* Can Do

Until now, most of our discussion has concerned what the *parent* can do to pay for college. Income and asset strategies, tax strategies, home equity loans—these are subjects that have little relevance for high school students. After all, in many cases, they have no income or assets, pay no taxes, and almost certainly don't own their own home. Is there anything *the student* can do to help pay for college?

The most obvious idea would seem to be for the student to get a job. However, under "Student Income and Assets" in Chapter Three, we explained that earning more than a certain dollar amount will decrease a student's aid faster than the earnings can be deposited in the student's bank account. After $13,232, every dollar a first-year student earns and saves can decrease his aid eligibility by 70 cents in the federal formula. Of course, if his family is not eligible for aid, the student should be out there earning as much as possible; but if his family stands a chance of qualifying for aid, the student's time would be better spent (at least under the current ridiculous law) by making the most of his educational opportunities.

There are, however, some very tangible ways a student can help pay for college. The first of these may make it sound like we've been paid off by high school teachers, but here goes anyway:

Study Like Crazy

It's the gospel truth. Good grades make a student desirable to the colleges. Yes, this will help you get in, but in these budget-tight times, good grades also translate directly into dollars and cents. As we said in Chapter Two, every tenth of a point a student raises her high school GPA can save her thousands of dollars in student loans she won't have to pay back later.

Even at the prestigious Ivy League schools, where students are supposedly awarded aid based only on their "need," applicants with high academic achievement do get preferential packaging—award packages with a higher percentage of grants and a lower percentage of loans.

If a student's dream is to attend an expensive private college, it isn't going too far to expect the student to contribute to help make that dream a reality. Parents are about to invest a sizable portion of all the money they have ever been able to save. It seems only fair that the student should be prepared to invest in his own future as well. And the single most productive way a student can invest in his future is by doing as well as possible during high school.

There are some colleges out there who state up front, "If you have a GPA of more than 3.5 and SATs of 1300 or above, we will offer you a full scholarship." There are other schools (more and more in recent years) that give out large merit-based grants, irrespective of need. These grants are not necessarily just for geniuses. We know of several colleges that award merit-based grants for students with B averages.

Take an SAT Review Course

Nothing can change a student's fortune *faster* than a big increase on the SAT. Look at it this way: it takes four years to accumulate your grades from high school. It takes six weeks to take a prep course. A study by FAIRTEST, published in *The New York Times,* showed that students who took these prep courses had an average improvement of over 100 points.

Every ten points a student can raise his score on the SAT can save his family thousands of dollars by increasing his desirability in the eyes of the FAOs, and hence, increasing the size of the aid packages they offer him. This is too important to leave to chance.

There are many companies that offer test preparation, some affordable and some quite expensive. We, of course, are partial to The Princeton Review course. If there are no preparation courses offered in your area, we suggest you at least buy a book, such as The Princeton Review's *7 Practice Tests for the SAT, 2027 Edition.* Books such as these will provide the student with valuable practice for the standardized test of their choosing. If money is a consideration, don't lose heart: the books are available at libraries and test prep companies often offer financial aid.

Take AP Courses

Many high schools offer advanced placement (AP) courses. By passing an advanced placement test at the end of the year, a student can earn college credits without paying college tuition. Not all schools accept AP credits, but many do, again enabling a student to save his family literally thousands of dollars. Some students are able to skip being a first-year in this way, thus cutting the entire cost of their college education by one quarter. Consult with the colleges you are interested in to see if they accept AP credits and with your high school to see which AP courses are offered and how to sign up.

Saving Money by Earning Credits on the CLEP Exams

The College Board has developed exams that—like AP tests—allow students who score high enough to earn college credits. These are offered under the College-Level Examination Program, more commonly known by its acronym: CLEP. There are currently 34 different CLEP exams, with at least one of them currently accepted by 2,900 colleges and universities. You earn the same number of credits you would earn by taking a course—simply by taking a test. This could potentially save you thousands of dollars in tuition.

Needless to say, this is a great option to explore, but you need to do your homework first. Some colleges don't award credits for CLEP exams at all, while others have fine print. It is up to the individual college to determine which exams can be taken, the minimum score you need in order to get credit, and the total number of credits the school is willing to give students for CLEP exams. Bear in mind that the minimum score needed on one test might be different than the minimum score on another test. And some colleges might not give you credit, but will use the test results to allow you to place out of entry-level courses or to fulfill core distribution requirements. Each test costs $97, and there are prep books and interactive tutoring websites available. For more information, visit clep.collegeboard.org.

Condense Your College Education

You have to be a little crazy to try this, but for motivated students it is sometimes possible to complete a four-year education in three years. The family may not realize big savings on the tuition itself (since some schools charge by the credit) but there will be savings on room and board, and the student will be able to get out into the workforce that much sooner.

A more reasonable goal might be to reduce time in college by half a year. By attending summer school (which is often less expensive than the regular terms) a student can reduce her time on campus by one full semester.

Even at half a year, this strategy may take its toll on the student. Academics are only one part of the college experience, and by accelerating the process, a student may lose out on some of the opportunities and friendships that make the college years meaningful.

Defer Admission

Many schools allow students to defer admission for a year. If the family is financially strapped, a student could use this year to earn money. You should always remember that at least under current law, student earnings above a certain dollar amount will reduce aid eligibility—thus for many students, this strategy could backfire. However, if the college the student really wishes to attend decides the family is not eligible for aid, and the family cannot shoulder the entire cost of college, this might be the only way the student could make up the difference. Be extremely careful in making a decision like this. If there is no reasonable plan for how you can meet the entire *four years'* worth of college bills, it may not make sense to begin the first year.

Go to School Part-Time

Some schools allow students to attend college part-time so that they can earn money while they are in school. Points to be aware of:

- Student loans become due as early as six months after the student stops taking classes or goes below half-time status. If the student takes too much time off between classes, she may have to start paying off the loans, even though she's still in school.

- The financial aid available for part-time students is much reduced. Particularly if the student is attending less than half-time, there will be little chance of substantial aid.

- Any money the student earns is going to be assessed by the colleges at a very high rate, thus reducing aid eligibility. You should consider carefully whether a job will actually help pay for college. It will depend on whether your family was judged eligible for aid and what kind of package you have been offered. If you were not eligible, or if the aid package left you with a substantial piece of "unmet need," then part-time study may make sense. However, before you take that course of action, ask the FAO what would happen if the student earned, say, $15,000 after taxes this year. Would the student's aid package remain the same, or would the extra income simply reduce the aid package by $4,000 or more?

Transfer in Later: Option 1

If a family is on a very tight budget, a good way to finance a four-year college education is to start with a two-year college education. Two-year public community colleges or junior colleges—where the College Board says the average in-state tuition for 2025–2026 was just $4,150—represent an outstanding way to save money. A student with a good academic record at a community college (perhaps earned while still living at home) can then transfer to a slightly more expensive state college for two more years to earn a BA. The total cost would be only a fraction of the cost of a private college and still thousands of dollars less than that of a four-year program at the state college.

Transfer in Later: Option 2

If a student really has her heart set on a particular private college but the family cannot afford the costs of four years' tuition, there is another option: the student could go to a public college for the first two years and then transfer into the private school. The student will get the private college degree at a much more affordable price. Obviously, the student would have to get accepted by the private school as a transfer student, and this can be quite difficult. Outstanding grades are a given. We will go into this strategy in more detail in Chapter Seven, "Innovative Payment Options."

Transfer in Later: Option 3
Inexpensive College, Pricey Graduate School

Extending the previous strategy, a student could attend an in-state public university during all four of the undergraduate years and then go to a top-of-the-line private graduate school. The undergraduate savings would be huge, but again, whether the student attends a private or a public undergraduate college, a compelling academic record is always very important to ensure acceptance.

The Senior Year

The family will complete its last standardized need analysis form in the spring of the student's junior year of college. Once that form has been filed, there are no longer any financial aid considerations to worry about. During the summer between junior and senior year, students who want to help out with the last year's tuition can earn unlimited amounts of money without hurting their eligibility for financial aid.

Of course, if the student goes straight on to graduate school, then the senior year of college becomes the first base income year for graduate school, and the process begins again.

Chapter Six

State Aid

States sometimes don't get the credit they deserve for their most pervasive and sweeping form of financial aid: an affordable college education for in-state residents through public state university programs. These programs are still terrific values (as we explored in Chapter Four, "How to Pick Colleges") and in some cases, the quality of education is at least as good as it is at the best private colleges.

However, it is the other kind of state aid that we are going to discuss here. It comes in the form of need-based and merit-based grants and loans to qualifying students who attend public *or* private colleges and universities within their own state. All 50 states have need-based financial aid programs for their residents, and more than 25 states now have merit-based awards as well. While some states are richer than others, the amount of money available for state aid is substantial; in some states, students can qualify for more than $10,000 each year in grant money alone.

To qualify for this aid, a student must generally attend a public university or private college within the student's state of legal residence. A few states have reciprocal agreements with specific other states that allow you to take aid with you to another state.

Note: In recent years, some states have eliminated or reduced their state grant programs as a result of budget deficits. For the latest information regarding the availability of state aid, you should contact the appropriate state agency, which you will find listed in a few pages. Be aware that some states (e.g., Alaska, Georgia, Illinois, Indiana, Kentucky, Montana, Nevada, North Carolina, North Dakota, Oklahoma, Oregon, South Carolina, Tennessee, Texas, Utah, Vermont, and Washington) award funds on a first-come, first-served basis.

Even If You Don't Qualify for Federal Aid, You May Qualify for State Aid

Because of the differences between the state aid formulas and the federal formula, it is sometimes easier to qualify for state aid. Federal aid is based on your adjusted gross income (along with information about your assets). In some states, however, aid is based solely on your taxable income (the AGI minus deductions) *without reference to your assets.*

Thus, if you miss out on federal aid because you have been industrious and managed to save enough to make investments, you may be able to qualify for state money anyway. In some states, it is possible to own a mansion, a business, and sizable investments and—as long as your *taxable* income is within state parameters—still qualify for thousands of dollars in aid.

There are too many states with too many different types of programs and formulas for us to go into each one separately. Suffice it to say, state aid is one of the more overlooked ways for middle- and upper-middle-class families to help pay for college. We estimate that thousands of these parents, under the impression they make too much money, never even apply.

How to Apply for State Aid

Some states use the data you supply on the federal FAFSA form to award their aid. Other states require you to complete a supplemental aid form that is processed directly by that state's higher education agency.

Confused? Your high school guidance counselor should have the correct forms for your situation. If, for some reason, forms are not available at your high school, or your guidance counselor doesn't seem to know what is what, contact your state agency (a list of all the state agencies with their addresses and phone numbers is at the end of this chapter).

The only time the forms you find at your high school might not be the right forms for you is when the student goes to school in one state but lives in another. If this is the case, again contact your state agency.

If your family is eligible for state financial aid, your state grant should appear as part of the aid packages you receive from the colleges sometime before April 15. Obviously, unless your state has reciprocal agreements, the state money will appear only in the aid packages from colleges in your own state. Families that are pondering several offers from schools within their own state sometimes notice that the amount of state money they were offered at each of the schools differs. This might be because aid is based not just on need, but also on the amount of tuition at different schools. A more expensive school will often trigger a larger grant. However, if you applied to two comparably priced schools within your own state, and one school gives you significantly less state aid than another, then something is amiss because you should be getting approximately the same amount of state aid at similarly priced schools.

Alternative State Loans

Some states make guaranteed student loans, much like the Stafford loans provided by the federal government. These are sometimes called "special loans." Again, if your state offers these loans and if you qualify, they will appear as part of your aid package.

Establishing Residency in a State

In-state rates are much cheaper than out-of-state rates at public universities; at the University of Vermont, for example, an out-of-state student pays $25,000 more than an in-state resident. So it should come as no surprise that students have tried over the years to establish residency in the state of the public university they were attending. Until recently, it was much easier for a student to establish residency in a state if he wished to take advantage of the in-state rates. It has since become much more difficult, with the exception of one or two states. We will discuss establishing residency in greater detail in the "Special Topics" chapter.

The State Agencies

Alabama

Alabama Commission on Higher Education
100 North Union Street
Montgomery, AL 36104
(334) 242-1998
www.ache.edu

Alaska

Alaska Commission on Postsecondary Education
P.O. Box 110505
Juneau, AK 99811
(907) 465-2962 or (800) 441-2962
https://acpesecure.alaska.gov

Arizona

Arizona Board of Regents
2700 North Central Avenue
Suite 400
Phoenix, AZ 85004
(602) 229-2500
https://azgrants.az.gov

Arkansas

Arkansas Division of Higher Education
101 E. Capitol Avenue
Suite 300
Little Rock, AR 72201
(501) 371-2000
https://adhe.edu

California

California Student Aid Commission
Grant Programs–Customer Service
P.O. Box 419027
Rancho Cordova, CA 95741-9027
(888) 224-7268
www.csac.ca.gov

Colorado

Colorado Commission on Higher Education
1600 Broadway, Suite 2200
Denver, CO 80202
(303) 862-3001
https://cdhe.colorado.gov/students

Connecticut

Connecticut Department of Higher Education
450 Columbus Blvd., Suite 707
Hartford, CT 06103
(860) 947-1800
www.ohe.ct.gov

Delaware

Delaware Higher Education Office
The Townsend Building
401 Federal Street, Suite 2
Dover, DE 19901
(302) 735-4000
www.doe.k12.de.us

District of Columbia

Office of the State Supt. of Education
Division of Higher Education &
Financial Services
1050 First Street NE
Washington, DC 20002
(202) 727-6436
https://osse.dc.gov

Florida

Florida Department of Education
Office of Student Financial Assistance
325 West Gaines St.
Tallahassee, FL 32399
(850) 245-0505 or (888) 827-2004
www.floridastudentfinancialaid.org
or www.fldoe.org

Georgia

Georgia Student Finance Commission
State Loans & Grants Division
2082 East Exchange Place
Tucker, GA 30084
(800) 505-4732
www.gsfc.georgia.gov

Hawaii

Hawaii State Postsecondary Education
Commission
2444 Dole Street, Room 209
Honolulu, HI 96822
(808) 956-7251
www.hawaii.edu

Idaho

Office of the State Board of Education
650 West State Street, Third Floor
Boise, ID 83720
(208) 334-2270
https://boardofed.idaho.gov

Illinois

Illinois Student Assistance Commission
1755 Lake Cook Road
Deerfield, IL 60015-5209
(800) 899-4722
www.isac.org

Indiana

Indiana Commission for Higher Education
101 West Ohio Street, Suite 300
Indianapolis, IN 46204
(888) 528-4719
www.in.gov/che

Iowa

Iowa Dept. of Education
475 SW Fifth Street
Suite D
Des Moines, IA 50309
(877) 272-4456 or (515) 725-3400
https://educate.iowa.gov

Kansas

Kansas Association of Student
Financial Aid Administrators
Kansas Board of Regents
1000 S.W. Jackson Street
Suite 520
Topeka, KS 66612-1368
(785) 430-4240
www.kansasregents.org

Kentucky

Kentucky Higher Education
Assistance Authority
100 Airport Road
Frankfort, KY 40601
(800) 928-8926
www.kheaa.com

Louisiana

Louisiana Office of Student Financial
Assistance
602 North 5th Street
Baton Rouge, LA 70802
(800) 259-5626
https://mylosfa.la.gov

Maine

Finance Authority of Maine
Maine Education Assistance Division
5 Community Drive, P.O. Box 949
Augusta, ME 04330-0949
(800) 228-3734
www.famemaine.com

Maryland

Maryland Higher Education Commission
217 East Redwood Street
Suite 2100
Baltimore, MD 21202
(410) 767-3300 or (800) 974-0203
https://mhec.maryland.gov

Massachusetts

The Massachusetts Office of Student
Financial Assistance
135 Santilli Highway
Everett, MA 02149
(617) 391-6070
www.mass.edu/osfa

Michigan

Michigan Higher Education
Assistance Authority
Office of Scholarships and Grants
P.O. Box 30462
Lansing, MI 48909-7962
(888) 447-2687
www.michigan.gov/mistudentaid

Minnesota

Minnesota Higher Education
Services Office
1450 Energy Park Drive
Suite 350
St. Paul, MN 55108-5227
(800) 657-3866 or (651) 642-0567
www.ohe.state.mn.us

Mississippi

Mississippi Office of State
Student Financial Aid
3825 Ridgewood Road
Jackson, MS 39211
(800) 327-2980 or (601) 432-6997
www.msfinancialaid.org

Missouri

Missouri Department of Higher Education
P.O. Box 1469
Jefferson City, MO 65102
(800) 473-6757
https://dhewd.mo.gov/

Montana

Montana University System
Office of the Commissioner of Higher
Education
560 N. Park Avenue, P.O. Box 203201
Helena, MT 59620
(406) 449-9124
https://mus.edu/che

Nebraska

Coordinating Commission for
Postsecondary Education
P.O. Box 95005
Lincoln, NE 68509-5005
(402) 471-2847
https://ccpe.nebraska.gov

Nevada

State Department of Education
700 E. Fifth Street
Carson City, NV 89701
(775) 687-9115
https://doe.nv.gov

New Hampshire

New Hampshire Department of Education
25 Hall Street
Concord, NH 03301
(603) 271-3494
https://education.nh.gov

New Jersey

HESAA
P.O. Box 545
Trenton, NJ 08625-0545
(800) 792-8670
www.hesaa.org

New Mexico

State of New Mexico
Higher Education Department
2044 Galisteo St.
Santa Fe, NM 87505
(800) 279-9777 or (505) 476-8400
https://hed.state.nm.us

New York

New York State Higher Education Services Corporation
99 Washington Avenue
Albany, NY 12255
(518) 473-1574 or (888) 697-4372
www.hesc.ny.gov

North Carolina

College Foundation of North Carolina
P.O. Box 41966
Raleigh, NC 27629-1966
(888) 234-6400
www.cfnc.org

North Dakota

North Dakota University System
Tenth Floor, State Capitol
600 E. Boulevard Avenue-Dept. 215
Bismarck, ND 58505-0230
(701) 328-2960
https://ndus.edu

Ohio

Ohio Dept. of Higher Education
State Grants and Scholarship Dept.
25 South Front Street
Columbus, OH 43215
(614) 466-6000
www.highered.ohio.gov

Oklahoma

State Regents for Higher Education
655 Research Parkway
Suite 200
Oklahoma City, OK 73104
(405) 234-4300
https://ocap.org

Oregon

Oregon Student Access Commission
3225 25th Street SE
Salem, OR, 97302
(541) 687-7400
www.oregonstudentaid.gov

Pennsylvania

Pennsylvania Higher Education Assistance Agency
P.O. Box 8157
Harrisburg, PA 17105-8157
(800) 692-7392
www.pheaa.org

Rhode Island

Rhode Island Office of the Postsecondary Commissioner
80 Washington St., 2nd Floor
Providence, RI 02903
(401) 736-1100
www.riopc.edu

South Carolina

South Carolina Higher Education
Tuition Grants Commission
111 Executive Center Drive
Suite 242
Columbia, SC 29210
(803) 896-1120
www.sctuitiongrants.org

South Dakota

South Dakota Dept. of Ed.
800 Governors Drive
Pierre, SD 57501
(605) 773-3134
https://doe.sd.gov

Tennessee

TN Higher Education Commission
312 Rosa Parks Avenue
9th Floor
Nashville, TN 37243
(800) 342-1663
(615) 741-3605
www.tn.gov/THEC

Texas

Texas Higher Education Coordinating Board
P.O. Box 12788
Austin, TX 78711-2788
(512) 427-6101
(800) 242-3062
www.highered.texas.gov

Utah

Utah System of Higher Ed.
The Gateway
60 South 400 West
Salt Lake City, UT 84101
(801) 646-4784
or (801) 646-4812
https://ushe.edu

Vermont

Vermont Student Assistance Corporation
Champlain Mill
P.O. Box 2000
Winooski, VT 05404
(802) 654-3750
(800) 882-4166
www.vsac.org

Virginia

State Council of Higher
Education for Virginia
James Monroe Building
101 North Fourteenth Street
Richmond, VA 23219
(804) 225-2600
www.schev.edu

Washington

Washington State Higher
Education Coordinating Board
P.O. Box 43430
Olympia, WA 98504
(360) 753-7800
www.wsac.wa.gov

West Virginia

West Virginia Higher Education Policy
Commission
2001 Union Carbide Dr., Bldg. 2000
South Charleston, WV 25303
(304) 558-2101
https://wvhepc.edu

Wisconsin

Higher Education Aids Board
PO Box 7885
Madison, WI 53707-7885
(608) 267-2206
www.heab.state.wi.us

Wyoming

University of Wyoming
Student Financial Aid
1000 East University Avenue
Dept. 3335
Knight Hall Room 174
Laramie, WY 82071-3335
(307) 766-2116
www.uwyo.edu

American Samoa

American Samoa Community
College Board of Higher Education
P.O. Box 2609
Pago Pago, AS 96799-2609
(684) 699-9155
www.amsamoa.edu

Guam

University of Guam
Financial Aid Office
University Drive
UOG Station
Mangilao, GU 96913
(671) 735-2288
www.uog.edu

Northern Marianas Islands

Northern Marianas College
P.O. Box 501250
Saipan, MP 96950
(670) 234-5498
www.marianas.edu

Puerto Rico

Council on Higher Education
Box 9023271
San Juan, PR 00902-3271
(787) 722-2121
www.ce.pr.gov

Trust Territory of Pacific Islands

Palau Community College
P.O. Box 9
Koror, Republic of Palau, 96940
(680) 488-2470
www.pcc.palau.edu

Virgin Islands

Board of Education
Box 11900
60B, 61 & 62 Dronningens Gade
St. Thomas, VI 00802
(340) 774-4546
https://myviboe.com

Part Three

Filling Out the Standardized Forms

Filling Out the Forms

Any prospective college student who wants to be considered for financial aid must complete the Free Application for Federal Student Aid (FAFSA). If you are applying to private colleges (as well as a few state schools and certain private scholarship programs) you will probably also have to complete the College Board's CSS Financial Aid Profile Application (CSS Profile).

After you finish completing your form or forms (usually online), you'll send the data to the processor, which then analyzes your information and sends a detailed report to the colleges you designate. The FAFSA processor also generates a report you can access online called the FAFSA Submission Summary (formerly known as the Student Aid Report or SAR). After you submit the CSS Profile form, you will be able to view a private online "dashboard" with a list of schools your information has been submitted to and, in some cases, additional steps you need to take. There will also be an option to view and print your submitted CSS Profile data.

In this part of the book, we will give you line-by-line guidance for filling out the 2027–2028 version of the FAFSA and tips for the key questions on the 2027–2028 CSS Profile form.

First Step: Decide Which Form(s) to Fill Out

As your child narrows down his choice of colleges, you should find out which financial aid forms are required by each of the schools. Don't rely on the popular college guides sold in stores for this information. These books sometimes get their facts wrong, and can contain incorrect or outdated information. You also shouldn't rely on information you receive over the telephone from the schools themselves. We are amazed at how often schools have given us misleading or wrong information over the telephone. If you must rely on information given over the telephone, get the name and title of the person you're talking to. In the financial aid process, Murphy's Law is in full effect, and when things do go wrong, remember it will always be your fault. The best filing requirement and deadline information comes from each school's own financial aid office website.

When applying to several schools, you should keep in mind that you are only allowed to file one FAFSA form per student per year. You don't have to fill out a separate FAFSA for each college being considered. The form (whether you use the popular online version or the paper version) will allow you to list the schools to which the student is applying. However if you will have more than one child in college in the same academic year, a separate FAFSA form for each child will need to be submitted. The same holds true with the CSS Profile form. If there is more than one child attending a school that requires the CSS Profile, then separate CSS Profile forms need to be completed. This Is because with the college aid process, an individual student and not their family is the aid applicant.

Sometimes the Schools Have Their Own Aid Applications as Well

To make things even more confusing, some of the schools have supplemental financial aid forms for you to fill out in addition to the forms we've just mentioned. For example, any undergraduate first-year applying for financial aid at the University of Pennsylvania must complete the Penn Financial Aid Supplement in addition to the FAFSA and the CSS Profile forms. Carefully check through the financial aid requirements of all the schools under consideration to see if there are any supplemental aid forms that you need to complete. For now, we are going to talk only about the FAFSA and the CSS Profile form.

Filling Out the Right Form

Make sure you are using the right version of the form. Don't laugh. It's actually quite easy to fill out the wrong form. That's because the filing period of the 2027–2028 academic year's FAFSA form will overlap for a number of months with the filing period of the 2026–2027 academic year's FAFSA form. Similarly, the different years' filing periods for the CSS Profile overlap for four months. The FAFSA form you want to file needs to correspond to the academic year for which you want to receive aid. If you submit the wrong version during these overlap periods, your forms will be processed but you will be up the proverbial creek.

Take Your Pick: Two Ways to File the FAFSA

Before you start in on the forms, you have an important choice to make as to what method you'll use to file the FAFSA. The Department of Education offers two options:

1. **The FAFSA on the Web (also known as the FOTW)**

2. **The downloadable PDF FAFSA**—Instead of using the electronic option, you can also download and print a PDF version, which you then fill out by hand and send by mail to the FAFSA processor.

While this choice will not affect how the processor calculates your SAI under the federal formula, there are a number of advantages to using the FOTW option:

- You can list up to 20 schools to receive your data (compared to only 10 with the PDF version).

- You don't need to worry if the post office lost your form or delivered it late.

- The online form provides a method that will allow the Internal Revenue Service (IRS) to transfer certain federal tax information (FTI) onto the FAFSA, once the individual whose data is being shared has provided their consent. This IRS Future Act Direct Data Exchange (FA–DDX) method replaces the more-cumbersome IRS Data Retrieval Tool (DRT) that was available prior to the 2024–2025 FAFSA. Use of the IRS FA–DDX will mean that responses for certain questions on the FAFSA related to Federal Tax Information (FTI) will not need to be inputted when the FAFSA is being completed by the student and/or their significant others (if applicable). We'll explain this in more detail later in this part of the book.

- Your FAFSA data will be processed faster.
- The skip logic built into the online form helps you to avoid submitting inconsistent data.
- You don't have to worry that some responses on the PDF version of the FAFSA will be incorrectly inputted by the processor.
- Once all the required data, consents, and electronic signatures have been provided when the FAFSA data is submitted to the federal processor, the student will instantaneously be able to see that vital number we've referenced often in the pages of this book: the Student Aid Index (SAI) under the federal methodology and the FAFSA Submission Summary.

Details on how to complete the FAFSA on the web or how to download the PDF version are available on the U.S. Department of Education's (DOE) comprehensive federal aid web page (studentaid.gov). The old www.fafsa.ed.gov site has been eliminated, and has been replaced with www.fafsa.gov which redirects to studentaid.gov/h/apply-for-aid/fafsa.

How Skip Logic Works on the FOTW

The FOTW utilizes "skip logic"—which means certain questions may not be asked based on your answers to previous questions. For example, if the student says he won't file a tax return, further questions about his tax return will be omitted. Because of this "skip logic," the questions on the online FOTW are not asked in the same order as they are on the PDF version. However, in the interest of clarity, and since some of our readers may still be using the PDF version, our line-by-line tips for completing the FAFSA questions that follow will be done in numerical order. Regardless of the version you file, the same questions will have the same question numbers. On the FOTW version, you can determine the corresponding number for a particular question by clicking on the ? icon near the response area for that question. Once you access the help content for that FAFSA question, the corresponding question number will appear at the beginning of that help content.

This Book's Approach to the FAFSA

The strategies in this chapter for answering each question on the FAFSA to the best advantage will apply for any version of the 2027–2028 FAFSA that you choose to file. A number of the tips in this chapter relating to the completion and filing of the FAFSA may apply only to the PDF version. If you are filing the FOTW, you should be sure to read our line-by-line instructions below, since the online "Help and Hints" text for the FOTW are not always as complete as the instructions on the PDF version. The PDF version of the form usually goes through a formal comment period and review process by the feds, which means that the final version of the 2027–2028 was not yet available as this book went to print. After the FAFSA is processed, the FAFSA Submission Summary that is generated will list your data in the same numerical order, regardless of the method you chose to fill out the form.

The New Incarcerated Applicant FAFSA Form

One of the few provisions of FAFSA Simplification that took effect beginning with the 2023–2024 academic year is the section of the law relating to incarcerated individuals being eligible to receive federal student aid. As a result of this provision, a slightly different Incarcerated Applicant FAFSA form has been introduced. This version of the FAFSA known only as the "Incarcerated Application Form" should only be completed if the applicant seeking aid is incarcerated in a correctional facility at the time the FAFSA is submitted. The questions on the PDF file versions of the regular 2027–2028 FAFSA and on the 2027–2028 Incarcerated Applicant FAFSA are expected to be basically the same. However, it is important to note that the PDF versions of these two forms will be sent to different post office boxes with different nine-digit zip codes and the Incarcerated Applicant FAFSA will have the words "Incarcerated Applicant Form" center-justified on the top of each page.

Second Step: Know Your Deadlines

Missing a financial aid deadline is worse than missing a mortgage payment. Your bank will probably give you another chance; the colleges probably will not. Schools process their financial aid candidates in batches. At most schools, student aid applications are collected in a pile until the "priority filing deadline" (set by the school) and then assessed in one batch. If you send in your application three weeks early, you will not necessarily be better off than someone who just makes the deadline. However, if your application arrives a day late, it could sit unopened in a small pile of late applications until the entire first batch has been given aid. Then, if there is anything left in their coffers, the FAOs look at the second batch on a rolling basis.

DEADLINE CHART

COLLEGE	Admissions deadline	Which standardized need analysis forms (FAFSA, CSS Profile) are required? When are they due at the processor?	Is there an institutional aid form required? If so, when?	Are income tax returns required? When? What year(s)?	Any other forms required? (Noncustodial form, business/farm supplement, etc.) When are they due?	Name of contact FAO at college & phone number

Meeting Deadlines

There are so many different deadlines to remember during the process of applying for college admission and financial aid that the only way to keep everything straight is to write it all down in one place. We suggest that you use the chart that appears on the preceding page.

You should realize that if a school requires both the FAFSA and the CSS Profile, the school's deadlines for filing these two forms may be different. If your earliest CSS Profile deadline is not until after the 2026–2027 FAFSA becomes available, it would be best to hold off on submitting either form until both are completed. This will give you a better opportunity to review all the data and resolve any inconsistencies between the two forms before submitting either of them. Keep in mind that while the information relating to the prior-prior year income will involve a time period that has long since ended, the asset information and other demographic details of your situation will be as of the date you submit the form.

Since the majority of students apply only to schools that require the FAFSA but do not also require the CSS Profile form, the strategies for completing both forms that follow will start with the tips for the FAFSA (so that those readers who do not need to complete the CSS Profile can skip it). However, for those students who must complete the CSS Profile with their earliest CSS Profile deadline after the 2027–2028 FAFSA becomes available, it would be best if possible to complete (but not submit) all parts of the CSS Profile before working on the FAFSA (as long as you do not risk missing any FAFSA deadline for any other non-Profile schools or state aid programs that may require an earlier submission than your earliest CSS Profile school's aid deadlines). This is because the FAFSA is child's play compared to the CSS Profile—which requires significantly more detailed information than the federal form. Or as one senior administrator at the College Board once said, using an analogy to a student's academic record to compare the two forms, "FAFSA is to grade point average as CSS Profile is to an academic transcript." To help ensure that your responses to similar questions on the two forms are consistent: in the Filling Out the 2027–2028 CSS Profile Form section that appears much later in this chapter, we provide guidelines to assist you in identifying and matching up your responses to those similar questions on both forms.

Note: In addition to the schools' deadlines, some state aid programs or private scholarship programs may have earlier deadlines than the priority deadlines set by the particular schools for the FAFSA, CSS Profile, and/or their own aid form. And some state agencies awards funds on a first-come, first-serve basis until their coffers are empty. (See Chapter 6, State Aid.)

There Are Three Types of Financial Aid Deadlines

1. The school, private scholarship program, or state agency says your application must be mailed (and postmarked) by a particular date.

   If filing a paper version: send the form by Priority Mail at the post office and make sure the postal worker and/or your payment receipt shows you the postmark on the envelope before you leave the post office. Priority Mail with 2–3 day delivery also provides a tracking number, provided you go to the window clerk.

2. Your application must be received and "date stamped" by the need analysis company by a particular date.

   In this case, you must factor in delivery time if mailing a paper form. Again, send the application by regular Priority Mail at the post office (provided you can track the delivery). If you are mailing the standardized form within two weeks of this type of deadline, use the U.S. Postal Service's more expensive "Express Priority" service (which assigns a tracking number and also guarantees delivery by a specified date). You cannot use FedEx or any of the other private carriers because standardized forms must be sent to a post office box. Since the FAFSA processor is located in a somewhat remote location, it may take two business days for your form to be delivered via Express Priority Mail.

3. Your standardized application must be processed and the results made available to the school, private scholarship program, or state agency by a certain date.

   To be on the safe side, allow four weeks processing time. If the deadline is March 1, for example, then you should submit the form (via some method that provides tracking or submission confirmation) to the need analysis company by February 1.

If you are filing a form online, then the first two types of deadlines will be the same; namely, the date you must transmit the completed form to the processor (since it will be considered received on the date you transmit it). Last-minute filers should be aware that the processors may be located in an earlier time zone which could affect the official receipt/transmission "date" for your form. So for example, a filer in Oregon would have to file a form online by 8:59 P.M. Pacific Time if the data is sent to a processor that uses Eastern Time for date-stamping the form. If the form were filed at, say, 9:04 P.M. Pacific Time, it would be considered as received the next day. If your form must be processed by a certain date, you should allow two to three weeks processing time.

If you are mailing any documents that must be postmarked by a certain deadline, know that the decades-long practice of the United States Postal Service (USPS) is to make the postmark the date when that piece of mail arrives at the first postal sorting facility. In the past, outgoing mail would almost always arrive at the same day at the sorting facility and so the mailing date would usually be the postmark date (provided of course, that it was mailed before the last pick-up time for the mailbox or post office from which it was mailed). As of December 24, 2025, this is no longer the case. A piece of mail is now much more likely to arrive at the first postal sorting facility a day or more after the date the item was mailed.

To avoid this, go directly to a USPS office and request a manual postmark at the retail counter when you deliver your piece of mail. This is the only way to ensure a day-of postmark: pre-printed labels or stamps generated by a USPS self-service kiosk, Click-N-Ship, a postal meter, etc., only list the date the label or stamp was generated, and that is not considered a postmarked date.

TIP 21:
Put together a list of which forms you must file and when they are due.

So When Is the Optimal Time to Submit the Aid Forms?

One of the most difficult things about financial aid is that the answers to most questions are: "It depends on your situation and other factors." While conventional wisdom holds that one should always file "as soon as possible after a certain date," the reality is that you should file at the appropriate time when you will demonstrate the greatest need for aid. So...

1. If you are applying for aid at one of the few schools (Florida State is one such school that comes to mind) that still awards financial aid on a first-come, first-served (FCFS) basis instead of setting a priority filing date, then you should file the 2027–2028 aid forms as soon as possible after the FAFSA becomes available. Be aware that the overwhelming majority of colleges no longer award funds this way, as they learned a long time ago it is better for their enrollment goals to leverage their aid by rationing their funds instead. If a school's aid requirements advise you to complete the forms "as soon as possible after X date but before Y date," then the Y date is the priority filing deadline and they do not award funds on a first-come, first-served basis.

2. If you reside in one of the states that awards state aid on an FCFS basis until funds run out, then you would want to file the 2027–2028 FAFSA and other required forms ASAP after the forms become available. Based on state aid information for the 2026–2027 school year, the applicable states were: Alaska, Georgia, Illinois, Indiana, Kentucky, Montana, Nevada, North Carolina, North Dakota, Oklahoma, Oregon, South Carolina, Tennessee, Texas, Utah, Vermont, and Washington. The other 33 states and the District of Columbia do not appear to have such policies (providing a fixed cut-off deadline to apply). However, the situation may change for the 2027–2028 award year's application processing cycle, so it's best to contact your state agency for full details. (See Chapter 6 for your state's contact info.)

3. If none of the colleges or your state agency award funds on an FCFS basis, the earliest school's deadline by which a standardized need analysis form must be sent to or received by the need analysis company becomes your overall deadline. In this case, you should file the form after it becomes available but before your earliest deadline, during the time period when your family contribution is likely to be the lowest number. Let's say your earliest deadline is January 31, 2027 for the 2027–2028 award year's application processing cycle, but you will be getting a large bonus check from your employer on January 15, 2027. You would be better off filing the form before the bonus money inflates your assets. Do you make estimated tax payments? You would be better off making that next payment and having the payment clear your account before you file so that your reportable assets are lower at the time you file.

Once the need analysis company has processed the data on your form, it sends such data and other information to all the schools you designated on that form. If the student subsequently decides to apply to some additional school(s) after you filed the standardized form(s), you will need to remember to send the data to the additional school(s). (We'll advise how to do this later.)

Regardless of your situation, keep in mind that the instructions for the 2027–2028 FAFSA say that you have until June 30, 2028 (that is, at end of the academic year for which you want aid) to fill out the FAFSA. What they mean is that the FAFSA processor is willing to accept and process the form until this date, but by then there will be virtually no money left at almost any college in the land.

Standardized Form Deadlines May Be Different from Individual Aid Form Deadlines

If you are applying to a school that asks you to fill out their own separate supplemental financial aid form in addition to a standardized form, make sure you know the deadlines for each form. Unfortunately, these deadlines are usually different. Even if they are the same, the standardized form may have a postmark deadline while the college form has a receipt deadline, or vice versa. The only way to keep all this straight is to read each college's financial aid requirements carefully and then use a deadline chart like the one we provided earlier in this Part.

Supplemental Forms at the Highly Selective Colleges

Some Ivy League schools, the "little Ivies," and many other selective schools have rather extensive financial aid forms of their own. The quantity of paperwork may seem daunting at first, but when you start answering the questions you will begin to notice that many of the questions on the forms are identical—designed to get more detailed responses to the questions already asked on the FAFSA and/or the CSS Profile form and to discover inconsistencies in your responses. Individual schools may also ask a few questions that may strike you as bizarre. This is less Big

Brotherish than it sounds. The FAOs are just trying to find recipients for restricted awards donated by alumni that the aid office would prefer to award before they tap their unrestricted funds.

Be aware that some schools may establish earlier admissions and/or aid filing deadlines than their normal deadlines for prospective students who wish to be considered for special scholarships. So if your child is an above average candidate for admission at a particular college, it is best to review the information on that school's admission office's website regarding institutional scholarships based on merit or a combination of merit and need to determine if there are earlier deadlines than the stated deadlines listed on the college's aid office website.

Third Step: Determine if Any of the Colleges You are Applying to Require the College Board's CSS Profile Application

Many private colleges and a handful of state schools will require applicants to complete the CSS Profile form in addition to the FAFSA to be considered for institutional aid as well as federal aid. While a PDF version of the FAFSA can be printed and submitted through the mail, the CSS Profile form can only be filed electronically via the Collegeboard.org website. Though it's possible to use the student's existing College Board account to complete the CSS Profile, we do not recommend parents use their child's account for a variety of reasons. For example, if the two biological or adoptive parents are no longer living together, the noncustodial parent could view all the intimate financial details of the custodial parent if their child's College Board account was used for the CSS Profile and the noncustodial parent knew the valid log-in information for that child's account. And so, it is best for another College Board "student account" to be created. When creating this additional College Board account—and only for purposes of creating this account and *not for purposes of registering for and completing the actual CSS Profile application for their child seeking aid*—a custodial parent will provide their own name and other requested information that applies to them as if they are a student *when creating this additional College Board profile*: Select "I am no longer in high school" and leave the "Where do you to go to school?" response blank when asked; and make sure to also leave any "parental information" blank *when creating this alternative College Board account.* A College Board "student account" merely allows one to access all the tools on the College Board web site. None of the information provided to create a College Board account will automatically pre-fill onto the actual CSS Profile form. And so once a parent uses their own College Board account to log into and start working on the CSS Profile online form, all questions on the actual CSS Profile form about the student must pertain to their child who is seeking aid. Information about the parent will be used to complete the parent sections of the CSS Profile form. Since this concept may seem confusing to many families, here is an illustrative example:

> Leslie Smith is a custodial parent of Mary Jones. Though Mary already has a College Board account, Leslie will create a new College Board account in Leslie's own name with responses that pertain to Leslie as if Leslie is a student. Then when going to the CSS

> Profile web page, Leslie will input the log-in credentials (i.e., email address and password) that Leslie established for Leslie's own College Board account. But after accepting the Terms and Conditions for the CSS Profile at the outset to access the actual CSS Profile form, all the questions and sections on the CSS Profile form itself that refer to the student applicant seeking aid need to be answered using Mary's information (e.g., the student's first name and last name need to be inputted as Mary and as Jones respectively) and all the questions in any Parent's sections of the CSS Profile need to be answered using Leslie Smith's (and if applicable, Leslie's spouse's) information.

However if you already started a CSS Profile application using your child's College Board account before you read this section of the book, this process for a parent to create and use an alternate College Board account to complete a CSS Profile will not work. This is because the system will eventually identify that a CSS Profile form in the same student's name has already been at least started. In that case, you will need to continue using the student's own College Board account to log in and do any further work regarding that student's CSS Profile.

For dependent students, parental information is required on the CSS Profile just as it is on the FAFSA. Yet some students who can be classified as independent students for federal aid purposes via the FAFSA may still find that parental information will be required on the CSS Profile; we'll get into this later.

But perhaps the most confusing part for children of divorced, separated, or never-married parents who are living apart is that many colleges requiring the CSS Profile will also require a noncustodial parent to complete their own CSS Profile application. To make things even more confusing, that noncustodial parent will need to first create their own College Board account. And unlike the student and custodial parent who can use the student's existing College Board account (though we do not recommend that), *the noncustodial parent must create their own College Board account* (as if they are a student), following our tips above on how to do that to access and complete their own CSS Profile. Don't worry, we'll get into this later as well.

There is a $25 fee for the CSS Profile (which includes one school report), with an additional $16 processing fee for each additional report—for a CSS Profile application submitted by the student and/or the custodial parent(s). A noncustodial parent will pay a $25 one-time processing fee for their version of the CSS Profile, regardless of the number of colleges that need it. Since you will have to pay this fee using a credit card or an electronic debit when you submit your completed CSS Profile data, you should carefully review each college's financial aid requirements in order to determine which ones (if any) need the CSS Profile information. Certain users may be eligible for a fee waiver for an unlimited number of CSS Profile schools. There are also some private scholarship programs that require the CSS Profile and those will set their own application filing deadlines.

Not Too Early

While counseling thousands of individual clients over the past 40 years, we've noticed that many families fit into two distinct categories: those who like to do things right away and those who like to wait until the last minute. When handling the CSS Profile application, either course of action could get you into trouble.

While you can register for, complete, and submit the 2027–2028 CSS Profile anytime on or after October 1, 2026, keep in mind that you will be paying a $16 processing fee for any school or program that you designate to receive your CSS Profile information. So it would make sense to wait a while to submit your completed CSS Profile to the processor until the student has a better idea of their list of schools. (You might also want to wait until you make any appropriate changes to your financials that could increase your aid eligibility!) While you can change the list of schools/programs that you have provided before you submit the form, you will be charged for any school that you have selected to receive your CSS Profile data at the time you submit your completed application to the processor. So unless the college requests the completion of the CSS Profile form in the early fall for an early decision or early action application (see Chapter 9, "Early Decision, Early Action, Early Notification, Early Read"), it is a good idea to wait to submit the CSS Profile until you are closer to your earliest school's or program's CSS Profile deadline. Otherwise, if you apply too soon you may be paying a fee for schools to which the child never decides to apply. Note: once you submit your CSS Profile for processing, you cannot electronically change any financial information. So unless a CSS Profile deadline is imminent, you should take your time, carefully read the online instructions, review our strategies, and double-check all your responses before you submit the original CSS Profile to the processor. And as mentioned earlier, you should wait to submit your CSS Profile until the FAFSA becomes available, if possible.

Once you submit the form, you can always add additional schools or programs to the CSS Profile at a later date (at an additional cost of $16 per school or program added unless you previously received a fee waiver). You will be asked any additional supplemental questions that are required by the school(s)/programs you wish to add that have not been previously asked. However, except for any comments you wish to add or change in the Special Circumstances section of the CSS Profile, you will not be able to electronically change any of the other CSS Profile responses originally submitted online to the processor.

Beginning with the CSS Profile application for the 2022–2023 award cycle, one may now submit explanations involving certain types of mistakes made when the original CSS Profile data was first submitted. (Prior to 2022–2023, one had to send any corrections directly an individual CSS Profile schools' financial aid office to alert them about the error on the form.) To use the CSS Profile system to report any correction, one will need to log back into the CSS Profile website using the log-in credentials for the College Board account that was used to submit the original CSS Profile for that award year. Then one will see a CSS Profile Correction icon that appears on the CSS Profile Dashboard for that application. After clicking on the icon, one will be asked to select a Reason for the Correction from a pull-down menu and then provide explanatory text about the nature of the Correction, with exact revised dollar amounts if applicable. Such corrections, once submitted, will then be sent by the College Board to all institutions that have or will receive the student's originally submitted CSS Profile data. Any issues or corrections that are specific only to a particular institution should be submitted either through an email message to the financial aid office or via a typed/hand-written letter mailed to the aid office (making sure to identity the name of the student, their date of birth, the student's status at the college—prospective student, currently enrolled student, etc.—and if already issued, the institution-specific student ID number assigned by that college). **KEY POINT:** You are only given one opportunity to submit corrections electronically. Be sure that all corrections are made during one online session for the CSS Profile.

Not Too Late

While you can now set up a free account on the College Board's website and then complete and submit the CSS Profile in one online session, it is still not a good idea to wait until right before your earliest school's CSS Profile deadline to get started. During peak processing periods, the College Board website may run slowly or be difficult to access. If additional supplements are required, you will also need some time to complete them and work out the logistics of getting the data to the appropriate schools by their deadlines.

And if a noncustodial parent is required to complete the Noncustodial parent Profile form, it would make sense for the student and the custodial parent to at least begin the CSS Profile process and complete the first few sections of their CSS Profile sooner rather than later so that the noncustodial parent has sufficient time to work on their own form. We will also provide more details later in this part of the book.

Fourth Step: Decide Whether You Can Get Your Taxes Done in Time to Fill Out the FAFSA and/or the CSS Profile Form

Prior to the 2017–2018 FAFSA and CSS Profile, most families had to estimate their base year income on the forms because they needed to file the aid forms before they could complete their tax returns for the "prior year."

However, with the switch to the use of prior-prior year (PPY) data on the standardized aid forms, most individuals who were required to file a tax return for the PPY will have done so before they need to file the forms. However, it would still be much better if you were not reading this chapter on the day of the deadline, because this is going to take more time than you think—if you want to maximize your aid. A ten-year-old child can fill out the form, but HOW you fill it out will determine your aid package. As you will soon find out, the questions involving PPY income only encompass a fraction of the data required to submit the forms. As such, you should begin gathering together all this information weeks before you plan to submit the aid forms.

Here are the records you will need:

1. Completed 2025 federal tax return (including all schedules), if filed. (If 2025 return not filed, see below.)
2. 2025 W-2 forms (if applicable)
3. Records of 2025 untaxed income (social security payments received, welfare payments, tax-exempt interest income, etc.)
4. Bank statements
5. Brokerage statements
6. Mortgage statements (for all properties other than the primary residence)
7. Student's social security number and driver's license (if available)
8. If you are an owner of a business, the business's financial statements or corporate tax return
9. Other investment statements and records (including any farm you own)
10. Records of child support paid to or received from former spouse

And if you will be filing the CSS Profile in addition to the FAFSA, you will also need:

11. Records of 2025 medical and dental expenses (must have been actually paid or charged on your credit card during 2025)
12. Mortgage statement(s) for your primary residence
13. Records of any post–secondary tuition paid or that will be paid during the 2026–2027 school year
14. Records of any educational loan payments made (or to be made in 2025 and 2026)
15. The amount of any financial aid awarded for the 2026–2027 school year (for any household member)

If you have NOT completed your 2025 tax return by the time you need to complete the aid forms:

Obviously, it will be easier to complete the 2027–2028 standardized aid form(s) if you first complete your 2025 tax returns and then file the aid form(s). However, if you are applying for aid at the relatively rare school that actually awards aid funds on a first-come, first-served basis and/or you are a resident of a state that awards state aid funds on a rolling basis until such funds are depleted, then you should not delay filing the aid forms if your tax return has not yet been completed. You should simply use your best estimates for your PPY information and submit the aid forms. (In this case, it would be helpful to have a copy of your 2024 return as well as a blank copy of the 2025 tax return as the line items on the tax returns changed.) However, you will want to file your tax return(s) as soon as possible (if required to do so), and then revise your estimated information reported on the aid forms as soon as you are able to do so.

If you are not required to file a U.S. tax return, you should not feel that it is necessary to do so in order to apply for aid. The financial aid application process and forms are designed to also accommodate those who do not file a U.S. tax return (or those who are only required to file a foreign tax return or those who are not required to file any return).

A Word About Confidentiality

The information you supply will go directly to the financial aid office and will stay there. You can trust them to keep information confidential. No one else at the school will see your personal data. And no one else at the school—not professors, students, or administrators—will know who is getting financial aid and who isn't.
Some parents are reluctant to share intimate details with a stranger. No matter how spectacular the details of your private life are, the FAOs have seen worse. And frankly, the FAOs are too busy coping with the needs of thousands of students to have time to make value judgments.

Currently, the only way the IRS can see a copy of your need analysis form is by getting a subpoena, although the laws could always change. However, the Secretary of Education now has the authority to verify the information on the FAFSA with the IRS.

Practice, Practice, Practice

If you're completing a paper form: it would be a good idea to make an extra copy for use as a draft version. Once you are satisfied with all of your entries, you can transfer the information carefully onto a new blank version. The PDF version of the FAFSA sent to the processor should be free of any corrections, comments in margins, or other stray marks. Otherwise, it may be rejected by the FAFSA processor. When you've finished, make a photocopy of the completed form and put it in a safe place before you mail the original to the processor.

If you're filing a form online: you should exercise care when inputting any responses. And be sure to review your responses before you hit the submit button. If you are in the habit of just dumping all of your financial records at your accountant's office, change your habits for the next four years. Photocopy every conceivably relevant document, and then dump them at your accountant's office.

Read ALL the Instructions

You should read all the instructions on the forms while working on them. In many cases, these instructions will be sketchy or misleading. Hopefully, this book will clarify what the forms do not.

If you're completing a PDF version of a form: make sure you use the proper writing implement. Also, be sure you complete the response areas the proper way. If they want a ●, don't give them a ✓ instead. Writing in the margins is forbidden. You are also not allowed to give a range of numbers for a particular item. For example, you cannot write down $700–$800. It must be an exact dollar amount.

And regardless of the way you file a form: use whole dollar amounts only. Do not include cents or decimals. When writing down the numeric equivalent of a single-digit date, the MMDDYYYY format is usually requested. Thus, January 9, 2025 would look like this: 01 09 2025.

Which Parent(s) Must Report Information on the 2027–2028 FAFSA and CSS Profile

Under FAFSA Simplification, new regulations were implemented for dependent students to determine which of the student's parents' information must be reported on the FAFSA. In most cases, the CSS Profile form will mirror these guidelines. Here is the gist of them:

- If the biological and/or adoptive parents of the student are living together, then information from both parents is required to be reported on the FAFSA and CSS Profile, regardless of their marital status and regardless of their genders.

- If the biological and/or adoptive parents are divorced or were never married *and in either case are living apart in separate residences*, then according to the FAFSA Simplification legislation the parent who "provides the greater portion of the student's financial support" will be the parent required to provide their information on a dependent student's FAFSA—even if the student does not live with them. For decades prior to the 2024–2025 FAFSA, the parent with whom the student spent the most time in the 12 months prior to the FAFSA being completed was the parent in such situations who was required to provide their information on the FAFSA. That is why many in the aid community still refer to the parent required to report their information on the FAFSA as the "custodial parent," even though the new rules under Simplification no longer involve any physical presence criteria.

  Unfortunately, the instructions on the 2024–2025 FAFSA merely repeated the vaguely written language in the law about "the greater portion of support" without defining how such support is to be determined. For the purposes of the 2024–2025 FAFSA, the USDOE did seem to clarify in a roundabout way that the period of support to be considered would be the 12 months prior to the FAFSA being completed and submitted. This is because the 2024–2025 FAFSA instructions referenced the "past 12 months" for a scenario related to the amount of support being equal, in which case the parent with the "greater income and assets" would be the parent required to complete the FAFSA. Separately, the USDOE has stated that the amount for child support paid for the applicant is to be considered part of the total support provided by the payer when determining who should complete the FAFSA.

  Nevertheless, there are still a number of unanswered questions that the USDOE is unlikely to answer by the time the 2027–2028 FAFSA instructions are finalized and the 2027–2028 FAFSA filing period begins. Such unanswered questions include: "How is support defined?" and "What happens if the amount of support is equal and one parent has greater income but fewer assets?"

NOTE: The College Board intends to follow the federal rules for such situations related to which parent's information should be listed on the regular CSS Profile completed by the parent and the student (and as such, if applicable, which parent previously referred to as the noncustodial parent would be required to submit the noncustodial parent's version of the CSS Profile).

- In cases where the parents of a dependent student are separated and living apart, there were statements made by many aid professionals in 2023 and 2024 as to what would constitute being "separated" for purposes of the new FAFSA under Simplification. Despite there being no specific language in the legislation, a rumor quickly circulated among members of the aid community that only legal separations would be recognized. If there were no separation agreement between the parents, then both parents' financial information would be required on the FAFSA, as they would be considered married. However, the USDOE—in response to a public comment made during one of the 2024–2025 FAFSA comment periods—reaffirmed its longstanding policy that both legal separations and informal separation would count for being considered separated for the purposes of the FAFSA and the FM. An informal separation occurs when the legally married parents of the student have "chosen to live separate lives, including living in separate households, as though they were not married." The Institutional Methodology will mirror this policy of recognizing both legal and informal separations for the purposes of classifying the marital status of parents who are separated and living apart, but not divorced, at the time the FAFSA is filed.
- If a divorced custodial parent or widowed parent is remarried (or the student's parents were never married, but now the biological or adoptive custodial parent is married to someone other than the student's other parent), then the information of the custodial parent and custodial stepparent is required to be reported. If this is the case, then when completing both the FAFSA and CSS Profile all references to "parent(s)" on the form will be applicable to the custodial parent and the custodial stepparent.
- If one of the student's biological or adopted parents is deceased and the surviving parent is not married, then only the surviving parent's information is reported.

Be aware that this determination is made based on the situation on the date the aid form is completed, not the situation during the prior-prior year. Given all the fine print, it makes sense to carefully review the applicable parts of the FAFSA and CSS Profile instructions as well as our guidance including any updates.

KEY POINTS: If the parents are living apart, one cannot randomly choose who to use as the parent on the FAFSA. Be aware that it is illegal to report the parental financial and other information of a parent on the FAFSA, if such parent does not meet the federal government's criteria for being a "parent" for purposes of completing that student's FAFSA. However, if you plan ahead, it may be possible to arrange the support provided by each parent so that the parent who will have the lower parent contribution in the federal aid formula will be the "parent" required to report their financial information on the FAFSA. For schools that require noncustodial parent information for their own aid funds, this planning approach may or may not save you any money since any increased federal grant aid may or may not reduce the amount of institutional need-based gift aid awarded dollar-for-dollar.

If the CSS Profile is required, it is critical that the same parent who is required to report their information on a student's FAFSA be the "custodial parent" for that student's CSS Profile form. And if that custodial parent is currently married to the student's stepparent, then that stepparent's information must be reported on both forms as well. More on this later, as well.

Don't Skip

Finally, don't skip any questions unless the instructions specifically tell you that you can. If you do not own a business, for example, put down "0" for any values related to a business. If you leave certain items blank on the PDF version of the FAFSA, the processor will just send the paper form back to you to correct. You can't afford to lose that time.

Getting Started If You Are Filling Out the Online FAFSA (FOTW)

FAIR WARNING: *FAFSA Simplification brought tectonic changes to the student aid landscape. Even if you have read a prior edition of this book or done independent research, we strongly recommend that you read this book's Introduction, Chapter One, and Chapter Three, as well as the preceding pages of Part Three if you have not already done so. This will ensure that you have up-to-date information.*

While there were major changes involving the questions on the FAFSA form and how federal aid eligibility would be determined due to the full implementation of the FAFSA Simplification legislation for the 2024–2025 award year and beyond, there were also major changes involving how the FAFSA application process works if one is filing the form online.

One of these changes is directly related to a key piece of legislation enacted in 2019 known commonly as the FUTURE (Fostering Undergraduate Talent by Unlocking Resources for Education) Act. This law includes provisions that allow the U.S. Department of Education to get one's income tax information directly from the IRS, provided one grants their consent for the Department to do so. This new process is known as the Future Act Direct Data Exchange (FA-DDX), with the federal tax information referred to as FTI. The pre-2024–2025 process involved accessing one's own tax information via the IRS Data Retrieval Tool (DRT) and authorizing the IRS to transfer it to the FAFSA. The new method means that new procedures must be followed to comply with IRS regulations concerning the protection and sharing of one's income tax information. For those completing the FAFSA online using the fafsa.gov website, one of the changes will be that those supplying information will need to use their own unique FSA ID (Federal Student Aid ID).

The FSA ID came into being in May 2015—and has been causing mass confusion ever since among parents, students, guidance counselors, and even financial aid officers. The FSA ID has always had several important functions: first, it can serve as a signature when you submit your FAFSA data. Second, it permits you to access your processed FAFSA data online at a later date and, if necessary, revise or correct it. Third, it permits you to apply for federal education loans online. Fourth, it allows you to access your federal education loan history via the National Student Loan Data System (NSLDS). And fifth, it allows you to complete the Agreement to Serve (ATS) for the federal TEACH grant program.

But now with FAFSA Simplification and the FUTURE Act, the FSA ID also serves as the sole method to provide one's consent to have the IRS share one's federal tax information (FTI) with the U.S. Department of Education for the online FAFSA. In addition to certain information listed on the IRS Form 1040 tax return, the FTI could also pertain to one not filing a return. (So as a reminder: one who is not required to file a tax return should not do so as there are some benefits that may accrue to those who do not file a tax return if not required to do so.)

Prior to the 2024–2025 FAFSA, one did not need to have an FSA ID (though it was beneficial). An applicant could just provide their identifiers (legal name, date of birth, and social security number) to start the online form. In addition to their information, they could also supply parental (or spousal) information, if required. After submitting the FAFSA electronically, users could print, sign, and mail a signature page to the processor who, upon receipt of the necessary signatures, would finalize the application. (For those supplying parental information, only one custodial (step)parent needed to sign; for those who were married, the spouse did not need to sign.) Alternatively, any required signatures could be provided through the use of an FSA ID unique to the individual(s) who needed to sign the form.

Under the new procedures for the 2024–2025 FAFSA and beyond, the online version of the FAFSA will no longer offer a signature page option. Those who submit without the necessary signatures will not receive an SAI (Student Aid Index) number until all signatures have been provided. Additionally, depending on the tax-filing status of the applicant, more individuals may be required to sign the FAFSA form than in the past. This is due to the necessary consents required for the FA-DDX process. Here's the scoop on who will be required to provide an FSA ID if the FAFSA form is being completed electronically:

- The student applicant seeking aid will always need their own unique FSA ID.

- For a dependent with only one parent required to provide parental information on the FAFSA, that parent will need their own unique FSA ID as well.

- For a dependent with both parents living together (whether they are married to each other or not), the situation will depend on how those parents filed their tax return for the PPY year (2025 is the PPY for the 2027–2028 FAFSA). If they filed a joint return, then only one parent needs a unique FSA ID. If they filed separately or did not file a tax return, then each parent will need to have their own unique FSA ID.

- For a dependent whose parent required to report information on the FAFSA is currently married to the student's stepparent, the necessary course of action will be very similar to the one immediately above involving two parents. Namely, if a joint return was filed by that parent with the stepparent for the PPY year, then only that parent needs a unique FSA ID. However, if a joint return was not filed, then both the parent and stepparent will need their own unique FSA ID.

- If the student is married (and therefore considered an independent student), the spouse will only need to have their own FSA ID if the student and their spouse did NOT file a joint tax return for the PPY year.

Even if only one parent is required to have an FSA ID per our guidelines above, we strongly recommend that if the parent of the dependent student required to report their information on the FAFSA is married, then both members of the married couple should have their own unique FSA ID. There could be glitches with the new procedures and the FSA ID may be needed for other tasks down the road.

Prior to the 2024–2025 application season, one needed a valid social security number to obtain an FSA ID. However, when the 2024–2025 FAFSA launched in late December 2023, a new system was introduced to allow such individuals lacking a social security to create their FSA ID. This new system had problems from the start preventing many students from completing the FAFSA online because their parent(s) who did not have a social security number could not obtain an FSA ID. After several months of failed workarounds, the USDOE threw up the white flag of surrender, announcing they would no longer require such individuals without a social security to have their identity verified in order to get an FSA ID for 2024–2025. For the 2027–2028 FAFSA, the feds are saying that such individuals will need to have their identity verified—even if they were able to use their unverified FSA ID with a prior year's FAFSA. However, as we went to press it remains to be seen if a new method to verify identity will work. Note though that if any person required to provide their financial and other information on the FAFSA is uncomfortable with the process of obtaining an FSA ID, then the PDF version of the FAFSA should be completed and mailed to the FAFSA processor.

To obtain an FSA ID (also known as a studentaid.gov account), you should visit the studentaid.gov web site. Once there, click on the words Create Account near the top right of the home page, just to the left of the magnifying-glass search icon and just above the large blue shaded area with images of various students and the vertical listing of POPULAR TOPICS. Once on the Create an Account page, click on the Get Started button. When creating your FSA ID, you will eventually be required to supply either an email address or mobile phone number. To have either your email address or mobile phone number verified—we'll cover this in more detail in a few paragraphs—you will want to be able to access your email account and/or your mobile phone when creating your FSA ID. You can choose to provide both a unique email address and a unique mobile phone when requested, but only one or the other is actually required. If you are supplying an email address, it is best to provide a personal email account address. Supplying your school's email address is especially not recommended, since that email address may expire once you are no longer attending your current educational institution.

You'll first be asked to supply some personal identifying information, including your name, date of birth, and social security number. Next, you'll be asked to create a unique username as well as a password. The passwords can be the same for multiple individuals, but each username created must be unique to an individual person. The username doesn't have to be your own name—if fact, it is probably not a good idea to do that. The 6 to 30 character username can be any combination of numbers and/or letters of the alphabet so long as no one else has already taken that exact same username for their FSA ID. (Note that the letters in your username are not case-sensitive as the system never distinguishes between an uppercase and lowercase letter.) The characters you type for your username will be fully visible when typed. You should carefully review the username you create for accuracy, as you will only be required to input it once when it is created.

For the 8 to 30 character case-sensitive password, you can use any combination of uppercase letters, lowercase letters, and numbers provided there is at least one uppercase letter, at least one lowercase letter, and at least one number between 0 (zero) and 9 as part of the password you create. Because the letters are case-sensitive, there are really 52 letters in the alphabet that can be used with the password (A, a, B, b, etc., etc.). You will be asked to enter and then re-enter your case-sensitive password, and the characters you type for your password will always be encrypted. There is however a "Show Text" option for your password, which we strongly recommend you always use so that you can be sure you typed what you meant to type when you either create your password or when you use your FSA ID at a later date. At some point, you will be asked to select four challenge questions and then supply your corresponding answer to each of the four questions. You will only type each respective answer once (which will be encrypted), so be sure to also use the option to display the encrypted text you typed. It is critical that you know the exact way you entered your answer to each of the four questions when you create the FSA ID. The validity of the answers does not matter. So for example: If you never left the United States in your life and you choose to use the question regarding the city in which you were born, you could supply the answer "London" even if you were actually born in Chicago. You will be fine as long as you remember if asked in the future that your answer to that question is London—or even london or LONDON—as your answers to your security questions are not case-sensitive. (The case of the letters used for an FSA ID password are the only case-sensitive letters applicable to the FSA ID system.) All that matters with the answer you provide for a security question is the character-by-character way you initially typed your answer when the FSA ID was created (or the way you typed any revised answer, if you choose to change your questions and/or answers in the future). This is because the security built into the FSA ID system uses character recognition for the answer to any security question (as well as with the username and password). So take your time when you create the FSA ID. Pick answers to the security questions that are easy for you to remember, but difficult for someone else to figure out. We do not recommend that you select a question that involves a multi-word answer. If you use multiple word answers to any question, you will then need to be able to recall—perhaps years later—if you used a space between words, as the system considers a space to be a separate character. (This can be confusing, as the FSA ID system does not allow spaces to be used between characters for the username or password.) The only special characters that should be used are those that are on the same keys as the digits (0 through 9) on a standard keyboard: !, @, #, etc.

At some point you will be asked if you wish to supply a mobile number. And eventually you will be asked to verify any email address and/or mobile number you supplied. To verify your email address, you can request that a message be sent to that email address with a 6-digit code (for one-time use) for you to enter on an FSA ID web page; to verify the mobile phone number, you will be texted a different 6-digit code to enter when asked. It may take a couple of minutes to be sent the code, so be patient. These codes will expire after a certain amount of time; if they do, you can request another code.

When attempting to have your mobile phone verified, do not panic if you see a message stating that the mobile phone number is already associated with an FSA ID/studentaid.gov account—even though you have not yet finished creating your FSA ID. This situation can occur if you have not had your phone number for more than ten years. Why? Since the FSA ID has been around since May 2015, it is possible that someone who used to have your mobile phone number created an FSA ID using your current mobile phone number. The Department of Education is aware of this problem (which will only get worse with time, given that with each new year, there's an increased likelihood that someone had your mobile phone number years ago and had an FSA ID as well). However, the USDOE currently has no method in place enabling you to verify your mobile phone number if another person's FSA ID is already associated with it. If you encounter this problem, forget about verifying your mobile phone number and just be sure to verify your email address. Once created, we recommend that you print on a piece of paper the username and case-sensitive password as well as all the security questions and answers as they were entered online. Then keep this paper in a secure place. Storing such information on your computer or device may be more convenient, but it is also more risky given identity theft issues involving the FSA ID which we will cover two paragraphs from now.

If you are wondering what you can do if you cannot remember your username or case-sensitive password and cannot find such information in your records, here is what you need to know. First of all, you will not want to use the "trial and error" method. If you provide the proper username but forget the password, the FSA ID will be locked after three unsuccessful attempts at guessing the password. You can however use the longstanding method to retrieve a forgotten username and/or to reset the password by providing the correct answers to the security questions which were established when the FSA ID was initially created (or when the security questions and answers were subsequently revised, if applicable). With this method, you will need to correctly answer both of the two of the challenge questions selected by the FSA ID system (out of the pool of the four questions you initially created). The system will not tell you if you got a question wrong, but it will eventually change the combination of the particular questions you are asked to answer, which can help if you've forgotten one (or two) of your four possible questions. Keep in mind that the answers to the security questions are not case-sensitive but your responses you type will appear encrypted—so you should be sure to use the option to see what you typed.

An alternate way to retrieve a forgotten password and/or to reset the password is to use your unique previously verified email address or your previously verified mobile phone number associated with the FSA ID. With this method, a new six-digit code is sent to your previously verified email address or previously verified mobile phone. To help remind one of this (while protecting one's personal information), the email account or mobile number that is currently stored in the FSA ID system is partially visible and partially encrypted. This method of using one's verified email address or verified mobile phone number is both a blessing and a curse. On the plus side, this option is easier to use than the security question method. On the other hand, the implementation of a verified email address and/or verified mobile number increases the chances that one's identity can be stolen. Keep in mind that if your FSA username and password combination can be ascertained by an identity thief, the crook can learn your legal name, date of birth, and other personal information including the last four digits of your verified Social Security Number (which is often used as a security check with financial institutions for their own client identification purposes). You need to also be aware that a verified email address can be used as a substitute username for the FSA ID system. Since it is relatively easy to acquire lists of email addresses, an identity thief using a phishing attack therefore only needs to get the corresponding password to be able to access one's personal information via the FSA ID system and other federal student aid web sites. So you need to carefully guard the username and especially the password you created. You should also never provide the password in response to any unsolicited email, phone call, or text message. The U.S. Department of Education may use an email message or mobile phone text message to contact you. But neither the Department nor any educational institution will ever ask you to provide your FSA ID username and/or password in response to their contacting you. If you are asked to access a website and enter your FSA ID log in information, be careful! The website is likely run by phishers hoping to fool you into providing your FSA ID password via their bogus website that often looks very similar to an official U.S. Department of Education web site. These phishing attacks will also frequently use scary language that your financial aid is in jeopardy if you do not immediately either provide your password outright or update your password immediately by inputting your current password (which is a bogus update system used only as a lure to get your current password). Keep in mind that financial aid is a decentralized system where aid is administered through the financial aid office of your college or other post-secondary educational institutions. So the school itself awards aid funds or certifies your eligibility for some federal aid programs. No aid is awarded directly to a student by the U.S. Department of Education itself. Therefore such comments in a phishing attack are not applicable to any student; the aid delivery system does not work the way that is implied in such bogus messages. To help protect yourself, you should therefore only access the Department of Education websites directly by your typing the URL into your browser or by using a known URL you saved on your device.

After you provide all the required data when you are creating an FSA ID, you'll hit the Submit tab. Once your identity is confirmed, the FSA ID you created can be used immediately to access the FAFSA online. The unique username and case-sensitive password combination you create is your actual FSA ID!

While your password will never expire, keep in mind that the U.S Department of Education at some point in the future may lock your FSA ID and require you to create a new password. This is done as a security precaution and can sometimes apply to everyone's FSA ID currently in the system. If this happens, you can simply add another character, delete a character (provided you still have the required minimum number), or change the case of one or two letters, so long as the new password is slightly different and meets the password criteria. Then you will likely need to again verify your newly created password and existing username. With this required password change (as opposed to the password reset), it will be unlikely that you will need to follow the procedures mentioned above to reset a forgotten password—unless you have to first reset your former password because you forgot it, as you will need an existing password before you are able to create a new password as required by the Department. Of course, you will want to revise the securely stored paper record of your FSA ID details you are keeping in a secure place, to reflect any new or reset password. And if the email account you originally decided to link to your FSA ID is no longer able to be used (for example, the student used their high school email address and have now graduated and so that email address expired) and/or for some reason, you no longer have the mobile phone number you linked to the FSA ID, you will want to be sure to log in to your FSA and update those items associated with your FSA ID.

And finally: be aware that in the unlikely event you do know your username and case-sensitive password AND you cannot recall the answers to at least two of your security questions AND your verified email address is no longer applicable (i.e., none of the ways to retrieve your forgotten username or reset your password can be used), you will need to contact the U.S. Department of Education (DOE) by phone at 1-800-4-FEDAID (1-800-433-3243) to fix the problem and speak with a live representative. It can take up to several weeks to have this issue resolved. So again, make sure you securely keep a paper record of the unique username, case-sensitive password, and the specific characters (including spaces if applicable) for the respective answer for each of the four security questions you chose. And be sure to use the actual FSA ID website to update your email address and/or mobile number if either or both are no longer able to be used. As you can tell by now, the FSA ID system has enhanced security measures to protect your sensitive information. It is not any way similar to a typical website where it is a far simpler process to retrieve a forgotten username or reset the password.

Moving Right Along

At the time we went to press, only a draft version of the 2027–2028 FAFSA was available. We have provided this draft version in Part Five to help you familiarize yourself with the layout of the print form. Remember though that this draft version is for informational purposes only and should never be submitted to the FAFSA processor.

When looking at this draft version, you will notice that in the right margin of each page of the form the text "Student," "Student Spouse," "Parent," "Parent Spouse or Partner," or "Preparer" appears vertically. This is due to a "roles-based" method being utilized for each person required to have their information provided on the form. The Department of Education also often uses a misleading term, "Contributor," to describe any individual with a role in the process—even though no "Contributor" is legally bound to contribute money toward the student's educational expenses merely by supplying their required information on the FAFSA. To avoid confusion, in the pages that follow we will often use quotation marks in regard to proper nouns (for example, "Student" or "Parent") to refer to the specific "Contributor" assuming a particular "role" on the FAFSA.

We do not expect many changes to the draft version regarding the questions or the ordering of them when the actual print version is released. Therefore, we have modeled our line-by-line references for the 2027–2028 FAFSA that follow based on the draft version. However, there may well be some important changes to the FAFSA instructions that accompany the form.

Because of this we recommend that before you begin working on the FAFSA or CSS Profile, you should first check for updates to this book via your online Student Tools. This will ensure that you get any late-breaking, post-print information and tips about the 2027–2028 forms from us. If you've not already done so, you will need to register this book (for free) to access this content. Details on how to do so and gain access to your Student Tools are explained on page vi in the section "Get More (Free) Content."

Our line-by-line tips that follow are presented in numerical order based on the question numbers and their subparts on the paper version of the FAFSA. However, we realize that the overwhelming majority of students now complete the online version of the FAFSA. As mentioned earlier, the skip-logic built into the electronic form will result in only the required questions being asked, though not in the same order as with the paper version.

With the electronic form for a dependent student, either the "Student" or the "Parent" required to report their information on the FAFSA can log into https://fafsa.gov, supply their FSA ID, and start the form. The person who starts the online FAFSA will then at some point invite their other "Contributors" to participate. The conventional wisdom is that students should begin the form, in part to initially determine if the student can be classified as an independent student. However, if the student will be considered a dependent student for the purposes of the FAFSA, we strongly recommend that the "Parent" required to report financial information on that student's FAFSA starts the form online before the student logs in and does anything with the FAFSA form. This is especially important if the student's biological or adoptive parents are not living together, as students frequently invite the incorrect parent to participate in the FAFSA process. Regardless of whether the parents are living together, there are other advantages to having the "Parent" contributor begin the form. Keep in mind that once any "Contributor" submits their part of the FAFSA to the processor, it may not be possible to change certain responses.

Filling Out the 2027–2028 FAFSA

Note: *If completing the PDF version of the FAFSA by hand, use block capital letters and follow the other guidance on page 1 of the PDF for the proper way to write your responses. On need analysis forms, "you" always refers to the student unless stated otherwise.*

1a.–1d. Student's name. By this, they mean the student applicant's name. This name must agree exactly (down to the appropriate middle initial for the middle name, if applicable) with the name listed on the student's social security card. It should also agree with the name of the student on the admissions application. If the first name is listed as Giovanni on the social security card, don't write down John on the need analysis form. Please be aware that if one is completing the FAFSA online via the FOTW and the student's FSA ID is provided to begin the FAFSA, the student's name and some other "identifiers" for that student will have some responses pre-filled using the "identifiers" provided when the student's FSA ID was created. However (if applicable), you will likely need to input the student's middle initial even if the first and last name are pre-filled.

If you have two children applying for aid, you must fill out two separate forms, even though the information will be largely identical. Do this even if the children are planning to attend the same college. This is because the student is the applicant, not the family or the student's parents.

1e. Student's date of birth. For a student who was born March 5, 2006, the correct answer should be "03 05 2006" not "3 5 2006."

1f. Social security number (SSN). By this, they mean the student's social security number. These days most students are required to have one. If the student does not have one but is eligible to get one, then apply for it immediately. Your form will be returned unprocessed if you supply an incorrect social security number, so be extra careful when listing it. Make sure the correct number agrees with the number on any admissions application. At some schools, students are still called up on the computer system by their social security number. The Department of Education will now check this number against the social security database. If the number doesn't match the name, there will be no aid until the problem is corrected and it does match. If you are applying to any college using the Common Application for admission and intend to apply for aid at any of your Common App schools, be sure that you list the student's correct SSN on the Common App, if asked for it. Otherwise, the college may not be able to "find" your processed FAFSA data until that glitch is resolved by your editing the Common App and providing the correct SSN.

1g. Individual Taxpayer Identification Number (ITIN). This question should only be answered if the student does not have a Social Security Number, but does have an ITIN.

2a. Student's mobile phone number. Remember to include the area code.

2b. Student's email address. Since high school email addresses are often deactivated after the student graduates, use a personal email address.

2c–2g. Address. Do not use a temporary address, such as that of a boarding school. Much of the mail you will receive from the colleges will be time sensitive. It's important that you get it quickly. Be sure to include a space when appropriate between different characters for the street address. It's fine to use standard abbreviations that are part of a street address (e.g. ST for the word "street). If completing the PDF version by hand and if any address is too long, then wrap the text onto the second line per the guidance on page 1 of the PDF file. When filling out question 2e—the student's home state—be sure to use the proper abbreviation. The form is now asking for the student's 9-digit Zip+4 zip code. If you do not know the last four digits, visit the U.S. Postal Service's website (usps.com) and use the Look Up a Zip Code tool with the student's address listed in 2c–2e. Be sure to use the proper country code provided in the FAFSA instructions.

3. As of today, what is your marital status? This refers to the student's marital status, not the parents'. Note: if you indicate that the student is "married/remarried," then questions 25 and 26 regarding the student's spouse income must be completed. Questions 27–29 must also be completed if the student did not file a joint income tax return with their current spouse for the 2025 tax year. Note that questions such as this one with circles to the left of each of the multiple-choice options are those where one must select the most appropriate single response.

4a. Your grade level during the 2027–2028 school year. The menu options for this question generated many comments from financial aid officers and state higher education agencies with the 2024–2025 FAFSA. This was mostly due to the confusing wording for the last menu option, which should only be used if the student is pursuing a graduate school or professional school degree above the bachelor's level. Those with an associate's degree should use the "Other undergraduate option" if they are pursuing a bachelor's degree (even though they may consider themselves a college graduate). Students who may have taken college credits while still in high school should still select "First year (freshman)" even if they enter college with advance standing. Be aware there may be certain aid programs only offered by the school to first-year and/or first-time college students. This question is likely also being used to determine annual borrowing limits for federal student loans. (We'll cover these annual borrowing limits later in Part Four, The Offer.)

4b. Will you have your first bachelor's degree before you begin the 2027–2028 school year? For most undergraduate students, of course, the answer will be no.

4c. Pursuit of an initial elementary or secondary teaching certification. If unsure, answer "Yes" as this may qualify the student for additional aid such as the federal TEACH grant. Remember that one can always change their mind before accepting such aid, which has some strings attached. But it is normally much easier to turn down aid offered than it is to ask for more later after the initial aid offer has been made.

5a.–5i. Student Personal Circumstances. These questions are here to also help establish whether an applicant is an independent student or a dependent student. Colleges that award a great deal of institutionally funded financial aid would prefer that their students were dependent. Independent students are much more expensive for a school since they usually require more financial aid.

Of course, it would be wonderful if a student can establish that she or he is independent, but there are several tough criteria to meet. If a student can truthfully select one or more of the options before the last one (i.e., "None of these apply") then he or she is undoubtedly independent for federal aid purposes for the 2027–2028 academic year—though one should carefully read the accompanying instructions on the FAFSA if selecting any response other than the last one. And one should be prepared to provide the financial aid office with the supporting documentation if any response other than "None of these apply" is selected.

Note that questions such as this one with squares to the left of each of the choices are those questions where one can select more than one response. (Obviously one cannot select "None of these apply" in addition to any other response.)

Comment: Outside of financial aid, a small difference in wording can mean the same thing and so similar words can be used interchangeably. But in the world of financial aid, similar words can mean very different things—and even the ordering of different words can mean something completely different. So the terms "Other Circumstances," "Unusual Circumstances," and "Special Circumstances" are <u>not</u> exactly interchangeable. We will now be discussing *questions on the FAFSA pertaining to the first two terms, which have slightly different meanings—although both terms involve situations where the student can ultimately be considered an independent student for federal student aid eligibility. The term "Special Circumstances" on the other hand refers to a situation with a completely different meaning involving information not reported on the FAFSA form—for example, a reduction or loss of income from the base year income reported to the FAFSA or a high medical expense—that can be used by dependent and independent students in an appeal process to request reconsideration of the initial aid offer (which we'll cover later in Part Four, The Offer).*

6a.– 6f. Student Other Circumstances. These questions apply to those students that are homeless or at risk of becoming homeless. If the answer to 6a is yes, then there are five follow-up responses. This is another way for a student to be considered independent and not be required to report any parental information on the FAFSA. However if the "None of these apply" response is selected, then the student will only be considered "provisionally independent," which means the applicant can proceed without needing to supply parental information for the time being. This is a change from past years for the FAFSA. If "None of these apply" is selected, the applicant should also contact the financial aid office at each college under consideration for further guidance. Be aware though that if at the end of the day it is subsequently determined that a student does not meet the criteria to be independent, then parental information will eventually need to be reported on the FAFSA at a later time to determine the applicant's eligibility for need-based student aid. This will be done as a "correction" to the FAFSA data previously submitted.

Note: Questions 7 and 8 can be skipped if the student meets the criteria for being an independent student by virtue of the student's age (born prior to January 1, 2004), student's marital status (married but not separated or remarried per question 3), or being a graduate / professional school student per question 4.

7. Student Unusual Circumstances. These questions involve situations that do not normally fit the criteria for a student to be classified as an independent student. Note that in terms of federal student aid, a "Yes" response for this question will trigger the student being considered "provisionally Independent" and so the student should contact the aid office(s) as well per above. Note that students who are homeless or at risk of becoming homeless should review their response to question 6 as documentable evidence of their housing situation by a third-party via one of the options other than "none of the these apply" as that will result in the student being considered "independent" instead of "provisionally independent."

8. Apply for a Direct Unsubsidized Loan Only? The wording of this question has generated a huge number of problems on the FAFSA in prior academic years due to applicants not understanding the dire repercussions of a "Yes" response to this question.

It may be tempting to assume that this question will offer applicants a roundabout way to avoid reporting parental information for a dependent student in order to get more aid—<u>*but you need*</u>

to resist that temptation! By selecting "Yes," the student will not be considered for any need-based aid. That means zero need-based grant aid—a type of aid that does not need to be paid back—and no work-study job and no subsidized Direct Loan. It also means a parent of such a dependent student will not be eligible to take out a parent PLUS loan. Nor will the dependent student be able to borrow additional funds via the Unsubsidized Direct Loan provisions that apply if the parent of a dependent student does not pass the parent PLUS loan's soft credit test. (We cover the different types of federal, state, and institutional aid programs including federal loans in detail in Part Four, The Offer.) As such, a "Yes" response should only be provided for this question as a last resort, with the full understanding that student aid will be limited to the dependent student Direct Loan annual borrowing limit, with interest charged on the total loan from the time the loan proceeds are disbursed.

Questions 9 and 10 are some of the questions on the FAFSA that only apply to independent students or provisionally independent students. Dependent students do not need to answer questions 9 and 10; nor do dependent students need to answer questions 18 and 21.

9. Family Size. With this question, the more family members the better. So be sure to carefully read the instructions and include all family members who meet the criteria mentioned in the instructions.

10. Number in College. As mentioned previously in Chapter 3, the federal aid formula will no longer automatically make an adjustment to the bottom line based on multiple family members being concurrently enrolled in college. One should still provide an accurate response to this question based on the FAFSA instructions, as some colleges will continue to take multiple students into account when awarding their own institutional aid funds. In a change from prior versions of the FAFSA, this question no longer stipulates that any other family members need to be attending at least half-time for at least one semester at a higher-education institution that can award students any type of federal student aid. However, many colleges will still use such criteria to make any multi-student adjustment. If an independent student is the only family member attending college, the response will be "01" as the applicant is always to be included for purposes of this question.

Unlike questions 9 and 10, which apply solely to independent students, questions 11–17 are to be answered by all applicants.

11. Student Demographic Information and 12. Student Race and Ethnicity. Be aware that these questions are for research purposes and do not affect your aid eligibility. Nonetheless these two questions generated many comments during the comment period for the 2024–2025 FAFSA, with many in the aid community questioning their inclusion on the form given FAFSA Simplification was supposed to minimize the questions asked and the responses to these questions do not affect the aid calculations. Be aware that your response for these questions will not be sent to any college that you list to receive your FAFSA data. If you are concerned about your privacy or have other issues related to question 12, there is no need to worry; just select "Prefer not to answer."

Note: Circle answer fields on the FAFSA involve questions with mutually-exclusive responses, so only one choice can be selected; square answer fields allow one to select more than one of the response options that apply.

13a.–b. Student's citizenship status. To get federal student aid, the student must be either a U.S. citizen or an eligible noncitizen (in most cases, the holder of a green card, although there are some exceptions; consult the instructions for the FAFSA). If the student will have an alien registration number by the time she starts school, but doesn't yet have one on the day you fill out the form, you should contact the financial aid offices of the schools she is interested in for further instructions on how to proceed.

If the student is not a U.S. citizen or eligible noncitizen (or is a U.S. citizen/eligible non-citizen living overseas), you may need to complete special aid forms in addition to the FAFSA or instead of the FAFSA. Ask the FAOs at the schools to which you are applying for more details.

14a.–b. Student's state of legal residence. This question can be very important if the student will be attending a college in their state of residence. Be sure to enter the proper two-character abbreviation for the student's state of residence along with your best estimate for when the student moved to that state. If the student was born in the state and has been living in the state ever since, enter the student's month and year of birth for the date. This second part of question 14 does not matter as much for students who have been living in the state for more than five years. This question is primarily being used to see if you meet the residency requirements to be classified as an in-state student for tuition purposes at a public higher-ed institution and/or to be eligible for state-funded student aid.

15. Parent Education Status. For versions of the FAFSA before 2024–2025, this question related to the highest level of education completed, which was important given that numerous colleges and some state higher-education agencies have aid funds designated for first-generation college students (often defined as those in which neither parent graduated from college). In the past, many colleges and state agencies would identify such students who met the definition of being first-gen based on the FAFSA responses. Since Simplification, the FAFSA provides two options regarding college attendance: if either parent ever attended any college as one option and if either parent completed college as another option. Note that this question relates only to the education of the biological or adoptive parents of the student (not any stepparent).

16. Parent Killed in Line of Duty. This question is being used to identify those students who may qualify for certain additional aid programs not available to all students. The instructions for the PDF version of the FAFSA or the help comments for an electronic version of the form will provide more guidance for this question and should be referred to before answering this question. This wording used at the outset for purposes of this question can be misleading as one's response can relate to one's legal guardian as well as one's parent who was killed in the line of duty. For all other questions on the FAFSA, a legal guardian is not considered a parent unless the guardian has adopted the student. If the response provided is "Yes," be prepared to submit additional supporting documentation as proof of such line-of-duty loss.

17a.–17f. Student High School Information. This question refers to the student's educational status before the first day of college. For most students, the answer will be "High school diploma," in which case additional information regarding the proper name, city, and state of the high school will need to be provided. If you are completing an electronic version of the form, the high school information will be matched with a database. If you encounter trouble and are still in high school, ask your guidance counselor for the exact way to enter the information. If you did not and will not receive a high school diploma, answer the questions accordingly.

Now that basic information has been provided about the student, it's time to move onto the more important questions on the FAFSA that follow question 17. If you briefly review the remaining questions that appear on the version of the 2027–2028 FAFSA that is reproduced in Part Five of this book, you will notice that many of the financial questions involving the student, the student's spouse, the student's parent, and that parent's spouse or partner are very similar, though the numbering of the questions is different. Be aware that not all of these questions for all four of these types of individuals (or "roles") will ever need to be completed. But since many of the questions that follow are indeed identical, for simplicity we will soon be discussing and providing tips and strategies for similar questions simultaneously. We will also provide the various question numbers associated with each of the tips that are similar for various "roles."

But before we get into the nitty-gritty details and provide our tips for answering specific questions, it is important to have a basic understanding regarding which individuals will be required to provide responses to some of these identical questions on the form. And if an electronic version of the FAFSA is being filed, it is also important to understand which significant others will need their own unique FSA ID.

Given the student is the applicant for aid, details regarding the student's income and possibly other benefit information for the student (and if applicable, the student's spouse) will be required. If an electronic version of the FAFSA is being filed, the student will always need their own FSA ID.

If the student is married, some demographic information regarding the student's spouse will be required in FAFSA questions 25 and 26. Not to worry. In addition to the identical questions for various individuals, we'll also soon cover these and any other questions specific to the significant other(s) of the applicant. If the student and the student's spouse *filed a joint return* in 2025 (the PPY year for the 2027–2028 FAFSA), then questions 27–29 will not be required of the spouse. And if the form is being completed electronically, the student's spouse will not need their own FSA ID (which we covered earlier in this part of the book). However, if the student and the student's spouse *did not file a joint income tax return*, then the student's spouse will need to supply responses for questions 27–29 based on their own (i.e., the student spouse's own) income tax filing situation for the PPY year. And if no joint return was filed for the PPY year and the FAFSA is being filed electronically, then the student's spouse will need their own unique FSA ID in addition to the student needing their own unique FSA ID.

If the student is unmarried and is a dependent student—that is, the student does not meet any of the criteria to be classified as an independent student or even to be temporarily classified as being provisionally independent—then some demographic information regarding one of the applicant's parents must be provided at a minimum in FAFSA questions 30 and 31.

Which parent's information must be provided for those two questions will depend in part on whether or not both biological or adoptive parents are living together (regardless of whether they are married or not).

If the student's parents are living together at the time the FAFSA is filed, then either parent's identity and contact information for questions 30 and 31 could be provided, with the responses for questions 42 and 43 needing to be completed using the other parent's identity and contact information. While it will not affect aid eligibility, there are some other situations where it may make sense to list one parent's information instead of the other's data for questions 30 and 31 if an electronic version of the FAFSA is being completed. This has to do with the FSA ID and the tax filing status and marital status. Specifically if the parents are married and filed a joint tax return for the 2025 PPY relevant to the 2027–2028 FAFSA, then only the parent who reported their information in questions 30 and 31 needs to have their own unique FSA ID. However, to be safe and since the other parent's FSA ID may be needed at a later date for a different task, we strongly recommend that both parents get their own FSA ID prior the FAFSA being completed, even though only one parent's FSA ID will need to be used for this scenario when completing and submitting the FAFSA. This way, if there is some glitch with one parent's FSA ID, the other parent's FSA can be used (though that other parent providing the FSA would then need to be the parent providing their information for FAFSA questions 30 and 31). If the parents filed a joint return for 2025, then questions 44 through 46 do not need to be completed as the joint tax return information will be reported in FAFSA 37 and 38.

But if those two parents living together did not and will not file a joint return for the 2025 tax year—because they were not married to each other at the end of the PPY year, because they chose to each file their own return using the "married filing separately" option, because they did not file a tax return because their income was below the threshold amount where they would be required to file a U.S. tax return, or for some other reason—**then both parents will need their own FSA ID if an electronic version of the FAFSA is being completed. And regardless of which version of the 2027–2028 FAFSA is being used, questions 44 through 45 will need to be completed using the income tax information for the parent listed in FAFSA 42 with that parent providing their own consent in FAFSA 46.**

However, if a dependent student's two biological or adoptive parents are *not living together* at the time the FAFSA is being filed, things get more complicated. First of all, there is the problem discussed earlier in this part of the book as to who is considered the "parent" of the dependent student applying for financial aid—given the lack of guidance to determine which parent has provided the greatest support. As a reminder, such students whose situation falls into this category should be sure to carefully review the instructions before completing the FAFSA or any other forms requiring "parent" information including but not limited to the CSS Profile. Please be aware that because policy guidance from the U.S. Department of Education may have been released after we went to press, your online student tools should be checked regularly.

Besides the issue of who is the "parent," there are still many other unanswered questions involving factors such as a) the tax filing status of that parent for the prior-prior tax year (PPY); b) whether or not that parent has legally married someone else (as well as when they got married); c) whether parents who are separated are legally separated; d) whether that parent's marital status changed from being separated without any court action at the end of the PPY year (i.e., being "informally separated") to being "legally separated" (via some court filing) but not divorced prior to the completion of the FAFSA; e) whether that parent of the student lost their spouse after the end of the PPY year and has not legally married another person as of the time the FAFSA is filed (and whether that spouse who passed away was the student's parent or was the student's step-parent); or f) some other situation where the tax filing status on the PPY tax return is not consistent with the current situation for the person considered the "parent" for purposes of the FAFSA.

Given that situations where the parents of a dependent student are not living together are more complicated (even before taking into account the financial aid implications) and given the large number of unanswered questions as we went to press that involve the completion of the FAFSA and other aid forms, we are going to just provide some general information now.

- The wording relating to questions 42 and 43 can easily be problematic. Remember that for these questions, the current spouse of the parent listed in question 30 will be that parent's "Spouse." For questions 42 and 43, that spouse can be either the biological or adoptive other parent OR it can be the stepparent who is married to the student's parent at the time the FAFSA is filed. (However, if the parent listed in question 30 is separated from the student's other parent or stepparent at the time the FAFSA is completed, then no responses should be provided for any of the Spouse or Partner questions 42–46.) **Key points:** While the applicable parents for question 15 are only to be the biological or adoptive parents, the word "parents" has a different meaning for the financial questions on the form that follow after the student's consent in question 29, since any reference to a parent can mean the stepparent currently married to the student's parent who is required to complete the FAFSA. However if stepparent information is required (and that person has not adopted the student), then such stepparent can only have the role of the Parent's Spouse. Therefore, that stepparent must be the individual listed in question 42. For that student's FAFSA, they cannot be the parent in question 30. This is a major change from pre-2024–2025 versions of the FAFSA with the use of (step)parent 1 and (step)parent 2 instead of the word "parent."

- If the parent in question 30 is married (and not legally separated) at the time the FAFSA is being completed *and that parent filed a joint income tax return in 2025 with the other parent or stepparent listed in question 42:* other than question 43 which must be answered, questions 44 and 45 should be left blank and consent from the (step)parent listed for question 42 need not be given in question 46. This is because the Federal Tax Information (FTI) for the person listed in question 42 will be reported on the joint tax return and the parent in question 30 will have provided the necessary consent in question 41 to have the FTI from the joint return transferred from the IRS. In this instance, it is not necessary for the person listed in question 42 to have their own FSA ID, though we still recommend their doing so.

- If the parent in question 30 is married (and not legally separated) at the time the FAFSA is being completed *and that parent did not file a joint income tax return in 2024 with the other parent or stepparent listed in question 42:* questions 43 through 45 must be completed by the other parent or stepparent and consent must be provided in question 46. And if an electronic version is being filed, that other parent or stepparent must have their own unique FSA ID. This same guidance would apply if the student's parents were unmarried but living together.

There are still some unanswered questions for those in situations in which a joint tax return was filed in 2025 by the parent listed in Question 30 and such parent is no longer married to or is separated from the person with whom they filed the joint 2025 return. This could occur for joint filers that have since separated, divorced, or become widowed. (The same would occur for an independent student who is no longer married to the person with whom they filed a joint return. Of course, this presumes the student can still be considered independent via some other criteria other than being married, in which case such a student would revert back to being a dependent student if no other criteria for independent status is met.)

One such question would be: How will the income tax information from such joint return be reported? While the electronic version of the 2027–2028 FAFSA could be filed with the person manually inputting only their share of information, it remains to be seen in what way or ways that share of the data is to be derived and inputted for the 2027–2028 FAFSA.

Then there are other unanswered questions that can also affect a large number of applicants, regardless of the student's parent(s) marital status: What FTI information will be transferred via the FA-DDX if an amended IRS 1040X tax return was filed? What information will be transferred if the IRS made corrections or adjustments to the original return (without the tax filer amending the return? In both cases, will the data transferred be from the original return or will it be the tax return data using the dollar amounts from the amended or IRS-corrected return?

As the answers were not available at the time we went to print, we suggest you carefully read the instructions and help comments for the 2027–2028 FAFSA.

Here are the questions we can answer:

What happens if one of the individuals required to provide their consent does not have an FSA ID and refuses to get one? *Answer:* only the PDF version can be used with the completed form mailed to the processor. This is because of the impact of the new "roles-based" method for completing the FAFSA. Veterans of the aid process will recall that the electronic versions of the FAFSA (for many academic years prior to 2024–2025) once permitted a student or the parent of the dependent to access the form, complete all the required questions, and then submit the data either by providing the required signatures (the student signature, and for a dependent student one parent's signature as well), using their respective FSA IDs, or by printing and mailing a signed "signature page" to the processor. This could all be done with one computer session. Yet with the new roles-based method that began with the 2024–2025 FAFSA, the student (one role) will now need to use their own FSA ID to log in, complete their section of the form and provide their consent (if an electronic version of the FAFSA is being filed). Then the parent of a dependent student (another role) will need to log into a separate session with their own unique FSA ID, complete the required parent information, and eventually provide their consent. And if that parent did not file a joint tax return for the PPY based year with the student's other parent or stepparent *and the other parent or stepparent is required to provide their information in the "Parent Spouse or Partner" section of the FAFSA,* than that person will need to log in with their FSA ID so that, in the role of that parent's "Spouse or Partner," they can provide their consent to have their FTI transferred from the IRS. (For a married independent student, the student's spouse need only log in with their own FSA and provide their consent if a joint tax return was not filed in the PPY year with the student.)

What happens if one parent refuses to provide their consent to have their FTI transferred by the IRS, if such consent is required? *Answer:* The FAFSA can be submitted, but no SAI number will be calculated, and so no need-based federal aid can be awarded by the financial aid office. However, if the consent is subsequently provided at a later date, then the SAI will be calculated. This is true whether the PDF version or an electronic version of the FAFSA is completed.

What happens if one is a victim of identity theft? *Answer:* In years past, such individuals could never use the IRS DRT given security concerns about the sensitive tax data if the IRS knew there were identity theft issues. But with the new method involving the FA-DDX, it appears that the IRS will transfer the data from the IRS tax return onto the form. However, this will only occur if the issues surrounding such identity theft have been resolved. If they are unresolved, then the data will need to be manually input on the FAFSA.

Now that we've covered the bases regarding who must provide information on the form, we are now going to first cover those questions on the FAFSA after question 17 that only are required of the student or that do not involve the student (or the student's spouse). Some of these parent questions will only be asked once of the parent, though some will be paired up, but only for the parent and the "Spouse or Partner." Then we will cover the matching questions that are basically the same questions for individuals in any of the four possible "roles" involved (i.e., student, student's spouse, parent and "other parent," who could be a stepparent).

23a.–23t. Which college(s) are getting the FAFSA for 2027–2028 academic year aid consideration? (Student question)

If you're completing the PDF version of the FAFSA: List up to 10 schools to which you want the FAFSA data sent. List only one school per line and don't cross out or skip any lines. You have a choice of writing in the complete name and address of the school or of listing the six-character code for the school. (The instructions printed above these questions on the FAFSA tell you how to find the codes.) The feds say that using the codes will speed up processing time. On the other hand, if you make a mistake when you write down the code, your information will not be sent to the school you wanted and you may not find out about the snafu until it is too late. Either way, we recommend that you take great care in writing down the information on the FAFSA. If you are applying to a particular branch or division of a university, be sure to specify that as well or use the correct code for that branch or division.

If you're filing the FAFSA online: List the codes (or search for the schools by name) for all the schools (up to 20) to which you want the data sent. After you input the code for a particular school, make sure that the name of the correct school appears on your screen.

Regardless of how you file the FAFSA: Some state higher education agencies do have policies regarding the ordering of schools on the FAFSA. You should therefore visit https://studentaid.gov/apply-for-aid/fafsa/filling-out/school-list to determine if the ordering of schools impacts state aid in your home state. If you are applying to more schools than can fit on the form, you should first list those schools with the earliest FAFSA deadlines. After your FAFSA has been processed, there are ways you can have the data sent to the colleges you were not able to list on the FAFSA. But you need to be careful when doing this as the instructions from the FAFSA processor assume that certain things will happen in real time, and they often do not. (We'll cover this important topic later in this part of the book.)

This seemingly straightforward question on the FAFSA nonetheless generated the most comments/complaints/requests for changes by far during the 2024–2025 FAFSA comment periods. The reason for the commenters' concern/frustration had to do with the 2024–2025 FAFSA no longer asking about the desired housing option for the student (On-Campus, Off-Campus, or With Parents), which have differing costs and therefore affect the amount of demonstrated need. The feds contend the housing question is not necessary to determine the SAI or Pell Grant eligibility, which is true. But the aid office must know the housing option to develop an aid offer. And if the FAFSA does not ask for this, the school will need to get the information elsewhere, which can be problematic. (For example, the admissions application is an option for prospective student, but what do you do with students already enrolled who are reapplying for aid for the next school year when housing options are likely to change?) No matter what happens with the 2027–2028 FAFSA, students need to be careful when providing this housing information on any document submitted to a college. If you are not sure, submit the "on-campus" response if the college offers university-owned housing, since the cost of attendance (and so the demonstrated need) will be higher than if "off-campus" is chosen.

The usual question about student interest in a work-study job on prior FAFSAs has also disappeared on the FAFSA (with numerous requests for reinstatement from commenters as well). As this information affects the types of aid awarded It is best to say "Yes" on any document submitted, especially as this does not commit the student (minds can be changed later). Also, any question about work-study has zero impact on the amount of grant or scholarship aid that will be awarded.

25a.–25g. Student Spouse Identity. (Married Independent Students only) Our tips for FAFSA question 1a.-1g. regarding the use of one's legal name and the listing of the proper Social Security Number or ITIN are basically the same.

26a.–26g. Student Spouse Contact Information. (Married Independent Students only) Refer to our tips for FAFSA questions 2a.–2g. for more guidance.

30a.–30g. Parent Identity (Dependent Students only) and **42a.–42g. Other Parent Identity** (If applicable). Before answering these questions as well the other "Parent" questions 31-35 (and if applicable, question 43 for the "Spouse or Partner"), you should carefully review the section "Which Parent(s) Must Report Information on the 2027–2028 FAFSA and CSS Profile" presented earlier in this part of the book, our comments following our tips for question 17, and the instructions on the FAFSA to determine who is the "Parent"—and if applicable, who is the "Spouse or Partner" (which can be a stepparent). Our tips for FAFSA question 1a.–1g. regarding the use of the legal name and the listing of the proper Social Security Number or ITIN are basically the same. However, if the parent has neither an SSN nor ITIN (for example, the parent is not a U.S. citizen and lives overseas), the FAFSA instructions may not cover this scenario, as the feds may release guidance after the start of the 2027–2028 processing cycle.

31a.–31g. Parent Contact Information. (Dependent Students only) and **43a.–43g. Parent Spouse or Partner Identity.** (If applicable) Refer to our tips for FAFSA questions 2a.–2g. for guidance.

32. Parent Current Marital Status. (Dependent Students Only) This question relates to the marital status of the parent(s) required to report their information on the FAFSA. The FAFSA instructions provide guidance on this question including help comments for some atypical situations involving some separated or divorced scenarios. However, if the parent required to report information on the form was separated or divorced from the student's other biological or adoptive parent, has not currently married, and the other parent is deceased, then answer widowed. If the stepparent of the parent required to report information on the FAFSA has passed away, then answer this question based on the parent's marital status in relation to the student's other biological or adoptive parent.

33a.–33b. Parent State of Legal Residence. (Dependent Students Only) Be sure to list the proper abbreviation. And if the parent required to report information is married, remarried, or unmarried but living with the other biological or adoptive parent of the student, provide the earliest date that either of the parents listed in question 30 or 42 (or the earliest date the parent or the stepparent) began living in the state—though no earlier than the Parent in question 30's month and year of birth.

34. Family Size. (Dependent Students Only) This question is used to help determine the Income Protection Allowance. You would like this number to be as high as possible. The more family members, the higher your allowance. The instructions on the first draft mention to include the student (whose name is on the FAFSA), the parent (listed in Question 30) the spouse of the parent in question 30 (if married or remarried), other children who live with the parent (or if they live apart from the parent due to college enrollment), as well other individuals who live with the parent. For any other children as well as for any other individual to be included in the family size, one must be currently receiving more than half their support from the student's parent(s) and expecting to receive more than half their support between July 1, 2027 and June 30, 2028. This question generated many comments given that certain categories of individuals previously considered family members were now not covered, such as: a) newborn babies (even if they are not yet born when you are filling out the FAFSA), b) half-siblings or stepsiblings of the student, and c) younger siblings (or half/step siblings) attending boarding school. The Department may issue additional guidance, so be sure to review the instructions for this question before you complete the FAFSA.

35. Number in College during the 2027–2028 award year. (Dependent Students Only) One of the biggest changes to the federal methodology is the elimination of the multiple-student adjustment, which was the one data element that had the greatest impact on aid eligibility prior to simplification. Under the old FM, if the parents were expected to contribute $20,000 to college, such contribution would be $20,000 with one dependent in college; $10,000 for each of two in college the same academic year; $6,667 for each of three concurrently enrolled in college, etc. Yet even though Simplification has eliminated this automatic adjustment for federal aid, it is still important that one provide an accurate response to this question based on the FAFSA instructions, as a number of colleges will continue to take multiple students into account when awarding their own institutional aid funds. So even though the SAI will not be adjusted for federal aid purposes for multiple students being enrolled, some parents who might not have qualified for any aid with only one child in college may find that with two children in school at the same time they do qualify for substantial amounts of institutional aid. This is why it is worth applying for aid each year, even if you were refused the first time. If one of your children is trying to decide whether to take a year off from college, this might be a factor when it comes time to make that decision if the college for the other child is making a multiple-student adjustment affecting institutional aid. In such a case, you want as much overlap as possible.

Note that this question no longer specifies that to be considered in college any other family members need to be attending at least half-time for at least one semester at a higher-education institution that can award students any type of federal student aid as it did in the pre-Simplification era. However, many colleges will insist on such criteria before making any multi-student adjustment. As in prior years, a (step)parent in college should never be included as a family member in college for this FAFSA question. However, if a (step)parent will be concurrently enrolled in a higher-education institution, some schools will make an adjustment for that expense. If this applies to you, be sure to explain this situation to the financial aid office. If the student is the only family member attending college, the response will be "01" as the applicant is always to be included, even if the student is taking a minimal course load.

18a.–18j. (Independent Students only) **and 36a.–36j.** (Dependent Students only) **Federal Benefits Received (in 2025 or 2026 by any member of the family).** As mentioned in Chapter Three, if a family member (included in the family size for the response to question 9 for an independent student or question 34 for a dependent student) receives any federal means-tested benefit (MTB) for at least one day during the prior two years, then assets will not be considered in the SAI formula provided all other criteria are met. One should select all menu options that apply to your situation. Otherwise, select the final option only: "None of these apply."

We'll now cover the matching questions for the four possible "roles" involving one's tax filing status and (if applicable) one's tax return information, which are questions 19 and 20 for the student; questions 27 and 28 for the spouse of an independent student (if applicable); questions 37 and 38 for the parent of a dependent required to report their information on the FAFSA; and questions 44 and 45 for the "other parent" i.e., the current spouse of that parent (if applicable). Remember: if you are completing the PDF version of the FAFSA, the student's spouse or the "Parent Spouse or Partner" will only need to provide responses for their respective questions involving tax filing status and tax return information if they did not file a joint tax return with their spouse in 2025. If they filed jointly, those questions for the spouse are to be left blank If an electronic version of the FAFSA is being filed, the questions for either the spouse of the student or the current spouse of the parent of the dependent student (if applicable) will not be asked due to the skip logic diagnosing the situation. Keep in mind as well that unlike versions of the FAFSA prior to 2024–2025 where an independent student could elect to report parental financial information on the FAFSA—since some aid programs such as special loans for graduate health profession students require such parental information—the FAFSA will no longer process such parental information if reported on the PDF version of the FAFSA nor will there be any opportunity to enter parental information on any electronic version of the FAFSA. In these instances, FAFSA Simplification will necessitate that such independent students will need to complete additional aid forms to provide such parent information to be considered for such special aid programs.

19a.–19c., 27a.–27b., 37a.–37c., and 44a.–44b. Tax filing status. *These questions are some of the most important questions on the entire form for many reasons, so you should be extra careful with your responses.* All students (dependent or independent) will need to provide the applicable responses for question 19.

However, if the student is *independent and is not required to answer "married" for the response to question 3 at the time the FAFSA is completed:* such responses in question 19 will serve as a diagnostic tool for an unmarried applicant to help determine eligibility for the Maximum Pell Grant (see Chapter 3 about this). And for a tax filer, the responses for question 19 for an unmarried independent student will also help determine whether or not student assets need to be reported on an electronic version of the form. (Not to worry if you are filing a paper FAFSA; if the assets you report are not required to determine the SAI based on your situation, the processor will ignore them in their calculations.) If an independent student is married, the responses to the question 19c. ("Did or will the student file a 2025 joint return with their current spouse") will determine whether or not an independent student's spouse will be required to a) complete questions 27–28 (responses to which will serve as additional diagnostic tools for Maximum Pell Grant eligibility or the exclusion of assets) and b) provide the FTI consent in question 29 (which will also necessitate the student's current spouse needing their own unique FSA ID if an electronic version of the FAFSA is being submitted).

For a dependent student required to report parent information on the FAFSA: the situation will be similar in regard to question 37 for the parent as question 19 is in regard to an independent student. And so the parent in question 30 will be required to complete the applicable parts of question 37. Such answers in question 37 will help determine Maximum Pell Grant eligibility and whether or not assets can be excluded. If such parent in question 30 selected "Married" or "Remarried" for question 32 regarding marital status, then the last subpart of question 37 regarding a 2025 joint tax return being filed or not with the current spouse, will determine whether or the spouse in question 42 will need to provide responses to questions 44 and 45 and provide consent in 46 (which will necessitate that Spouse needing their own FSA ID if filing online). If the parent in question 30 selected "Unmarried and both legal parents living together," then the "Spouse or Partner" questions 44 and 45 as well as the consent in question 46 will need to be completed (with an FSA ID needed for the other parent as well if an electronic version of the FAFSA is being used). If the parent in question 30 was able to select "Single," Separated," "Divorced," or "Widowed" as their response to question 32, then even though the response to the last subpart of question 37 will be "No" whether or not the parent in question 30 filed a return, all the questions in the "Spouse or Partner" section of the form (questions 42 through 46) need not be answered.

As you can see, there are many moving parts involved with these questions. But if you look carefully at the 2027–2028 version of the FAFSA reproduced in Part 5 of this book, you will notice that the second subpart of this question—applicable to those who indicate at the outset of this question that they did not and will not file a 2025 IRS 1040 (the common U.S. personal income tax return) or 1040-NR (used by non-resident aliens)—looks very different (and is more simplistic) if you are comparing the Student and Student Spouse subparts to the same subpart for the "Parent" or the "Spouse or Partner" where many response options are provided. This discrepancy generated many comments during the comment period last year, with many aid professionals questioning if it was an oversight by the USDOE to not use the same menu options and text for all "roles" on the form. There were also comments about the lack of specificity. Be aware that for a non-tax filer, the FA-DDX will supposedly confirm the individual did not file a tax return.

Regardless of whether you are filing the paper version or the electronic version of the FAFSA, it is imperative that you provide correct responses for all the applicable subparts of these questions that apply to your situation. Remember that questions regarding one's tax filing status refer to one's 2025 tax filing situation; the questions regarding marital status relate to one's situation on the day the FAFSA is being signed and submitted.

With an electronic version of the form, such responses will trigger the skip-logic programmed into the application to ask only the relevant questions. This will make it much easier to complete the FAFSA, and so the electronic version should be used if at all possible. But remember that with such electronic versions: all individuals who need to provide consent if required per our many tips above—i.e., the student; if applicable, the spouse of an independent student if they did not file a 2025 joint tax return with the student; the parent of a dependent student; and if applicable, the Spouse or Partner (which can be the stepparent married to the parent in question 30) if such Spouse or Partner did not file a joint 2025 tax return with that parent—will need to have their own unique FSA ID in order to provide their consent with the electronic version of the FAFSA. If any one person who must provide consent does not have an FSA ID, then an SAI will not be calculated until such FSA ID is obtained and consent is provided for the electronic form. If one who must provide consent is unable or unwilling to obtain an FSA ID before you start working on the form online, then the paper PDF version of the FAFSA should be completed and mailed to the applicable address listed on the form.

For any individual who did not file a tax return: Be aware that for a non-tax filer, the FA-DDX will supposedly confirm with the IRS that such individual did not file a tax return. However, other documentation may be required. Depending on the reason for not filing, an unmarried independent student may or may not need to complete questions 20–22 while a married independent student will likely need to answer such questions. The spouse of the student may or may not need to answer 28 depending on their reason for not filing. However, if the student is a dependent student: they will still need to complete question 22 on the paper version of the form. If a dependent student is filing an electronic version of the FAFSA: the student may be asked to complete question 22, but likely only if the student starts the FAFSA or if the parent in question 30 is required to answer question 40. If the parent in question is unmarried and is a non-tax filer who is not living with the student's other biological / adoptive parent, questions 38–40 may or may not need to be answered depending on the reason for non-filing. For if the parent in question 30 is married and the "other parent" in question 42 is a non-filer: depending on their reason for not filing, question 45 may or may not need to be answered. Be aware however that the wording of the instructions on the 2027–2028 version of the FAFSA reproduced in Part Five of this book should not be relied upon for guidance as to which questions can be skipped on the 2027–2028 FAFSA. There is a possibility that such wording on the final version of the 2027–2028 FAFSA may change for all four questions.

20a.–20p., 27a.–27n., 38a.–38p., and 45a.–45n. Tax Return Information (Note that these questions may still need to be completed even if no 2024 U.S. personal tax return was or will be filed). By the time the FAFSA filing period begins, most individuals who were required to file a 2025 IRS 1040 or 1040-NR will have done so. *For those filing an electronic version of the FAFSA:* this will mean that the FA-DDX should work once the necessary consent is provided—and the applicable person(s) Federal Tax Information (FTI) will be transferred by the IRS onto the form. However, you will never be able to see the dollar amounts that have been transferred. (If you are concerned about this transferred data being masked, you can determine the data being transferred by requesting a freely available transcript of your 2025 tax return from the IRS by visiting https://www.irs.gov/individuals/get-transcript, making sure to request your "return transcript" for the year ending December 31, 2025.) Unlike previous years when the entire FAFSA application could be completed online in one session: the new roles-based initiative will require that each person needing to provide consent for the FA-DDX will need to log in separately onto the FAFSA website and provide their consent. (Remember that the spouse of an independent student need not provide their consent if they filed a 2025 joint return with the student. A (step)parent who is considered the spouse of a dependent student's "Parent" in question 30 need not provide their consent if they filed a 2025 joint tax return with the student's "Parent" in question 30. The FA-DDX tool will then attempt to retrieve the data from the IRS. If the tool does not work for one of the individuals attempting to transfer their data, that person will be given the opportunity to manually enter their tax return information and the data will be considered valid for purposes of the SAI. Supposedly the system has been designed so that if FTI was not transferred initially, the FA-DDX system will try a second time to transfer the data after the FAFSA was submitted and processed. In such an instance, a new FAFSA Submission Report will be generated to reflect the data transferred from the IRS replacing your manually-inputted data. So if you are concerned about data being transferred and prefer to manually input your information, be aware that the system will soon replace your manually-inputted tax return information with the FA-DDX data from the IRS. So it would be better to get that transcript as explained above and use the FA-DDX from the outset, if able to do so. As a reminder: the FAFSA Submission Report is a summary of the information submitted. It is the output document available to the student applicant, that will replace the Student Aid Report (or SAR) output document for FAFSAs relevant to academic/award years prior to 2024–2025.)

However, there will be some scenarios in which the FA-DDX will not work after the consent is provided. This would involve individuals who filed a joint return in 2025 but with a person to whom they are no longer married at the time the FAFSA is completed (e.g., a recently-widowed parent of a dependent student, a parent who is considered separated from the parent with whom they filed jointly in which case only one person's share of the joint tax return data will likely need to be manually-inputted). Inability to use the FA-DDX can also happen with someone who filed their 2025 tax return late and the return has not yet been processed by the IRS, which is more likely if a paper tax return was mailed to the IRS and/or the FAFSA filing period somehow starts in November or December. Though if you are not required to file a tax return because your income is too low, you should not do so. Of course, those who file a foreign tax return will also not be able to use the FA-DDX.

However even if the FA-DDX works, it would still be a good idea to have an understanding regarding how the various transferred items influence the calculations and aid eligibility. And if you had a qualified rollover from an IRA or other qualified retirement plan rollover in 2025 or you reported any grants, scholarships, or Americorps benefits on the 2025 tax return you should realize there may be glitches with the FA-DDX that could affect aid eligibility and will require special attention. On the hand, if you are filing electronically and are unable to use the FA-DDX or you are filing the paper FAFSA, you will surely need to know how to answer these questions properly since you will have to manually input the data. If filing the paper version, keep in mind that an attempt will be made by the processor to use the FA-DDX if possible, in which case the manually-inputted data will be replaced with the federal tax information (FTI). And if the paper version is being completed: one will need to be very careful to make sure that answers are provided by all the applicable individuals with every required consent provided as well, so that the FA-DDX tool with the IRS can be utilized.

Note well: The FA-DDX will be transferring the number of the dependents on the respective tax return for each of the "roles" being completed even though there is no such question on the FAFSA. The number of dependents and the number of tax filers on the return (i.e., 2 if filing jointly and 1 for other filing statuses) will be added together. (The final sum may be an aggregate number if the student's spouse or the Parent's "Spouse or Partner," filed a separate return from the student or the parent in question 30 respectively.) This final sum will then be compared to the family size reported on the FAFSA. If the two numbers do not agree, that is OK. But be prepared to be able to explain the discrepancy. Initially the feds thought the number derived from the tax returns could be used to determine the family size (and so that question could be eliminated), but have scrapped that idea for a number of reasons. For example, divorced parents may alternate claiming their child as a dependent (i.e., one parent claims the child in even years, the other in odd years) regardless of where the child lives or the amount of support provided.

Before you begin inputting any responses for these questions, we recommend you review Chapter 3 where we cover the various types of income and other tax return data that appear on the applicable lines of the first two pages of the IRS 1040 and the numbered schedules. You should also refamiliarize yourself with the various lettered schedules, especially those that you filed with your 2025 return.

If you are manually inputting your responses, you should view the IRS line references on the 2027–2028 FAFSA; you'll want to look for that line item on your return as well as the various schedules and then input the relevant responses. If a particular subpart for these questions involves a response for a specific dollar amount and that subpart does not apply to your tax return situation, then be sure to enter a 0 (zero) inside the last response square to the right. And list only whole dollar amounts (no cents) for any of your dollar-amount responses other than zero.

The first subpart of these questions involves the tax filing status. The response for this question can be found on the top of page 1 of the 2025 IRS 1040.

So that you can follow along for the remaining subparts of these questions on the 2027–2028 FAFSA reproduced in Part Five, we will cover the subparts from the left subpart directly across to the right subpart, and then go down to the next subpart below those two subparts starting on the left side of the form again, etc.

The income earned from work question(s) will be used to determine the payroll tax deduction and the employment allowance. Per the IRS line references this question will capture W-2 income as well as the net profit from a business that files Schedule C (either as a sole proprietor or as a single-person LLC) and the net profit from a farm reported on Schedule F. For this income earned from work subpart only: if there is a loss showing on line 3 of Schedule 1 (which reflects the profit or loss from any Schedule C and/or a loss on line 6 of Schedule 1 (which reflects the profit or loss reported on Schedule F), treat any such loss as being 0 (zero) when summing up the items to include for this income earned from work FAFSA subpart question. In other words, do not reduce any positive numbers by subtracting any negative amounts reported on line 3 or line 6 of Schedule 1.

The 2027–2028 FAFSA continues to elicit some commentary regarding a potential oversight by the USDOE involving those individuals who work at a partnership and receive an IRS Form 1065 (Schedule K-1) that contains a profit amount on Line 14 with an accompanying Code A on that K-1. That profit amount would be subject to self-employment taxes. Given the instructions for the income earned from work subpart of the FAFSA: such individuals will not have their self-employment taxes paid considered for purposes of both the payroll tax and employment allowance expense items in the FM—as will occur with those reporting income subject to self-employment on Schedules C or F. It remains to be seen if the final version of the 2027–2028 FAFSA will make an adjustment to include such earnings. If no change is made by the feds with the 2027–2028 FAFSA and you have partnership income subject to self-employment taxes: You should contact the financial aid office(s) at the applicable colleges and explain this situation, especially if the school only requires the FAFSA form to apply for aid. Be aware that the aid formulas roughly take into account only half of one's self-employment taxes paid, given the other half is already claimed as an adjustment to income on Schedule 1 that reduces one's Adjusted Gross Income. The aid office may be able to make an adjustment to your SAI via an appeals process you are permitted to initiate. Be aware that if you are applying to any school that requires the CSS Profile: the IM will still account for such income earned from work at a partnership to derive the IM's deduction for payroll taxes paid. The IM's calculation of this expense item more closely follows the actual amount of payroll taxes that are paid than the FM's workaround calculation using the FA-DDX tool that does not properly reflect the amount of payroll taxes paid in some situations.

The next subpart about tax-exempt interest is straightforward: you either report the amount on line 2a of the IRS 1040 or list 0 (zero) in the far right response box if there is no amount showing on line 2a.

However, the next four subparts can be tricky for a number of reasons, regardless of whether you are completing the paper or electronic version. (This is true even if the FA-DDX tool is used for an electronic version and you do not need to manually enter tax return data for most of the subparts of this question.) Here are the ways these subparts can get complicated. If you have any amounts on your 2025 tax return regarding IRA or pension/annuity distributions: You may need to do a little math and have a basic understanding of certain provisions in the IRS tax code, if you have any such dollar amounts listed for lines 4a, 4b, 5a, and/or 5b on the return. If the amount derived after either mathematical function is performed by subtracting the amount in the right margin of the return (line b) from the corresponding amount in the left margin (line a) for that same line number (i.e., 4 or 5) is a positive, then a positive number will be entered for that subpart if you are manually inputting your data. But if the amount derived after your subtraction calculation for line 4 and/or your separate subtraction calculation for line 5 is a negative number: then enter (zero) in the far right response box on the FAFSA for that corresponding subpart for your manually-entered response relating to the applicable IRS line references. (Backstory: In most cases a negative number will happen if there is no dollar amount reported in 4a and/or 5a, but there is a dollar amount listed in the far right column on that same IRS line of the return. This is because IRS regulations stipulate it is not necessary for a tax filer to report any amount in the a portion (i.e., 4a or 5a) towards the left margin for the line item if the entire amount of the distribution was taxable. The taxable portions of line 4 and 5 are reported in the far right column with all your other types of taxable income and have the letter b following the applicable line number). If your calculation results in a negative number: Do NOT list the negative number as your response for that FAFSA subpart. Any such negative amount related to IRS line 4 or 5 would be assumed to be a positive dollar amount that would incorrectly inflate your income in the SAI calculations. (Don't worry If your FTI data is being transferred via the FA-DDX on an electronic FAFSA; the programming will provide for a 0 (zero) value to be entered for that data element.) Veterans of the aid process in prior years may recall that previously one would add any amount on 4a to the amount on 5a and then subtract the amounts on 4a and 4b to derive an answer for the combined line numbers. This is no longer the case as responses for IRS Form 1040 line 4 and line 5 are no longer comingled together into one combined dollar amount on the FAFSA. Separate responses are now required of tax filers for each of these two distinct types of income on the tax return.

KEY POINT! The following text applies even if you are completing an electronic version of the FAFSA and can use the FA-DDX to have the IRS transfer your FTI data onto the form instead of manually inputting such data onto the FAFSA. If you had a "qualified rollover"—that is, you took a distribution from one qualified retirement plan and returned the funds withdrawn to the same plan or another qualified plan within 60 days and met all the other IRS fine print for the return of the funds to be considered a "qualified rollover"—you want to be sure that your responses on any version of the FAFSA reflect the correct dollar amount of that rollover for the applicable IRS line reference. (There are separate subparts on the FAFSA for line 4 and line 5 rollovers.) Be aware that the FA-DDX will not be sophisticated enough to detect the rollover from your tax return information. While the 2025 IRS 1040 has introduced checkboxes (Box 1 for both line items 4c and 5c) to indicate a rollover, no dollar amount is listed on page 1 of the return. Since no rollover amount will be transferred by the FA-DDX, you will still need to indicate any rollover and manually input the dollar amount on the online FAFSA when prompted. The amount of the rollover is important so that the processor will not assume you have extra untaxed income that can inflate your SAI. The amount of the rollover will reduce the calculated "untaxed portion..." that is entered for the applicable FAFSA subpart dollar-for-dollar. If you have a rollover, you will want to be sure you have the supporting documentation from the plan administrator that accepted the rollover of funds. The financial aid office will almost certainly want documentary evidence of the rollover. And if you had a qualified rollover in 2025 and a college requires a copy of your IRS Form 1040 tax return transcript, make sure to print the word "Rollover" next to the applicable line if it is not already listed on the transcript. If submitting a transcript of the return, the tax filer(s) for that return should sign the transcript received from the IRS before the transcript is sent to the school. WARNING: If you had a qualified rollover in 2025 and you do not enter any amount or the wrong amount for these two subparts on the FAFSA about "...rollover into a qualified plan," you will likely have to obtain a paper original version of your "FAFSA Submission Summary" (FSS) via regular mail by calling the Federal Student Aid hotline at 1-800-433-3243. Best to request a couple summaries, in case you make a mistake. (The version emailed to you by the feds will not suffice.) Then you will need to correct the paper FSS and mail it back to the processor. Since this will lead to delays with schools getting your correct data and correct SAI number, you need to exercise extra care if you had any qualified rollover in 2025.

The Adjusted Gross Income (AGI) and income tax paid questions are straightforward for the next two subparts. Be sure to refer to the correct line references on the final version of the 2027–2028 FAFSA for guidance. If the adjusted gross income is a negative number, be sure to fill in the oval with the minus sign inside of it that appears just to the right of the response boxes for the dollar amount of the AGI; do not use parentheses to indicate a negative number.

Unlike question 18 and question 36 which apply to both the 2025 and 2026 calendar years regarding the Earned Income Credit (EIC), this item that is part of question 20 and question 38 applies only to the 2025 tax return. Here the receipt of the 2025 EIC is used to help determine if the "applicable person" can meet one of the methods to qualify as a "single parent" for the purposes of Max or Min Pell Grant eligibility. (See the "Maximum Pell, Minimum Pell, and the SAI Disconnect" section toward the beginning of Chapter Three for more details.) The online FAFSA's skip-logic may determine that a response for this EIC item is not needed for a variety of reasons, so don't be surprised if you never see this item. However if asked about this item online or you are completing the paper FAFSA: Be aware that a "Don't know" response will be assumed to be the equivalent of a "No" response. So if a 2025 tax return has not yet been filed for some reason, it would make sense to estimate your eligibility for the EIC if you need to provide a response.

The subparts regarding IRA deductions/self-employed qualified retirement plans as well as the education tax credits involve items on certain lines of the numbered schedules of the IRS 1040. These are also straightforward.

The next subpart regarding Schedule A, B, D, E, F, and H will be used to help determine if you qualify to be exempt from assets being considered in the SAI calculations. Note this subpart for question 20 only matters if the student is an independent student. With this subpart, a "Don't know" response will assume to be "Yes," so as with the EIC subpart earlier it is best to determine the appropriate response instead of answering "Don't Know" if your answer will affect the calculations. We discuss these various lettered schedules as well as Schedule C in Chapter Three of this book when we discuss the various criteria to avoid having to report assets on the aid form.

Be aware that if your 2025 return has not yet been filed and the only reason you would need to answer "Yes" to this subpart (if it would impact required asset reporting on the FAFSA) would be due to your completing Schedule B: then if the IRS does NOT require your filing Schedule B with your return because the amount of interest and dividend income is below the $1,500 threshold for interest and below the $1,500 threshold for dividends requiring such Schedule B to be filed, such Schedule B should not be completed and submitted with your return.

The next subpart involves Schedule C, which is another question to help determine if you can be exempt from reporting assets. Just as with the Adjusted Gross Income subpart, if your response is a negative number, be sure to fill in the circle with the minus sign inside of it that appears to the right of the response squares where the dollar amount is listed.

Just as with the Earned Income Credit subpart discussed earlier, the next subpart regarding the amount of college grants, scholarships, or AmeriCorps benefits reported as income to the IRS is only asked of the student and the parent (and not the other two roles). Be aware that any amounts reported will reduce income in the FM.

The last subpart of these questions involves the Foreign Income Exclusion reported on Schedule 1. Due to the FAFSA Simplification legislation, this item that reduces one's Adjusted Gross Income (AGI) for certain U.S. tax filers will now be added back to the AGI in the FM calculations. Given that this item if reported on the tax return can only be a negative number (which is why this IRS line item already has parentheses printed in Schedule 1), it is strange that the circle with the minus sign is listed on the form, as it is unnecessary. However, if this exclusion applies to you, be sure to fill in that circle.

That does it for the income and tax subparts on the form. There are two remaining financial questions we are going to cover. Be aware that even if you are filing an electronic version of the

FAFSA, these questions may still need to be manually input on the form if required; this will be true even if the FA-DDX tool will be transferring Federal Tax Information (FTI) onto the form.

NOTE: These next two questions are only in the Student role and Parent role parts of the FAFSA, as they should be. This is because if the respective question needs to be answered and the student is married/remarried or the parent is married/remarried/unmarried but living with the student's other legal parent, then the response involves a "*combined amount*" as explained on the FAFSA for these two questions.

21. (Independent Students only) or **39.** (Dependent Students only) **Annual Child Support Received.** Under FAFSA Simplification and starting with the 2024-2025 award year, child support received is now considered an asset. As such, child support payments received will no longer be considered untaxed income in the FM as was true for eons of prior academic years. If you meet the qualifying criteria to be exempt from reporting assets on the FAFSA and are completing an electronic version of the FAFSA, this question will not be asked due to the skip logic. However if assets do need to be reported either because you are completing the paper version of the form (where assets need to be reported even though they may eventually be excluded in the SAI calculation by the processor if you meet all the criteria for their exclusion) OR because with the skip-logic it has been determined that you do not meet the criteria for assets to be excluded when completing an electronic version of the FAFSA: then any child support received must be reported as a separate "asset category" for an independent student in question 21 and in question 39 for a dependent student's FAFSA. This should be the amount you actually received during the applicable year, not the amount you were supposed to receive. (If you must answer this question AND you did not receive any child support during the applicable year, then enter zero in the far right response box.)

This child support received question generated a fair number of comments during the 2024–2025 comment period given the use of the "last complete calendar year" term in the explanatory text for this question. Some who provided comments felt that child support received should be the 2022 base income year for the 2024–2025 form. However since child support is now considered an "asset" (at least in the FM, even though it is really a form of income received) and since other types of assets for the purposes of the FAFSA and other aid forms involve their value on the date the form is submitted to the processor: the use of child support received in the base income year is likely not happening.

But since child support received could never just pertain to the amount received on the date the FAFSA is submitted (as is the rule for determining the proper value for all other reportable assets), a workaround was created that would look at child support received during the "last complete calendar year." *So unless there is some change in the language for this question on the FAFSA:* This would mean that if you complete and submit the form electronically between the time it becomes available and the time the ball drop occurs in New York City to ring in 2027—remember the processor time stamps forms submitted electronically using Eastern

Time—then the applicable "last complete calendar year" in this scenario would be 2025, as the 2026 calendar year has not yet completely ended. If you are mailing in the paper FAFSA, you would need to have the form postmarked no later than December 31, 2026, to be able to report the amount of child support received in 2025 on the FAFSA. But if you have already sung "Auld Sang Syne" and then complete and submit or mail the FAFSA sometime thereafter, the "last complete calendar year" would then be 2026 as you completed the form in 2027. So this can be another aid planning strategy for those required to report assets on the form related to an additional factor affecting the ideal time to submit the FAFSA (see our tips earlier in this part of the book regarding the optimal time to submit the aid forms) if you have a situation where the amount of child support received differs significantly between calendar year 2025 and 2026. Be aware that if you did not receive any child support, then your response should be 0 (zero) unless you are not required to answer this question on an electronic version of the FAFSA.

22a.–c. (All Students) or **40a.–c.** (Dependent Students only) **Student Assets.** On an electronic version of the FAFSA, an independent student who was not required to answer the previous question 21 about child support due to meeting the criteria of being exempt from reporting assets will also not be required to answer this question. However, if the parent of a dependent student was not required to answer question 39 about child support, and that parent began the FAFSA form, then neither the student in question 22 nor the parent in question 40 will be required to answer these questions about assets. However, if you are required to report assets....

We don't intend to repeat all the advice we gave under "Assets and Liabilities" in Chapter Three. Look through that chapter again—it could save you some serious money. Remember not to list retirement provisions such as IRA accounts. Under the federal financial aid formula, assets in retirement provisions are protected from assessment. You should be sure to read the FAFSA instructions carefully for details about what types of assets to include and what types you should exclude.

Understand that real estate (other than your home) is considered an "investment" for purposes of the FAFSA. Be aware that for the question relating to investments as well as the questions regarding businesses and farms, you are to list their "Net Worth," which is defined as their current value minus the current debt outstanding on the assets. If the net worth for a particular question is a negative number (or if you have no assets for that asset category), then list "0" in the far right response box for that question. You should also keep in mind that you are not allowed to deduct credit card debt from the value of your assets—only debts secured by reportable assets will reduce the value of such assets for these questions.

Be careful not to double-count assets. While the instructions for the FAFSA may seem confusing, keep in mind that an asset belongs to you or to your child. Don't list the same asset twice. If you have set up a bank account "in trust for" your child, it is legally part of your assets as long as your social security number is listed as the taxpayer I.D. However, if the asset is under the child's name (or in your name "as custodian for" the child—most likely in a regular UTMA or UGMA account) it will be assessed severely. (Consider consulting a financial advisor who is an expert on the aid eligibility formulas to discuss your options.)

Regarding the reporting requirements involving 529 savings plans, 529 pre-paid plans and Coverdell Education Savings Accounts, please refer to our detailed treatment of these tax-advantaged assets that appears in Chapter 2. Be sure to carefully read the instructions for the 2027–2028 FAFSA if you have any funds in any of these special tax-advantaged plans for the benefit of yourself, the student, and especially other family members before answering question 22 and/or question 40 if you are required to answer them.

If you have a passbook loan, remember to include the net worth of the account (the value of the account before the passbook loan minus the amount of the passbook loan outstanding) as part of "investments," instead of as part of the "cash, savings, and checking" subpart of this question.

Do not include your home if it is your primary residence. If you own "other real estate," even if you do not own your primary residence, include this other real estate as part of your "investments" response but remember to subtract any mortgages or other debts secured by the property from the value of the real estate. In other words, only the equity of any other real estate (the value of any property minus the debt on it) becomes part of your "investments" response. If you own your primary residence but rent out a part of it, the proportionate share of the total equity for that part of the home that is rented out is to be included as part of the response as well unless a) you rent out the part of the property to a relative OR b) there is no separate entrance to the rented portion OR c) there is no separate bathroom or kitchen.

Owners of businesses and farms should also read our advice on this subject (in Chapter Nine, Special Topics). Remember that if you are a part-owner, you should list only your share of the net worth.

Please check your free online student tools (see page vi), as there may be updates on this topic as a result of late-breaking developments.

24a.–c. (Required for all students), 29a.–c. (Student's spouse, if applicable), 41a.–c. (Required for all dependent students), and 46a.–c. ("Other parent," if applicable). Consents and Signatures.

IMPORTANT! *As mentioned previously in this part of the book: all students as well as the parent of a dependent student required to report their information on the FAFSA that is named in question 30 must always provide their consent for the FA-DDX transfer tool and sign off on their responses for their role on the form. For the 2027–2028 FAFSA: Any person who is considered* *the Parent's Spouse or Partner and is named in question 42 must only provide their consent and sign off on their responses for their role if they did NOT file a 2025 joint personal income tax return with the parent named in question 30. The spouse of an independent student listed in question 25 must only provide their consent and sign off on their role on the form if the student did NOT file a 2025 joint personal income tax return with them.*

If you need to also complete the CSS Profile and/or any other detailed institutional aid forms with financial responses required, it would be best to delay signing off on the FAFSA until such other forms are completed (if at all possible). Indeed if you need to complete the CSS Profile as well for at least one school under consideration, it would be even better to complete the CSS Profile first—but not submit it —and then use that data to help with the completion of the FAFSA. Completing all the various forms first, if possible, before any of them are submitted will significantly minimize the likelihood of your submitting conflicting information that will require the submission of additional documents to resolve the conflict and could delay the receipt of aid. HOWEVER: the advice in this paragraph should NOT be followed if you: a) are at risk of missing any aid deadline OR b) have any issue related to living in a state that awards state aid on a first-come, first served basis and/or applying for aid at college that awards fund on a first-come, first-served basis. In such cases, meeting the deadline or submitting a form as soon as possible will trump any reason to complete all the aid forms first before submitting any one of them.

If one or more of the required consents for the FAFSA are NOT provided: then the form can be submitted but no SAI will be calculated until all the required consents are provided. Note that the consent to transfer the Federal Tax Information using the FA-DDX tool needs to be done, even if no tax return was required to be filed.

If an electronic version of the 2027–2028 FAFSA is completed: the required consents and signatures were likely already done using the respective person's unique FSA ID to provide consent for the data being submitted for their unique role in the process. Remember that unlike in years past, there will be NO option to mail in a signature page with the "wet signature" to the processor. If one of the individuals required to provide their own consent and sign the FAFSA will not apply for an FSA ID or is unable to obtain one, then an electronic version should NOT be completed and submitted. In this situation, the paper PDF version should be completed and mailed to the processor; however, all the required individual who need to provide their consents and sign the form will need to do so. Otherwise, no SAI will be calculated until all the required consents and signatures are provided. Exception: There is only one workaround as stated earlier in this part of the book, which only applies to a situation where *the two biological or adoptive parents of a dependent student are married and filed a joint 2025 tax return:* if the parent who wishes to take on the role of "parent" on the FAFSA is unable or unwilling to obtain an FSA ID, but the other parent is willing and able to obtain an FSA, then these two biological or adoptive parents who filed a 2025 joint income tax return can exchange their "roles" on the form with the spouse taking on the "parent" role on the FAFSA and vice versa. This should be done before any responses pertaining to the "parent" role are inputted. This exception will not work if a stepparent is involved; nor will it work if a joint 2025 U.S personal income tax return was not filed.

An electronic version provides the benefits of eliminating any postal delivery delays as well as providing notification in real time that your data has been submitted. It also has the skip logic and will not permit a person to submit their data unless all the required responses for their "role" are supplied on their part of the application. Nonetheless if you have no choice than to use the paper route, here's what you need to know before about the Consent and Signature questions before you prepare your paperwork for mailing to the processor.

If the paper version has been completed: With this version of the FAFSA, it is imperative not only that all the required signatures based on the roles be provided as explained above but also that each signature is dated. Equally important: It is critical that the circle to the left of the one-line Consent Statement on the far left of the respective person's Signature and Consent question is completely filled in before the form is mailed to the processor. While other responses on the paper form can be filled in electronically, including the consent response circle, only a "wet signature"—that is a hand-written signature done in cursive with a dark-ink ballpoint pen (i.e., dark blue or black ink)—will be acceptable for the signature of each person required to sign the form. Digital signatures should not be used to sign a paper FAFSA form.

47a–.d., 48a.–e., 49a.–b. FAFSA preparer information. You can skip these questions if you are filling out the FAFSA on your own.

FINAL CHECKS IF YOU ARE MAILING THE PAPER PDF VERSION OF THE FAFSA TO THE PROCESSOR

Be 100% certain that all the required responses to the questions, the required consents, and the required "wet" signatures with signature dates have been provided—and that all responses on the form are legible. Any incomplete or unreadable responses will cause processing delays. The Notes pages that appear at the end of the PDF file and the text on the 14-page FAFSA Form itself will provide guidance regarding the questions that may be skipped given your situation. But there are number of decision-trees involved with the Notes and instructions on the form, so that is why you should double- and triple-check your responses. Indeed we recommend that, if possible, at least two sets of eyes review the form to make sure responses to all the required items have been provided. If a question requires a dollar value but does not apply to your situation (e.g., you have no tax-exempt interest income), then be sure a 0 (zero) was entered in the far right column.

Be sure that you make a photocopy of your completed form for your records. Since scanners may slightly damage the paper so that your completed form will not be able to be scanned properly by the processor, we recommend that you make a paper photocopy of all the pages of the completed form and then scan the photocopy to create a digital record. When mailing the form, make sure you are mailing *all pages* of the original version of the FAFSA with the "wet" signature(s), and that you are not mailing the photocopy with photocopied signatures to the processor. Do NOT staple the pages together. Double check to be sure that all the pages are submitted in numerical order by the pre-printed page number in the lower right concern of each page. Submit all pages of the FAFSA form itself even if some pages, such as those for the preparer, have no required responses on them. However it is NOT necessary to send any of the instruction pages or Notes pages that are part of the PDF file.

Since you will be sending the form to a post office box, you will not be able to send the form using a private delivery service such as FedEx or UPS; such private companies cannot deliver anything to a post office box. We do recommend that at a minimum you use Priority Mail—and that you place your completed form in a sealed envelope before placing the sealed envelope inside U.S. Postal Service's (USPS) cardboard mailer (with red trim). If you need to have your completed form received by the processor in less than two weeks then we recommend you use the U.S. Postal Service's more-expensive Priority Express Mail option (formerly known as Express Mail) placing your sealed envelope inside that USPS cardboard mailer (with blue trim). Note that even with Express Priority Service it may take a few days for your mailer to be delivered, as the processor is in a remote location. In either case, your cardboard mailer containing your completed FAFSA should be taken to the post office and you should use either the window service staffed by USPS postal worker or use an automated postal machine inside the post office's lobby. This should be done for two reasons: 1) You want a tracking number and 2) You want to avoid mail being stolen out of streetside post-office boxes.

If using Priority Mail or Express Mail with a window employee or an automated USPS machine: a tracking number will be generated on your receipt. You can then use that tracking number to track delivery via the free tracking service available at usps.com specifying that you want to track your item throughout the delivery process. There is then no need to pay extra for Certified Mail or Return Receipt Requested Service given you have a tracking number. If going to a window employee, the tracking number and receipt serve as proof of the date you mailed the paper form to the processor if a postmarked-deadline is applicable. As mentioned earlier, one should only use a window employee if facing a postmark deadline. Note that if you choose to mail your form out via regular first-class mail—which we do NOT recommend—you will need to be sure to affix sufficient postage given the large number of pages involved which may lead to extra-charges due to envelope size or thickness above the extra charges for the extra weight. If you use regular first-class mail with the Certified Mail–Return Receipt Requested options, the mailing cost will be not much less than the cost of the Priority Mail service. So better to use Priority Mail at a minimum.

That does it for the FAFSA. Congratulations! If none of the schools to which you are applying require the CSS Profile form, skip ahead to the section "Are You Done?" that follows our CSS Profile tips. Otherwise, let's go to the CSS Profile form.

Filling Out the 2027–2028 CSS Profile Form

As we predicted back when FAFSA Simplification was announced, as of the 2024–2025 award year, there has been a greater decoupling between the federal methodology and the College Board's institutional methodology. The former is used to determine eligibility for federal student aid based on the data reported on the FAFSA and the latter is used by a number of schools—especially the very selective private colleges and a few flagship state universities—to determine eligibility for institutional aid based on data reported on the College Board's CSS Profile. This will make it much more difficult to maximize aid at those schools that require completion of the CSS Profile in addition to the FAFSA.

To ensure the best results, we recommend reading the Introduction, Chapter One, Chapter Three, and the preceding pages of this Part Three before you start filling out the CSS Profile. That's because it is critically important that FAFSA data match CSS Profile data: inconsistencies will likely cause delays in the aid office's review, and will likely result in requests for additional documentation to resolve the conflicting information

Since there is no urgency to complete the 2027–2028 CSS Profile immediately after its filing period officially begins on October 1, 2026—the earliest CSS Profile deadline is usually November 1 for some Early Decision or Early Action Schools—it would be best to delay filing the CSS Profile for as long as possible. Forget what you may have previously read in the media about "the sooner you file, the more money you will get." Forget what the high school guidance counselor may have told you in the spring of 2026 about submitting the aid forms as soon as possible. Also, be aware that the schools that require the CSS Profile are the more selective schools in the country. It would be a waste of money for the aid office at such schools to hire, train, and pay extra personnel to carefully review all the aid forms of all the applicants for admission, since they know that in a few weeks a significant percentage of students who applied will not be accepted. There is zero advantage in being among the first to complete and submit the CSS Profile in early October.

This recommendation to delay even starting work on the CSS Profile online is especially critical for those families in which both biological or adoptive parents of a dependent student are alive but not living together. As we discussed earlier, the Department of Education had not yet issued clear guidance regarding the criteria to determine which parent provided the "greater support" for determining which parent is required to complete the FAFSA. By now you may be thinking: "That's the FAFSA, what does it have to do with the CSS Profile?" The answer is: Plenty!

The way the CSS Profile works is that after logging in and accessing the form, one first provides some basic information about the student. After that, a student who must provide parental information on the CSS Profile is asked to provide information about all parents (and if applicable), all stepparents currently married to (but not separated from) one of the student's parents. For a number of prior versions of the CSS Profile, the form would then ask the applicant to select the parent(s) and, if applicable, the stepparent with whom the student spent the most time in the past 12 months from the list of all the parents and stepparents one had just provided. If the biological or adoptive parents of the student were living apart but both living, that parent with whom they spent the greater amount of time would be known in financial aid circles as the "custodial parent." If they were married, their spouse would be called the "custodial stepparent." The parent with whom the student spent the lesser amount of time in the past 12 months would be referred to as the "noncustodial parent" and their spouse, if any, would be known as the "noncustodial stepparent." Following that for a situation where the parents are living apart: the skip logic would then begin to preliminarily set up all the sections that would need to be completed by the student and the parent with whom the student spent the most time (and, if applicable, the student's spouse).

The CSS Profile, not having a paper version, utilizes robust skip logic in this way. However, as we mentioned earlier, many CSS Profile schools also require a separate application from the *other* parent. This means that if a college you've selected requires a CSS Profile from the parent who provides the lesser support, the CSS Profile application system will then make it technologically possible for that parent to be able to complete their own CSS Profile. That version for that parent to complete will ask many, but not all, of the same questions as the version the student and the parent who provides greater support would complete. (If you are confused, don't worry. We will be soon be providing more specific guidance about how to complete the various sections of the CSS Profile.)

Unfortunately, unlike the pre-Simplification years when there was a "custodial parent" term and a "noncustodial parent" to distinguish between parents, no such terminology has yet been developed, for example, to easily describe "the parent required to report their information as the 'parent'" on the FAFSA. To avoid confusion, we will still use the old lingo such as "custodial parent" to mean the parent who must supply information as the "Parent" on the 2027–2028 FAFSA and the parent who must always provide information on the CSS Profile, if your child is applying to at least one CSS Profile school. And if that parent is remarried: we will refer to that stepparent as the "custodial stepparent"—who would be known as the parent's "Spouse or Partner" on the 2027–2028 FAFSA. Isn't it great how the one adult who is defined in two words in the new world of FAFSA Simplification is assigned a moniker that can be so misleading? We will often keep quotation marks around the terms "custodial parent," "noncustodial parent," and "noncustodial stepparent," so that you will know the player in the aid process to whom we are referring.

We'll also continue to refer to the parent who does not automatically have to complete the CSS Profile as the "noncustodial parent" (since that is the term the College Board is still using). However be aware that most, but not all, schools that require the CSS Profile will want separate CSS Profile application data if the two biological or adoptive parents are living apart and both are still alive. Finally, as a reminder, the criteria for determining which parent must provide information on the 2027–2028 FAFSA is no longer based on physical custody but rather on the yet-to-be fully defined concept of "greater amount of financial support."

Keep in mind that with the CSS Profile's sophisticated skip logic set up to match information from the separately submitted CSS Profile applications of biological or adoptive parents living apart, changing which parent is going to be the "custodial parent" who must provide information for any and all schools under consideration that require the CSS Profile as well as on the FAFSA (and therefore by default, changing which parent will be the "noncustodial parent") is going to get messy! In such a case, it is likely that any data inputted and saved may get deleted, meaning that any work done will have been a waste. You will have to reset the parent configuration and start over from scratch (if that will even be possible).

But if having to flip the biological or adoptive parents on a partially completed CSS Profile not yet submitted isn't bad enough, be aware that things can get much worse. If you're the type of person who has to take care of any task as soon as it can be done or thinks mistakenly that there is some advantage to being among the first to submit their CSS Profile, you'll hit a huge problem if the wrong parent completed and submitted their version of the CSS Profile: electronic corrections cannot be made to change the inputted data once the CSS Profile data is submitted to the processor.

The College Board has stated that to avoid confusion, they will follow the Department of Education's policy: the parent providing the greater support is the one who must always provide parental information on the CSS Profile. That would make the CSS Profile's "custodial parent" the person assuming the "parent role" on the FAFSA.

Our recommendation to delay the completion and submission of the CSS Profile is not about encouraging procrastination. We are just advising you engage in a strategic delay given the unintended consequences that can occur if you act too fast. Best to think of the Latin expression, *festina lente*, which translates to: Make Haste Slowly! At any rate, once you're ready to begin, have no fear: what follows is detailed guidance on the types of questions you will be asked.

The CSS Profile is a much more detailed form than the FAFSA. And for those schools that require it, the responses you provide on the CSS Profile are likely to be even more important than your FAFSA data, given the CSS Profile application determines the eligibility for the large amounts of need-based gift aid awarded out of the school's own coffers.

Since repetition fixes firmly, if a "noncustodial parent" must also complete a separate CSS Profile form (which, to avoid confusion, we will refer to as the "Noncustodial parent Profile" in this book, even though the College Board does not use that exact term), the student and their "custodial parent" need to begin working on their CSS Profile in order for the "noncustodial parent" to be able to complete and submit their own CSS Profile form. We'll discuss this issue in more detail in the following pages. In the meantime, be aware that the "noncustodial parent" should never complete another FAFSA for the same student, though they may need to report their information on a FAFSA for a different student for which they would be considered the parent providing the greater support.

The CSS Profile has much more sophisticated skip logic than the FAFSA. So it is critical that the early sections of the CSS Profile be properly completed. Otherwise, the wrong questions will be asked—and likely many questions that should be asked will not be generated by the skip logic. As you progress through the form, the initial questions at the start of each section will further refine the questions you will be asked to complete. Certain responses in one sub-part of a section may also immediately generate additional follow-up questions on the same screen.

Because the CSS Profile is so personalized, it is impossible to provide you with line-by-line tips for every possible question you will be asked. However, the information in Chapter 3, the line-by-line strategies for the FAFSA, and the recommendations and suggestions that follow should have you thinking the right way in order to answer the questions to your best advantage. Yet while many questions on the CSS Profile are similar to those on the FAFSA, here are some important differences that you should realize before you begin work on the CSS Profile.

1. On the CSS Profile form, real estate (other than your primary residence) should not be included as an "Investment." It will be listed in a separate category as "Other real estate." Exception: if part of the primary residence is rented and is considered part of your "Investments" response for the FAFSA, on the CSS Profile you will provide the total value and total debt for the primary residence in the Housing Section of the CSS Profile. Then you will simply list the percentage rented out to others when asked. The CSS Profile processor will do the calculations to segregate the percentage considered the home and the percentage that will be considered other real estate when the data is submitted. So you should not provide the value and debt of the rented share of the home on the CSS Profile form as other real estate. If you do, that rented share will be assessed twice. However, since we have not seen the new version of the CSS Profile yet, be sure to carefully read the CSS Profile Help Comments if this situation applies to you.

2. Regarding certain assets, the CSS Profile requires you to list "What is it worth today" (value) and "What is owed on it" (debt) separately. The College Board will then do the subtraction for you to determine your net assets.

3. Even if you can skip the asset questions on an electronic version of the FAFSA, you must answer all the asset questions on the CSS Profile applicable to your situation.

4. Unlike the FAFSA form that only asks for financial information of the "custodial parent" (and if applicable, the stepparent residing with the "custodial parent"), the CSS Profile process provides schools the opportunity to request detailed information from the "noncustodial parent" (and if applicable, the stepparent residing with the "noncustodial parent") when the student's biological or adoptive parents are no longer living together. However, the "noncustodial parent's" detailed personal and financial information will go on a separate CSS Profile application. Be aware that responses provided on the "noncustodial parent's" own "Noncustodial parent Profile" will not correspond to the FAFSA

data, since the "noncustodial parent" should never complete a FAFSA for that particular student.

5. In most cases, students completing the FAFSA who are considered independent do not need to provide parental financial information on the FAFSA. However, depending on the student's situation and the school's aid policies, an independent student may need to provide parental information on the CSS Profile if the student wishes to be considered for institutional aid.

6. List whole dollar amounts; do not list cents. Do not use the dollar sign—just list the dollar amount. Do not use commas to separate numbers. For example, $53,205 should be listed as 53205. Use the minus sign before any negative numbers; do not use parentheses.

7. Since the overwhelming majority of our readers live in the United States, the CSS Profile tips that follow do not cover the CSS Profile questions that may be asked of international students. Most of these international questions do not correspond to items on the FAFSA, since only students classified as international who are U.S. citizens or eligible non-citizens living outside of the United States or its possessions are normally eligible for federal student aid programs funded by the U.S. federal government.

Getting Started

As we suggested, it would be a good idea for a separate College Board student account to be created for the express use of completing the CSS Profile. (See "Third Step: Determine if Any of the Colleges You are Applying to Require the College Board's CSS Profile Application" earlier in this part of the book.) It would be best for the parent's email address and phone numbers to be listed as the "student's email address" and "student's phone number" for the preliminary questions at the beginning of the CSS Profile. However, the other identifiers—the actual student's name, the student's date of birth, the student's social security number, etc., need to be provided in the **Getting Started** section at the beginning of the CSS Profile. We simply recommend the parent's email address and phone number be used instead. From our experience counseling families, we know parents constantly have a problem with their child not being diligent in viewing their emails, answering their phone, and responding to voicemail messages.

And if the "Noncustodial parent Profile" is required by at least one college, the CSS Profile instructions will mention at some point that the "noncustodial parent" needs to create their own College Board account. However, since only a "student" and not a parent can create a College Board account, this means that "noncustodial parent" needs to create another College Board "student account" (so there may be three College Board accounts if the "custodial parent" followed our suggestion above). There's no need to worry if you have three accounts for the same student. There will be a separate email address and password to log into each account.

As long as the respective parents do not share the log-in details for the "student" account they created, their information will not be available to anyone else (unless another person has ready access to the email account they listed when they created the College Board account).

Once you get to the sign-in page for the CSS Profile application and log into your College Board account, you will want to select the correct application for the year you are seeking aid, as the CSS Profile for two different school years will both be available until sometime in February 2027. Be sure to select the 2027–2028 version if you are seeking aid for the fall 2027 and/or spring 2028 school year. Due to the skip logic built into the CSS Profile application, you should carefully follow the instructions and help comments so that the proper questions will be generated based on your individual situation. Since the CSS Profile is a more detailed form than the FAFSA, it is best for the "custodial parent" of a dependent student to complete the CSS Profile form instead of the student to better ensure that the proper questions are generated.

In the **Getting Started** section of the CSS Profile that appears shortly after you log onto the form with the College Board account you will be using to complete the form, you will first notice that some questions are required; these are denoted by an asterisk (*) in a red font appearing next to any questions on the form. However, we recommend that you answer all of the questions on the CSS Profile form, even the optional ones, such as the student's social security number, if applicable to your situation.

As you begin to fill out the CSS Profile, you may experience déjà-vu—because many of the questions seem identical to the questions on the FAFSA—but be sure to carefully read the questions and any help comments that may appear on the screen as you complete the CSS Profile form. Be aware that many of the questions on the CSS Profile will correspond exactly to the questions on the FAFSA. However, in some cases, similarly worded questions may require a different response as we explain in the text that follows.

As we went to press, information regarding the exact questions and the ordering of the sections for the 2027–2028 CSS Profile was not yet available. We are making an informed guess regarding the data that will be required for the various sections of the form. We have used the same ordering of the sections in the text that follows that was used for prior versions of the CSS Profile.

In our comments that follow, we have tried to anticipate the most common questions you are likely to be asked. But remember that because of the skip logic built into the form, you very well may not be asked all the questions that we cover below. For example, if the student's parents do NOT own their own home, they will not be asked questions regarding its value or purchase price.

For clarity, on the pages that follow, we may have boldfaced references to particular questions you may be asked for a particular section of the CSS Profile. However, the exact wording of such questions may well differ on the actual CSS Profile form you view online. Once all the key identifiers are completed on the first few pages, you will be asked to confirm them. Keep in mind that it is still fine at this stage—and even preferable—for a parent of the student to supply their email address and phone number as if they are those of the student, regardless of which College Board account is used to complete the CSS Profile.

However, the other information at the start of any CSS Profile needs to be accurate information regarding the student so that the aid office at a school receiving your submitted CSS Profile data will be able to match the processed CSS Profile data with the student identifiers supplied to the aid office as a result of the admissions application or enrolled student database. Keep in mind that these CSS Profile responses will also be asked of the "noncustodial parent" at the start of the "Noncustodial parent Profile," if that is required. All the responses used to identify the student need to match so that the respective versions of the CSS Profile applications will be linked up by the processor. In that way, the colleges will get the data from both processed forms and know which CSS Profile form matches up with which "Noncustodial parent" CSS Profile form. As with the regular CSS Profile, the "noncustodial parent" can use their email address and phone number for those "student" questions.

On the next page of the CSS Profile (and the "Noncustodial parent Profile"), there will be questions to determine if the student is an independent student for federal aid purposes. However, as mentioned earlier, some students completing the CSS Profile may still be asked for parental data even if they could skip the parent questions on the FAFSA. Carefully read those questions and select "Yes" or "No" for each one based on the how those questions apply to the student (and not the student's parent).

For students where both biological or adoptive parents are living together (whether or not they are married and regardless of their gender), the next section is straightforward, as you will provide information about both adults. However, for students where the two parents are living apart, you will need to provide the names of both biological parents and any stepparents (provided the stepparent is alive and still married to that parent). So you may need to list as many as four significant adults in the student's life if both parents are remarried. If any parent is deceased, indicate that as well. Make sure all the required adults are listed.

You will then be asked some follow-up questions to ascertain who is the "custodial parent" and who is the "noncustodial parent." As mentioned earlier, it is critical that the parent required to report their information on the FAFSA is the same parent who is selected as the one who provides more than half of the student's support on the CSS Profile. If there is a discrepancy, this will cause major problems down the road, especially if the forms are submitted with this conflicting information. You may be asked to confirm this information. It is advisable to alert the "noncustodial parent" about this potential problem as well.

Be aware that if there was only one biological or adoptive parent of the student at the time the student was born or adopted, respectively, and that sole parent is not married and living with the student's stepparent, then the response areas for the name, date of birth, etc. of the second parent should be deleted by clicking on the "X." This will trigger a follow-up question with menu options to determine why a second parent is not listed. Select the best option for your situation—but be prepared to provide appropriate supporting documentation to the college, such as a birth certificate or the adoption papers. In this way, "noncustodial parent" information will be waived if it is otherwise required. And if that sole parent is married to a stepparent, then the stepparent's info needs to be listed as a stepparent (not a parent).

Since the application's skip logic will now take over to determine if the rest of the form is going to be considered the student and "custodial parent's" CSS Profile or if it will be "Noncustodial parent Profile" (if such a form is required), it cannot be stressed enough how important the responses in this **Parent Information** section are, especially for any family situation in which the student's two biological or adoptive parents are no longer living together. Some basic information about any "noncustodial parent," if applicable, will be requested a bit later on the CSS Profile. The data on this one webpage about the "noncustodial parent" that appears on the CSS Profile with the student's and "custodial parent's" detailed information is NOT the "Noncustodial parent Profile form." That form requires a separate College Board account to access and will be completed by the "noncustodial parent."

The **Academic Information** section that follows for the CSS Profile will first ask questions about the student applicant's enrollment during the 2026–2027 school year and then will require you to list at least one school that requires the CSS Profile for the 2027–2028 school year. Be sure to select the appropriate status for the student. If the student will be a first-year student, select the proper admissions application option. If the student is applying Early Decision 1 to a CSS Profile school, it would be best to hold off on listing any other colleges here unless they have a CSS Profile deadline before the ED school's admission decision is known. In this way, fees can be minimized if accepted. And if not, you can still select "Early Decision" in this section if the student is applying ED2 to another school. Once this section is completed and saved, the "noncustodial parent" can complete and submit their entire "Noncustodial parent Profile," even if the regular CSS Profile is not yet submitted (provided at least one of the saved schools requires a CSS Profile from the "noncustodial parent.") "Noncustodial parents" do not provide a list of schools to receive their data; the processor will automatically make sure that their data goes to those schools that require the online "Noncustodial parent Profile," even if more schools are added at a later date by the student or "custodial parent" on their version. If a waiver is needed because the "noncustodial parent" will not complete the "noncustodial parent Profile," the home page for the CSS Profile form before one signs in has details on the procedures to follow. Be aware, each school may have their own waiver procedures as well.

For the remaining questions on either the CSS Profile or the "Noncustodial parent Profile," the word "parents" refers to the parent(s), and, if applicable, their spouse, who is to provide information on that particular form. So for example, if both parents are divorced and remarried: the "parents" for the CSS Profile will be the "custodial parent" and "custodial stepparent" for most questions, similar to "Parent" and "Spouse or Partner" on the FAFSA. And for the "Noncustodial parent Profile," the word "parents" refers to the "noncustodial parent" (and if applicable, the "noncustodial stepparent") who should not provide their information on a FAFSA for that student.

The next section of the form, **Parent Details**, will show the name of the person whose information is being requested on that web page listed at the top. Be aware that as with any other web page on the form requiring at least one response, all the required responses on that web page must be completed in order to save the information and proceed. If you leave a web page before all the required responses are provided, you will likely get a warning; but in any event, if you go to another page before the data can be saved, all the inputted data on that web page will not be saved.

Be honest, but humble, when listing occupations. If true, be sure to indicate if you are a veteran of the U.S. Armed Forces. You should then provide the appropriate responses for any applicable retirement programs if you will receive any funds from such programs at some point in the future, even if not doing so now. If you have previously contributed to IRAs, 401(k)s, 403(b)s, a TDA plan, and/or other tax-deferred retirement plans, you should indicate that you have these retirement plans. Then list the current value of such plans in the appropriate response areas. If applicable, list zero if no funds have ever been contributed to such plans or there are no longer any funds in these plans. Be aware that most colleges do not factor such dollar amounts into account when determining your eligibility for aid.

After the preliminary sections are completed, the more detailed financial and other information will be requested. Unless the student is an independent student not required to provide parental information on the CSS Profile, the next few sections of the CSS Profile (as well as the "Noncustodial parent Profile") will pertain to income, expenses, and assets of the parent(s) or parent/stepparent required to provide such information. Unlike the FAFSA, these questions go into much more detail. Care should be taken with each question due to the skip logic that generates follow-up questions for each section.

The **Parent Income** section begins with questions about the PPY 2025 tax return status. However, before you input any data, you should read the remaining text in this section about 2025 income. Tax filers should simply refer to individual IRS line references, schedules, or numbered forms that appear on the CSS Profile form for each question, and input the appropriate responses that appear on the return. While most of these questions are optional, you should answer all of them to avoid possible problems later on in the aid process. Most of these IRS line items will appear in the far right column of the IRS 1040 and its schedules and numbered forms, but there are some others not in that far right column that should also be carefully inputted. (e.g., IRS 1040 Line 2a regarding tax exempt interest). If any line item is blank on the return, enter 0 (zero) for the corresponding CSS Profile question. If you had any qualified rollovers with IRAs or other retirement plans, be sure to enter the correct amount you rolled over so that the processor will deduct the rollover when calculating your income. Some, but not all, individual adjustments to income are requested; though the total adjustments to income amount on

Line 26 of Schedule 1 of the IRS 1040 is asked as well. Those individual adjustments to income above Line 26 with questions on the CSS Profile will be considered untaxed income in the IM aid formula. The other adjustments are not, but do reduce your AGI.

Most likely, your earliest CSS Profile deadline will not be until November 1, 2026. So if you are on extension and won't file your 2025 tax return until the extension deadline of October 15, 2026, if at all possible, you should wait to complete the PPY income questions until your 2025 return(s) are completed. That way, you will be able to use completed tax return data. If you are not required to file a return, then use your best estimates about your other income items. If you used the FA-DDX on the FAFSA, it will not be possible to compare the answers to similar tax return questions between the two forms due to encryption on the FAFSA. Otherwise, make sure you provide similar responses for the 2025 adjusted gross income and U.S Taxes paid questions on both forms.

Once you complete all the appropriate responses relating to the 2025 tax return, you should click on the tab to save your work and continue, since the CSS Profile may time you out if you do not change screens in a certain time period. However, it would be a good idea once the 2025 tax data is saved to then navigate back to that screen and double and triple check your figures to be sure the proper answers from your return were entered in the correct response areas.

The next screen in the **Parent Income** section will ask questions about **income earned from work**. If you only were required to report information about one parent on the FAFSA (and no step-parent data is required on the FAFSA) ***and*** you were able to use the FA-DDX tool, follow the instruction on the CSS Profile to complete this item, which is the sum of amounts on certain line items on your tax return and/or W-2s. As mentioned earlier in our FAFSA tips, the CSS Profile and the IM will still consider partnership income subject to self-employment taxes as part of one's response for their income earned from work. The CSS Profile will also ask for each person's own income earned from work instead of a combined amount that can apply to some but not all employment-related situations on the FAFSA.

If applicable: when answering questions about Social Security benefits, exclude any benefits you received that were reported on the 2025 tax return and therefore are reported on the prior CSS Profile web page. Also exclude any benefits the parent received for the student and exclude any benefits the parents received for any dependent that will be in college during the 2027–2028 school year. So if the parents filed a 2025 return, this question should only include the benefits *paid to the parent* for the benefit of a minor child or other dependent who will not be in college in the 2027–2028 school year.

Be careful when answering the question on this web page about pre-tax deductions from your salary and other untaxed income. The amount of voluntary pre-tax contributions to a 401(k), 403(b), or other tax-deferred plans listed on any W-2 form are no longer required to be reported on the FAFSA, but are required on the CSS Profile. Do not include contributions to IRAs and other plans deducted on the tax return that should have been reported on the prior web page. Unlike the FAFSA, the CSS Profile asks questions about HSA contributions that do not appear on your tax return as they are deducted pre-tax from your salary (and oftentimes, but not always, are listed on your W-2 form). Any 2025 HSA deduction claimed on Line 13 of Schedule 1 and considered part of FAFSA question 89a should not be reported in the **Parent Contribution** section, but on its own Schedule 1 section item instead. Any 2025 alimony received, taxable or untaxed, is to be reported in the **Parent Income and Benefits** section—*though any taxable portion needs to also be reported earlier on its own Schedule 1 section item.* The processor will subtract any Schedule 1 alimony from the total amount listed in the Benefits section to determine the untaxed amount, if any. Do not include any 2025 child support received in this CSS Profile section. It will be reported later in a separate **Child Support** section.

Unlike the FAFSA, the 2027–2028 CSS Profile also requires information regarding the "recent year" (2026) aka the "prior year" or "PY" and possibly the "anticipated year" (2027). Yet these questions are not as detailed as the 2025 PPY ones. Because similar data is requested for these 2026 and 2027 income questions, our tips are the same for both years.

Since your 2026 income tax returns will likely not be completed until after your earliest CSS Profile deadline—even for regular decision schools—there is no question of getting into trouble if your figures are off a bit. In most cases, the colleges will be awarding aid using your 2025 PPY income year data rather than your projections for the PY year and/or the year after the PY year. However, some schools have been known to reduce aid if income for either year is larger than income listed for the PPY base income year. Of course, if 2026 and/or 2027 income will be significantly less than 2025 income, you should explain the situation in the Explanation and Special Circumstances Section (ES) towards the end of the form. You should contact the financial aid office directly as well. Using "professional judgment," the FAOs may ignore the PPY income and focus instead on the projections you have made for the years after the base income year. And be prepared to provide supporting documentation. Anyone who is out of work or even just feeling that her employment situation is unstable should read our section about "The Recently Unemployed Worker" in the "Special Topics" chapter.

When projecting the 2026 and 2027 income, be conservative. Don't talk about a raise you are supposed to get but haven't yet received. If you are out of work, give the FAOs the worst-case scenario. If you are self-employed, use your expected NET business income, not the gross receipts. If you just took a job at a lower salary or you know you will have less overtime or a smaller bonus in the coming year, make sure the figures reflect this. If you are already aware of any extreme changes in your situation compared to 2025, you should probably write to the individual FAOs directly rather than relying on them to take these projections on the CSS Profile into account.

For **2026 and 2027 Income earned from work**: These questions are not quite the same as the 2025 questions on an earlier web page. For the 2025 PPY income from work questions, such amounts for tax filers are used to calculate expense allowances in the aid formulas. Here they count as income questions, *even for tax-filers*. Be careful not to double-count your income. If you project that you will be contributing to deferred compensation provisions next year [such as 401(k) or 403(b) plans], you should include the contributions as part of your regular income earned from work for that year—and exclude them from the 2026 and 2027 **untaxed income and benefits** responses.

For **2026 and 2027 other taxable income** questions: make a rough projection of your other taxable income for the respective years (see Chapter 3, Lines 2b and 3b, and Schedule 1, Lines 1–6, for our suggested strategies)—include interest, dividend, taxable alimony, etc. and subtract any losses. Include the taxable portion, if any, of your social security benefits. Use a minus sign if the sum is a negative number.

For the **2026 and 2027 untaxed income** questions: the CSS Profile instructions will advise you about the types of untaxed income to include. However, despite what they say, do not include any adjustments to income that are considered untaxed income in the federal or institutional aid formulas, such as IRA contributions. Their inclusion would overstate your income for 2026 and/or 2027. Also, do not include 2026 and/or 2027 taxable combat pay, which should be included as part of your income from work. If applicable, include only the sum of the untaxed portion of your social security benefits plus any benefits you received or will receive for any person who will NOT be enrolled in college in 2027–2028. You should also be sure to include child support that will be received for all children, not just the student, in 2026 and/or 2027.

You will be asked to explain the types of untaxed income if your response is a number other than 0 (zero).

The last subsection in Parents Income will ask about various need-tested benefits received, if any. The responses should be consistent with FAFSA 36. As with the FAFSA, remember that Supplemental Security Income (SSI) is NOT the same as the social security program with its retirement, death, and disability benefits.

The next section on the CSS Profile, **Child Support**, first asks two preliminary questions: the first about such payments paid in 2025 and 2026 and then the second regarding 2025 payments received. If you answer yes to either question, follow-up questions will be asked about annual (not monthly) support. Be sure to read them carefully, as some will ask about total support for all children while others will only apply to the student. Any 2025 support received for all children response should be the same as the response for FAFSA 39, if any such response on the FAFSA is an amount greater than zero.

The next section on the CSS Profile, **Household Information**, refers to your living arrangements for your primary residence. Answer the preliminary question accordingly, and remember that in this section the word "home" only refers to your main domicile, which is likely your legal address. If you do not own your primary residence, the questions in the section are straightforward. But, if you do indeed own your home, please refer to our strategies in Chapter 3 regarding value and debts on the home. Be sure to report the total value as well as total debt currently outstanding, even if part of this "home" is rented out to others. You will be asked to also give the year purchased and the purchase price. This is a check on the value of your home. Using the Federal Housing Index Multiplier and other tools, the colleges can see if you have low-balled the value of this property. If you inherited the house, the purchase price is "0." If you built the house yourself, the purchase price is the cost of the house plus the cost of the land. For the "Amount owed on home" question, include the amounts owed on any mortgage(s) plus the balance owned on any home equity line of credit (HELOC). You will then be asked to list the total amount owed on the home. And if the total owed is more than just the primary mortgage, you'll need to then report the amount owed on the primary mortgage in a follow-up question.

The next CSS Profile section, **Parent Assets**, involves various subsections for different types of assets. When answering these questions, it is critically important that you don't double count assets by listing the same assets in different subsections or questions on the CSS Profile. Qualified retirement accounts listed earlier on the CSS Profile are not to be reported here. Just as with the FAFSA, it will be helpful to review the asset section in Chapter Three before you answer these questions.

Regarding **"investments":** unlike the FAFSA (which considers other real estate as part of your investments), the CSS Profile only considers financial assets such as stocks, bonds, mutual funds, CDs, etc. as investments. For the preliminary question regarding parental assets held in the names of their children, be sure to read the CSS Profile instructions for this section carefully before you provide any dollar amounts in the **Parent Asset Details** subsection. If you have any debt outstanding secured by these investments, such as margin debt, deduct the amount of such secured debt; however, be sure to mention you reduced the value of your investments by the dollar amount of this debt in the **"Special Circumstances"** section at the end of the CSS Profile. The **Cash, checking and savings** amount reported should agree with your answer for the same asset category as in FAFSA 40. The next CSS Profile subsection pertains to other real estate. If any of the situations mentioned apply, you will then be asked to provide additional information. If you rent out part of your home and the equity in that portion rented out is required to be reported as part of your investments on the FAFSA (see Part 3, "Additional Financial Information"), the ONLY applicable statement regarding this situation with your home to be selected is the last one about renting out a portion of the primary residence. You will then simply indicate the percentage rented out; the processor will then divide the total value of your home and total debt previously reported in the **"Housing Details"** section earlier in the CSS Profile into the proper portion considered to be your home and the portion that will be considered other real estate. The top three statements should only be checked if you own real estate other than your primary residence that cannot be classified as business property. Answer the detailed follow-up questions accordingly. Given the uncertainty regarding the reporting of certain assets on the FAFSA that may be different on the CSS Profile, look carefully at the questions as they appear on the CSS Profile.

The next and final asset subsection begins with the **"Parent Business/Farm Setup."** If you do not own or have a partial interest in any corporation (other than shares in a publicly-traded company), or in any partnership, or in any farm, or if you are not self-employed, then most likely you will not be selecting any of the statements on this web page. Be aware that if you are only a "limited partner" in a partnership, the value of your stake in the limited partnership should be considered as part of your CSS Profile and FAFSA investments, and not as a business entity for this set-up page—though you should also mention this fact in the **Special Circumstances** section of the CSS Profile. If you have any activity reported on Schedule C of the 2025 IRS 1040 with such net income or loss from this activity also reported on Line 3 of Schedule 1 of the IRS 1040, this activity is considered a "business" on the CSS Profile and you should select the appropriate statement. You will then be asked to provide the number of different entities in which you are involved.

If you do need to report information on any business or farm, it will be helpful to first refer to Chapter 9, "The Four Types of Business." If applicable, you will also need to have copies of any 2025 corporation or 2025 partnership returns available, as well as any financials about any farm ownership. With any questions involving dollar amounts such as assets, debts, revenue, and expenses, be sure to list only the proportionate share of those items on the CSS Profile and not the total figures for the entity—unless, of course, you own 100% of it either individually or jointly with the other "parent" on that CSS Profile (who may be a stepparent). The percentage owned by the "parents" should be reported as well as the separate percentage owned by other relatives (by blood or marriage). However the definition of other family members for other questions about the entity may be different, so be sure to read the fine print in the CSS Profile instructions for these questions. Be aware that if you have an ownership stake in a farm that is organized and operates as a partnership or corporation that files a separate tax return (IRS 1065, 1120 or 1120S), then that ownership stake should be reported as a business and not as a farm.

The **"Parent Expenses"** section that follows next on the CSS Profile first asks about various types of expenses you may have incurred in 2025 and/or 2026. Follow-up questions involve annual figures (unless otherwise stated). Regarding **medical and dental expenses not paid by insurance**: be sure to refer to Chapter 3, "Optional Expenses," for our suggested strategies. These expenses are among the most underreported by parents. Use all the IRS allowable expenses. These include medical or dental expenses you've charged on a credit card during the year, even if you haven't paid for them yet. We find that many families forget about health insurance premiums deducted from their paycheck and medical-related transportation costs. However, do not include insurance premiums that are deducted on Line 17 of Schedule 1 of the 2025 1040. After you have figured out 2025 expenses, estimate 2026 as best you can if final numbers are not yet available. If either number is more than the threshold percentage of your total income for the corresponding year specified in the CSS Profile instructions for these two questions, list that total number you calculated. Otherwise, enter 0 (zero) if instructed to do so. Regarding the **repayment of parents' educational debt**: be sure to read the instructions carefully for this type of expense and only include payments on those types of loans specifically mentioned. If you are asked questions about alimony paid in this section or elsewhere, read the fine print. If the alimony is paid to an ex-spouse other than the student's parent and the question does not cover that situation, mention this fact and mention the alimony paid amount for 2025, 2026, and 2027 in the **"Special Circumstances"** section. Parents of international students may need to provide monthly or annual amounts for various household expenses.

For the next CSS Profile section, **"Household Summary"**: be aware that unlike FAFSA 34 and 35 regarding household size and the number in the college, the CSS Profile does not ask these two similar questions. The enhanced skip logic built into CSS Profile now indirectly derives this data based on responses in this and other sections of the form. At the start of this section, the names of the student and the "custodial parents" (or the "custodial parent" and also, if applicable, the "custodial stepparent") will appear. As you continue to the next web page, the **"Dependent Summary"** subsection will appear. If you have determined there is no other family member who qualifies as a member of the household—but be sure to read all the fine print in the instructions for this section—you can then click on "Save and Continue" and you will advance to the CSS Profile section regarding the student's income. However, if there is any other family member who can be considered a member of the household, enter their identifying information one at a time until all the additional family members' information is inputted and appears on this web page. After reviewing this data for accuracy (and editing any incorrect responses), you can click on the Save and Continue tab to advance to the more detailed questions regarding each of the other family members' year in school in 2026–2027 and 2027–2028. If a family member is in grades K–12 for a given year, follow-up questions will ask if the student attends or will attend a private school. If so, additional questions will appear asking about the amount of various costs paid by the parent and the amount of any gift aid awarded. The responses to these questions will be used to determine if you qualify for a deduction against income for these tuition payments (see Chapter 3, "Elementary and Secondary School Tuition"). And if another family member is in college in 2026–2027 or will be in college in 2027–2028, then information will be asked about the enrollment. **NOTE WELL:** this is the only section on the CSS Profile now used to determine if another family member will be concurrently enrolled during the 2027–2028 academic year in a higher education institution for purposes of determining the parent contribution per student (see Chapter 3, "Multiple College Students"). Because the size of the household, the ages of the other family members (see Chapter 3, "College Board Asset Allowances"), possibly their K–12 educational expenses paid, and *especially the number of family members in college (excluding the student's parents)* impact the parent contribution for the student in the IM aid formula, it is critical that your situation be properly represented in this section of the form before the CSS Profile is submitted to the processor. Independent students on the CSS Profile may be asked slightly different questions about other household members.

For the CSS Profile's **Student Income** section: the 2027–2028 CSS Profile will now ask questions in various subsections about **the student's 2024 tax return status,** as well as questions about the student's 2025 income. Just as with the parents, if the student is on extension until October 15, 2026, it would be better to wait to complete the CSS Profile until the 2025 tax return is prepared (though the FAFSA may need to be filed earlier with estimated figures if at least one college under consideration and/or the student's home state government awards funds on a first-come, first-served basis). Unlike the parents, for tax-filers, the specific questions regarding certain IRS line items to be listed on the CSS Profile do not include any questions regarding wages or self-employment income. These items are to be reported in the **Student income earned from work** question, asked on the CSS Profile of both tax filers and non-filers. For other 2025 income questions: be sure you do not include benefits paid to the parent for the student in the untaxed social security benefits question in this section. And for a student who has attended college before 2026–2027, be sure to list any 2025 income earned in a college work-study program (that is part of the CSS Profile income earned from work figure listed), a co-op program, as well as the amount of any taxable grants or scholarships reported on the student's 2025 tax return in the appropriate CSS Profile question. (This CSS Profile question about taxable grants and scholarships will likely agree with the similar question in FAFSA 20.)

Unlike the **Parent Income** section on the CSS Profile, students will not be asked any questions about their 2026 income. However, the **Student Expected Income and Benefits** subsection asks questions about income for the summer of 2027 and during the 2027–2028 school year. Be conservative with your estimates here as your responses may trigger a higher student contribution from income in the IM (see Chapter 3, "Student Resources")—and be sure to exclude work-study earnings!

The **Student Resources** subsection in the **Student Income** section includes some very important, though tricky, questions about various contributions from others to assist with college costs. (On the "Noncustodial Parent Profile," some of these questions are the only ones for that form's somewhat awkwardly-named **"Student Income"** section.) For the response to the question on either version of the CSS Profile regarding **The student's parents:** for dependent students, list only the amount you feel you can contribute from your current income and assets. Do NOT include any amounts you intend to borrow. Independent students should list only a minimal figure if any help is expected; otherwise list "0."

For the question about **"Other relatives...:"** before answering this question, you should review the section "Direct Payments to the School" in Chapter 3. And be sure to carefully read the CSS Profile help comments before you answer this question.

For the question regarding **Scholarships and grants from (other) sources..."** (see Chapter 7, "Outside Scholarships" and "National Service"): when answering this question, you should not include any outside awards unless you are 100% certain you will be receiving the money. For the **tuition benefits** question: if there will be no tuition benefits, enter "0." If there will be benefits, but the amount of the benefits will be based upon the school attended, list the least amount of the benefit that you would receive based on your list of colleges under consideration that require the CSS Profile. Some questions apply only to international students. Answer appropriately if asked. Depending on responses in the Parent Details section, questions regarding **Veteran's benefits** may also be asked. Read these questions carefully before you enter your responses.

The **Student Assets** section is arranged in almost the same way as the **Parent Assets** section earlier on the CSS Profile. However, the questions in the **Student Assets Types** subsection are different. For the CSS Profile, a student's trust is treated as a separate category from other investments, while a parent's trust is included as part of the parent's investments. If you answer "Yes" to the statement in the **Student Asset Types** subsection about the existence of a trust, additional questions about the trust and its value will eventually be asked. You should realize that when the word trust is used for this **"Student Asset Types"** question, it is not referring to a regular type of bank account that is maintained by one person "in trust for" another person. In that case, such an asset held by a parent reporting information on any aid form "in trust for" the student (and/or anyone else) should be reported as a parent asset and not as a student asset. For the **"Has Retirement accounts"** question: most students don't have IRAs, Keoghs, or other retirement accounts, so most likely your answer for this will be "No." Otherwise, answer accordingly.

Whether or not any statement in the **Student Assets Types** subsection is answered in the affirmative, all students will be asked about the current amount of their **Cash, savings, checking account, and deposit accounts**. Your response should be the same as the similar component of FAFSA 22, unless you were eligible to skip the FAFSA asset questions (if you filed the FAFSA on the Web) because you met the FM criteria to be exempt from reporting assets. In that case, you should follow the instructions on the CSS Profile to answer this questions as well as any other questions about the student's other assets including...

Student investments: Remember that for purposes on the FAFSA, the investment component of FAFSA 22 would include the equity in other real estate and the value of a student's trust(s). So if the student has any financial investments, the figure provided on the CSS Profile for the investment value may or may not agree that FAFSA question.

Regarding the **Student Real Estate** subsection: If the *student* owns any real estate, then select the statement(s) that apply. Then answer the follow-up questions about each property. For any jointly-owned property, list only the student's (and if applicable, the student's spouse's) share.

For the **Student Businesses and Farms**: The same tips for a parent's business and/or farms apply.

Be aware that most dependent students going to college immediately after high school will likely not select any statements in the **Student Real Estate** and the **Student Businesses and Farms** subsections because they do not yet own such types of assets.

Student Home: If you are asked any of these questions and the student does not own his or her primary residence, you should go back and check your prior responses in the earlier sections of the CSS Profile, as the student likely will not be asked these questions, which apply to some independent students. Otherwise, answer accordingly. As we explained in more detail in our comments regarding a parent's home, the questions regarding current value, year of purchase, and purchase price also serve an audit check to be sure you have not low-balled the value of real estate.

Most dependent students will not be asked questions in the **Student Expenses** section, which are primarily for independent students. For **Student's medical and dental expenses**: if the parents paid the medical and dental expenses for the student, don't include them here—do refer to the CSS Profile instructions before answering this one.

Explanations and Special Circumstances

We already mentioned a number of situations that should be explained here. You should also provide details regarding any other CSS Profile items that you are required to explain. Otherwise, we suggest that you leave this section blank. It is far more effective to send a separate letter to each college explaining any unusual circumstances. Be aware that if you select any option other than "None" from the list of special circumstances listed in this section you will then need to provide some written comments below that list and explain the applicable circumstances. You should, of course, select "Other" if any of your special circumstances is not applicable to any on the menu options on the list.

That about does it for the most common sections and questions on the CSS Profile you are likely to be asked. Unfortunately, you may not be finished with the CSS Profile form just yet. Depending on the colleges and the programs you designated to receive your CSS Profile (which are listed in the **Academic Information** section), there may be one or more additional questions that you have to answer at the request of one or more of the listed schools. If you are asked any of these questions, they will appear in the **Supplemental Questions** section, which may be broken down into subsections depending on the questions being asked.

At the time we went to press, the pool of available questions for this section had not been finalized. Nor had many individual colleges decided which additional questions, if any, they would be requiring of CSS Profile applicants. As such, it is impossible for us to give you any specific advice regarding questions that may appear in this section of your CSS Profile form.

It seems a safe bet to assume, however, that the majority of questions in this part of the CSS Profile will either be asking for further details regarding items previously listed on the CSS Profile or about additional assets or resources not previously reported. After reading Chapter Three and this part of the book, by now you should have a very good idea of the strategy you should be applying in order to maximize your aid eligibility. If you also keep the following points in mind, any questions in this section should not pose too much of a problem for you:

- Read the questions carefully. Answer them honestly, but do not disclose more information than required. If a yearly amount is requested, be sure you provide data for the requested calendar or academic year.
- Avoid overstating or double-counting assets or income (especially if you are estimating).
- Remember to include all allowable expenses or debts.
- Keep your responses consistent with other data previously listed on any form.

Keep in mind that only those colleges that select a particular question for this section will receive your response to that question. However, beginning with the 2018–2019 CSS Profile, this section no longer provides information as to which college is requesting which supplemental questions from the pool of available questions. So if you are completing the CSS Profile with more than one college listed, it is hard to know which schools are getting the various responses in this section, if any. And if you add any additional colleges or programs to a previously submitted CSS Profile for that student, only new questions not previously asked by another college that was already on the CSS Profile will be asked. So if a school you are now adding to the CSS Profile requests applicants to answer these questions, you will not know all the questions being asked by that school you are adding, unless none of your colleges listed in any previous submission asked any questions in this section and you are only adding that one school at this time.

Are You Done?

Congratulations! Save your data and/or put your work aside for a day (unless the form is due that day!). You've earned a rest. Tomorrow, look the forms over very carefully. Are you happy with the numbers? If you finished the CSS Profile and saved your CSS Profile data online, it would be best to make sure all the answers are consistent with the answers you gave on the FAFSA (assuming you did not need to submit the CSS Profile before the FAFSA became available). In addition, do your answers on the CSS Profile and the FAFSA agree with any supplemental aid forms required by the colleges? Go online today and check to see if your stock or bond investments have lost any value. If so, revise your figures downward.

When you are convinced that everything is ready, carefully review your data again before you submit any online form or mail/fax/upload any paper aid document. Date any paper form, sign it, and make photocopies for your records. When submitting your CSS Profile information, be sure you have credit card or bank account information handy as you will likely be charged a processing fee. If you are filing the PDF FAFSA, mail the original form via "Priority Express Mail" to the processor. Track delivery via the usps.com free tracking service.

Your FAFSA Submission Summary (FSS) from the government should be available in three to four weeks (or sooner for online filers). Once you submit your CSS Profile data, you will be able to save and print the submitted info.

The FSS Document

If you filed the PDF version of the FAFSA and did not provide an email address, you will receive a multi-page form sent by the government called the FAFSA Submission Summary (or FSS) a few weeks after you send in your 2027–2028 FAFSA to the processor. (You can also retrieve the FSS online at fafsa.gov, provided you have a verified FSA ID for the student.) If you filed the FAFSA and provided a student email address on any version, you will need to retrieve your FSS electronically as no paper FSS will be mailed to the student. No matter which method you used, check the information on the FSS carefully to make sure it agrees with the information you entered on the FAFSA. Be sure that the FSS includes the correct names of the colleges to which you are applying for aid. If you are applying for aid at more colleges than you could list on the original FAFSA, and/or you have decided to add some additional schools, and/or the processor did not list a correct school, you will need to get the FAFSA data to those additional schools. You should call the FAOs at each of the schools not listed, explain the situation, and ask them how to proceed. Be sure to keep a record of the person you spoke with at each college as well as a summary of what was discussed. They will probably tell you one of two ways to get the data to them:

1. By sending them a copy of the 2027–2028 FSS. While a number of schools will accept your data this way, you should be sure to mention that the school is not listed on the FAFSA when you call the aid office. Since you should always have at least one original FSS for your records, you should call (800) 433-3243 to request a duplicate 2027–2028 FSS if you received an original SAI in the mail.

2. By revising the FSS. Because the online version allows you to maintain a list of up to 20 schools (and only 10 schools appear on the paper version of the FSS) it is probably better to revise the list online (at www.fafsa.gov) since you can list more schools this way. If you're sending back the FSS to the processor, use Priority Express Mail and track delivery. Be sure to carefully follow the instructions so that the processor will make the necessary corrections. If you already listed the maximum number of schools on the FAFSA, you will be substituting the unlisted school(s) for one or more of the schools previously listed. Before you do this, however, you should make sure any school you are substituting out has received your FAFSA information before you remove them. If you are mailing the FSS back to the processor, make a photocopy for your records. Within a few weeks after mailing, you will receive a new FSS which you should again review for accuracy. If you still have not been able to get all the schools listed after this first round of revising, keep repeating the process until every school gets the FAFSA data. Of course, if you have to do the process more than once, you should give preference on your first revision to those schools with the earliest deadlines.

   Note: If you substitute one school for another, the originally listed school will no longer receive any revised data that you send back to the processor. Therefore, if you have to correct or change any items other than those schools currently listed on the FAFSA, you may need to put the original school(s) no longer listed back on the new FSS that is generated and send it back to the processor.

If you haven't received a FSS within three weeks of filing, call (800) 433-3243 during business hours for a status report. Be sure to have the student's social security number handy when you call.

Two Moments of Truth

The FSS will tell you if you qualify for a Pell Grant. Don't panic if the FSS says you are ineligible. This is a federal grant for lower-income families and many people do not qualify. Just because you didn't get a Pell Grant does not mean you won't qualify for any aid at all. The Pell is often the toughest type of aid to get.

The FSS will also tell you your Student Aid Index (SAI).

Here's what that area with the SAI information on the FSS will look like:

February 7, 2027	F 211 2425
	DRN: 9755
Wright Price 123 Main Street Anytown, ST 12345	Student Aid Index (SAI): 008920*C

Remember that your SAI only applies to the federal methodology. There is no dollar sign and only a vague reference to how a college will use the index number to determine aid eligibility at that school. In this example, the Student Aid Index for one year for this student was determined to be 8920 by the FAFSA processor.

Note: If you filed the FAFSA online, your SAI figure may be provided to you along with your Data Release Number right after you submit your FAFSA for processing.

Counting Chickens

Unfortunately, the federal SAI is not necessarily the number the colleges will elect to use. Schools that asked you to fill out the CSS Profile form will most likely be using the institutional methodology to determine the family contribution. This figure could be lower or higher than the federal number. The institutional contribution figure is never provided by the CSS Profile processor.

The Verification Process

"Verification" is the financial aid version of an audit, although the process is generally much more benign. Years ago, either the federal processor or the colleges themselves could select students for verification, and each college had to verify a minimum of 30% of their applicants. Only the federal processor will determine who must be selected for verification, but schools can also select additional students.

With the full implementation of FAFSA Simplification, the U.S. Department of Education (USDOE) announced that they would no longer be using the algorithm they utilized for awards years prior to 2024–2025 to determine which applicants are selected for verification. That algorithm made it more likely for one to be selected for verification if one was eligible for a Pell Grant and/or one either did not use or was unable to use the IRS Data Retrieval Tool (DRT) to have their tax return information transferred onto the FAFSA. The USDOE has further stated that they will be developing a new algorithm upon reviewing the data from FAFSAs submitted once Simplification was implemented. However, it is very likely this past practice will remain: once the algorithm is developed for use in future years, the USDOE will keep the algorithm confidential, with very few USDOE employees having access to it. As in the past, one will never be able to predict with 100% certainty what scenarios will result in one being selected for verification.

However this much is known as we went to press: On page 1 of the FSS there will be text alerting the applicant they have been selected for verification. Additionally, there will be an asterisk (*) that will be listed after one's SAI (per the example above) to denote such selection. More details about what to do should one be selected for verification will be provided on one's FSS. And as in the past, the verification process will be handled by the financial aid office of the applicable school(s).

If you are selected for verification, and you chose not to use (or were unable to use) the FA-DDX tool or the FA-DDX could not be used to transfer tax information if you filed the paper version of the FAFSA: you will likely be required to send the school either a signed copy of your complete 2025 income tax return (including all schedules and attachments) or an official IRS transcript of your return(s).

The schools may also ask for documentation of certain benefits if you receive them or information about child support received. You will likely also have to fill out a Verification Worksheet so that the colleges can double-check the number of members in your family.

While the IRS audits a minuscule percentage of taxpayers, financial aid verification is relatively commonplace. At some schools, 100% of the applicants are verified. Thus, if you receive a notice of verification, this does not mean that it is time to book plane tickets to a country that does not have an extradition treaty with the United States. It is all routine.

Revising Your Information

If the numbers on the FSS are different from the numbers you sent in a PDF FAFSA, you will probably want to revise them immediately. The FSS will give you instructions on how to correct errors made either by the processor or by you. You will also want to revise immediately if you receive any notice stating that your FAFSA could not be processed, if there are comments on the FSS that there were problems with the processing, or if you need to change the list of schools. The responses that were processed from your FAFSA data will appear in boldface type on your FSS.

How to Update Your Data

While the instructions to the FSS tell you how to handle revisions, these instructions may conflict with the procedures many colleges would prefer you to follow. To find out the correct way to revise your FSS, you must call the FAOs at all of the colleges still under consideration. In general, the FAOs will tell you to do one of two things:

1. Revise the FSS and send the revisions to the processor. (Most likely response.)
2. Revise the FSS and send all pages of the FSS directly to the FAO.

When you call the FAOs, ask when they expect you to do this. See if you can hold off until you know for sure what college the student will be attending. If you received the FSS in the mail and a college requires a physical copy of the FSS before the student is sure of his educational plans, you should request a duplicate FSS for your records by calling (800) 433-3243. A duplicate FSS is free, so we suggest you call for a few duplicate copies just in case.

The question numbers on the FSS should correspond exactly to the question numbers on the FAFSA. To help you in your revisions, you can refer to your photocopy of the FAFSA, as well as to the detailed instructions we gave for completing each line of the FAFSA form. The FSS processors prefer you to use a dark-ink ballpoint pen for any revisions on the paper FSS. The asset information should be the net asset figures at the time you completed the original FAFSA, not the net asset figures on the day you are revising. You should therefore revise your asset information only if a mistake was made when the FAFSA was originally filed.

After you send your FSS revisions to the processor, a new version of the FSS with the revised data will be generated. Look over the new FSS data to make sure it's accurate. It is best to revise your FSS information electronically if at all possible.

The CSS Profile Acknowledgment

After you transmit your CSS Profile data to the processor, you will be able to view and print a file that summarizes your responses to most of the CSS Profile questions. Follow the directions regarding revisions, if necessary.

Applying to More CSS Profile Schools

If after transmitting the CSS Profile data to the processor you decide to apply to additional schools that require the CSS Profile form, you can have the data sent to the additional schools by accessing your CSS Profile dashboard with your College Board email address and password for the account used to file the original CSS Profile. Details on how to add additional schools will then be provided. You will also have to get the FAFSA data to these schools by revising the FSS.

What to Do If You Get a Notice Saying Your Form Could Not Be Processed

Your need analysis form may get rejected for any number of reasons, but the most common are forgetting to answer one of the questions or not signing the form.

If your paper FAFSA is returned to you unprocessed, the main thing is to get it back to the processor as fast as possible. Even if the screw-up was your fault, you will minimize the odds of missing out on aid if you snap into action immediately. The processor may though send an incomplete version of their report to all the colleges, so you will still be in the running. To be on the safe side, contact the individual schools to let them know what is happening.

In some cases, the processor will question specific items because they are unusually low or high for a "typical family" with your income level. Don't feel you must change a number if it is really correct. If the item is correct, you may need to rewrite the exact same information when revising your FSS.

As always, photocopy any new information you send to the processor, and send it Priority Express Mail unless you are revising the FAFSA form online (with the latter being the preferred method given audit checks will be done online to resolve any conflicting information). And be sure that you follow all instructions to the letter.

If Your SAI Is Much Higher than You Expected

Somehow, no matter how prepared you are, seeing the federal SAI in print is always a shock. Remember that the colleges do not expect you to be able to pay the entire amount out of current income. If they deem your resources sufficient, they expect you to liquidate assets each year that your child is in college and they may expect you to have to borrow money on top of that. Your SAI is designed to include money that you have earned in the past (assets) and money that you will obtain in the future (loans) as well as the income you are currently earning.

Remember that your family contribution could be lower or higher than the SAI printed on the FSS. This will be especially true if the school uses the institutional methodology in awarding their own aid funds. Remember also that colleges have broad latitude to change the SAI in either direction. This is where negotiation can come into play. Consult Part Four, "The Offer." We know of one case in which the number in the FM was judged to be $24,000. The school brought the actual number down to $13,000.

In addition, some state aid formulas differ from the federal formula. We know of another case in which the number was judged to be $99,999, but the family managed to receive $5,000 a year in state aid because of quirks in the state's formula.

If you have followed our guidance in Part Five and used the worksheets provided in your online student tools to compute your federal Student Aid Index, you should not be surprised by the number on the FSS. If there is a large discrepancy between what you thought your SAI would be and what the FSS says it is, then someone may have made a mistake. Go through your worksheets carefully, and double-check to see that the information on the FAFSA form you filed agrees with the numbers you used in the worksheets. Also, make sure that these numbers agree with the numbers on the FSS if you filed the PDF version of the FAFSA. If an error was made on the FAFSA, start revising.

The Next Step: Supplying Completed Tax Returns

Some colleges will not give you a financial aid package until they've seen your taxes for the first base income year. Others will give you a "tentative" package, subject to change when they see the final numbers. And some may want to see 2026 returns too, especially if your income declined in 2026 and you are appealing the aid package(s).

It is in your best interest to get your taxes done as fast as possible. Prod your accountant if he is dragging his heels. Better yet, if you are not reading this book at the eleventh hour, plan ahead. During the fall of senior year in high school, let your accountant know that you are going to need your 2026 taxes done as soon as possible this year if you are planning to appeal based on a reduction in income.

Find out whether the colleges that you are interested in really do want to see your tax return. In many cases, the answer will be yes. In a few cases (such as New York University), they will not want your tax return unless you are randomly selected for verification. We recommend that you not send a return unless it is required. Why give them more information than they need?

The most effective time for negotiation with the FAOs is before May 1, the Universal Reply Date by which most colleges require you to commit to attend. Obviously, you will have more bargaining power if you can still decide to go to another school. The FAOs are much less likely to compromise once you are committed to their college.

The School's Own Aid Forms

The standardized need analysis forms are probably not the only financial aid forms you will have to complete. Many selective colleges have their own institutional aid forms as well with deadlines that may differ from those of both the standardized forms and the admissions applications to the schools themselves. The purpose of these forms is sometimes difficult to comprehend, since in many cases they ask many of the same questions you have already answered on the FAFSA or the CSS Profile form all over again. Some counselors suspect this is intentionally designed in an attempt to reveal discrepancies.

More Detailed Information

However, the individual school forms do ask for some new information. In general, they are looking for more specific breakdowns of your income and assets. Exactly what kind of assets do you have? How liquid are they? In addition, you will often be asked about your other children's educational plans for the current year and the year to come.

While neither the FAFSA nor the CSS Profile form ask income and asset information about "noncustodial parents," many of the individual schools will want to know all the financial details of that parent. Some may ask the "noncustodial parent" to complete their own "noncustodial parent form" instead of the "Noncustodial parent Profile." If you own your own business, you may need to fill out the paper College Board Business/Farm Supplement. We'll cover both of these situations in more detail in the "Special Topics" chapter of this book.

These institutional aid forms may also ask questions to determine eligibility for specific restricted scholarships and grants. In general, these scholarships are left over from a different era when private citizens funded weird scholarships in their own name. The colleges hate administering these restricted scholarships—they would much rather be allowed to give money to whomever they feel like.

Be Careful

Take the time to be consistent. Your answers on these institutional aid forms may be compared to other information you've supplied elsewhere. Small differences, especially if you are estimating, are acceptable, but anything major will cause serious problems. Get out your photocopies of any previous aid forms you've completed and make sure you are not diverging.

Much as you may feel that your privacy is being invaded, do not skip any of the questions. This is the colleges' game and they get to make the rules. If you don't answer, they don't have to give you any money.

Send these requested items to the schools themselves, completing the form online (preferred method), via fax (if permitted), or by using Priority Mail at the post office. You can also use a private delivery service if you are sending items to a street address (as opposed to a PO Box). If you are sending any supplementary information (such as tax returns), make sure that the student's name and his or her college ID number or social security number are prominently displayed on all documents. This is especially important if the student's last name is different from either of his parents'.

The IDOC Service

Some schools may now require you to submit your income tax returns and other documents to the College Board's IDOC service. (This stands for "institutional documentation," but nobody calls it that.) After your documents are received by the IDOC processor, they will be made available electronically to those schools that require them in this format. If at least one of your schools is utilizing the IDOC service, you will likely receive an email notification from the College Board. Required documents can now be either uploaded online (preferred) or mailed to the IDOC service. Make sure all required signatures are provided. Be extra careful that you submit the tax returns (and W-2s and/or 1099s if requested) for the correct calendar year. Finally, some additional documents required by a college using IDOC (e.g., a Student Non-tax Filer's Statement or a Verification Worksheet) may be a fill-in form that can be completed and submitted online with electronic signatures.

Part Four

The Offer and Other Financial Matters

On the day that the offers from colleges arrive there will be many dilemmas for parents. One of the most vexing is deciding whether to steam open the letters from the colleges or wait until the student gets home from school. We can set your mind at ease about this dilemma at least. You can usually tell an acceptance letter from a rejection letter even without opening it—acceptance letters weigh more. This is because as long as you met your deadlines, you should receive financial aid packages in the same envelopes the acceptance letters came in. Most colleges will need a commitment from you before May 1. This gives you only a few weeks to sift through the offers, compare them, and—if possible—negotiate with the FAOs to improve them.

The details of an aid package will be spelled out in the award letter. This letter will tell you the total cost of one year's attendance at the college, what the college decided you could afford to pay toward that cost, and what combination of grants, loans, and work-study the college has provided to meet your "need."

On the following page you will find a sample award letter from Anytown University located in Anytown, State.

ANYTOWN UNIVERSITY

OFFICE OF FINANCIAL AID

FIRST NOTICE

Academic Year
2027-2028
Budget Assumptions
Resident Dependent Single
Identification Number
U123456789
Award Date
March 20, 2026

Wright Price
123 Main Street
Anytown, ST 12345

OFFER OF FINANCIAL AID

After careful consideration, the Financial Aid Committee has authorized this offer of financial assistance for the award period indicated at left. The decision was made after careful consideration of your application.

To accept this offer, you must complete, sign, and return the white copy of this form within four weeks of receipt. This award is subject to cancellation if you do not respond by the specified date.

If you choose to decline any part of this offer, please place a check mark in the "DECLINED" box for the corresponding part of the package.

Be sure to review the terms and conditions of the award as described in the Financial Aid booklet enclosed.

DECLINED		FALL 2027	SPRING 2028
❐	Anytown University Scholarship	$20,975.00	$20,975.00
❐	Federal SEOG Grant	$500.00	$500.00
❐	Estimated Federal Pell Grant	$2,720.00	$2,720.00
❐	Recommended Federal Direct Loan	$1,750.00	$1,750.00
❐	Federal Work-Study	$665.00	$665.00
	TOTAL	$26,610.00	$26,610.00

FAMILY RESOURCES		SUMMARY	
Parent's Contribution	$980.00	Total Estimated Budget	$56,000.00
Student's Contribution	$1,800.00	Less: Family Contribution	$2,780.00
Other Resources	0.00	Financial Need	$53,220.00
TOTAL FAMILY CONTRIBUTION	$2,780.00	TOTAL FINANCIAL AID	$53,220.00

Jane Doe, Director

Note that in this case, the family contribution was set at $2,780. The total cost of attendance at Anytown for that year was $56,000. Thus, this family had a remaining "need" of roughly $53,220 which was—in this case—met in full with a mixture of grants, loans, and work-study.

This was evidently a high-need family, and received an excellent package: $48,390 in grants (outright gift aid, which did not need to be repaid), $1,330 in work-study, and $3,500 in loans for the year.

Not all colleges will meet the entire remaining "need" of every student, and there may have been a number of reasons why the package was so good in the case of the sample student in the report above. Perhaps this was a particularly bright student or the impoverished grandchild of a distinguished alum.

The Different Types of Financial Aid in Detail

Let's examine the different types of financial aid that you may be offered in the award letter. An acceptance of the aid package does not commit you to attending the college, so be sure to respond by the reply date (certified mail, return receipt requested, as always). You are allowed to accept or reject any part of the package, but there are some types of aid that should never be rejected.

Grants and Scholarships: These should never be rejected. This money is almost always tax-free and never has to be repaid. Grants and scholarships come in different forms.

The Federal Pell Grant: This grant is administered by the federal government, and like all federal aid, is awarded only to U.S. citizens or eligible noncitizens. The Pell is primarily for low-income families. You automatically apply for the Pell Grant when you fill out the FAFSA. The size of the award is decided by the federal government and cannot be adjusted by the colleges. If you qualify, you will receive up to $7,395 per year, based on need.

The Federal Supplemental Educational Opportunity Grant or SEOG: This is a federal grant that is administered by the colleges themselves. Each year, the schools get a lump sum that they are allowed to dispense to students at their own discretion. The size of the award runs from $100 to $4,000 per year per student.

Grants from the Schools Themselves: The colleges themselves often award grants as well. Since this money comes out of their own pocketbook, these grants are, in effect, discounts off the sticker price. And because this is not taxpayer money, there are no rules about how it must be dispensed. Some schools say they award money solely based on need. Many schools also give out merit-based awards. There is no limit on the size of a grant from an individual school. It could range from a few dollars to a full scholarship. Obviously, richer schools have more money to award to their students than poorer schools.

State Grants: If a student is attending college in his state of legal residence, or in a state that has a reciprocal agreement with his state of legal residence, then he may qualify for a state grant as well. These grants are administered by the states themselves. The grants are based on need, as well as on the size of tuition at a particular school. Thus, the same student might find that his state grant at the local state university would be smaller than his state grant at a private college. These grants vary from state to state but can go as high as $9,000 per year or more.

Scholarships from the School: Some schools use the words *grants* and *scholarships* more or less interchangeably, and award scholarships just like grants—in other words, based on need. Other schools give scholarships in their more traditional sense, based on merit, either academic, athletic, or artistic. Some schools give scholarships based on a combination of need and merit.

The only real difference as far as you are concerned is whether the scholarship is used to meet need or whether it may be used to reduce your family contribution. If the school wants you badly enough, you may receive a merit-based scholarship over and above the amount of your need.

The Teacher Education Assistance for College and Higher Education (TEACH) Grant Program: This federal grant program provides grants of up to $4,000 per year to students who intend to teach full-time in a high-need field in a private elementary or secondary school that serves students from low-income families. To qualify, you must attend a school that has chosen to participate in the program and meet certain academic achievement requirements along with other requirements. It is important to note that failing to complete all of the service requirements (e.g., teaching four years within eight years of completing the program of study for which you received the grant at designated schools) will result in the amount of all TEACH grant funds received being converted to a Federal Direct Unsubsidized Stafford Loan.

Outside Scholarships: If you have sought out and won a scholarship from a source not affiliated with the college—a foundation, say, or a community organization—you are required to tell the colleges about this money. Often the scholarship donor will notify the colleges you applied to directly. In most cases, the schools will thank you politely and then use the outside scholarship to reduce the amount of grant money they were going to give you. In other words, winning a scholarship does not mean you will pay less money for college; your family contribution often stays exactly the same.

By notifying the colleges about an outside scholarship before getting your award letter, you ensure that the outside scholarship will be included as part of your package. This is not very satisfactory because you have effectively given away an important bargaining chip.

If you have managed to find and win one of these scholarships, you may feel that you deserve something more than thanks from the school for your initiative. By telling the FAO about an outside scholarship for the first time when you are negotiating an improved package, you may be able to use the scholarship as a bargaining chip. Some schools have specific policies on this; others are prepared to be flexible. In some cases, we have seen FAOs let the parents use *part* of that money to reduce the family contribution. In other cases, FAOs have agreed to use the scholarship to replace loan or work-study components of the package instead of grants from the school.

Federal Work-Study: Under this program, students are given part-time jobs (usually on campus) to help meet the family's remaining need. Many parents' first inclination is to tell the student to reject the work-study portion of the aid package. They are concerned that the student won't have time to do well in class. As we've said earlier, several studies suggest that students who work during college have as high or higher grade point averages as students who don't work.

We counsel that you at least wait to see what sort of work is being offered. The award letter will probably not specify what kind of work the student will have to do for this money. You will get another letter later in the year giving you details. In many cases these jobs consist of sitting behind a desk at the library doing homework. Since students can normally back out of work-study jobs at any time, why not wait to see how onerous the job really is? (A minuscule number of colleges do have penalties for students who fail to meet their work-study obligations, so be sure to read the work-study agreement carefully.)

While work-study wages are usually minimum wage or slightly higher, they carry the important added benefit of being exempt from the aid formulas; work-study wages do not count as part of the student's income. Other earnings, by contrast, may be assessed at a rate of up to *50 cents on the dollar*. In addition, each dollar your child earns is a dollar you won't have to borrow.

Some colleges give you the choice of having the earnings paid in cash or credited toward the next semester's bill. If your child is a big spender, you might consider the second option.

Loans: There are many different kinds of college loans, but they fall into two main categories: need-based loans, which are designed to help meet part of a family's remaining need; and non-need-based loans, which are designed to help pay part of the family contribution when the family doesn't have the cash on hand. The loans that will be offered as part of your aid package in the award letter are primarily need-based loans.

The best need-based loan, the federally-subsidized Direct Loan, is such a good deal that we feel families should always accept it if it's offered. No interest is charged while the student is in school, and repayment does not begin on Direct Loans until the student graduates, leaves college, or dips below half-time status. Even if you have the money in the bank, we would still counsel your taking the loans. Let your money earn interest in the bank. When the loans come due, you can pay them off immediately, in full if you like, without penalty. Most college loans have some kind of an origination fee and perhaps an insurance fee as well. These fees are deducted from the value of the loan itself; you will never have to pay them out of your pocket.

Here are the different types of loans in order of preferability.

Federal Direct Loans: Formerly known as Stafford Loans, there are two kinds of Direct Loans. The better kind is the *subsidized* Direct Loan. To get this, a student must be judged to have "remaining need" by the college. The federal government subsidizes the loan by not charging any interest until the six-month grace period ends after the student graduates, leaves college, or goes below half-time attendance status. (Formula: Cost of Attendance minus SAI minus financial aid accepted by the student equals Remaining Need)

The second kind, known as an *unsubsidized* Direct Loan, is not based on need. Once the loan proceeds are disbursed, the student will be charged interest that one can either pay while in school or allow to accrue until the end of the grace period, where it is added to the principle once repayment on that Direct Loan begins. Virtually all students who fill out a FAFSA are eligible for these unsubsidized Direct Loans.

A full-time dependent student may be eligible to borrow up to $5,500 as a first-year, up to $6,500 as a sophomore, and up to $7,500 per year for the remaining undergraduate years. However, for all of these annual limits, at least $2,000 must be unsubsidized in any year.

A full-time independent undergraduate can borrow up to $9,500 as a first-year (of which at least $6,000 must be unsubsidized), up to $10,500 as a sophomore (of which at least $6,000 must be unsubsidized), and up to $12,500 per year for the remaining undergraduate years (of which at least $7,000 per year must be unsubsidized).

What happens if an undergraduate student is awarded a subsidized Direct Loan, but the amount is less than the maximum subsidized amount? In this case, the student can borrow up to the amount of her remaining need with a subsidized Direct Loan and, if wanted, can also take out an unsubsidized Direct Loan for the remainder of the total annual borrowing limit.

All Direct Loans for new graduate/professional schools are unsubsidized. For such students who have not taken out any federal education loan for that specific program of study prior to July 1, 2026: the annual maximum is $20,500 for graduate students and $50,000 for professional school students. Those contemplating graduate/professional school in the future should also refer to Chapter Eight ("Managing Your Debt"). Note that as we went to press, a judge had just issued a stay related to certain loan provisions under OBBB3.

The interest rate for a newly originated Direct Loan is pegged to the 10-year Treasury Note rate with the rate fixed for the life of that loan. For any Direct Loan originated during the 2026–2027 academic year, that will be 6.52% for an undergraduate and 8.07% for a graduate/professional school student.

The rates for new Direct Loans originated during subsequent academic years will be based on the last 10-year Treasury Note auction in May prior to the start of that subsequent academic year. However, there are interest rate caps for Direct Loans (that would only apply to newly-originated loans taken out in subsequent academic years) should the 10-year Treasury Note rate rise significantly. For undergraduates, the cap will be 8.25%—with a 9.5% cap on Direct Loans for graduate/professional school students.

Because the government guarantees the loans, parents are never required to cosign a Direct Loan.

Starting in the 1994–95 academic year, under a law proposed by President Clinton, some of the Stafford loans were funded directly by the government and administered by the schools—thus eliminating the role of private lenders such as banks. This program, referred to as the William D. Ford Federal Direct Loan Program, co-existed with the Federal Family Education Loan Program (FFELP) for a number of years. The schools would decide which program they would have Stafford borrowers use to get their loan proceeds and the majority of such loans (in terms of loan volume) were originated with FFELP private lenders as the middleman. However, as part of the Health Care and Education Reconciliation Act of 2010, all new Stafford loans disbursed after June 30, 2010 would be via the Direct Loan program. That is why the name changed from a Stafford Loan to a Direct Loan, though the name Stafford Loan is still sometimes used.

Once you have decided on a college and accepted the aid package, the FAO will tell you how to go about obtaining the loan funds. You will have to fill out a promissory note, and because the process can take as long as six weeks, it may be necessary to apply for the loan by mid-June for the fall term.

The College's Own Loans: These loans vary widely in preferability. Some are absolutely wonderful: Princeton University offers special loans for parents at very low rates. Some are on the edge of sleazy: numerous colleges have loan programs that require almost immediate repayment with interest rates that rival VISA and MasterCard. While these types of loans do not normally appear as part of an aid package, a few colleges try to pass them off as need-based aid to unsuspecting students and their parents. Remember that you are allowed to reject any portion of the aid package. It is a good idea to examine the terms of loans from the individual colleges extremely carefully before you accept them.

Financial Sleight of Hand

As we've already said, there are two general types of college loans: a need-based loan (such as the subsidized Direct Loans we've just been discussing) is meant to meet a family's "remaining need"; the other kind of loan is meant to help when families don't have the cash to pay the family contribution itself.

By its very nature, this second type of loan should not appear as part of your aid package. As far as the colleges are concerned, your family contribution is your business, and they don't have to help you to pay it. However, a number of schools do rather unfairly include several types of non-need-based loans in their aid package, including the unsubsidized Direct loan we just discussed and the federal PLUS loan (Parent Loans for Undergraduate Students), which is intended to help those parents of dependent undergraduate students who are having trouble paying their family contribution. Virtually any biological or adoptive parent (or even, if applicable, a step-parent who is the spouse of the "Parent" listed on that academic year's FAFSA form) can get a PLUS loan—provided the federal government thinks the parent is a good credit risk.

Thus when a college tries to meet your need with a PLUS loan, the college is engaging in financial aid sleight of hand, ostensibly meeting your need with a loan that was not designed for that purpose and which you could have gotten anyway, as long as your credit held up. If you are offered a PLUS loan as part of your need-based aid, you should realize that the college has really *not* met your need in full. An aid offer that includes a PLUS loan used to meet the student's need is not as valuable as an offer that truly meets a family's demonstrated need.

With the PLUS loans, repayment normally begins within 60 days of the date the loan was made. However, legislation now permits a PLUS loan borrower to delay repayment on a PLUS loan taken out for a student until that student leaves school or drops below half-time status. You will need to elect to defer payment when applying for a PLUS loan.

Non-Need-Based Loans

While the other types of college loans won't be part of your aid package, this seems like a good place to describe a few of them, and they are certainly relevant to this discussion, for as you look at the various offers from the colleges, you will probably be wondering how you are going to pay your family contribution over the next four years. Most families end up borrowing. There are so many different loans offered by banks and organizations that it would be impossible to describe them all. College bulletins usually include information about the types of loans available at the specific schools, and applications can usually be picked up at the colleges' financial aid offices or be filed online. Here's a sampling of some of the more mainstream alternatives (we'll talk about a few of the more offbeat loans in the next chapter):

PLUS Loans: We've already discussed some details of PLUS loans above. As credit-based loans go, the PLUS is one of the better options. However due to some unresolved issues as we went to press (as well as many complications involving PLUS loan) due to the implementation of the One Big Beautiful Bill Act, be sure to consult the Student Tools (see page vii) if you're considering a PLUS loan for the first time OR you already have any outstanding PLUS loan(s) or other federal education loan(s), including any taken out for your own education.

For PLUS loans originated during the 2026–2027 academic year, the interest rate will be fixed at 9.07%—which is a bit more than the 7.9% rate that had been charged on fixed rate

Direct PLUS loans originated prior to July 1, 2013. For loans originated for the 2013–2014 academic year and beyond, there is a cap of 10.5% (that would apply only to newly-originated PLUS loans taken out in subsequent academic years should the 10-year Treasury Note rate rise significantly).

When we suggest the PLUS loans to some of our clients, their immediate response is, "There's no way we'll qualify; we don't have a good credit rating!" Before you automatically assume you won't qualify, you should realize that the credit test for the PLUS is not as stringent as it is for most other loans. You don't have to have excellent credit to qualify. You just can't have an "adverse credit history" (i.e., outstanding judgments, liens, extremely slow payments). Even if you fail the credit test, you may still be able to secure a PLUS loan provided you are able to demonstrate extenuating circumstances (determined on a case-by-case basis by the lender) or you are able to find someone (a friend or relative) who can pass the credit test, who agrees to endorse (i.e., cosign) the loan, and who promises to pay it back if you are unable to do so.

In 2014, the Department of Education relaxed the credit requirements necessary to receive the loan.

If you are rejected for the PLUS loan and are unable to get a creditworthy endorser, there is still another option available to you. In this case, dependent students can borrow extra Direct Loan funds over the normal borrowing limits. First- and second-year students can get an additional $4,000 per year, while those in the third year and beyond can get an additional $5,000 per year. In all cases, these additional Direct Loan funds must be unsubsidized. Obviously, this approach is going to put the student deeper in debt. However, if you need to borrow a few thousand dollars to cover the family contribution and are unable to get credit in your name, this strategy may be your only option.

State Loans: Some states offer alternative loan programs as well. The terms vary from state to state; some are available only to students, others only to parents; many are below market rate. Unlike state grants, state loans are often available to nonresidents attending approved colleges in that state.

Lines of Credit: Some banks offer revolving credit loans that do not start accruing interest until you write a check on the line of credit.

Discover Student Loans [www.studentloan.com or (800) 788-3368]: These loans to students do not have any origination fees. But such traditional loan charges are built into the interest rate charged, which is pegged to the 90-day London Interbank Offer Rate (LIBOR). Unlike the federal education loans in which all borrowers for a particular loan are charged the same interest rate, these loans, as well as other private loans, will have an individual borrower's interest rate based on the borrower's (and, if applicable, the cosigner's) credit history. There is a $1,000 minimum loan amount. A cosigner is required for almost all undergraduates, especially those who do not have a positive credit history. Note that this is one of the few loan programs that a foreign student can take advantage of, but they must have a credit-worthy cosigner, and that cosigner must be a U.S. citizen or permanent resident.

Sallie Mae Smart Option Student Loans [www.salliemae.com or (800) 695-3317]: These cosigned private student loans require payment of interest while the student is in school and during the 6-month separation period before repayment. Cosigners may only be required for first-year students. The interest rate is pegged to the prime rate and will vary depending on the credit rating of the student (and, if applicable, the cosigner) as well as the school attended. This program offers a 0.25% interest rate reduction for students who elect to have their payments made automatically through their bank and a 0.25% interest rate reduction for students who receive all servicing communications via a valid email address.

This is only a partial listing of the different loans available. When choosing which type of loan to take out, you should consider all of the following questions:

- What is the interest rate and how is it determined?
- Is the interest rate fixed or variable, and if variable, is there a cap?
- What are the repayment options? How many years will it take to pay off the loan? Can you make interest-only payments while the child is in school? Can you repay the loan early?
- Who is the borrower—the parent or the student?
- Are there origination fees?
- Is a cosigner permitted or required?
- Will having a cosigner affect the interest rate and/or origination fees?
- Is the loan secured or unsecured? The rates on a loan secured by the home or by securities are generally lower, but you are putting your assets on the line.
- Is the interest on the loan tax-deductible?

On balance, the PLUS loan is probably the best of all these options. Unless you are able to secure more favorable terms from a state financing authority's alternative education loan program, then the only reasons to consider the other types of non-need-based loans, besides the PLUS loan, are if you prefer having the loans in the student's name or if the student is an independent student.

Should You Turn Down Individual Parts of an Aid Package?

Some parents worry that by turning down part of the financial aid package they are endangering future aid. Clearly, by refusing a work-study job or a need-based loan, you are telling the FAOs that you can find the money elsewhere, and this *could* have an impact on the package you are offered next year. In our experience, we can't remember many times when we thought it was a good idea for a family to turn down grants, scholarships, need-based loans, or work-study.

Certainly Not Before You Compare All the Packages

Before you turn down any part of a single financial aid package, you should compare the packages as a group to determine your options.

The Size of the Package Is Not Important

Families often get swept up by the total value of the aid packages. We've heard parents say, "This school gave us $12,000 in aid, which is much better than the school that gave us only $7,000." The real measure of an aid package is how much YOU will have to end up paying, and how much debt the student will have to take on.

Let's look at three examples:

School A:

total cost—$30,000
family contribution—$11,000
grants and scholarships—$14,000
need-based loans—$3,000
work-study—$1,000
unmet need (what the parents will have to pay in addition to the family contribution)—$1,000
value of the aid package—$18,000
money the family will have to spend—$12,000
need-based debt—$3,000

School B:

total cost—$29,000
family contribution—$11,000
grants and scholarships—$17,000
need-based loans—$500
work-study—$500
unmet need—$0
value of the aid package—$18,000
money the family will have to spend—$11,000
need-based debt—$500

School C:

total cost—$25,000
family contribution—$10,500
grants and scholarships—$10,750
need-based loans—$3,250
work-study—$500
unmet need—$0
value of the aid package—$14,500
money the family will have to spend—$10,500
need-based debt—$3,250

School A and school B gave identical total dollar amounts in aid, but the two packages were very different. School B gave $17,000 in grants (which do not have to be repaid), while A gave only $14,000. School B would actually cost this family $11,000 with only $500 in student loans. School A would cost the family $12,000 with $3,000 in student loans. Leaving aside for the moment subjective matters such as the academic caliber of the two schools, school B was a better buy.

School C would cost this family $10,500 in cash. On the other hand, this school also asked the student to take on the largest amount of debt: $3,250.

You've probably noticed that the sticker prices of the three colleges were almost totally irrelevant to our discussion. After you've looked at the bottom line for each of the colleges that have accepted the student, you should also factor in the academic quality of the schools; perhaps it is worth a slightly higher price to send your child to a more prestigious school. You should also look at factors like location, reputation of the department your child is interested in, and the student's own idea of which school would make her happiest. In the end, you'll have to choose what price you're willing to pay for what level of quality.

Is the Package Renewable?

An excellent question, but unfortunately this is a very difficult question to get a straight answer about. Of course there are some conditions attached to continuing to receive a good financial aid package. Students must maintain a minimum grade point average, and generally behave themselves.

It also makes sense to avoid colleges that are on the brink of bankruptcy, since poor schools may not be able to continue subsidizing students at the same level.

Bait and Switch?

Most reputable colleges don't indulge in bait-and-switch tactics, whereby students are lured to the school with a sensational financial aid package that promptly disappears the next year.

We have found that when parents feel they have been victims of a bait and switch, there has often been a misunderstanding of some kind. This might occur when parents have two children in school at the same time. If one of the children graduates, the parents are often surprised when the SAI for the child who remains in college goes up dramatically. This is not a bait and switch. The family now has more available income and assets to pay for the child who is now in college alone.

Sometimes, schools minimize work-study hours during the first year so that students have a chance to get accustomed to college life. Parents are often shocked when the number of work-study hours is increased the next year, but again this is not a bait and switch. It is reasonable to expect students to work more hours in their junior and senior years.

Negotiating with the FAOs

Once you've compared financial aid packages and the relative merits of the schools that have said yes, you may want to go back to one or more of the colleges to try to improve your package.

We are not saying that every family should try to better their deal. If you can comfortably afford the amount the college says you must pay, then there is little chance that the college is going to sweeten the deal—it must be pretty good already. College FAOs know just how fair the package they have put together for you is. If you are being greedy, you will not get much sympathy. It is also a good idea to remember that the average FAO is not making a great deal of money. Parents who whine about how tough it is to survive on $400,000 a year will get even less sympathy.

However, if you are facing the real prospect of not being able to send your child to the school she really wants to attend because of money, or if two similarly ranked colleges have offered radically different packages and your son really wants to go to the school with the low package, then you should sit down and map out your strategy.

Negotiate While You Still Have Leverage

After you've accepted the college's offer of admission, the college won't have much incentive to sweeten your deal, so you should plan to speak to the FAO while it is clear that you could still choose to go to another school. Similarly, you will not have much leverage if you show the FAO a rival offer from a much inferior college.

Try to make an objective assessment of how badly the college wants you. Believe us, the FAOs know exactly where each student fits into their scheme of things. We know of one college that keeps an actual list of prospective students in order of their desirability, which they refer to when parents call to negotiate. If a student just barely squeaked into the school, the family will not be likely to improve the package by negotiating. If a student is a shining star in one area or another, the FAOs will be much more willing to talk.

In the past few years, colleges—especially the selective ones—have become more flexible about their initial offer. Now that FAOs from the different colleges are limited in their ability to sit down together to compare offers to students, the "fudge factor" by which they are willing to improve an offer has increased. We heard one FAO urge a group of students to get in touch with her if they were considering another school. "Perhaps we overlooked something in your circumstances," she said. What she meant of course was, "Perhaps we want you so much we will be willing to increase our offer." This FAO represented one of the most selective schools in the country.

Be Prepared

Before calling, gather as much supporting evidence as possible. If you've received a better offer from a comparable school, have it in front of you when you call and be prepared to send a copy of the rival award letter to the school you are negotiating with. (They will probably ask to see it, which brings up another point: don't lie!)

If you feel that the school has not understood your financial circumstances, be ready to explain clearly what those special circumstances are (such as high margin debts or any other expenses that are not taken into account by the aid formula, support of an elderly relative, or unusually high unreimbursed business expenses). Any documentation you can supply will bolster your claim.

If your circumstances have changed since you filled out your need analysis form (for example, you have recently separated, divorced, been widowed, or lost your job), you should be frank and let the FAOs know.

Keep in mind that on the FAFSA, you are always required to report your "prior prior year" (PPY) income for the snapshot colleges use to determine your "need"—but colleges are permitted under U.S. Department of Education regulations (although not required) to use *another* 12-month period if they deem it more "representative" of the parent's current situation. How will the schools know they should consider using another 12-month period? By your telling them! If you are making less money, you should alert the individual schools. You could explain your changed circumstances in a letter—but probably the best thing to do is to wait until *after* you get a financial aid package to send that letter so that you can see what the initial offer based on the higher PPY income will be. Some schools may have an additional appeal form to complete.

If you are requesting that the school consider using another 12-month period, you'll need to be prepared to provide documentation. Some schools will want you to fill out special appeals forms they've created. Provide as much detail and documentation as you can so they understand your situation.

This doesn't mean you get to decide *which* 12-month period they use. However, you can always appeal and suggest another 12-month period (and by the way, it doesn't have to be a 12-month calendar year period).

All this is easier to accomplish if you are a salaried employee than if you are a freelancer whose income varies routinely. Because of the large number of parents who are expected to appeal this year, you should send in your appeal shortly after the financial aid package arrives.

The Call

Unless you live within driving distance of the school, your best negotiating tool is the telephone. The FAOs will find it hard to believe that you need more money if you can afford to fly to their college just to complain to them.

If possible, try to speak with the head FAO or one of the head FAO's assistants. Make sure you write down the name of whoever speaks to you. It is unlikely that he will make a concession on the telephone, so don't be disappointed if he says he will have to get back to you or if he asks you to send him something in writing.

Some telephone tips:

- Be cordial and frank. Like everyone, FAOs do not want to be yelled at and are much more likely to help you if you are friendly, businesslike, and organized.
- Have a number in your head. What would you like to get out of this conversation? If the FAO asks you, "All right, how much can you afford?" you do not want to hem and haw.
- Be reasonable. If the family contribution you propose has no relation to your SAI, you will lose most of your credibility with the FAO.
- Avoid confrontational language. Rather than start off with, "Match my other offer or else," just ask if there is anything they can do to improve the package. Also avoid using words such as "negotiate" or "bargain." You're better off saying you wish to "appeal" the award and then present your facts. Any new information not previously presented could bolster your case, especially if you can provide supporting documentation.
- If you are near a deadline, ask for an extension and be doubly sure you know the name of the person you are speaking to. Follow up the phone call with a letter (certified mail, return receipt requested) reminding the FAO of what was discussed in the conversation.
- Parents, not students, should negotiate with the FAOs. Some colleges actually have a question on their own financial aid forms in which the parents are asked if they will allow the colleges to speak to the student rather than the parents. Colleges prefer to speak to students because they are easier to browbeat.
- Read through this book again before you speak to the FAO. You'll never know as much about financial aid as she does, but at least you'll stand a good chance of knowing if she says something that isn't true.
- If you applied "early decision" to a college and that college accepts you, you are committed to attend, and you won't have much bargaining power to improve your aid package. If you applied and are accepted "early action," you are not required to attend that school, and it is in your interest to apply to several other schools in order to improve your bargaining position. We discuss both of these options in more detail in the "Special Topics" chapter.

The Worst They Can Say Is No

You risk nothing by trying to negotiate a better package. No matter how persistent you are, the school cannot take back their offer of admission, and the FAOs cannot take back their aid package unless you have misstated your financial details.

Accepting an Award

Accepting an award does not commit a student to attending that school. It merely locks in the award package in the event the student decides to attend that school. If you haven't decided between two schools, accept both packages. This will keep your options open for a little longer. Be careful not to miss the deadline to respond. Send your acceptance certified mail, return receipt requested, as always. Above all, don't reject any award until you have definitely decided which school the student is going to attend. If a school's aid package has not arrived yet, call the college to find out why it's late.

If you have been awarded state aid as part of the aid package at the school of your choice, but the award notice you received from the state agency lists the wrong college, you will have to file a form with the state agency to have the funds applied to the school you chose.

Now That You Have Chosen a School

By the time you have chosen a college, you will already be halfway through the second base income year. Now that you understand the ins and outs of financial aid, you will be able to plan ahead to minimize the apparent size of your income and assets and be in an even better position to fill out next year's need analysis forms. The first application for financial aid is the hardest, in part because you're dealing with a number of different schools, in part because it is a new experience. From now on, that first application will serve as a kind of template.

Chapter Seven

Innovative Payment Options

Innovative Options

We've already discussed the mainstream borrowing options and methods for paying for college. Over the years, colleges, private companies, public organizations, and smart individuals have come up with some alternative ways to pay for college. These ideas range from the commonsense to the high-tech, from good deals for the family to self-serving moneymakers for the colleges and institutions that came up with them. Here is a sampling.

Transfer in Later

Every year a few parents make an unfortunate decision: they send the student off to a college that didn't give them enough aid. After two years of tuition bills, they've spent their life savings, and the banks won't lend them any more money. The student is forced to transfer to a public university. The result? A diploma from the student's own State U. that could end up costing the family more than $175,000. The parents paid private school prices for a state school diploma.

What if they had done it the other way around? The student starts out at a state school, paying low prices. She does extremely well, compiling an outstanding academic record and soliciting recommendations from her professors. In junior year, she transfers to a prestigious private college. Even if the cost were exactly the same as in the previous example, she now has a diploma from the prestigious private school, at a savings of as much as $75,000 over the regular price.

This scenario won't work without the part about the "outstanding academic record." Prestigious private colleges will almost certainly not be interested in a transfer student with a B average or less. The other thing to bear in mind is that aid packages to transfer students are generally not as generous as those given to incoming freshmen.

Both of these points must be factored into a decision to start with a public college and transfer into a select private college. However, if a student really wants a diploma from that selective private college, and the family can't afford to send her for all four years, then this is a way for her to realize her dream. Anyone interested in this tactic should be sure to consult the individual schools to see how many transfer students are accepted per year, what kind of financial aid is available to them, and how many of the credits earned at the old college will be accepted by the new college.

Cooperative Education

Over 900 colleges let students combine a college education with a job in their field. Generally, the students spend alternate terms attending classes full-time and then working full-time at off-campus jobs with private companies or the federal government, although some students work and study at the same time. The students earn money for tuition while getting practical on-the-job experience in their areas of interest. This program differs from the Federal Work-Study Program in which the subsidized campus-based jobs are probably not within the student's area of interest, and take up only a small number of hours per week. After graduating, a high percentage of cooperative education students get hired permanently by the employers they worked for during school. Companies from every conceivable field participate in this program. The federal government is the largest employer of cooperative education students.

Getting a degree through the cooperative education program generally takes about five years, but the students who emerge from this program have a huge head start over their classmates; they already have valuable experience and a prospective employer in their field. They owe less money in student loans, and they are often paid more than a new hire.

If you are eligible for financial aid, you should contact the financial aid office at any college you are considering to determine the effect of cooperative earnings on your financial aid package.

Short-Term Prepayment

Recently, some colleges have been touting tuition prepayment as the answer to all the ills of higher education. In the short-term version of tuition prepayment, the parent pays the college the entire four years' worth of tuition (room and board are generally excluded) sometime shortly before the student begins freshman year. The college "locks in" the tuition rate for the entire four years. Regardless of how much tuition rises during the four years, the parent will not owe any more toward tuition.

Since most parents don't have four years of tuition in one lump sum, the colleges lend it to them. The parents pay back the loan with interest over a time period set in advance. The colleges love this arrangement, because it allows them to make a nice profit. If you pay the entire amount without borrowing, the colleges invest your money in taxable investments, which (because of their tax-exempt status) they don't have to pay taxes on. If you borrow the money from the college, they charge you interest on the money you borrow. Whatever course you pursue, the revenue the colleges earn from these prepayment plans more than make up for any tuition increases.

Is Prepayment a Good Idea for the Parent?

While the colleges may tell you that you will save money by avoiding tuition increases each year, your savings, if any, really depend on what interest rates are doing. If you would have to borrow the money to make the prepayment, the question to ask yourself is whether your after-tax cost of borrowing will be less than the tuition increases over the four years. If so, prepayment may make sense.

If you can afford to write a check for the entire amount of the prepayment, the question to ask yourself is whether the after-tax rate of return on your investments is higher than the rate at which tuition is increasing. If so, then prepayment makes no sense.

Any prepayment plan should be examined carefully. What happens if the student drops out after one year? What happens if the program is canceled after only two years? What is the interest rate on the loan you take out? Is the loan rate fixed or variable, and, if variable, what is the cap? These are a few of the questions you should ask before you agree to prepayment.

However, unless the interest rates are extremely low—*and will remain low over the four years your child is in college*—prepayment may end up costing you more money than paying as you go.

ROTC and the Service Academies

The Reserve Officer Training Corps has branches at many colleges. To qualify for ROTC scholarships you generally need to apply to the program early in the senior year of high school. Competition for these awards is keen, but if a student is selected, he or she will receive a full or partial scholarship plus a living allowance. The catch, of course, is that the student has to join the military for four years of active duty plus two more years on reserve. While on active duty, many students are allowed to go to graduate school on full scholarship. A student can join a ROTC program once he's entered college, but will not necessarily get a scholarship.

To qualify for the four-year scholarships, students must be U.S. citizens; have a high school diploma (or equivalent); at least a 2.5 GPA; an SAT score of 1000 (out of 1600) or an ACT score of 19; must pass a physical; and they must also impress an interviewer.

The service academies (the U.S. Military Academy at West Point and the U.S. Naval Academy at Annapolis are probably the best known) are extremely difficult to get into. Good grades are essential, as is a recommendation from a senator or a member of Congress. However, all this trouble may be worth it, for the service academies have a great reputation for the quality of their programs and they are absolutely free. Again, in exchange for this education, a student must agree to serve as an officer in the armed forces for several years.

Outside Scholarships

Opinions are divided about outside scholarships. The companies that sell scholarship databases say there are thousands of unclaimed scholarships sponsored by foundations, corporations, and other outside organizations just waiting to be found. Critics charge that very few scholarships actually go unclaimed each year, and that the database search companies are providing lists that families could get from government agencies, the local library, or the internet for free.

Certainly it must be said that many scholarships in the search services' databases are administered by the colleges themselves. There is almost never a need to "find" this type of scholarship. The colleges know they have this money available, and will match up the awards with candidates who meet the requirements attached to the awards. It is in the colleges' interest to award these "restricted" scholarships since this frees up unrestricted funds for other students. Every year, colleges award virtually *all* the scholarship money they have at their disposal.

It must also be pointed out that when you notify a college that you have won an outside scholarship (and if you are on financial aid you are required to tell the school how much you won), the college will often say thank you very much and deduct that amount from the aid package they have put together for you. As far as the colleges are concerned, your "need" just got smaller. Thus if you hunt down an obscure scholarship for red-haired flutists, it will often not really do you any monetary good. Your family contribution (what the colleges think you can afford to pay) will stay exactly the same. The FAOs will use the outside scholarship money to reduce your aid (often your grants).

This is not to say that there aren't circumstances when outside scholarships can help pay for college, but you must be prepared to fight. If you have found outside scholarships worth any significant amount, you should talk to the FAO in person or on the phone and point out that without your initiative, the college would have had to pay far more. Negotiate with the FAO. He may be willing to let you use part of the scholarship toward your family contribution, or at least he may improve your aid package's percentage of grants versus loans.

We've talked to people who've had terrible experiences with the scholarship search companies and we've talked to other people who swear by them. Just keep in mind that this type of aid accounts for less than 5% of the financial aid in the United States. Of course, 5% of the financial aid available in the United States is still a lot of money.

We do recommend, however, that you steer clear of any scholarship search firm that promises you'll get a scholarship or your fee will be refunded. These guarantees are not worth the paper they're printed on. When you read the fine print, you'll discover that you need to send them rejection letters from each and every scholarship source they recommended to you. Many of these donors don't have the time or the resources to tell you the bad news, so you'll never get the proof you need to claim your refund. The Federal Trade Commission has closed down a number of these firms after receiving numerous complaints from students and parents who didn't get their money back.

Innovative Loans

The very best type of loans, as we've said before, are the government-subsidized student loans. We've also already discussed home equity loans and margin loans (both of which reduce the appearance of your assets) as well as some of the more popular parent loan programs.

There is one other type of loan that can help you write the checks:

Borrow from Your 401(k) Plan or a Pension Plan

If you are totally without resources, the IRS may allow you to make an early withdrawal of money without penalty from a 401(k) plan to pay for education. However, rather than get to this desperate situation (which will increase your income taxes and raise your income for financial aid purposes), it would make a lot more sense for you to take out a loan from your 401(k) plan or from your pension plan.

Not all plans will allow this, but some will let you borrow *tax-free* as much as half of the money in your account, up to $50,000. There are no penalties, and this way you are not irrevocably depleting your retirement fund. You're merely borrowing from yourself; in many cases, the interest you pay on the loan actually goes back into your own account. Generally, the loan must be repaid within five years. However, if you lose your job or change your employer, this loan will become due immediately, so you should exercise some caution before you proceed.

This kind of borrowing will not decrease your assets as far as the FAOs are concerned because assets in retirement provisions are not assessed anyway. However, if you've come to this point, your non-retirement assets are probably already fairly depleted.

A self-employed individual can borrow from a Keogh plan, but there will almost certainly be penalties, and the loan will be treated as a taxable distribution. Loans against IRAs are not currently permitted.

Loans Forgiven

A few colleges have programs under which some of your student loans may be forgiven if you meet certain conditions. At Cornell University, for example, Tradition Fellows, who hold jobs while they are in college, are given awards that replace their student loans by up to $4,000 per year in acknowledgment of their work ethic. Even federal loans can be forgiven under certain circumstances. Head Start, Peace Corps, or VISTA volunteers may not have to repay all of their federal loans, for example.

Moral Obligation Loans

Here's a novel idea: the college makes a loan to the student, and the student agrees to pay back the loan. That's it. There is no *legal* obligation to pay back the money. The student has a moral obligation to repay. Several schools have decided to try this, and the results, of course, won't be in for some time. At the moment, when a student repays the loan, the repayment is considered a tax-deductible charitable contribution. The IRS will probably have closed that loophole by the time your child is ready to take advantage of it. Nevertheless, this is a wonderful deal because it allows the student flexibility in deciding when to pay the loan back, and does not affect the child's credit rating. If your college is offering this option, grab it.

Payment Plans and Financing Options

Many families have difficulty coming up with their Family Contribution in one lump sum each semester. There are a number of commercial organizations that will assist you with spreading the payment out over time. Some of these programs are financing plans that charge interest and involve repayment over a number of years. Others are simply payment plans in which you make 10 or 12 monthly payments during the year. These plans may require you to begin making payments in May or June prior to the start of the fall semester. A nominal fee (about $50) is usually charged for these plans. Many schools have developed their own deferred payment plans as well. These programs can vary tremendously from college to college.

The college financial aid office or bursar's office should be able to provide you with information regarding all your payment options, as well as the names of those commercial plans (if any) that can be used at their school. Be sure to read the fine print before you sign up for any of these programs.

Tuition Refund Insurance

Writing that check for the first tuition bill is a sobering experience for most families. Given the large outlay of funds involved, it may make sense to take out a tuition refund insurance policy to protect yourself if the student is forced to withdraw in the middle of a term. Most colleges do give partial refunds when a student has to withdraw. How much money you get back from the college itself depends on how far into the term the student is when he/she withdraws, as well as the policies of the individual school. (There are no federal regulations governing how much money must be refunded, if any.)

Tuition refund insurance—also known as tuition insurance—is designed to make up the difference. For an insurance premium of normally $350 to $500 per academic year, you can have peace of mind that any non-refunded payments for tuition and possibly room and board are not a total loss.

Bear in mind that if the student withdraws midway through the term—regardless of the reason—the school will probably not permit the student to finish the coursework after the semester is over. More than likely, the only option will be to re-enroll for the course in a future term.

For medically-related withdrawals you can often get up to 100% of what the college doesn't refund if you have taken out a tuition refund insurance policy. For mental health issues, you can often get up to 60 or 70%. Some policies also offer coverage if the student is forced to withdraw for other reasons—such as a death in the family or an employment-related relocation of the parents. Keep in mind that as the academic term progresses, you will get back less money from the school. So if there are issues that make the student's ability to complete the term unlikely, it makes sense to make a decision sooner rather than later—and to notify the school through the proper channels and withdraw relatively quickly.

Of course, if the student is at a lower-priced state school or is getting a lot of financial aid, tuition refund insurance makes less sense. But at the very least, you should carefully review the college's refund policy. And if you are considering purchasing a policy, you should be sure to read all the fine print since some refund policies will not pay a benefit if the student withdraws due to a pre-existing medical condition that was present within a certain time period before the policy was purchased.

National Service

One of the nontraditional methods of educational financing has been the AmeriCorps program (www.Americorps.gov). Since it was established in 1994 during the Clinton administration, more than a quarter million individuals have participated in this national service program designed to encourage young people to serve in educational, environmental, or police programs or in programs to assist the elderly or the homeless. In return for taking part in national service, a participant receives training, a living allowance at the minimum wage, health insurance, child care, and up to $6,495 per year in educational grants.

While we think this is a generally great idea, the program in its current form has a few problems from a financial aid standpoint. First, if a student joins this program after he or she has graduated, the student will not be able to use money from this program to pay college bills directly. Students would have to come up with the money in the first place. Only later could AmeriCorps grants be used to pay back loans that the student had taken out along the way. Second, with a maximum of only $6,495 per year in grant money, national service may not be the most economically efficient way for a student to pay back student loans. Unless national service appeals to you for altruistic reasons, you may be able to repay loans faster by taking a job outside of AmeriCorps and putting yourself on a minimum wage allowance. Finally, for students who participate in the program prior to college and who demonstrate need when they apply for financial aid, the AmeriCorps grants may simply reduce those students' "need" in the aid formulas and not the family contribution. This is why many higher education organizations have criticized references to national service as a student aid program. As we went to print, an executive order was in place to eliminate this program, but the court had issued a stay on that termination. Once this has been resolved, we will provide an update in your online student tools; see page vi for instructions on how to access these for free.

Marketing Gimmicks Arrive on Campus

Some colleges have begun incentives that owe more to the world of retailing than to the world of the ivory tower. Among the offers you may find:

- discounts for bringing in a friend
- rebates for several family members attending at the same time
- discounts for older students
- reduced prices for the first semester so you can see if you like it
- option of charging your tuition on a credit card

Chapter Eight

Managing Your Debt

For many people, there is really no choice: if you or your child want a college education, you have to go into debt. But it turns out that there are a number of choices to make about how you go into debt and how you eventually pay it off. Most parents and students assume they have no control over the loan process. Unfortunately, this assumption may cost them thousands of dollars.

In previous chapters, we've discussed the different kinds of loans that are available. Of course, the most common types of loans are a Direct Loan (for undergraduate and graduate/professional school students), a PLUS Loan (for parents of undergraduates), and a GradPLUS Loan (for graduate/professional school students), all of which are different types of federal education loans that are part of the William D. Ford Federal Direct Loan Program. Direct Loans for students used to be known as Stafford Loans, and such Direct Loans may still be referenced by their former name.

In this chapter, we'll provide more information on how to select the best loans, as well as how to pay off these loans once you are required to do so.

Please check your free online student tools (see page vi), as there may be updates on this topic as a result of late-breaking developments.

As usual, this advice comes with our standard caveat: we can't recommend any specific course of action since we don't know your specific situation. These strategies are only meant to steer you in the right direction. Please consult with your accountant or a financial aid planner.

Before You Borrow

Smart financial planning dictates that you always borrow at the lowest possible cost. So the first type of loan to consider is usually the subsidized Direct Loan. For Direct Loans originated during the 2026–2027 school year, the rate will be fixed for the life of the loan at 6.52% for an undergraduate student's Direct Loan and at 8.07% for a graduate/professional student's Direct Loan.

As far as loans go, this is a great deal since the government pays the interest on a subsidized Direct Loan while a student is in school. And if you wish to pay off a subsidized Direct Loan before the student leaves school, graduates, or drops below half-time enrollment, no interest will be charged at all. Be aware that only an undergraduate student may now be eligible for a subsidized Direct Loan.

Next in desirability is the unsubsidized Direct Loan. Unlike the subsidized Direct Loan, the unsubsidized Direct Loan charges the student interest from day one. The decision whether or not to take out this type of loan depends on other factors. For example, let's say you have funds for school in a bank account that's earning 1% in a bank; in that case, it makes no sense to take out a loan in which you're paying more interest than you're earning by keeping those funds in a bank. Conversely, if you don't have the funds to pay for school, and other loans would carry a higher interest rate, then the unsubsidized Direct Loan makes sense.

And for paying the education expenses of a dependent undergraduate student, the last federal loan option available is the PLUS loan—in which one of the student's parents is the borrower. With interest charged from the time the loan funds are disbursed at a fixed rate that is higher than the fixed rate for an unsubsidized Direct Loans, this is the costliest of the federal education loan options.

There are two other types of loans available which can be broken down into two categories: the first is offered by state educational financing authorities such as MEFA in Massachusetts or CHESLA in Connecticut. Depending on the eligibility criteria, some of these loans allow state residents to borrow funds for schools both in-state and out-of-state. Some also make such loans available if an out-of-state student is attending a participating school within the state that offers the loan. Most have a fixed-rate option that is sometimes lower than some federal loan options. The second category involves private alternative loans, generally offered by banks or other private lenders. While these mostly variable rate-loans can start out lower than the Federal options, if interest rates rise appreciably they can become very costly. And unlike housing debt, in which you can convert a variable rate home equity line of credit into a fixed-rate loan before interest rates start to rise, these education loans normally cannot be refinanced with another fixed-rate education loan.

But what if you're an independent undergraduate student? The first two most attractive options offered above—that is, a Direct Loan and then a state loan, which may well require a co-signer if you need additional funds above the Direct Loan annual borrowing amount—should be considered in the same hierarchy. Compared to most dependent undergraduate students, independent undergrads can borrow an additional $4,000 for each of the first two years and an additional $5,000/year for the third year and beyond via the Direct Loan program should additional funds be needed. Though as explained earlier (see Part 4, "The Different Types of Financial Aid in Detail"), these additional amounts per year will be unsubsidized. But that's it for federal education loans for independent undergrads, since there are officially no parents in the picture who can take out PLUS loans. Even if a parent of an independent undergraduate wants to take out a PLUS loan for their child, they cannot do so since PLUS loans are only for parents of dependent students.

What about graduate students? Beginning with the 2012–2013 academic year, graduate and professional school students are no longer able to take out subsidized Direct Loans. They can still take out unsubsidized Direct Loans (up to $20,500 per year, and possibly even more for health profession students), but the up-to-$8,500 subsidized Stafford that existed in 2011–2012 and before is no longer available. However, all unsubsidized Direct Loans for graduate students will continue to have a fixed-interest rate—albeit at a higher rate than for undergrads. (8.07% for new loans originated during the 2026–2027 academic year.)

Graduate School Considerations

Those considering going on to graduate school, which for purposes of this chapter will include any professional school such as a law school, medical school, business school (MBA), etc., should consider borrowing the maximum amount of subsidized Direct Loans for which they are eligible as an undergraduate. This is because any money you borrow for graduate or professional school will have interest charged from the get-go. So you would be better off preserving funds in your nest egg while the student is an undergraduate, and using them instead in graduate school when the cost of borrowing is higher.

And what if you're taking time out for a few years between an undergraduate program and graduate school? With a subsidized Direct Loan no longer available to graduate students, one would be better off making minimum payments on their education loans, possibly by choosing a repayment option other than the standard one (which we'll cover shortly). Provided you have the discipline.

When you go back to school, the amount of any subsidized Stafford, Perkins, and Direct Loans that qualify for an in-school deferment will be frozen at the amount owed when you return to school until you graduate, leave school, or drop below half-time status.

So you're better off stockpiling the cash for graduate school, rather than paying off these loans quickly. This will reduce your overall interest charges. And you'll also minimize or even avoid origination fees on new loans by borrowing less for graduate school or not borrowing at all. And if you are borrowing less for graduate school, the weighted average of all the loans together will ensure a lower overall rate than if you pay off lower-interest loans early and then have to take out higher-interest loans such as a 8.07% unsubsidized Direct Loan (for graduate/professional students) or a 9.07% GradPLUS loan (which we will soon discuss). These fixed rates are for new loans first disbursed between July 1, 2026 and June 30, 2027.

Note: For your prior loans to again qualify for an in-school deferment, you will have to go back to the holders/servicers of your prior federal education loans and let them know you're back in school. You will also have to meet all other criteria based on your enrollment status. Each loan holder/servicer will send you a form to be completed by the school you will be attending, so that you'll again be eligible for the in-school deferment to suspend payments while in school and so that the government will again pay all the interest on any subsidized Stafford or Subsidized Direct Loans as well as any Perkins loans while in school.

Certain Graduate/Professional school students are eligible for two federal loans: the Direct Loan and the GradPLUS loan (which is only available to those who already had a Direct or GradPLUS loan originated prior to July 1, 2026 for their school's same program of study and who meet other conditions to be grandfathered under the OBBBA's Interim Exemption, explained in further detail in your Student Tools). Unlike independent undergraduate students, grandfathered graduate or professional students can therefore borrow their entire cost of attendance via the federal education loan programs if no other aid is awarded. Note: Similar to a parent taking out a PLUS loan, a student borrowing through a GradPLUS loan must pass a credit test or have an eligible creditworthy cosigner to obtain the loan. Perkins and Direct Loans do not require any such credit test.

Note: As of now, no new Perkins loans can be originated or disbursed.

How to Pay Off Your Loans

As soon as a student graduates, the clock starts ticking. The government gives you a six-month grace period to find a job and catch your breath—and then the bills start arriving. You might think that at least this part of the process would be straightforward: they send you a bill, you pay. But in fact, there are a bewildering number of repayment options, as well as opportunities, to postpone and defer payment.

Overriding all of this is one simple maxim: the longer you take to pay, the more it costs you. Putting it in practical terms, choosing to lower your monthly payments will stretch out the amount of time you'll be making these payments, and ultimately add thousands of dollars in interest to your bill. Sometimes this is worth it, as we'll see.

It's impossible for us to predict exactly what your monthly payments will be, since everyone owes different amounts, and borrowed on different terms. Just to give you a ballpark figure, someone who owes $15,000, at an average rate of 8% would have 120 monthly payments of about $182. Someone who owes $50,000 would have 120 monthly payments of about $607.

The only way to defer these student loan payments long-term is to stay in school. As long as you are at least a half-time student at an approved post-secondary school, you can keep those bills at bay forever. If you get a job and then later decide to go on to graduate school, your loan payments may be deferred while you are in graduate school, and resume as soon as you get out.

Above All, Avoid Default

When all the loans come due, and a few personal crises loom as well, there's a very human urge to shove the bills in a drawer and hope for the best. This is absolutely the worst possible thing you can do.

The default rate on government guaranteed student loans is still somewhat high at the moment. This might give you the erroneous impression that a default is no big deal. You should realize that a large portion of defaulted loans comes not from college loans, but from loans made to students of "bogus" trade schools with three initials and two faces. These trade schools are often scam operations designed to fleece the federal government by preying on immigrants and poor people. A new arrival to this country may not care about or understand the importance of his credit rating, but you certainly do.

When people get into economic trouble, they tend to get very reticent, and often don't ask for help. Even though you may feel embarrassed, it is much better to call your lender and explain the situation than to miss a payment with no explanation.

As you will see, there are so many different payment options that there is really no need for anyone ever to go into default. If you lose a job, or "encounter economic hardship," you should apply for a temporary deferment (suspension of principal and interest payments for a specified time) or something called *forbearance,* which can include temporary suspension of payments, a time extension to make payment—even a temporary reduction in the amount of monthly installments. Many lenders will draw up new repayment plans, or accept a missed payment as long as you inform them ahead of time.

Work *with* the lender. Or rather, lenders. If you have loans from more than one lender (the Perkins loans are administered separately from the Stafford or Direct Loans), one lender isn't necessarily going to know what's happening with the other, unless you tell them.

It can take years to build up a good credit rating again once you've loused it up. Meanwhile, you may not be able to get credit cards, a mortgage, or a car loan. And if you're in default, getting additional loans for graduate school can be difficult, if not impossible.

The Different Payment Plans

If you are repaying Perkins loans, Stafford loans, Direct Loans, Supplemental Loans for Students (SLS), PLUS, or Grad PLUS loans, there are up to seven repayment options at present. When you pick an option, it is not for life. You can switch payment plans at any time. Here is a brief summary of the current options. If these change during budget reconciliation, we will provide updates in your online student tools; see page vi for instructions on how to access these for free. For more details, contact your lender(s).

Standard repayment: The loans must be repaid in equal installments spread out over up to 10 years. This is a good plan for people who have relatively little debt, or have enough income to afford the relatively high payments.

Extended repayment: The loans must be repaid in equal installments over a period that can extend up to 25 years. The increased time period reduces monthly payments, but long-term interest expenses go up dramatically.

Graduated repayment: Loan payments start out low and increase over time. The payments must always at least equal the monthly interest that's accruing. This is a good plan for young people whose earnings are low, but are expected to increase over time. Over the lifetime of the loan, interest expenses are much higher.

Income-sensitive repayment: This option allows payments that are initially low, but increase as income rises. The lender works with the borrower to establish a payment schedule that reflects the borrower's current income. The payments are adjusted annually to accommodate changes in the borrower's income. This option is available only to borrowers who took out Stafford, PLUS, or Grad PLUS loans from private lenders years ago.

Income contingent repayment: This option is available only to borrowers with federal Direct Loans but does not cover parent PLUS loans. In this plan, the payments are based on a combination of the borrower's level of debt and current income. With this (and the following two options), payments can be lower than the monthly interest accruing (which is called *negative amortization*). Of course, this can add substantially to the final cost of long-term interest expenses. To counter this, at the end of 25 years, the government will forgive any unpaid balance. But don't start jumping for joy: the IRS may tax you on this unpaid balance. Thus, if the government were to forgive a $10,000 remaining debt, a person in the 25 percent tax bracket would have to come up with at least $2,500 in additional taxes that year.

Income-based repayment and **Pay As You Earn:** Under these options, the required monthly payment will be based on your income during any period when you have a partial financial hardship. The monthly payment may be adjusted annually. The maximum repayment period under these plans may exceed 10 years. If you meet certain requirements over a specified period of time, you may qualify for cancellation of any outstanding balance. The amount of any loan canceled may be subject to income taxes. Parent PLUS Loans are not eligible. Only Direct Loans qualify for Pay As You Earn.

Loan Consolidation

Government regulations allow you to consolidate all your education loans from different sources into one big loan—often with lower monthly payments than you were making before. As usual, the catch is that the repayment period is extended, meaning that you end up paying a lot more in interest over the increased life of the loan. However, you can always prepay your loans without penalty.

The loans that can be consolidated are: the Stafford, Direct Loans, SLS, Perkins, PLUS loans, GradPLUS loans, and loans issued by the government's programs for health-care professionals. You can't consolidate private loans from colleges or other sources in the federal consolidation program.

How It Works

A consolidation loan can be paid back using one of the plans outlined above. In some cases, loan consolidation doesn't make sense—for example, if you are almost done paying off your loans. For the most part, student loans can be consolidated only once, and in most cases, it would be better to wait to do this until a student is completely finished with school.

You also don't have to consolidate all your loans. The rules on how your new interest rate will be calculated change constantly, so you'll need to get up-to-date information from your lender.

Before you consolidate any loans, you should also consider these factors:

- How will the interest rate be calculated?
- Are you better off excluding some loans from consolidation to get a better rate and/or to prevent the loss of some benefits with some of your loans?
- Will consolidating your loans later give you a better or a worse interest rate?
- Can you consolidate your loans(s) more than once?
- Do you have to consolidate your loans with a private lender? Do you have to consolidate your loans directly with the government? If you have a choice between the two, which consolidation plan is the best deal for you?
- If you are consolidating unsubsidized and subsidized loans together, will this affect your ability to have the government pay the interest on your subsidized loans should you go back to school?

Loan Discharge and Cancellation

The Direct Loan, the GradPLUS, and the PLUS loan programs have various provisions in which the loan can be discharged or canceled. While some provisions hopefully do not happen to you in the near future (e.g. you become permanently disabled or die), loans may also be forgiven for performing certain types of service (teaching in low-income areas, law enforcement, nursing, working with disabled or high risk children and their families in low-income communities, etc.).

One of the provisions of the College Cost Reduction and Access Act has expanded Direct Loan forgiveness in exchange for public service. Borrowers who take public sector jobs in the government, the military, certain non-profit tax-exempt organizations, law enforcement, public health, or education, may be eligible—after making 120 on-time payments after October 1, 2007—to have the remaining balance of their Direct Loans forgiven. Direct GradPLUS and Direct PLUS loans can also be eligible for this program known as Public Service Loan Forgiveness (PSLF).

Those with Stafford loans borrowed through banks (not borrowed through the Direct Loan program from the government via the financial office of your school) may be able to take advantage of this new provision by consolidating, or even re-consolidating, into a Direct Consolidation Loan.

The Smartest Loan Strategy

All federally guaranteed education loans can be prepaid without any penalty. This means that by paying just a little more than your monthly payment each month, you can pay down the loan much faster than you might have thought possible, and save yourself a bundle in interest.

Obviously, if you're going to do this, try to prepay the loans with the highest interest rates first. It wouldn't make sense to prepay your 5% Perkins loan if you're paying 10% on an unsecured bank loan, or 12% on some huge credit card bill.

However if you are eligible for the Public Service Loan Forgiveness (PSLF) program that we just discussed, prepaying loans does NOT make sense. You want to pay the least amount of money with PSLF because, after 10 years, the remaining balance will be forgiven. But because it takes 10 years before your loans are eligible to be forgiven, it is critical that you understand all the requirements before you go into repayment as there is plenty of fine print. For example, only loans in the Direct Loan Program are eligible for discharge. These are the Direct Loan—which is confusing because it is not the only loan in the William D. Ford Direct Loan Program—and the Direct GradPLUS Loan (both for students) as well as the parent PLUS Loan. Being in the wrong repayment plan can disqualify you, as can many other things if you do not understand all the rules in advance. Many borrowers have learned the hard way that after 10 years of repayment, they are ineligible to get tens of thousands of dollars forgiven simply because of some technicality many years earlier. You don't want to be another one of them, so you need to do your homework to benefit from the PSLF program.

Chapter Nine

Special Topics

Divorced or Separated Parents

The breakup of a marriage is always painful, and some parents are understandably reluctant to share their pain with strangers. We know of one set of parents who went through four years of need analysis forms without ever telling the college that they were divorced. Unfortunately, by not telling the schools about the divorce, those parents lost out on a great deal of financial aid and put themselves through unnecessary hardships in paying for college.

No matter how painful or unusual your personal situation is, the FAOs have heard worse, and you will find that being upfront about such problems as refusal by a former spouse to pay alimony or to supply needed financial aid data to the schools will make the financial aid process easier. While the FAOs are quite expert at understanding the convoluted and intricate family relationships that arise out of divorce or separation, you will find that the aid formula itself tries to fit these complex relationships into a few simple categories. The result is completely baffling to most parents.

Who Are the Parents Required to Report Financial Information on These Aid Forms?

The formula doesn't really care who the biological or adoptive parents of a student are. Ultimately, the formula wants to know only which parent provided the greater portion of financial support for the student completing the FAFSA. This parent gets the honor of completing the standardized need analysis form. And according to federal guidelines, it is this parent whose financial information will be used to determine the parents' contribution to college.

Soap Opera Digest

Let's say that Mr. and Mrs. Jackson separated two years ago. Their only daughter Jill receives the majority of her support from Mr. Jackson and will be attending college next year. While some standardized aid forms may ask a few vague questions about Mrs. Jackson, as far as the federal financial aid formula is concerned, Mr. Jackson is the only parent whose income and assets are to be reported on the FAFSA. This counts as a family of two under the aid formula.

Let's say that Mr. Jackson gets a divorce from Mrs. Jackson and then marries another woman, Francine. The aid formula will now want to look at the assets and income of Mr. Jackson *and* the assets and income of his new wife as well. The instructions to the need analysis form will tell Mr. Jackson to provide information about himself as well as Francine, even if he just married her last week. Francine's income and assets will be assessed just as heavily as Mr. Jackson's, even if she didn't meet Jill until the day of the wedding, and even if they signed a prenuptial agreement stating that she would not be responsible for Jill's college expenses. This is now a family of three in the eyes of the FAOs, assuming Mr. Jackson has continued to provide the greater portion of Jill's financial support.

What if Mr. Jackson's new wife has a 10-year-old child of her own, Denise, from a previous marriage, who will also come to live with Mr. Jackson and be considered Mr. Jackson's and Francine's "dependent" child? Now there is a family of four. Neither of the *previous* spouses will be considered for assessment by the federal formula. When it comes time for Denise's college education, Mr. Jackson's assets and income will be assessed just as heavily as Francine's, provided Mr. Jackson and Francine provided the greater portion of Denise's financial support.

Let's suppose that Mr. Jackson also had a son, James, from a much earlier marriage. The son has never lived with him, but Mr. Jackson provides for more than half his support and James is boarding away year-round while in college. Even though the son has never lived with him, James is considered part of Mr. Jackson's family by the federal guidelines because Mr. Jackson provides for more than half his support and James is living apart from Mr. Jackson because of college enrollment. We now have a family of five for aid purposes.

Since James is attending college, he would also be included as part of the number of family members attending "college, graduate/professional school, or other post-secondary school." This could help to reduce the Jacksons' family contribution for Jill's college expenses, even though the SAI is no longer reduced by the multiple student adjustment (see Chapter 3).

Number of Dependents

As you know from reading the rest of this book, the more family members you can include on the need analysis form, the lower your SAI will be. This number will not necessarily coincide with the number of dependents you claim on your tax return. Let's say you have a son applying for financial aid who receives more than half support from you, but your spouse claims him as a dependent on the IRS Form 1040 because of a divorce agreement. This other parent is entitled to claim your son as a dependent, and you are not. You will have one more member of your family than you have dependents. The colleges are used to this situation. You may have to explain, and possibly provide documentation, but they will understand.

In either case, when it is time for college, you'll list financial information on the FAFSA in your "role" as the "parent," and your ex will not be assessed by the federal financial aid formula.

A Quick Summary

Because parents find all this so confusing, and because the information they receive from others is often contradictory or misleading, we're going to summarize the key points:

1. The parent who provides the greater portion of financial support for the student completing the FAFSA is considered the "Parent." This parent is not necessarily the parent who was initially awarded custody in the divorce agreement.

2. Siblings (including stepsiblings and half-siblings) can be considered part of the custodial parents' household provided they

    a. are a "dependent child" who lives with the Parent *or*

    b. are a "dependent child" who lives apart from the Parent due to college enrollment.

3. A stepparent who resides with the custodial parent will be treated in the federal methodology as if he/she were the natural parent. On the FAFSA, this stepparent will have the role of the "Other Parent."

Read the instructions carefully when you complete the aid forms. If a college challenges your application by trying to disallow some members of your household, don't automatically assume that they are right and you are wrong. When you speak to the FAO, refer to the section in the instructions to the aid form on which you based your decision.

Will an Ex-Husband or Ex-Wife's Assets and Income Ever Be Used to Determine the Family Contribution?

Parents are always concerned that the colleges will look at the other biological or adoptive parent's income and assets and decide that the student is ineligible for aid, even if the ex-spouse refuses to help pay for college.

The vast majority of colleges will never even ask to see income or asset information from a parent who is not required to supply financial information on the FAFSA. While the CSS Profile form asks a few questions about the other biological or adoptive parent, the processor does not take this information into account when calculating the parent contribution for that student's CSS Profile, completed by the same parent who was the "Parent" on the FAFSA, and most colleges will not take the matter any further. (Of course, if you received alimony or child support from your ex, this will appear as part of your financial information.)

However, a number of colleges do require that you fill out their own supplemental forms. Some schools that use the CSS Profile form will require that a separate aid form be completed by the other biological or adoptive parent. The colleges that ask for this information tend to be the most selective, including all the Ivy League schools. If your child applies to one of these schools, you may find that the other biological or adoptive parent's income and assets will indeed have a bearing on how much a college ultimately decides your family contribution ought to be.

Even if this is the case, you should not lose heart. Some types of aid must, by law, be awarded without reference to the student's other biological or adoptive parent. These include the Pell Grant, the Direct Loan, and some forms of state aid.

As of the 2005–2006 CSS Profile, some schools have required the student's other biological or adoptive parent to complete a separate CSS Profile form. Details about this online form will be provided at some point at the beginning of the CSS Profile process. Other schools may still choose to accept or require their own form which, following completion, should then be sent directly to the financial aid office of any school that requires it.

To find out if any additional forms are required, consult the college's own financial aid instructions on the aid office's website.

What If the Ex-Husband or Ex-Wife Refuses to Fill Out the Form?

Most schools that require financial information about former spouses will not process your application for aid until you have supplied *all* the information they requested. If your ex refuses to supply the information you need to apply for aid, you have two options.

First, try to use reason. Your ex may be worried that merely by filling out the form, he/she is accepting legal responsibility for paying for college. Point out to your former spouse that on the form they are to complete, there is a question that asks, "How much are you willing to pay?" By writing down "0," the parent expresses a clear desire to be left out of this responsibility.

It is also worth noting that even if a college decides to assess the other biological or adoptive income or assets, this does not mean that the parent will ever get a bill from the college. Yes, the family contribution will probably be larger, but the bill for tuition will go, as always, to the student or the parent who provided their financial information on the FAFSA. There is no legal obligation for the ex-husband or ex-wife to help pay for college unless an agreement was signed beforehand.

The second option, if that parent refuses to cooperate, is to get a waiver from the colleges. Each college that requires financial information from that parent will establish their own waiver request procedures. The FAOs can decide at *their* discretion to waive this requirement if it is really clear that that individual can never be persuaded to help. You are going to have to make a strong case to get colleges to give you that waiver. This is the time to pull out all the dirty laundry—alcoholism, physical or mental abuse, chemical dependency, abandonment, chronic unemployment, and so on. Send the FAO the required item(s) presenting your case, and include any documentation from agencies or third parties (such as an attorney, guidance counselor, or member of the clergy) that supports your case. Follow up with a phone call, and do this as soon as possible after you've decided to apply. Any information you supply will be confidential and will not go farther than the financial aid office. This will *not* jeopardize your child's chances for admission. It may, however, get you the aid you need to send your child to the school.

Is There an Agreement Specifying a Contribution from an Ex?

You may find this question included on your need analysis form. Be very careful how you answer it. If there is an agreement, and you have every reason to expect that your ex will honor that agreement, then say yes and give the figure. However, if there is a *disagreement* as to what your ex originally agreed to provide, then it would be calamitous to say yes. The colleges will assess your ability to pay based in part on this figure. If your ex then refused to pay, you would be in bad shape. If you are not sure you can count on your ex-spouse to provide the promised money, then write "no" on the form and write a letter explaining the situation to the various colleges.

The Other Biological/Adoptive Parent's Information

You should NEVER send this data to a school unless it is required. Read the individual college's financial aid instructions carefully. Some always require it, while others want it only if you've recently divorced or separated or if your ex has claimed the child as a tax deduction in the past few years. The information on this form should agree with that on any other forms that have already been sent in—the need analysis form and tax returns. If you and your ex still have assets held in common, make sure that your proportionate shares of these assets as reported on your need analysis forms add up to the whole. Alimony and child support figures should also agree.

Remarriage

A stepparent's income and assets will be assessed by the FAOs just as severely as if he/she were the natural parent—even if there is a prenuptial agreement to the contrary. This being the case, it may make sense to postpone marriage plans until after your child is out of the base income years. A couple that decided just to live together while their children were in college might easily save enough money to take a round-the-world honeymoon cruise when it was all over.

Note: a few colleges give you the option of using the financial information of either your former spouse or your new spouse to determine eligibility for the school's own grant money.

The Difference Between Being Divorced, Legally Separated, or Just Separated

For financial aid purposes, there is absolutely no difference provided you are living apart. If you are not legally separated, you may be asked to provide documentation to show that you no longer live together.

If You Are in the Process of Separating or Getting a Divorce

We have actually known of cases in which a couple separated or divorced in order to get more financial aid. This is taking the pursuit of free money way too far. We know of another couple that pretended to separate to qualify for more aid. Aside from the moral implications (you have to wonder what kind of warped view of life the children will bring away from that experience), this is also illegal.

However, if your situation has become impossible, and there is absolutely no choice but to separate, then you should try to take financial aid into account as you consider your legal options. An agreement by the soon-to-be ex-spouse to provide for your child's education could be an expensive mistake.

Let's say that a father formally agrees to pay $10,000 per college year for his daughter's education. Many colleges will say thank you very much and decrease their aid packages by $10,000. If this is an amicable separation, it might be better if no agreement were made on paper. The father could then voluntarily gift money during the year, thus preventing any loss of aid eligibility. If the separation is not amicable, and the mother is afraid she will never see the money unless there is an agreement in writing, it would be infinitely better if the father made one lump-sum payment to the mother toward college. In this way, the money becomes part of her overall assets, which can be assessed at up to only 5.65% a year. If a significant amount of money is involved, it would be best to consult with a professional, due to the "greater portion of financial support" criteria involving which parent needs to fill out the FAFSA.

Avoid Acrimony

A couple in the midst of splitting up is not always in the most rational frame of mind. It is essential, however, that you try to keep your heads clear, and prevent the education of your children from becoming one more brickbat to hurl back and forth.

Cooperation is the most important part of the process. We have seen parents childishly miss financial aid deadlines just to spite their former spouse. The person who really loses out when this happens, of course, is the child.

Transfer Students and Graduate Students

The process of applying for financial aid as a transfer student or a graduate student is very similar to applying for aid as a freshman in college. However, there are a few differences that should be discussed:

- Deadlines for transfer and graduate students are often different from the deadlines for regular undergrads. Check your applications carefully for the specific deadlines.

- If you have previously attended any colleges, you may need a financial aid transcript sent from each one of them to the schools you are applying to, especially if you are transferring during the middle of the academic year. A financial aid transcript is not the same thing as a transcript of your academic record (which you will probably need as well). You will have to send financial aid transcripts even if you received no financial aid from the previous schools.

The colleges want to look at these records in part to see what kind of a deal you were getting at your previous school, and in part to see how much you've already borrowed, for there are aggregate limits to certain types of aid.

The best way to go about getting financial aid transcripts is to pick up blank copies from the school to which you are applying, which come already addressed, ready to be sent back to the school. You can then mail these forms to the schools you previously attended. You'll have to keep on top of the process to make sure the transcripts are sent. The records offices at colleges are often worse than the motor vehicle bureau.

- Some colleges have separate aid policies for transfer students. Often, priority is given to students who began as first-year students. This is particularly true if a student transfers in the middle of the year; the FAOs will have already committed the bulk of their funds for that school year.

- It may help if you have some kind of bargaining chip—for example, if there is another school that is also interested in you. Your *previous* school won't be much of a bargaining chip since you have probably already given them a compelling reason for why you wanted to leave.

- It will certainly help if you've maintained a high grade point average. In particular, students who are transferring to a "designer label" college from a less well-known school will need good grades and good recommendations.

Graduate and Professional School Financial Aid Tips

Graduate and professional school aid is parceled out in much the same way as college aid but the ratio of grants to loans to work-study is unfortunately very different. Grant money is less plentiful.

The paperwork you will be asked to fill out varies widely. All schools require the FAFSA, but many schools will also require the CSS Profile form or some other aid form that asks questions similar to the CSS Profile form.

Fortunately, all graduate school students will find they now meet the federal government's independent student test. If you are a graduate student, you are independent by definition for federal aid purposes—even if your parents still claim you as a dependent on their tax returns and you still live at home.

However, a few of the very selective schools will insist on seeing parent information anyway. The Harvard Law School FAOs, for example, require parents' financial data even if the student is 28 years old and the parents have long since retired to the Sun Belt. Though the schools may refuse to give you any of their own money, you can still qualify for federal loans since you meet the federal regulations for independent status.

If you are planning on law school, medical school, or business school, taking on large amounts of debt is, although unpleasant, possible for many individuals. However, if you are planning on, say, a PhD in philosophy, you should be very cautious about borrowing large amounts of money. An alternative to borrowing is to find gift aid that is not administered by the financial aid office—in graduate school, some fellowships are administered by department heads instead. In addition, students sometimes find opportunities to teach or work on professors' grant projects.

If you are thinking of attending a graduate or professional school, please refer to your student tools, given late-breaking developments and the impact of the One Big Beautiful Bill Act on borrowing.

Colleges' Special Needs: Academically Gifted, Under-Represented Population Groups, Athletes, Legacies

While financial aid is based on *your* need, it is always wise to remember that it is also based to some extent on what *the colleges* need. If you fit a category a particular college is looking for, your package is going to be much better than if you don't.

Preferential packaging comes in many forms. Perhaps the FAO will decide that your Student Aid Index, as computed by the need analysis computer, is a bit high. Perhaps you will be offered an athletic scholarship or a non-need-based grant.

Whatever the school chooses to call it, you are being offered a preferential package—more grant or scholarship money, less loans and work-study.

No Time for Modesty

In many cases, these are not scholarships or grants for which you can apply. The schools themselves select the recipients with a keen eye toward enticing high-caliber students to their programs. It is therefore crucial that the student sell herself in her application. This is no time for modesty. For example, a promising student violinist should make sure that one of her application essays is about the challenge of mastering a difficult instrument. This should be backed up by recommendations from music teachers, reviews of her performances that have appeared in newspapers, and a listing of any awards she has won. If a student is offered one or more of these merit-based grants or scholarships, it is important to find out if these awards are one-time-only or whether they are renewable, based on performance. If renewable, just how good does the student's performance have to be in order to get the same package next year?

Bargaining

Colleges are particularly likely to increase their offer if they really wanted you in the first place. Students with excellent academic records are in an especially strong position to bargain. See Part Four, "The Offer," for more details.

Financial Aid for the Academically Gifted

Some awards come directly as a result of test scores. The National Merit Scholarship Program will award over $20 million in scholarships to about 6,930 students who score extremely well on the PSAT/NMSQT.

At schools where all aid is based on need, a National Merit finalist will not necessarily get one penny of aid unless "need" is demonstrated. Other schools, however, automatically give National Merit finalists a four-year free ride—a full scholarship.

Some awards come as a result of the student's performance in college. For instance, the Harry S. Truman Scholarship is mostly awarded to full-time college juniors.

Merit grants based on academic performance in high school are becoming more widespread as time goes on. We believe this trend will continue as colleges begin to compete in earnest for the best students. However, most of the money awarded to students with high academic performance is less easy to see. It comes in the form of preferential packaging.

Athletes

In general, it is up to the student to tell the colleges why the student is special through his or her application.

Athletes, however, should get in touch with the athletic department directly. When you go to visit the school, make it a point to meet the coach of the team you are interested in. Do not assume that a school is not interested in you merely because you have not been approached by a scout during the year. Get your coach to write letters to the schools you are interested in. Don't sell yourself short either—an average football player might not get a scholarship at Notre Dame, but the same applicant at Columbia might get a preferential package. Even if the school does not award athletic scholarships per se (Columbia, like the rest of the Ivy League, does not), many FAOs bend the numbers to come up with a lower family contribution for an athlete the school particularly wants.

Remember, too, that football is not the only sport in college. Schools also need swimmers, tennis players, long-distance runners, and the like.

Under-Represented Population Groups

Students from population groups that have historically been under-represented on college campuses are now a growing demographic in higher education as colleges seek a more diverse student body. This change in the applicant pool has sometimes created new challenges for schools as they strive to balance their budgets while remaining dedicated to a more inclusive student body.

Because of this anticipated increased demand for aid, it will be more important than ever for applicants to meet financial aid deadlines, to build a strong academic record in high school, and to maintain good grades in college to ensure continued funding.

Fortunately, at most schools, once on campus, students will find resources and support services designed to help them stay in school—ranging from mentors to work-study programs. The colleges have made it very clear that they remain committed to retaining the students they admit—and many will go to extraordinary lengths to keep them. As with most facets of college life, however, students who take the initiative will be more likely to get help.

Historically Black Colleges and Universities (HBCUs) and Hispanic-Serving Institutions (HSIs) are also experiencing challenges meeting their financial needs. A number of these institutions are among the finest schools in the country. But minority students with high need applying to these schools need to be aware that many of them don't have the financial aid resources of other schools with larger endowments. In some cases, a minority student with high need may find that he or she will get a larger aid package elsewhere. As we mentioned earlier, it is important for all students to apply to at least one financial safety school.

Legacies

Many colleges will go out of their way for the children of alumni. If the student's parents' circumstances are such that they cannot pay the entire cost of college, they should not be embarrassed to ask for help. At many schools it will be forthcoming.

Running Your Own Business or Farm

As we have already mentioned, the tax benefits of running your own business or farm are considerable: you are allowed to write off legitimate expenses, put relatives on your payroll, and possibly claim a percentage of your home for business use. The financial aid benefits are even better: your business or farm assets are assessed at a much lower rate than personal assets. This is because the colleges recognize a business's need for working capital. Thus a business's net worth (assets minus liabilities) of $50,000 will draw roughly the same assessment as a $20,000 personal asset.

If you have been planning to start your own business, now might be a good time!

The Four Types of Businesses—C Corporation, S Corporation, General Partnership, Sole Proprietorship

A **C corporation**'s profits are taxed at the corporate rate. C corporations must file an IRS 1120 corporate income tax return. The profits from a C corporation owned by a parent should not be included on the standardized financial aid forms, but the assets and liabilities may need to be listed. The owner of an **S corporation** (short for subchapter S) files an 1120S corporate income tax return, but also reports profits and losses on his own personal income tax return on schedule E. On the aid forms, the owner may have to report assets and liabilities as well as profits (or losses). A parent who is part of a **general partnership** reports profits and losses to the IRS on schedule E of the 1040. For aid purposes, she reports net profits (or losses) and possibly assets and liabilities on the need analysis form.

A **sole proprietor** reports profits and losses to the IRS on schedule C of the 1040. Again, profits (or losses) and possibly assets and liabilities must also be reported on the need analysis form. A **farmer** is treated like a sole proprietor but reports profits and losses to the IRS on schedule F of the 1040. Farmers who live primarily on their farm should be sure to exclude the value of the farmhouse when reporting the farm's net worth on the FAFSA.

Keep in mind that whatever business arrangement you have, you should never report your gross revenues on the standardized aid forms. Your net income (or net loss) is what counts—gross receipts less your deductible business expenses.

Financial Aid Strategies for Business and Farm Owners

Before the first base income year begins, it would make sense to accelerate billings, and take in as much cash as possible in advance. Try to defer expenses into the base income year. The idea, of course, is to minimize your income and maximize your expenses for the snapshot the college financial offices will be taking of your business. During the base income year itself, you might decide finally to do that remodeling or expansion you've been thinking about. In the last base income year, you will want to reverse the process you began before the first base income year: accelerate expenses and defer income until after the colleges have taken their last snapshot.

Starting a Business or Farm

The beginning years of a business are very often slow. Many businesses lose money in their first couple of years until they develop their niche and find a market. Parents who dream of starting their own company often feel that they should wait until after the kids are done with college before they take on the risk of an entrepreneurial enterprise. If you always dreamed of starting your own business, but have decided to wait until after the children are done with college, think again.

The perfect time to start a business is just before your child starts college. Consider: you'll have high start-up costs (which will reduce your assets) and low sales (which will reduce your income) for the first couple of years. If you time it right, these years will coincide exactly with the base income years, which means you will be eligible for substantially increased amounts of financial aid. Any business assets will also be assessed at a lower rate than personal assets. Like many businesses, yours may well start to be profitable within four years—just as your child is finishing college.

In effect, the college will be subsidizing the start-up costs of your business. This strategy is obviously not for everyone. A business must be run with the intention of showing a profit or it risks running afoul of the IRS. If you are merely indulging in a hobby, your farm or business losses may be disallowed. In addition, most schools that use the institutional methodology will disallow losses when determining eligibility for the school's own funds.

Any new business contains an element of risk, which should be carefully considered before you start. On the other hand, if you wait until your children are done with college, you may not have enough money left to start up a lemonade stand.

Estimating Your Company's Assets and Liabilities on the Aid Form

Owners of businesses sometimes overstate the value of their assets by including intangibles such as goodwill and location. These are important elements if you were to sell the company, but irrelevant to the need analysis formula. You are being asked to list only the total value of cash, receivables, inventory, investments, and your fixed assets (such as machinery, land, and buildings).

If your net worth is negative, you will list "0" on the FAFSA for that question. On other forms, you should list the total debts even if they exceed the total assets, but you will find that most colleges will not subtract a negative net worth from your total assets.

The Business/Farm Supplement

Many schools require the owner of a business or farm to fill out a paper version of the College Board's Business/Farm Supplement. Since this statement is not analyzed by a central processor you can send signed photocopies of the completed form to any school that requests it. The form more or less mimics the IRS forms you will probably be sending the colleges anyway. Some other schools may insist on your completing their own business supplement even though such forms will look very similar to the College Board's version. If you are not the sole owner, be careful to distinguish between questions that ask for the business's total income, assets, and liabilities, and questions that ask for your proportionate share of the business's income, assets, and liabilities.

High expenses during the base income years will help to maximize financial aid. However, large business purchases cannot be deducted all at once under IRS rules. There are several different methods to depreciate your fixed assets. During the college years, accelerated depreciation probably makes the most sense, especially during the critical *first* base income year. As always, however, you should consult with your accountant, and perhaps a financial aid consultant as well.

If You Own a Significant Percentage of the Stock of a Small Company

A parent who owns more than 5% of the stock in a small company could report this asset on the standardized need analysis form under "other investment," but it would be much more beneficial to report it under "business and farm." If you own a significant part of a small company, accountants argue that you can be said to be a part-owner of the company. Most colleges will go along with this. The advantage, of course, is that the value of the stock will be assessed less heavily as a business asset than it would have been as a personal asset.

Selling Your Business or Farm

A huge capital gain from the sale of your business or farm will probably wipe out any chance for financial aid. On the other hand, if you are receiving a huge capital gain, you don't need aid. If possible, delay the sale until you are out of the base income years, but if the offer is good enough, take it and enjoy the feeling of never having to look at a need analysis form ever again. Oh, yes, and expect a call almost immediately from the fundraisers at your child's college. It's amazing how fast good news travels.

Putting Your Child on the Payroll

This is a good tax move since it shifts income to the child, who may pay tax at a reduced rate. From a financial aid standpoint, however, increasing your child's income can backfire. Each year, up to 50% of the child's income gets assessed by the FAOs. Once the income reaches a certain amount (see Chapter 3, "Student Income"), it may disqualify your family from receiving aid, or at least reduce the amount you receive.

If you are not eligible for aid, by all means consider putting your child on the payroll. A self-employed parent who hires a son or daughter does not even have to pay social security taxes on the child's earnings until the child turns 18.

The Recently Unemployed Worker

If you have been terminated or laid off, or if you have received notice that you will be terminated or laid off, or if you are a self-employed person who cannot make a living due to harsh economic conditions, then you should be sure to point this out to the FAO.

Many schools can use what is called "professional judgment" to increase aid for the child of a recently unemployed worker. Instead of using the base income year (when you may have been gainfully employed) they can elect to look at your projected income for next year. Since you are now unemployed, your projection will be understandably bleak. Your child's college will probably want to see some sort of documentation (e.g., termination letter from your employer, unemployment benefits certification, etc.). Taking these extra steps could be worth thousands of dollars in aid.

How Do You Let the Colleges Know Your Projection for Next Year?

You will be asked on the CSS Profile form to project your income for the coming year. Project conservatively. You may be out of work for a while, so assume the worst-case scenario. Do not project based on a tentative job offer; if it doesn't come through, you will be making much less than the colleges will think based on your over-optimistic projections.

If all the schools to which you are applying require the CSS Profile form, then the schools will get your projected income from the College Board's analysis. Just remember to mention your work status in the "Explanations/Special Circumstances" section of the form.

Contrary to what the CSS Profile instructions say, you should not list any deferred compensation—401(k), or 403(b)—or contributions to IRAs or Keoghs as part of your untaxed income in the sections about the prior year (PY or the year after the PY). Do, however, list your gross wages, including any deferred compensation as part of your projected income from work.

The reason you should not include these items as untaxed income is that by doing so, you would be overstating your income. For example, let's take married parents with projected gross wages of $30,000 (and no other income) who made a $4,000 deductible IRA contribution. If this couple followed the instructions, they would be listing a total income of $34,000 ($30,000 income earned from work, plus $4,000 untaxed income). Obviously, they should only be reporting their total income—$30,000.

If your child is applying to schools that do *not* require the CSS Profile form, then you should send them a separate letter detailing your changed employment status and a projection of next year's income. When listing your projections, you should break them down into separate categories: father's income from work (if any), mother's income from work (if any), income from unemployment benefits, and all other taxable and untaxable income.

In fact, it wouldn't be such a bad idea to send copies of this letter even to the schools that require the CSS Profile form, since the FAOs at these schools sometimes miss comments written in the "Explanations/Special Circumstances" section of the form.

If You Lose Your Job While Your Child Is in College

Call or write a letter to the FAO explaining what happened as soon as possible, and include some form of documentation. It will probably be impossible for the FAO to revise your aid package for the current semester, but this will give them warning that you will be needing more aid next semester.

Other Disasters

If you are a nonworking parent who has been financially abandoned by a spouse, if you've had an accident that cost you a lot of money in unreimbursed medical expenses, if you lost your second job, if you received a pay cut or reduction in overtime, if you recently separated from your spouse, if your business lost its major client, if you became disabled, or had a major casualty or theft loss, you should be sure to notify the FAO immediately—even if the school year has already begun. Many schools have emergency aid funds for just these situations.

Independent Students

If a student is judged to be independent, the need analysis companies assess only *the student's* income and assets. The income and assets of the parents do not even have to be listed on the form. Obviously, this can have a tremendous impact on financial aid. Most students have limited resources, and so the aid packages from the colleges have to increase dramatically if they are to meet the student's entire "need."

Parents often erroneously believe that by not claiming the student as a dependent on taxes, their child will be considered independent for aid purposes—but this is not the case.

It is in the school's interest to decide that a student is not independent since independent students need so much more aid. In fact, a student is presumed to be dependent unless he meets certain criteria. The rules change from year to year (in general, going from stringent to more stringent). For the 2027–2028 academic year, you are automatically considered independent for federal aid purposes if:

A. You were born before January 1, 2004.

B. You are a veteran of the U.S. Armed Services or you are currently serving on active duty in the U.S. Armed Forces for purposes other than training.

C. When you are age 13 or older: both of your parents are deceased, you are/were in foster care, you are/were an orphan or a ward/dependent of the court, or you were a ward/dependent of the court until age 18.

D. You have children who will receive more than half their support from you between July 1, 2027 and June 30, 2028 OR you have dependents (other than your children or spouse) who live with you and receive more than half of their support from you, from the time you complete the 2027–2028 FAFSA through June 30, 2028.

E. You are a graduate or professional school student in 2027–2028.

F. You are married.

G. As of the day you complete the FAFSA, you are an emancipated minor or you are in legal guardianship as determined by a court in your state of legal residence.

H. At any time on or after July 1, 2026, your high school or school district homeless liaison determined that you are an unaccompanied youth who is homeless, the director of an emergency shelter program funded by HUD determined you were an unaccompanied youth who was homeless, or the director of a runaway or homeless youth basic center or transitional living program determined that you were an unaccompanied youth who was homeless or self-supporting and at risk of being homeless.

Meeting any one of these conditions makes you an independent student for federal aid purposes. However, the schools themselves may have their own, even tougher rules. A few schools (these tend to be the most expensive private colleges) state flat out that if the student is under 22 years old, he is automatically dependent unless both parents are dead. Beyond the criteria listed above, students with unusual circumstances may (or may not) be considered independent. See our comments in Part Three ("Filling Out the Standardized Forms") regarding questions 6 and 7 on the FAFSA.

These schools and others may insist that the parents fill out the parents' information section of the CSS Profile form and/or other aid forms, even if the student meets the federal rules for independence. To find out if this is the case at the schools you are interested in, consult the individual school bulletins. This will also give you an early clue as to whether a school uses the federal definition of independence, or a more rigid definition of their own.

If you don't meet the rules for independence, but have special circumstances, the FAOs have the authority to grant independent status on a case-by-case basis. To convince schools to do this requires extensive documentation. If the student has been abandoned by his parents, letters from a social service agency, court papers, or letters from a guidance counselor or member of the clergy acquainted with the situation may tip the scales.

If You Meet the Federal Requirements, but Not the School's Requirements

A student can meet the federal requirements for independence without meeting the school's own requirements. In this case, an undergraduate student may qualify for Pell Grants, other types of federal student aid including Direct Loans, and possibly some state aid based on his status as an independent student. The school's own grant money, however, will be awarded based on his status as a dependent student, taking his parents' income and assets into account.

Independence and Graduate School

Graduate schools generally have more flexible rules about independence, and anyway, graduate students are usually no longer minors. Some graduate schools (particularly law schools and medical schools) will continue to ask for parents' financial information in awarding their own money. Even if the school will not grant independent status, virtually all students will meet the federal guidelines and be eligible for federal aid. The borrowing limits on the Direct Loans rise in graduate school, making these very worthwhile. Graduate students can borrow up to $20,500 per year and even more for certain health profession students. Graduate and professional school students are also able to borrow additional funds under the federally-sponsored GradPLUS Loan Program. This program allows such students to borrow the difference between the Cost of Attendance and any other financial aid (including loans) that has been received. Terms for the GradPLUS are somewhat similar to the PLUS loan for parents.

Establishing Residency in a State

Establishing residency in another state is probably worthwhile only if the school you want to attend is a public university with lower in-state rates. The difference between in-state and out-of-state rates can be more than $25,000. It is true that in-state residents also may qualify for additional state grant aid available for students who attend public or private colleges, but this will generally be less than $4,000 a year—sometimes a lot less. In addition, most private colleges that meet a student's entire need will replace any money you might have gotten from the state anyway with their own funds. In this case, changing your state of residence is not worth the trouble.

Whether you will be able to pull this off at all is another story. Each state has its own residency requirements and, within those requirements, different rules that govern your eligibility for state grants and your eligibility for in-state tuition rates at a public university. These days, the requirements are usually very tough and they are getting tougher. There are some states, Michigan for example, where a student cannot be considered an in-state resident unless her parents pay taxes and maintain a primary residence in that state. Period. To find out about the requirements to qualify for in-state tuition for a school in a particular state, consult the financial aid office at that school.

Planning Ahead

If you decide you need to do this, you should begin investigating the requirements even before you apply to schools. Write to the individual state universities to ask about their rules, and set about fulfilling them before the student arrives at college. If the parents live in different states, it might be worth considering with which parent the child should spend the base income year.

Early Decision, Early Action, Early Notification, Early Read

Some colleges allow students to apply early and find out early whether or not they have been accepted. You are allowed to apply **early decision** to only one school, because your application binds both you and the school. If they decide to admit you, you are committed to attend. The schools like early decision because it helps them to increase their "yield"—the percentage of students they accept who ultimately decide to attend. An early decision candidate must apply by as early as mid-October and will find out if he has been accepted, rejected, or deferred as early as the first week of December.

Early decision applicants may also need to apply early for aid. You should be sure to consult the college's admissions literature for early decision financial aid filing requirements. Provided that you meet your deadlines, you should receive an aid package in the same envelope with your acceptance letter.

Early action is an admissions option in which you are notified early of your acceptance but are not bound to attend the school. You have until the normal deadline in May to decide whether to attend. The financial aid package, however, will usually not arrive in your mailbox until April and at many (but not all) schools you usually file for aid as if you were a regular applicant. (Note: some colleges refer to this option as non-binding early decision.)

Early notification is offered by many colleges that use rolling admissions. As the admissions committee makes its decisions, it mails out acceptance letters. Generally, you still have until the normal deadline to let the colleges know if you are accepting their offer. You apply for aid as if you were a regular applicant. Financial aid packages may arrive with acceptances or they may come later.

Some of these schools may try to put pressure on you by giving you an early deadline to decide if you are coming. If they are just asking you to accept the financial aid package, that's fine. An acceptance of the aid package does not commit you to attend the school. However, if they are trying to force you to accept their offer of admission before you've heard from your other schools, stall. Call the school and ask for an extension. Make sure you get the name and title of the person you speak to on the phone, and send a "we spoke and you agreed" letter via certified mail to confirm.

What Are the Financial Aid Implications of These Programs?

Early decision: For a high-need or moderate-need family, early decision is a big gamble, because you are effectively giving up your bargaining position. By committing to the school before you know what kind of aid package you will receive, you lose control of the process. It is a bit like agreeing to buy a house without knowing how much it costs. If the school has a good reputation for meeting a family's need in full, then this may be acceptable. However, even if the aid package they offer meets your need completely, you may not like the proportion of loans to grants. The school will have little incentive to improve the aid package since the child is already committed to attending.

If the aid you are offered is insufficient, there is a way to get out of the agreement, but this will leave you with little time to apply to other schools. We recommend that any student who applies to one school early decision should have completely filled out the applications to several other schools in the meantime. If the student is rejected or deferred by the early decision school—or if the aid package is insufficient—then there will still be time to apply to other colleges.

Early action: Even if a student is accepted early action, the student should probably still apply to several comparable schools. If one of these schools accepts the student as well, this will provide bargaining leverage with the FAOs, particularly if the second school's aid package is superior.

Early notification: The only financial aid implications of early notification occur if you are being squeezed. If a college is putting pressure on you to accept an offer of admission before you have heard from other schools, the college is also taking away your potential to negotiate an improved aid package. Fight back by asking for an extension.

The Early Read

Some schools say that, as a courtesy, they will figure out your Student Aid Index for you early in the fall if you submit your financial data to them—even if you aren't applying to their school. On the face of it, this seems like an offer too good to pass up.

However, you should understand that by letting them perform this early read, you are giving up complete control over the aid process. Your financial data is now set in stone, and if your child applies to that school, there won't be much you can do to change it (in any of the ways we have set forth in this book). We think you are better off figuring out your SAI for yourself using our worksheets, or hiring a financial aid consultant (see Chapter Eleven). Letting the colleges figure out your SAI is a bit like letting the IRS figure your taxes.

Aid for the Older Student

People who go back to school later in life often say they get more out of the experience the second time. We've found that from a financial aid standpoint, things are actually just about the same. Returnees still have to apply for aid and demonstrate need just like any incoming freshman. They are awarded aid in the same fashion.

The major difference is that they were probably employed at a full-time job during the base income year. If an older student is returning to school full-time, he should point out to the FAOs that there is no way he can earn as much money while he is in school. The first base income year is just not very representative in this case. Older students are probably independent by now, but they should not be surprised if some schools ask for their parents' financial information. Old habits die hard.

Two strategies for older students that should not be overlooked:

1. Let your company pay for it. Many companies have programs that pick up the cost of adult education.

2. Life credits! Some colleges will give you free credits for your life experience. We can't think of a better form of financial aid than that.

International Students

For students who are not U.S. citizens or eligible noncitizens (see instructions in the standardized need analysis forms), financial aid possibilities are severely limited. No federal aid is given to nonresident aliens. However, the schools themselves are free to give their own grants and scholarships.

You should check with the individual schools to find out their filing requirements. Many colleges require that you complete special aid forms designed solely for international students—even if the student is a U.S. citizen or eligible noncitizen. Some of these colleges will also require a certificate of finance (which is issued by the family's bank certifying how much money the family has) and proof of earnings.

Because you are dealing with the vagaries of *two* separate postal systems, you should begin the application process as early as possible.

Note: The CSS Profile will have special questions for international students, so many schools may now require international students to complete the CSS Profile form as well.

Foreign Tax Returns

The standardized need analysis form is not equipped to deal with foreign currency, so you will have to convert to U.S. dollars, using the exchange rate in effect on the day you fill out the form. There are special instructions in the forms that apply if you fit this category. Some colleges will ask to see your actual tax return, and they will insist that it be translated into English. Believe it or not, there is someone in your country's tax service whose job it is to do this, though it may take a while for you to find him.

Note: The filing of a foreign tax return by the custodial parent(s) will automatically make a dependent student ineligible for the Maximum Pell Grant criteria to exclude assets (see Chapter 3).

Study Abroad

There are two general types of study abroad programs:

1. Programs run by your own college

2. Programs run by someone else

In the former case, there is usually no problem getting your school to give you the same aid package you would normally receive. While some of these programs are a bit more expensive than a year on campus, the cost is usually not that much greater.

In the latter case, you may have more difficulty. At some schools, you may be eligible only for federal aid. To avoid an unpleasant surprise, call on your FAO to find out what the aid consequences of a year abroad in another school's program would be.

To the Professional

A word to the guidance counselors, financial planners, stockbrokers, accountants, tax advisors, and tax preparers who may read this book:

We spoke recently to a broker from one of the big firms who said, "We don't take financial aid into account in our investment advice because . . . well, frankly, we assume that none of our clients are eligible."

This is dangerous thinking. These days, lots of people are eligible for financial aid, including (we happen to know) two of his clients. While no one can be an expert at everything, we think it would be a good thing if brokers, accountants, tax advisors, tax lawyers, and counselors knew a bit more about financial aid strategy—or were willing to admit to their client when they didn't know.

Our intent here was to give *the parent and child* an understanding of the aid process and some idea of the possibilities for controlling that process. If you can use this as a resource tool as well, we are just as happy. We would caution you, however, that this book is by no means encyclopedic, and the rules change almost constantly. To be truly on top of the situation you would have to subscribe to industry newsletters, read the *Federal Register,* attend the conventions, develop your own contacts at the colleges, and then take what those contacts tell you with a large measure of salt.

Or you could just hire a consultant to train you to become a financial aid consultant and to keep you abreast of the latest developments. For more details on such training, refer to the "About the Authors" section which follows the Glossary at the back of this book.

Chapter Ten

Less Taxing Matters

The Good News

There are many tax benefits under the United States income tax code that provide much-needed help to give lower income and middle-income families help in raising their children and paying for the costs of higher education. Unfortunately, the regulations are truly complex and some of the goodies are mutually exclusive. The purpose of this section is to provide you with a basic summary regarding many of the benefits now available for education and raising children. But because of all the fine print, for all the important details, we recommend that you refer to the appropriate IRS publications, including but not limited to IRS Publication 970, and/or that you consult with a competent professional.

- Coverdell ESAs (formerly called Education IRAs) have a $2,000 annual contribution limit per beneficiary (who must be under the age of 18). Though no tax deduction will be granted for these contributions (which must be made in cash), the funds will grow tax-deferred and there will be no taxes owed on withdrawals used to pay for qualified higher education expenses. Be aware that the IRS definition of qualified expenses differs for each of the various federal tax benefits and can change from year to year, so be sure to read the fine print. Withdrawals from Coverdells can also be made tax-free if the funds are used to pay for qualified private elementary and secondary school expenses as well as for college or graduate school. The definition of "education" expenses also includes certain withdrawals to cover computers, internet access, and some other related expenses. While there are income limits as to who can contribute to a Coverdell, parents with higher incomes may be able to take advantage of a loophole in the law. Since the tax code states that the income limits apply to the "contributor" and does not state that the parent must be the contributor, families may be able to get someone else (whose income is below the limits) to fund the account. This benefit phases out between $190,000 and $220,000 for couples filing jointly and between $95,000 and $110,000 for others.

- Withdrawals from qualified state tuition programs (i.e., Section 529 plans which include both pre-paid plans and tuition savings accounts run by state governments) are tax-free if the funds are used for qualified higher education expenses. Under the tax law in effect through 12/31/25, up to $10,000 per year can be withdrawn free of federal taxes for certain elementary and secondary school expenses, though some states consider such distributions to be subject to state income taxes. Such distributions from 529 plans for qualified secondary school expenses during a base income year may cause problems for those otherwise eligible for financial aid because any distributions for the benefit of the student applying for aid will be considered part of the student's untaxed income.

- Currently, the annual tax credit parents can receive for qualifying dependents under the age of 17 at the end of the calendar year is $2,000 per child. This benefit is potentially available to married parents filing jointly with an Adjusted Gross Income below $400,000 and for others with an AGI below $200,000. Up to $1,600 of the Child Tax Credit is refundable, meaning you may be able to claim a partial credit even if you have no federal income tax liability. For a dependent qualifying child age 17 or above, there is a $500 credit with the same income thresholds, though this credit is only nonrefundable.

- Parents of college students have been eligible for a federal tax credit of up to $2,500 per student per calendar year, which is known as the American Opportunity (Tax) Credit or AOTC. (In 2009, this credit replaced the Hope Credit, which had been in existence for many years.) To qualify for the maximum AOTC, one must pay at least $4,000 towards qualified expenses, as the credit is based on 100% of the first $2,000 in expenses paid during the tax year plus 25% of the next $2,000 in expenses paid. Up to $1,000 of the AOTC per student per year can be refundable. The income phase-out ranges for the AOTC are higher than with the prior Hope Credit. For married couples filing jointly, the AOTC begins to phase out once the "Modified Adjusted Gross income" crosses the $160,000 threshold and completely phases out at $180,000. For others, the corresponding income amounts are $80,000 and $90,000, respectively. (Modified AGI is a taxpayer's AGI increased by any foreign income that was excluded.) Be aware that married parents who file separately are not eligible to claim any of the federal education tax credits, which include the AOTC as well as the Lifetime Learning Credit, which will be discussed shortly. The American Opportunity Credit is available for only the first four years of undergraduate postsecondary education for a given student (including any years the Hope Credit was claimed for that same student). A student who pays for her own educational expenses may also be eligible for this credit, provided she is not claimed as a dependent on someone else's tax return.

- In addition to the AOTC, there is currently another education tax credit known as the Lifetime Learning Credit or LLC. Currently, the amount of this non-refundable credit is equal to 20% of the first $10,000 of qualified expenses paid each tax year. The phase-out and cutoff income amounts for the LLC are identical to those for the AOTC. Unlike the 4-year American Opportunity Credit, the Lifetime Learning Credit can be claimed for an unlimited number of tax years, provided one meets all the other criteria. It is therefore possible for a parent to take this credit for a few years, provided he claims the child as a dependent on his tax return. Years later, the student herself could claim the Lifetime Learning Credit on her own tax return if she goes back to school and meets the other criteria for the credit. In contrast to the AOTC, the Lifetime Learning Credit can also be used for graduate studies.

- For most (but not all) taxpayers, claiming the American Opportunity Credit will result in a larger tax benefit than claiming the Lifetime Learning Credit. However, given the fine print and differing eligibility criteria, you (or your tax preparer) should still do the math and compare the results just to be sure.

- It is important to note that the above two tax benefits involve tax credits and not merely deductions against your taxable income. As such, they are much more valuable since they reduce your tax liability dollar-for-dollar. While the American Opportunity Credit can be claimed for each qualifying child in the same tax year, the maximum amount of the Lifetime Learning Credit you can take each year will not vary based upon the number of students in college. In determining the size of the credit, qualifying educational expenses will only represent "out-of-pocket" costs paid. So, for example, scholarships and grants that are awarded will reduce the amount of educational expenses used to determine the size of the credit. In many cases, however, expenses paid from the proceeds of a loan will qualify as out-of-pocket expenses. This is true even if the expenses were "paid" with a student loan, as the regulations focus on the amount of expenses paid but not necessarily who paid them. Unlike the LLC in which expenses are limited to tuition and mandatory fees as a condition of enrollment, AOTC expenses can include required "course materials" (like books, supplies, and equipment) and possibly even a computer if it is needed as a condition of enrollment. For those students who receive so much grant and scholarship aid that they equal or exceed the qualifying educational expense for the purposes of these educational tax credits, it may be possible to still qualify for such credits by claiming some of the gift aid as earned taxable income to the student. This "loophole" is explained in detail in the aforementioned IRS Publication 970, which covers all the educational tax benefits. Given the fact that most students can have considerable earned income—up to $14,600 in 2024 and up to $15,000 in 2025 before there is any tax liability—the viability of this loophole has increased. Just always run the numbers—or have an accountant do so—to determine the most beneficial course of action.

- There is also a waiver of the 10% penalty on withdrawals from regular IRAs and Roth IRAs prior to age 59 1/2, provided the withdrawals are used to pay qualified post-secondary education expenses. Withdrawals can cover your own educational expenses (including grad school) as well as those of your spouse, child, or grandchild. Withdrawals from traditional IRAs will, of course, still be considered part of your taxable income. The section of the tax code pertaining to withdrawals from Roth IRAs is more complicated. While there are no special provisions regarding higher education expenses, distributions of the original contributions to Roth IRAs are not subject to tax or penalty. Distributions involving the earnings in a Roth IRA are, however, subject to taxes unless other criteria are met. (For example, the distribution is made five years after the initial contribution and the taxpayer is at least 59 1/2 years of age.) It is assumed that the first dollars distributed represent the initial contribution to the Roth IRA. Because the rules regarding IRAs and Roth IRAs contain so much fine print, you should consult the appropriate IRS publications or a professional tax advisor if you are contemplating any distributions from these plans. And remember, any distributions (other than rollovers) from retirement accounts are required to be reported as income on the FAFSA and CSS Profile, whether taxable or not.

- The 2001 tax law expanded the availability of the deduction of student loan interest paid on qualified educational loans. Taxpayers will still not need to itemize deductions to claim this benefit, which increased to $2,500 in 2002 and beyond. The modified adjusted gross income thresholds for the full deduction in 2025 have been set at $85,000 for single filers and $170,000 for joint returns. The maximum amount of this deduction then gradually phases out until the income reaches the upper limit of $100,000 for single filers and $200,000 for joint filers, at which point it is no longer available. Currently, there is no limit as to how many years this deduction can be claimed, provided all the qualifying criteria are met for a given tax year. Qualifying educational loans can be those incurred to cover your own post-secondary expenses, as well as those of your spouse or any other dependent at the time the loan was taken out. If you are claimed as a dependent on someone else's tax return for a particular year, however, you cannot claim this deduction.

And now . . .

The Bad News

When the Economic Growth and Tax Relief Reconciliation Act of 2001 (that established many of the above-mentioned educational tax benefits) was first enacted, politicians from both sides of the aisle were patting themselves on the back. But now that the dust has settled, the truth of the matter is that the changes have been so complicated that many experts have stated that the major beneficiaries of all these changes are the tax preparers and accountants across the country.

We used to tell our clients to look before they leapt. But since 2002, we now tell them to look both ways, since the 2001 tax law and subsequent legislation are anything but tax simplification. Some of the provisions may still expire in a few years. And given the constant budget battles in Congress, there is nothing to prevent new legislation from being introduced that would impact some of these educational tax benefits.

Going . . .

Though the income restrictions on many of these benefits have been loosened in recent years, many families are going to discover that they still don't qualify for them. Indeed, whenever news breaks about new or enhanced education tax breaks, a number of our clients will call to ask what we think, already assuming the increased benefits will apply to them. We often have to burst their bubbles and tell them they won't be able to qualify because their income is still too high or they do not meet all the criteria.

Many families who could qualify may also fail to get the maximum benefits simply because they don't understand all the fine print. The regulations are rather extensive and the timing of certain transactions is very important. For example, let's say your child will be graduating at the end of the 2026–2027 academic year. If you're overly eager and pay the spring 2027 tuition bill as soon as you get it in mid-December 2026 (instead of waiting until January 10, 2027 when it's due), you won't be able to claim the American Opportunity Credit or Lifetime Learning Credit in 2027 for that child simply because you paid the money too soon. That mistake might have cost you as much as $2,500 as you can only claim the credit for the tax year in which you make the payment. If the college insists on payment before you sing "Auld Lang Syne," consider going on a payment plan for the final semester. Installment payments made after the new tax year begins may allow you to claim the credits for another tax year, provided you meet all the other criteria.

There's also the linkage among the different provisions. To prevent some tax-payers from hitting the jackpot, the benefit you receive from one of the tax benefits can often eliminate your eligibility for other goodies. For example, you can't claim both the American Opportunity Credit and the Lifetime Learning Credit during the same tax year for educational expenses paid for the same child. You can, however, claim the American Opportunity Credit for one undergraduate student and the Lifetime Learning Credit for an older sibling in graduate school on the same year's tax return (provided you meet all the other criteria). In addition, if you claim the American Opportunity Credit or the Lifetime Learning Credit for expenses paid with funds withdrawn from a section 529 plan or Coverdell ESA, part or all of the funds withdrawn may no longer qualify for tax-free treatment unless you forego claiming the credit. You can still withdraw funds from these plans and claim an education tax credit for the same student in the same tax year, but you'll have to pay some of the qualified expenses (as defined by the IRS for the credit you are claiming) with funds from other accounts and/or loans. Finally, many of the provisions are not available to married couples who file separate returns.

. . . Going . . .

Then there is the impact of these provisions on financial aid. For example, the Lifetime Learning Credit and any non-refundable portion of the American Opportunity Credit will reduce your aid eligibility under the institutional methodology. Since these credits reduce your U.S. income taxes paid (an expense item in the IM formula), your available income will be higher and so your IM SAI will go up as well. While the amount of the credit will still be greater than the amount of aid that is lost, the value to you of those credits is reduced under the institutional formula for any base income year.

Other provisions are potential financial aid traps. As mentioned earlier in this book, distributions from IRAs and other retirement accounts (other than rollovers) boost your income, thereby reducing your aid eligibility. It also remains to be seen how some IRA withdrawals will impact eligibility. For example, will the conversion of a regular IRA to a Roth IRA be considered a special circumstance taken into account by an FAO when awarding aid? Because these provisions often change from year to year, the Department of Education, the College Scholarship Service, and most college financial aid offices still have not finalized their policies as to how to handle most of these items. We therefore recommend that those families who are interested in maximizing aid eligibility avoid discretionary withdrawals from retirement accounts until they are out of the base income years.

Reminder: Most traditional financial advisors (e.g., accountants, financial planners, attorneys, stockbrokers, etc.) rarely take financial aid implications into account when making recommendations. Now more than ever before, you should investigate how such advice will affect your aid eligibility before you proceed.

. . . Gone

Even if you qualify for these benefits and are still ahead of the game after factoring in the reduced aid, the various tax provisions may still not save you any money by the ninth inning. For the big question still remains: "Will these tax benefits save you any money in the long run?" While many families are saving money on their taxes, many colleges have realized that fact and have just raised their tuition even higher to follow suit. So the jury is still out on how much these provisions will actually help any family or student pay for college.

Chapter Eleven

Looking for a Financial Aid Consulting Service

Looking for a Financial Aid Consultant

At this point you may be rubbing your hands together and saying:

"I'm ready. Bring on those need analysis forms!" or you may be saying:

"I'd rather eat cement than ever look at those forms."

You know quite a lot about the financial aid process and you know how to take control of that process. You also know yourself, and if you don't want to get any more familiar with this subject than you already are, you can hire someone to do it for you.

What a Financial Aid Consultant Does

A good financial aid consultant will do far more than simply fill out the forms. Anyone can throw together numbers on a paper. Principally, you hire a consultant to examine your entire financial situation ahead of time and make recommendations to increase your aid eligibility. A good consultant will know the specific rules that govern aid in your state, will be up-to-date on the constantly changing regulations that govern tax law and financial aid, and will assist you to complete the forms to maximize your aid eligibility.

There are several different kinds of professionals who may offer their services to guide you through the financial aid process: accountants, financial planners, tax lawyers, tax advisors, and financial aid consultants (who specialize in this field alone).

Why Your Accountant May Say He Is Willing to Do the Form Even If He Doesn't Want To

Accountants want you to come back to see them next year. Even if your accountant hates preparing need analysis forms and even if he knows very little about the financial aid process, he will probably tell you that he'll do the forms for you. He's afraid that if he says no, you'll go to another accountant and he'll lose your regular business.

Why You May Not Want to Let Him

At stake are tens of thousands of dollars. You do not want to be your accountant's guinea pig. If your need analysis form is his first, or even his tenth, you may not get the best aid package possible.

Of course, there are accountants, tax lawyers, and financial planners who have made it their business to learn the ins and outs of financial aid. The problem is finding out whether you are dealing with one of these knowledgeable experts or a rank beginner *before* you place your child's future in his hands. How do you find a competent person?

Ask Your Friends for Referrals

There is no licensing organization in this field, and asking your local Better Business Bureau about prospects will only reveal the most egregiously bad apples. The best way to find a good aid consultant is to ask your friends for a referral. This is far better than responding to an unsolicited sales pitch you receive in the mail or by phone. Some questions to ask your friends:

- Did the consultant give them the forms in time to meet deadlines?
- Was he available throughout the year for planning?
- Did he give them an idea of what their Student Aid Index would be, and was it reasonably correct?
- Did he provide them with strategies to maximize aid for the coming year?

It's always hard to know what kind of packages a family would have received had they *not* gone to a professional for help, which makes objective comparison difficult. However, if your friends came away from the experience feeling that the professional knew the process inside and out and that they had been well taken care of, then you are probably in good hands.

Fees can be expensive, but if a professional can find ways to increase your aid eligibility by thousands of dollars, even a relatively expensive fee is a bargain.

Be cautious with professionals who try to sell you financial products. They may be more interested in selling you financial investment instruments you may or may not need than in getting you the most aid. You should also be suspicious if a consultant promises that you'll receive a certain amount of aid before reviewing your situation. And pass immediately on any professional who tries to steer you toward anything illegal. Please report any unprofessional behavior to the Better Business Bureau immediately.

Some Questions to Ask the Professional

Before you engage anyone to give you financial aid advice, you might want to ask a few of the following questions:

- What is the name of the state grants awarded here in __________?

Any professional who does financial aid consulting should certainly know the name of the state grants offered by your home state. Each state calls its grants something else, and each state has its own set of rules as to who qualifies for these grants. If the professional doesn't even know the names of the grants, he probably doesn't know the rules under which they are dispensed either.

- Should we put assets in the child's name?

A competent professional should know that student's assets are assessed at a much higher rate than parents' assets. If the family is eligible for aid, putting money in the child's name can be a very expensive mistake.

- Which year's income and assets do the colleges look at?

To determine what a family can afford to pay for college in the academic year of 2027–2028, for example, the colleges look at the income from the *prior-prior* year; in this case, 2025. They look at assets as of the day the need analysis form is completed.

- What is the difference between a GradPLUS loan and a PLUS loan?

Both are sponsored by the federal government, but the GradPLUS loan is made to students, while the PLUS loan is made to parents.

- Could you explain a couple of terms for us?

Go to the glossary and pick a few terms at random. An experienced professional should have no difficulty defining those terms.

One Question Not to Ask:

- Could you tell us if we qualify for aid?

Of course this is the one question you really want answered, but no competent consultant could answer this question without a detailed analysis of your situation.

Chapter Twelve

Looking Ahead

Future Trends in College Finance

The world of financial aid and college finance is always in flux. Making any predictions whatsoever is dangerous. However, it is safe to say that college tuitions will continue to rise at a rate faster than that of overall inflation. And now more than ever before, there is a huge difference between just applying and applying smart. The aid is still available, but the mechanics of securing it will continue to become more complicated, with more hurdles than ever before.

The Prior-Prior Year

One of those hurdles: the decision to change the timing of the all-important "snapshot" that the FAFSA and, if applicable, the CSS Profile asks you to take of your finances. By changing that first snapshot from the year before the student enters college (known as the "Prior year" or PY) to two years before the student enters college (known as the "Prior-prior year" or PPY), the U.S. Department of Education, as well as the school, have enhanced their ability to require more extensive documentation, ensuring the validity of student and parent information. In the past, much work was spent in the aid offices resolving discrepancies between estimated PY income reported on the aid forms and the actual PY income figures on completed tax returns. So with this administrative burden sharply reduced, the U.S. Department of Education could require college aid officers to spend more of their time reviewing other data elements besides the PPY income reported on tax returns.

Identity Theft

Another hurdle has occurred due to advances in technology. As the financial aid forms have moved online (from the paper and snail-mail route), the dangers of cyber theft and identity theft have greatly increased. Because the aid forms contain your entire financial history, dates of birth for various individuals and social security numbers for the student and any custodial parent or stepparent required to report their finances on the FAFSA, it's more important than ever to take all precautions to make sure your passwords are robust and that you keep any log-in information secure. Unfortunately, the Department of Education still uses the student's social security number as an identifier for colleges to retrieve students' processed FAFSA information. This means that prospective students using the Common Application for their admissions purposes will need to enter their social security number on the Common App if they are applying for aid at any school(s) that accepts that admissions form. Otherwise, such schools may not be able to find the student's processed FAFSA data on their system.

Because the aid forms and supporting documents contain social security numbers and other information valuable to identity thieves, one cannot be careful enough. To better protect yourself and your significant others, keep these following tips in mind:

Do not send copies of tax return files by email. It is more secure to send them by fax or even postal mail—unless you are uploading the documents to a school using their own secured school document system or the school is using a third-party app such as the College Board's IDOC service.

Remember that neither the government, the College Board, nor the colleges will EVER ask you to provide a password in response to an email.

The Rise of "Free" Tuition

A few states have offered free tuition for community college for some time—but in the spring of 2017, New York became the first state to offer free tuition for up to four years of college (i.e., through the first bachelor's degree). This is, of course, great news—and more states may follow. But while these announcements get a lot of headlines, it is important to understand that going to these schools is by no means free. For example, in New York, this offer only covers tuition, not room and board, books, etc. And at most state universities, it turns out that room and board expenses are higher than the tuition itself. There may also be bundles of string attached to such awards. So be sure to read all the fine print about qualifying for such funds and maintaining eligibility, as well as if there are any requirements that must be met after leaving school. You should also be aware of the maximum benefit that can be awarded under the state program.

FM and IM Divergence

Even though federal regulations have become more liberal over the last few years in terms of defining a student's "need" (for example, treating child support received as an asset instead of as income), more and more colleges are becoming increasingly conservative when it comes to awarding their own funds. More and more schools are asking additional questions about the existence of (and distributions from) 529 plans that are owned by individuals other than the student's parents (such as a rich aunt or grandparent). Even though such 529 plans do not have to be reported on the aid form as an asset, colleges want to know about them, taking the position that a student with a sizable 529 plan funded by Aunt Mary should obviously be in a position to pay more.

The Importance of Planning Ahead

If history has taught us anything, it is that it is never too early to start planning ahead for college costs. At whatever stage you are reading this book, there are some tangible strategies you can use to help take control of the financial aid process and minimize college costs. The purpose of this book has been to show you those strategies. We hope they will make the dream of a college education a reality.

Good luck!

Part Five

Worksheets and Forms

Calculating Your Student Aid Index (SAI)

We realize that the pages of tables and worksheets that follow may seem a little intimidating. There are some online resources that claim you can estimate your SAI by consulting a single chart. Unfortunately, these charts are overly simplistic and frequently do not provide an accurate SAI number. Calculators on various websites all too often make assumptions that may not be applicable to one's situation or use flawed logic, resulting in a case of "garbage in, garbage out" with incorrect or misleading results being generated regarding the SAI and Pell eligibility.

When you submit your completed FAFSA, you provide the federal processor with very specific information. However, you will not be required to complete tables and worksheets such as the ones that follow. The processor will simply take your data and run it through a computer program that automatically does all the calculations that we are about to show you.

So Why Should You Bother to Calculate the SAI On Your Own?

There are two excellent reasons.

First, by making the calculations yourself, you will be able to see how the formula works; it is amazing how small changes in the way you list your financial information can produce big changes in the final result.

Second, by having an *accurate* idea of what your Student Aid Index will be, you can make informed decisions about which schools to apply to, how to answer questions on the individual school aid forms like, "How much do you think you can afford to pay for college?" and what early steps you can take for next year.

Ughhhh

If these worksheets fill you with dread, you can always hire an independent financial aid consultant to do these calculations for you. Details on how to find one are in Chapter Eleven.

The Standard Disclaimer

While we believe that these worksheets and tables are accurate, they have not been approved by the U.S. Department of Education. In addition, the worksheets and tables regarding calculation of income have not been approved by the IRS and should not be used to calculate your tax liability for your income tax return.

Before you begin: *If you are certain that you meet the criteria for Maximum Pell eligibility via either of the two scenarios we discussed in the "Maximum Pell, Minimum Pell, and the SAI Disconnect" section towards the beginning of Chapter 3, then your SAI will be 0 or less. If* *this situation applies to you, there is no need to complete these tables and worksheets that follow to calculate your SAI. However, if you meet the criteria for the Minimum Pell (but not the Maximum Pell), then you should proceed, as one's "calculated SAI" will be used in part to determine eligibility for aid programs other than the Pell Grant.*

Our Tables and Worksheets for Calculating the Student Aid Index for a Dependent Student

Please note that by TAXABLE INCOME, we mean income that the IRS considers subject to possible taxation, even if the IRS does not require that a tax return be filed because the income is below a minimum level determined by them. As such, it is possible to pay no tax on a small amount of taxable income. UNTAXED INCOME or NONTAXABLE INCOME refers to income that is never subject to income tax. Some income items, such as social security benefits, can be considered either taxable income or untaxed income, depending on the taxpayer's total income.

Unless otherwise indicated, all references in this worksheet to specific IRS line numbers relate to those lines on the 2025 IRS 1040 form. To avoid confusion, we suggest that you refer to Chapter Three for more detailed descriptions of these various items. If the student's biological or adoptive parents are living apart, please consult Part 3, "Which Parent(s) Must Report Information" if you are unsure whose income should be listed on this worksheet.

The worksheets and tables that follow are based on the federal formula for calculating the SAI for the 2027–2028 award year. Before you start completing any of the tables or worksheets, you should be sure to read all the important tips below as well as the additional instructions that appear on the various tables and worksheets.

Some important tips for completing the worksheets:

1. Round off all figures to the nearest dollar. If any line item is not applicable to you, enter 0 (zero).

2. All income/expense items relate to yearly amounts. Do not use monthly or weekly figures. All asset/liability items relate to current amounts.

3. Since the 2027–2028 SAI will be using "prior-prior-year" income (see Chapter 1, "The First Base Year Income"), all references to income on the Tables and Worksheets in Student Tools should be completed using 2025 income amounts. Most likely, by the time you are completing these Tables, you will have already completed the 2025 Federal income tax returns if required to file a return. If that is the case for the student's parents (or parent and stepparent) required to report information on the FAFSA, then most likely you can skip the calculations for the Parents' Adjusted Gross Income (Table 3) and Parents' U.S. Taxes Paid (Table 6). Simply go to the last line of that respective Table and just list the dollar amount reported on the corresponding line of your U.S. individual

income tax return(s). If separate tax returns were already filed by the Parent and the Parent's Spouse/Partner required to report financial information on the FAFSA, list the combined amounts for the AGI (IRS 1040 Line 11a) on the last line of Table 3 and list the combined amount of U.S. Taxes Paid (IRS 1040 Line 24) on the last line of Table 6. Please remember that one's marital status for purposes of the FAFSA is the marital status on the date the FAFSA is filed, not the status at any time during the prior-prior year. If separate returns will be but have not yet been completed: Tables 3 and 6 should be completed for each person, with the last lines then combined to determine the appropriate amount to list on the Parents' Contribution Worksheet. If the Parent completed a 2025 tax return but the Parent's Spouse/Partner will not complete a 2025 tax return due to low income (or vice versa), then Tables 3, 4, 5 and 6 should be completed using the applicable tax filer's information only. If the Parent and/or the Parent's Spouse/Partner: a) filed a tax return with Puerto Rico or another U.S. territory b) earned income in a foreign country; c) filed a foreign tax return and/or d) worked for an international organization (such as the UN, the World Bank, or the IMF) without being required to report such earned income on any tax return, then visit this USDOE webpage (https://studentaid.gov/help/foreign-tax-return) for guidance on determining the amounts to be used for Income Earned From Work, Adjusted Gross Income, and U.S Taxes Paid.

Exception: If 2025 federal tax individual income tax returns were completed as married filing jointly and the Parent or the Parent's current spouse is now separated, divorced, or widowed from that other adult with whom they filed jointly, then the entire Adjusted Gross Income table should be completed using only that person's share of the respective items to determine that person's share of the Adjusted Gross Income (AGI). To calculate the last line for the U.S. Taxes Paid table: use the proportionate share of the AGI that you listed on the last line of the AGI table. Divide that number by the joint AGI figure reported on the actual tax return. The number you have just calculated should then by multiplied by the combined amount of U.S. Taxes paid on the joint return (IRS 1040 Line 24) to determine that person's share of the U.S. taxes paid.

4. Be aware that the tables (as applicable) must be completed (in order) *before* you can begin work on the Parents' Contribution Worksheet. Table 13, if applicable to the student, should be completed *before* you begin work on the Student's Contribution Worksheet.

5. When completing the Income Earned From Work tables, be sure to enter the appropriate amounts under the proper column. Do not combine the amounts into one column, unless our instructions state to do so.

6. Any number in parentheses should be subtracted from the number above it.

7. The earnings portion of any qualified withdrawals from Coverdell ESAs (Education IRAs) and Section 529 state savings accounts, as well as the increase in the value of any tuition credits redeemed since the time of purchase for Section 529 prepaid plans, will

not be considered as part of the student's or parent's non-taxable income. Therefore, do not include any "earnings" or any qualified withdrawals from these accounts on any tables or worksheets.

8. We suggest that you check your math. Even better, you should consider having another family member review your completed tables and worksheets for accuracy. Even if your SAI is higher than the cost of attendance, you should still consider applying for aid since the FAOs may take other factors into account, you may be eligible for state aid benefits not based on the SAI formula, and/or you may have made an error in your calculations when doing these worksheets.

Analyzing Your Numbers

Instead of thinking of the SAI as a definitive number for the amount you will be expected to pay toward college in a given year, you should think of the SAI as a rough approximation for financial aid planning purposes. Until you receive a finalized award package from a school, it is impossible to know for certain the final number for what you will need to contribute. So instead of thinking of absolutes, it would be better to think in terms of probabilities. For example, if the SAI you calculate is quite a bit lower than the Cost of Attendance for the applicable school(s) under consideration, it would be better to focus on using those applicable strategies outlined earlier in the book to lower your SAI and complete the aid forms. This will increase the probability of your receiving more aid and will be more beneficial than trying to figure out exactly how much aid you will receive before admission and aid decisions are known. Similarly, if your SAI is significantly higher than the cost of attendance for all schools under consideration, then it is likely—though not certain—that you will not receive any need-based funds in a given year. While you should still apply for aid (as strange things sometimes can happen with the aid process, especially with state and/or institutional aid), you should also have a backup plan (i.e., applying to lower cost schools and/or to schools where there is a high probability the student will receive merit-based aid).

You should also remember that although the federal formula under FAFSA Simplification will no longer make an adjustment to take into account multiple students in the family being in college (see Chapter 3), schools awarding their own institutional need-based aid may choose to make a multiple-student adjustment. So your actual contribution could be much lower than the calculated SAI when more dependents are in college. And if you are applying to schools that use the Institutional Methodology (IM), the family contribution derived in the IM may well be very different from the SAI.

TABLE 1
Parents' Income Earned From Work

If there is no "Parent Spouse/Partner" required to provide information on the FAFSA (a "one-parent" situation for the SAI formula), only the left column should be completed. However, see the Note in italics below if a joint return was or will be filed.

If this will be a "two-parent" situation for the SAI—that is, the "Parent" (per USDOE regulations) AND either the other biological or adoptive parent are living together regardless of marital status OR the "Parent" for the purposes of the FAFSA is currently marred to (and not separated from) the student's stepparent—then provide information in each person's respective column only if the "Parent" and the "Parent Spouse/Partner" for the FAFSA did NOT and will NOT file a joint tax return with each other during the base income year (which is 2025 for the 2027–2028 award year). See Note below in italics as well. If the Parent has filed or will file a joint tax return with their current spouse for the base year, then complete only the left column with the combined income from work amounts for lines A–D.

NOTE: If a joint return was filed, but the parent or stepparent required to provide information on the FAFSA is no longer married to the person with whom they filed the joint return (i.e., they are now either separated, divorced or widowed from the person with whom they filed jointly), then only the Parent's or the Parent Spouse's (stepparent's) share of the respective types of income from work should be listed in the appropriate column.

	Parent	Parent's Spouse/Partner
For Lines B and C, list losses as zero.		
A. Wages, tips, salary, and other compensation subject to income tax (IRS 1040 Line 1z)	$ ________	$ ________
B. Business income: self-employment (Schedule 1, Line 3)	+ $ ________	+ $ ________
C. Farm income (Schedule 1 Line 6)	+ $ ________	+ $ ________
D. **TOTAL INCOME EARNED FROM WORK** (Sum of Lines A through C)	**$** ________	**$** ________

TABLE 2
Dependent Student's Income Earned from Work

Table 2 should always be completed if the dependent student completed an IRS Form 1040 tax return for the base income year. For the most part, Table 2 need not be completed if a dependent student for the base income year did not file their own IRS Form 1040 tax return AND was not required to file their own IRS Form 1040 tax return. (See exceptions below.)

This is because the processor will assume that a dependent student who is a non-filer will have a Student's Contribution from Income of 0 (zero). As such, it will also not be necessary to perform any of the calculations in Table 7 or complete the Student Contribution from Income section of the Student Contribution Worksheet. You can simply list 0 as the Student's Contribution from Income on the appropriate line of that Worksheet. However, unless a dependent student's parent required to provide information on the FAFSA meets at least one of the three criteria to be exempt from asset reporting (see "The Criteria to Exclude Assets in the FM" section in Chapter 3), then the Student Contribution from Assets section of the Student Contribution Worksheet will need to be completed.

Exceptions apply if the student did any of the following for the base income year:

- earned income in a foreign country
- worked for an international organization (such as the United Nations, the Work Bank, or the International Monetary Fund) without being required to report such earned income on any tax return
- filed a tax return with Puerto Rico or another U.S. territory

If any of these occurred, use your applicable financial document (if necessary, converting any foreign currency amounts to U.S dollars) in conjunction with the guidance found on this USDOE page (https://studentaid.gov/help/foreign-tax-return) to determine the dependent student's Total Income Earned From Work to list on Line D of this Table.

For Lines B and C, list losses as zero.

		Student
A.	Wages, tips, salary, and other compensation subject to income tax (IRS Line 1z)	$ ________
B.	Business income: self-employment (Schedule 1, Line 3)	+ $ ________
C.	Farm income (Schedule 1, Line 6)	+ $ ________
D.	**TOTAL INCOME EARNED FROM WORK** (Sum of Lines A through C)	**$** ________

TABLE 3
Parents' Adjusted Gross Income

If you have already completed your U.S. income tax return, in most cases you can skip completing this table and simply list the amount reported on Line 11a of the first page of the IRS Form 1040 of the tax return for the base year on Line C (Adjusted Gross Income), which appears on the bottom of the next page. However:

- IF separate base income year tax returns were filed by the Parent required to report financial information on the FAFSA
- AND that parent's current spouse or partner (provided that partner is the dependent student's other biological or adoptive parent) is also required to report their financial information on the FAFSA
- THEN please refer back to the earlier "Our Worksheets for Calculating the Student Aid Index for a Dependent Student" in this Part Five, specifically tip #3, for guidance on completing this table.

You should also refer back to tip #3 if a joint base year tax return was filed by the Parent and/or the Parent's Spouse/Partner required to report financial information on the FAFSA, but such individual is no longer married to the person with whom they filed that joint return. In other words, their marital status with regard to the other person with whom they filed that joint base year tax return is separated, divorced, or widowed.

Helpful hint: List losses, if any, in parentheses and subtract them.

Sum of:

Taxable wages, tips, salary, etc. (IRS Line 1z)	$ ______	
Taxable interest (IRS Line 2b)	+ $ ______	
Dividend income (IRS Line 3b)	+ $ ______	
Taxable refunds of state and local income taxes, if any (Schedule 1, Line 1)	+ $ ______	
Alimony received (Schedule 1, Line 2a)	+ $ ______	
Father and/or mother's income or (loss) from self-employment (Schedule 1, Line 3)	+ $ ______	
Capital gain or (loss) (IRS Line 7)	+ $ ______	
Other gains or (losses) (Schedule 1, Line 4)	+ $ ______	
Taxable IRA distributions (IRS Line 4b)	+ $ ______	
Taxable IRA pensions, and annuities (IRS Line 5b)	+ $ ______	
Rents, royalties, estates, partnerships, and trusts, etc. (Schedule 1, Line 5)	+ $ ______	
Farm income or (loss) (Schedule 1, Line 6)	+ $ ______	
Unemployment compensation (Schedule 1, Line 7)	+ $ ______	
Taxable social security benefits (IRS Line 6b)	+ $ ______	
Other taxable income (Schedule 1, Line 9)	+ $ ______	
A. Gross Income		$ ______

A. Gross Income (Line A from previous page) $ ________

ADJUSTMENTS TO INCOME

Sum of:

Educator expenses (Schedule 1, Line 11)		$ ________
Certain business expenses for reservists, performing artists, and fee-basis government officials (Schedule 1, Line 12)	+	$ ________
Health savings account deduction (Schedule 1, Line 13)	+	$ ________
Moving expenses (Schedule 1, Line 14)	+	$ ________
Deductible part of self-employment tax (Schedule 1, Line 15)	+	$ ________
Self-employed SEP, SIMPLE, and qualified plans (Schedule 1, Line 16)	+	$ ________
Self-employed health insurance deduction (Schedule 1, Line 17)	+	$ ________
Penalty on early withdrawal of savings (Schedule 1, Line 18)	+	$ ________
Alimony paid (Schedule 1, Line 19a)	+	$ ________
IRA deductible contributions (Schedule 1, Line 20)	+	$ ________
Student loan interest deduction (Schedule 1, Line 21)	+	$ ________
Archer MSA Deduction (Schedule 1, Line 23)	+	$ ________
Other adjustments (Schedule 1, Line 25)	+	$ ________

B. Total Adjustments (Schedule 1, Line 26) ($ ________)

C. ADJUSTED GROSS INCOME $ ________
(Gross Income [Line A] minus Total Adjustments [Line B])
2025 IRS 1040, Line 11a

TABLE 4
Parents' Untaxed Income

Sum of:

A.	Deductible IRA, SEP, SIMPLE, Keogh payments (Schedule 1, IRS 1040, total Lines 16 and 20)	$ ________
B.	Tax-exempt interest income (IRS 1040, Line 2a)	+ $ ________
C.	Untaxed portions of IRA distributions (IRS 1040 Line 4a minus 4b [excluding rollovers])	+ $ ________
D.	Untaxed portions of pension, and annuity distributions (IRS 1040 Line 5a minus 5b [excluding rollovers])	+ $ ________
E.	Foreign earned income exclusion (Schedule 1, IRS 1040, Line 8d listed as a positive number)	+ $ ________
F.	**TOTAL UNTAXED INCOME** (Sum of Lines A through E)	**$** ________

TABLE 5
Parents' Income Offsets

Sum of:

A.	Education tax credits (Schedule 3, IRS 1040, Line 3 plus IRS 1040, Line 29)	$ ________
B.	Parents' taxable earnings from Federal Work-Study	+ $ ________
C.	Parents' grant and scholarship aid included in adjusted gross income. (Include AmeriCorps benefits, as well as grant or scholarship portions of fellowships and assistanceships)	+ $ ________
D.	**Total Income Offsets** (Sum of Lines A through C)	**$** ________

TABLE 6
Parents' U.S. Taxes Paid

Adjusted Gross Income (from Table 3—Line C)	$ ________	
Minus: Total Itemized Deductions (same as the bottom line on Schedule A of IRS 1040) (If you do not/will not itemize deductions, use the following numbers based on your tax filing status: Single—$15,750 Head of Household—$23,625 Married filing jointly or Qualifying Surviving Spouse—$31,500 Married filing separately—$15,750	– ($ ________)	$ ________
Minus: Qualified business income deduction (IRS 1040, Line 13)		– ($ ________)
Taxable Income (If zero or less, skip charts below and enter zero on the last line of this table.)		$ ________

Use the Taxable Income figure listed above with the appropriate chart below based on your tax filing status to calculate your U.S. Income Tax Liability. Enter the result at the end of the four tax charts. (Tax charts are based on 2025 tax rates). Then subtract any nonrefundable tax credits to determine a rough approximation of U.S. Income Taxes Paid.

Use if your filing status is **Single**

If your taxable income is: *Over—*	But not *over—*	*Income taxes paid is—*	*of the amount over—*
$0	$11,925	10%	$0
$11,925	$48,475	$1,192.50 + 12%	$11,925
$48,475	$103,350	$5,578.50 + 22%	$48,475
$103,350	$197,300	$17,651.00 + 24%	$103,350
$197,300	$250,525	$40,199.00 + 32%	$197,300
$250,525	$626,350	$57,231.00 + 35%	$250,525
$626,350	—	$188,770.65 + 37%	$626,350

Use if your filing status if **Married filing jointly or Qualifying Surviving Spouse**

If your taxable income is: ***Over—***	**But not** ***over—***	***Income taxes paid is—***	***of the amount over—***
$0	$23,850	10%	$0
$23,850	$96,950	$2,385.00 + 12%	$23,850
$96,950	$206,700	$11,157.00 + 22%	$96,950
$206,700	$394,600	$35,302.00 + 24%	$206,700
$394,600	$501,050	$80,398.00 + 32%	$394,600
$501,050	$751,600	$114,462.00 + 35%	$501,050
$751,600	—	$202,154.50 + 37%	$751,600

Use if your filing status is **Married filing separately**

If your taxable income is: ***Over—***	**But not** ***over—***	***Income taxes paid is—***	***of the amount over—***
$0	$11,925	10%	$0
$11,925	$48,475	$1,192.50 + 12%	$11,925
$48,475	$103,350	$5,578.50 + 22%	$48,475
$103,350	$197,300	$17,651.00 + 24%	$103,350
$197,300	$250,525	$40,199.00 + 32%	$197,300
$250,525	$375,800	$57,231.00 + 35%	$250,525
$375,800	—	$101,077.25 + 37%	$375,800

Use if your filing status is **Head of the household**

If your taxable income is: *Over—*	**But not *over—***	***Income taxes paid is—***	***of the amount over—***
$0	$17,000	10%	$0
$17,000	$64,850	$1,700.00 + 12%	$17,000
$64,850	$103,350	$7,442.00 + 22%	$64,850
$103,350	$197,300	$15,912.00 + 24%	$103,350
$197,300	$250,500	$38,460.00 + 32%	$197,300
$250,500	$626,350	$55,484.00 + 35%	$250,500
$626,350	—	$187,031.50 + 37%	$626,350

U.S. Income Tax Liability	$ ________
Plus: Additions to tax (IRS 1040, Schedule 2, Line 1z)	+ $ ________
Plus: Alternative minimum tax (IRS 1040 Schedule 2, Line 2)	+ $ ________
Subtotal	$ ________
Minus: Tax Credits (IRS 1040 Line 21)	– ($ ________)
Subtotal (IRS 1040 Line 22)	$ ________
Plus: Other taxes (IRS 1040 Line 23)	+ $ ________
U.S. Taxes Paid (IRS 1040 Line 24)	**$** ________

TABLE 7
Payroll Tax Allowance

This table should be completed by utilizing the Total Income Earned from Work amount(s) you previously calculated on Line D of Table 1 for Parent(s) using the appropriate category (A, B, or C), which are mutually exclusive for Step 1. If the student is dependent and has filed or will file a tax return for the base income year, then the student sections in Steps 1 and 2 should also be completed using the student's Income Earned from Work amount you calculated on Line D of Table 2. Such amount(s) for income earned from work on Line D will be used in conjunction with the federal methodology's "Medicare tax" and "Old-age, survivors, and disability insurance (OASDI) tax" rate schedules. Additional instructions follow before and after Step 2.

Step 1: Medicare's Hospital Insurance (HI) Program Tax Rate

A. If a "one-parent" situation with no Parent Spouse/Partner required to provide financial information on the FAFSA:

1.45% of parent income earned from work up to $200,000		$__________
2.35% of parent income earned from work over $200,000	+	$__________
Equals: PARENT'S MEDICARE TAX PAID		**$**__________

B. If Parent filed as Married-Filed Joint Return (with current Spouse):

1.45% of parent income earned from work up to $250,000		$__________
2.35% of parent income earned from work over $250,000	+	$__________
Equals: PARENT(S)' MEDICARE TAX PAID		**$**__________

C. If Parent filed a separate return from current Spouse/Partner:

1.45% of left-column income earned from work up to $125,000		$__________
1.45% of right-column income earned from work up to 125,000	+	$__________
2.35% of left-column income earned from work over $125,000	+	$__________
2.35% of right-column income earned from work over $125,000	+	$__________
Equals: PARENT(S)' MEDICARE TAX PAID		**$**__________

D. If Dependent Student (Tax-filers only):

1.45% of dependent student income earned from work up to $200,000		$__________
2.35% of dependent student income earned from work over $200,000	+	$__________
Equals: STUDENT'S MEDICARE TAX PAID		**$**__________

For Parent: Use the appropriate category (AA or BB), which are mutually exclusive for Step 2.

Step 2: Old-age, Survivors, and Disability Insurance (OASDI) Tax Rate

AA. If Single Parental Income:

6.2% of parent's total earned income up to Contributions and Benefit Base of $176,100 for Tax Year 2025. $__________

OR

If parent's income exceeds $176,100, the capped amount is $10,918. $ 10,918

BB. If Two Parental Incomes (or Joint Return):

6.2% of parent's total earned income up to Contributions and Benefit Base of $352,200 for Tax Year 2025. $__________

OR

If parent's income exceeds $352,200, the capped amount is $21,836. $ 21,836

CC. If Dependent Student:

6.2% of student's total earned income up to Contributions and Benefit Base of $176,100 for Tax Year 2025. $__________

OR

If student's income exceeds $176,100, the capped amount is $10,918. $ 10,918

For Step 1:

- The dollar amount on the Equals: PARENT'S or PARENT(S)' line item for the applicable category (A, B, or C for the parent(s)) should be listed on the "Medicare Taxes Paid" (From Table 7 – Step 1) line item in the Expenses & Allowances section of the Parent's Contribution Worksheet.
- The dollar amount on the Equals: STUDENT'S MEDICARE TAX PAID (in D for the student), if any, should be listed on the "Medicare Taxes Paid" (From Table 7—Step 1) line item in the Expenses and Allowances section of the Dependent Student's Contribution Worksheet

For Step 2:

The lesser of the calculated dollar amount OR the pre-printed capped dollar amount for the applicable category (AA or BB for the parent) should be listed for the "OASDI Taxes Paid" (From Table 7—Step 2) line item in the Expenses & Allowances section of the Parent's Contribution Worksheet. The lesser of the calculated dollar amount OR the pre-printed capped dollar amount (in category CC for the student), if any, should be listed for the "OASDI Taxes Paid" (From Table 7—Step 2) line item in the Deductions Against Income section of the Student's Contribution Worksheet.

TABLE 8
Employment Allowance

To complete Table 8, refer to the bottom line on Table 1 to obtain the appropriate "Income Earned From Work" figure.

IF YOU COMPLETED ONLY THE LEFT COLUMN ON TABLE 1

Total income earned from work × 0.35 = $ ___________

The maximum employment allowance is $5,200. If the number calculated above is greater than the maximum allowance, the maximum number instead of the calculated number should be listed on the Parent Contribution from Income Worksheet (Allowances Against Parent's Income section).

IF YOU COMPLETED THE LEFT AND RIGHT COLUMNS ON TABLE 1

Income earned from work in left column of Table 1 × 0.35 = $ ___________

Income earned from work in right column of Table 1 × 0.35 = + $ ___________

The maximum employment allowance is $5,200. Take the sum of the two numbers. If that sum is greater than the maximum allowance, the maximum number should be listed instead of the calculated number on the Parent Contribution from Income worksheet (Expenses & Allowances section).

TABLE 9
Income Protection Allowance

Family Size (including student)	Income Protection Allowance Amount
2	$30,300
3	$37,720
4	$46,590
5	$54,970
6	$64,290

(Note: For each additional family member, add $7,260.)

TABLE 10
Business/Farm Net Worth Adjustment

Business and farm net worth for the parent(s) is somewhat sheltered in the aid formula. To determine the proper amount to list on the adjusted net worth of businesses and/or farms line in the Parent Contribution from Assets section, first determine the net worth of the business/farm and then use the conversion rates below. See Chapter 3, "What About My Farm?" and "Ownership of a Business." If you are a part-owner, use only your share of the net worth for the calculations.

Please check your free online student tools (see page vi), as there may be updates on this topic as a result of late-breaking developments.

Net Worth (NW) = Assets minus Liabilities

If you do not have a current balance sheet available for the business and/or farm, you can use the following guidelines:

Business and/or farm assets (Include cash, investments, receivables, inventories, land and buildings, machinery and equipment net of accumulated depreciation, and other assets. Do not include the value of intangible assets such as goodwill.) $ ____________

Minus: Business and/or farm liabilities (Accounts payable, mortgages on land and buildings, other debts) ($ ____________)

Net Worth (NW) (if negative, list 0) $ ____________

Now that you have a net worth figure, use the adjustment table below to calculate the adjusted business/farm net worth.

Helpful hint: The ADJUSTED NET WORTH figure that you calculate should be smaller than the Net Worth figure.

Business or Farm Adjustments	
If Net Worth (NW)	**Adjusted Amount Is**
Less than $1	$0
$1 to $180,000	$0 + 40% of NW of business/farm
$180,001 to $540,000	$72,000 + 50% of NW over $180,000
$540,001 to $905,000	$252,000 + 60% of NW over $540,000
$905,001 or more	$471,000 + 100% of NW over $905,000

ADJUSTED BUSINESS/FARM NET WORTH $ ____________
(This figure will be listed on the adjusted net worth of businesses and/or farms line in the Parent Contribution from Assets section.)

TABLE 11
Asset Protection Allowance

Age of Older Parent in Household	Two-Parent Family	One-Parent Family
34 or less	$0	$0
35–39	$0	$0
40–44	$0	$0
45–49	$0	$0
50–54	$0	$0
55–59	$0	$0
60–64	$0	$0
65 or more	$0	$0

TABLE 12
Parent's Contribution

Adjusted Available Income	Total Parents' Contribution
Less than –$8,900	–$1,958
–$8,900 to $22,600	22% of AAI
$22,601 to $28,300	$4,972 + 25% of AAI over $22,600
$28,301 to $34,000	$6,397 + 29% of AAI over $28,300
$34,001 to $39,900	$8,050 + 34% of AAI over $34,000
$39,901 to $45,600	$10,056 + 40% of AAI over $39,900
$45,601 or more	$12,336 + 47% of AAI over $45,600

PARENTS' CONTRIBUTION WORKSHEET

Income Addition & Offsets

PC1.	**PARENTS' ADJUSTED GROSS INCOME** *(From Table 3—Line C)*	$ ________
PC2.	**PARENTS' TOTAL UNTAXED INCOME** *(From Table 4—Line F)*	$ ________
PC3.	**PARENTS' TOTAL INCOME ADDITIONS** *(Line PC1 plus Line PC2 above)*	$ ________
PC4.	**PARENTS' TOTAL INCOME OFFSETS** *(From Table 5—Line D)*	($ ________)
PC5.	**PARENTS' TOTAL INCOME** *(Line PC3 minus Line PC4 above)* *(Can be a negative number)*	$ ________

Expenses & Allowances

(For explanations consult Chapter 3, "Expenses")

Sum of:

	U.S. Taxes Paid *(From Table 6)*	+ $ ________
	Medicare Tax Paid *(From Table 7—Step 1)*	+ $ ________
	OASDI Tax Paid *(From Table 7—Step 2)*	+ $ ________
	Employment Allowance *(From Table 8)*	+ $ ________
	Income Protection Allowance *(From Table 9)*	+ $ ________
PC6.	**TOTAL EXPENSES AND ALLOWANCES**	($ ________)
PC7.	**PARENTS' AVAILABLE INCOME** *(Line PC5 minus Line PC6)* (Can be a negative number)	**$** ________

Instructions for Listing Assets and Debts on the Next Page

(For explanations consult Chapter 3, "Assets and Liabilities")

If the parent of a dependent student required to report financial information on the FAFSA meets the criteria to have parent and student assets exempt from being required to be reported on the FAFSA (see the section "The Criteria to Exclude Assets in the FM" in Chapter 3), then skip to line PC15 on this Worksheet and enter the digit 0 (zero) as your response for Line PC15. Additionally, you can leave the entire Student's Assets and Liability section blank and enter the digit 0 (zero) as your response for Line SC7. CONTRIBUTION FROM ASSETS that appears toward the end of the DEPENDENT STUDENT'S CONTRIBUTION WORKSHEET, which follows after Table 13.

List only your share of assets and liabilities for this section. Do not include the home, retirement accounts, annuities, or insurance products.

For 529 plans as well as Coverdell Education Savings Accounts (formerly known as Education IRAs): include the current value of any 529 plans (prepaid plans and/or savings plans) and/or the current value of any Coverdells for the benefit of the student that are owned by the Parent or Parent's Spouse/Partner required to report financial information on a dependent student's FAFSA. Coverdell ESAs or 529 plans owned by a dependent student should be included as part of the parent assets (and not as a student asset on the DEPENDENT STUDENT'S CONTRIBUTION WORKSHEET). Do not include the value of any 529 plans and/or Coverdells owned for the benefit of the student's siblings as part of your responses for any of the following parent asset categories.

Parents' Assets

Sum of:

	Cash, savings and checking accounts	+ $ ________
	529 plans (see instructions on previous page)	+ $ ________
	Coverdell ESA (see instructions on previous page)	+ $ ________
	Investments other than real estate	+ $ ________
	Market value of real estate other than the home	+ $ ________
	Child support received in most recent calendar year	+ $ ________
PC8.	**TOTAL PERSONAL ASSETS**	$ ________

Parents' Debts

Sum of:

	Debts owed on real estate other than the home (Add principal balance(s) outstanding on mortgages plus home equity line(s) of credit outstanding plus other debts against real estate.)	$ ________
	Other debts against assets listed above (margin debt, passbook loan, etc.)	+ $ ________
PC9.	**TOTAL PERSONAL DEBTS**	($ ________)
PC10.	**PERSONAL NET ASSETS** *(Line PC8 minus Line PC9)*	$ ________
PC11.	**ADJUSTED BUSINESS/FARM NET WORTH** *(From Table 10)*	$ ________
PC12.	**TOTAL NET ASSETS** *(Line PC10 plus Line PC11)*	$ ________
PC13.	**ASSET ALLOWANCES** *(From Table 11)*	($ ________)
PC14.	**REMAINING ASSETS** *(Line PC12 minus Line PC13)*	$ ________
PC15.	**CONTRIBUTION FROM ASSETS** *(If Line PC14 is a negative number, enter -0-; otherwise, multiply the amount on Line PC14 by 0.12.)*	$ ________
PC16.	**ADJUSTED AVAILABLE INCOME** *(Line PC7 plus Line PC15)* *(If Line PC7 is a negative number, Line PC16 will be less than Line PC15.)*	$ ________
PC17.	**PARENTS' EXPECTED CONTRIBUTION** *(Refer to Table 12 and use the Adjusted Available Income amount on Line PC16.)*	$ ________

TABLE 13
Student's U.S. Taxes Paid

If the student completed a base income year tax return: Skip to the last line on this Table 13 and list the amount from Line 24 of the IRS 1040 at the end of the table.

If the student has not yet filed but will file their own tax return: Complete this table using your best estimates.

If the student did not and will not file a tax return: Skip Table 13 and list 0 (zero) on line SC8 on the "DEPENDENT STUDENT'S CONTRIBUTION WORKSHEET" that follows. You should also skip the "Student's Income" and "Deductions Against Income" sections on that student worksheet.

Standard Deduction Worksheet

Student's wages, tips, salary, and other compensation subject to tax (similar to IRS 1040—Line 1z)	$ ________
Student's earned income from self-employment or farming (similar to Schedule 1, Lines 3 and 6)	+ $ ________
	+ $ 450
SUBTOTAL	$ ________
Minus: 1/2 Self-employment tax paid (if any)	($ ________)
A. TOTAL	$ ________
B. Minimum amount	$ 1,350
C. Enter the larger of Line A or B	$ ________
D. STANDARD DEDUCTION (enter the smaller of Line C or $14,600)	$ ________
Student's wages, tips, salary, and other compensation subject to tax (IRS 1040—Line 1z)	$ ________
Student's other taxable income (IRS 1040—Sum of Lines 2b, 3b, 4b, 5b, 6b, 7a, and 8)	+ $ ________
Adjustments to income (if any) (Schedule 1, Line 22)	($ ________)
E. ADJUSTED GROSS INCOME (2025 IRS 1040—Line 11a)	$ ________
Minus: Standard deduction (From Line D above)	($ ________)

F. TAXABLE INCOME (Line E minus Line D) $ ___________

Use the Taxable Income figure listed above with the table below to calculate the student's U.S. Income Taxes.

If your taxable income is: *Over—*	But not *over—*	*Income taxes paid is—*	*of the amount over—*
$0	$11,925	10%	$0
$11,925	$48,475	$1,192.50 + 12%	$11,925
$48,475	$103,350	$5,578.50 + 22%	$48,475
$103,350	$197,300	$17,651.00 + 24%	$103,350
$197,300	$250,525	$40,199.00 + 32%	$197,300
$250,525	$626,350	$57,231.00 + 35%	$250,525
$626,350	—	$188,770.65 + 37%	$626,350

U.S. Income Tax Liability (using tax table above) $ ___________

Plus: Additions to tax (IRS 1040, Schedule 2, Line 1z) + $ ___________

Plus: Alternative minimum tax (IRS 1040 Schedule 2, Line 2) + $ ___________

Sub-total $ ___________

Minus: Tax Credits (IRS 1040 Line 21) ($ ___________)

Sub-total (IRS 1040 Line 22) $ ___________

Plus: Other taxes (IRS 1040 Line 23) + $ ___________

STUDENT'S 2025 U.S. TAXES PAID (IRS 1040 Line 24) $ ___________
(List in the Deductions Against Income section on the Dependent Student's Contribution Worksheet that follows)

DEPENDENT STUDENT'S CONTRIBUTION WORKSHEET

Student's Income

If the student did not file a base year tax return: Skip this page of the worksheet, make sure -0- is entered on Line SC8, and proceed with the "Assets and Liabilities" section on the next page.

If the student did file a base income year return: If applicable, subtract the amount of any federal work-study earnings (reported on Line 1a of the IRS Form 1040) and/or subtract the amount of any taxable grants, scholarships, or AmeriCorps benefits (reported either as part of Line 1z of the IRS Form 1040 and/or on Line 8r of Schedule 1 of the IRS 1040) from the Adjusted Gross Income amount (Line 11a on a completed IRS 1040 or line E on Table 13). This will derive the "Student's modified AGI" amount to be listed below. If neither of these two types of income apply, then the AGI on Line 11a of the IRS 1040 equals the "Student's modified AGI" to be listed below for the purposes of this worksheet.

	Student's modified AGI	$ ________
	Student's untaxed income *(Refer to Table 4 for types of untaxed income to include as attributable to the student.)*	+ $ ________
SC1.	**TOTAL INCOME** (sum of the above)	$ ________

Deductions Against Income

	U.S taxes student will be expected to pay *(From last line of Table 13 or from Table 6, as applicable to the student)*	$ ________
	Student's Medicare Tax *(from Table 7—Step 1)*	+ $ ________
	Student's OASDI Tax Paid *(Refer to Table 7—Step 2)*	+ $ ________
	Adjustment for negative parent AAI [If Line PC16 of the Parent's Contribution Worksheet is negative, enter that negative number as a positive amount; otherwise, enter -0- (zero)]	+ $ ________
	Income Protection Allowance	+ $ 12,200
SC2.	**TOTAL DEDUCTIONS AGAINST INCOME** (sum of the deductions above)	($ ________)
SC3.	**AVAILABLE INCOME** (SC1 minus SC2, but if negative enter -0-; use this SC3 amount to complete SC8 on the next page.)	$ ________

Student's Assets and Liabilities

If the dependent student's parent who is required to report financial information on the FAFSA meets the criteria to be exempt for asset reporting and so did not provide asset information on the Parent's Contribution Worksheet, then you should skip this section, list -0- on Line SC7 below and then proceed to Line SC8 (which should already have been completed).

Otherwise, please read on and complete this section to derive the amount for SC7. Note that if the student owns their own (or a share of a) business and/or farm, follow the instructions on Table 10, using the student's business/farm asset and liability information to determine the student's "Adjusted business/farm net worth" amount to be listed below. Do not include the business/farm debt again on Line SC5 below.

	Cash, savings, and checking account	$ ________
	Uniform Gifts to Minors Act and custodial accounts	+ $ ________
	Investments other than real estate	+ $ ________
	Market value of any real estate	+ $ ________
	Adjusted business/farm net worth	+ $ ________
SC4.	**TOTAL ASSETS** (sum of the above)	$ ________
SC5.	TOTAL DEBTS (Any debts against assets listed above)	($ ________)
SC6.	**TOTAL NET ASSETS** (SC4 minus SC5; if negative, enter -0-)	$ ________

Student's Contribution

SC7.	CONTRIBUTION FROM ASSETS (SC6 × 0.20)	+ $ ________
SC8.	CONTRIBUTION FROM INCOME (SC3 × .0.50)	+ $ ________
SC9.	OTHER GIFTS AND SCHOLARSHIPS RECEIVED OR AWARDED	+ $ ________
SC10.	**STUDENT'S CONTRIBUTION** (Sum of SC7, SC8, and SC9)	$ ________

CALCULATED SAI FORMULA

Parent Contribution (PC17 from Parent's Worksheet) + Student Contribution (SC10 above) = SAI

Sample Forms

2027–28

FAFSA® Form
Free Application *for* Federal Student Aid

July 1, 2027 – June 30, 2028

Federal **Student Aid**

An OFFICE of the U.S. DEPARTMENT of EDUCATION

OMB No. 1845-0001

For help in filling out the FAFSA form, go to StudentAid.gov/fafsahelp or call 1-800-4-FED-AID (1-800-433-3243).

Student

▶ ***The student must complete this section.***

Questions 1–24 apply to the student. ***All questions are required*** *except in some circumstances (see "Can I skip any questions?", on page 4).*

1 Student Identity Information

[See Notes page 21.]

The student's full legal name, for example, as it appears on their Social Security card.

First name

Middle name

Last name

Suffix *(e.g., Jr. or III)*

Date of birth ___ / ___ / ____ *MM DD YYYY*

Social Security number (SSN) ___-__-____

Individual Taxpayer Identification Number (ITIN) ___-__-____

If the student does not have an ITIN, leave this field blank.

2 Student Contact Information

[See Notes page 21.]

Mobile phone number ___-___-____

Email address

Continue on next line.

Permanent mailing address

Continue on next line.

Include apt. number.

▶ *If you are currently incarcerated, enter your inmate identifying number at the end of your mailing address.*

▶ *If you are homeless or have no stable address, provide an address where you can reliably receive mail.*

City

State

Postal (ZIP) code

Country

3 Student Current Marital Status

[See Notes page 21.]

○ Single (never married) ○ Married (not separated) ○ Remarried ○ Separated ○ Divorced ○ Widowed

4 Student College or Career School Plans

What year will the student be in college when they start their classes for the 2027–28 school year?

○ First (freshman) ○ Second (sophomore) ○ Third or higher (junior and up) ○ Graduate-level (such as a master's or doctorate)

Will the student already have a bachelor's degree when they start their college classes for the 2027–28 school year? ○ Yes ○ No

Will the student be pursuing an initial teaching certification at the elementary or secondary level? ○ Yes ○ No

Student

7

The above is a reprint of a draft of the 2027–2028 FAFSA. It is for informational purposes only. DO NOT SEND IN.

2027–28

5 Student Personal Circumstances

[See Notes page 21.]

Select all that apply.

- ☐ The student is currently serving on active duty in the U.S. armed forces for purposes other than training.
- ☐ The student is a veteran of the U.S. armed forces.
- ☐ The student has children or other people (excluding their spouse) who live with the student and receive more than half of their support from the student now and between July 1, 2027, and June 30, 2028.
- ☐ At any time since the student turned 13, they were an orphan (no living biological or adoptive parent).
- ☐ At any time since the student turned 13, they were a ward of the court.
- ☐ At any time since the student turned 13, they were in foster care.
- ☐ The student is or was a legally emancipated minor, as determined by a court in their state of residence.
- ☐ The student is or was in a legal guardianship with someone other than their parent or stepparent, as determined by a court in their state of residence.
- ☐ None of these apply.

6 Student Homelessness

[See Notes page 22.]

At any point in 2026 or after, has the student faced one of these situations?

- ○ They didn't live with a parent or guardian, and they were homeless.
- ○ They didn't live with a parent or guardian, were supporting themselves, and were at risk of becoming homeless.
- ○ They didn't face either of these situations.

If the first or second option above was selected, did any of the following determine the student was homeless or at risk of becoming homeless? *Select all that apply.*

- ☐ Director or designee of an emergency or transitional shelter, street outreach program, homeless youth drop-in center, or other program serving those experiencing homelessness
- ☐ The student's high school or school district homeless liaison or designee
- ☐ Director or designee of a project supported by a federal TRIO or GEAR UP program grant
- ☐ Financial aid administrator (FAA)
- ☐ None of these apply.

7 Student Unusual Circumstances

► *See "Can I skip any questions?", on page 4.*

Do unusual circumstances prevent the student from contacting their parents or would contacting their parents pose a risk to the student? *This information will help us evaluate the student's ability to pay for school.* ○ Yes ○ No

A student may be experiencing unusual circumstances if they:

- Left home due to an abusive or threatening environment;
- Are abandoned by or estranged from their parents;
- Have refugee or asylee status and are separated from their parents, or their parents are displaced in a foreign country;
- Are a victim of human trafficking;
- Are incarcerated, or their parents are incarcerated, and contact with the parents would pose a risk to the student; or
- Are otherwise unable to contact or locate their parents.

If the student does not have a safe, stable place to live because of such circumstances, they may be considered a homeless youth and should review the answer to question 6.

8 Parents' Refusal to Provide Information

► *See "Can I skip any questions?", on page 4.*

Are the student's parents refusing to provide their information on this FAFSA form? ○ Yes ○ No

This response must be "No" for the student to be eligible for a Federal Pell Grant and most other types of federal aid. If the answer is "Yes," a financial aid administrator at the student's college will determine their eligibility for a Direct Unsubsidized Loan only. If the student is approved for this option, they will not qualify to receive other types of federal student loans (including Direct Subsidized Loans), federal grants, or Federal Work-Study programs.

9 Family Size

► *See "Can I skip any questions?", on page 4.*

How many people are in the student's family?

☐☐ *Include the student (and spouse), the student's dependent children (even if they live apart temporarily, such as due to attending college), and other people living with the student now. Include these dependent children and other people only if the student will provide more than half of their support between July 1, 2027, and June 30, 2028.*

10 Number in College

► *See "Can I skip any questions?", on page 4.*

How many people in the student's family, including the student, will be in college between July 1, 2027, and June 30, 2028?

☐☐

Student

8

The above is a reprint of a draft of the 2027–2028 FAFSA. It is for informational purposes only. DO NOT SEND IN.

2027–28

11 Student Demographic Information

*The answers will not affect the student's eligibility for federal student aid, be used in any calculations, or be shared with the schools to which the student applies. They will be **used for research purposes only**.*

What is the student's sex? ◯ Male ◯ Female

12 Student Race and Ethnicity

*The answers will not affect the student's eligibility for federal student aid, be used in any calculations, or be shared with the schools to which the student applies. They will be **used for research purposes only**.*

What is the student's race and/or ethnicity? *Select all that apply. If you select "Other," you may enter more than one category in the entry boxes.*

☐ **American Indian or Alaska Native**

☐ Other: [ ]
Enter name of enrolled or principal tribe(s) (Navajo, Blackfeet, Mayan, Nome Eskimo Community, etc.)

☐ **Asian**

☐ Chinese ☐ Asian Indian ☐ Filipino ☐ Vietnamese ☐ Korean ☐ Japanese

☐ Other: [ ]
Enter Pakistani, Hmong, Afghan, etc.

☐ **Black or African American**

☐ African American ☐ Jamaican ☐ Haitian ☐ Nigerian ☐ Ethiopian ☐ Somali

☐ Other: [ ]
Enter Trinidadian and Tobagonian, Ghanaian, Congolese, etc.

☐ **Hispanic or Latino**

☐ Mexican ☐ Puerto Rican ☐ Salvadoran ☐ Cuban ☐ Dominican ☐ Guatemalan

☐ Other: [ ]
Enter Colombian, Honduran, Spaniard, etc.

☐ **Middle Eastern or North African**

☐ Lebanese ☐ Iranian ☐ Egyptian ☐ Syrian ☐ Iraqi ☐ Israeli

☐ Other: [ ]
Enter Moroccan, Yemeni, Kurdish, etc.

☐ **Native Hawaiian or Other Pacific Islander**

☐ Native Hawaiian ☐ Samoan ☐ Chamorro ☐ Tongan ☐ Fijian ☐ Marshallese

☐ Other: [ ]
Enter Chuukese, Palauan, Tahitian, etc.

☐ **White**

☐ English ☐ German ☐ Irish ☐ Italian ☐ Polish ☐ Scottish

☐ Other: [ ]
Enter French, Swedish, Norwegian, etc.

☐ **Prefer not to answer**

13 Student Citizenship

[See Notes page 22.]

Citizenship status

◯ U.S. citizen or national ◯ Eligible noncitizen ◯ Neither U.S. citizen nor eligible noncitizen

A–Number

A[ ]

If the student is an eligible noncitizen, provide their A-Number.

14 Student State of Residence

State, country, or military location

[ ] *Usually, this is the state where the student lives while not attending school. If the student lives in Canada, enter the province code. For any other foreign country, enter FC.*

Date the student became a resident

[ ] / [ ]
MM YYYY

If the student was born in their state of residence and hasn't moved out of state since, enter the student's date of birth. Otherwise, enter the date the student moved to their state of residence.

Student

9

The above is a reprint of a draft of the 2027–2028 FAFSA. It is for informational purposes only. DO NOT SEND IN.

2027–28

15 Parent Education Status

Did either of the student's parents attend or complete college?

○ Neither parent attended college ○ One or both parents attended college, but neither parent completed college ○ One or both parents completed college ○ Don't know

16 Parent Killed in Line of Duty

[See Notes page 22.]

Was the student's parent or guardian killed in the line of duty while (1) serving on active duty as a member of the U.S. armed forces on or after September 11, 2001, or (2) performing official duties as a public safety officer? ○ Yes ○ No

The student may be eligible for additional Federal Pell Grant funds once their eligibility is confirmed by their college or career school.

17 Student Completion of High School

[See Notes page 22.]

Will the student be done with high school when they start their college classes for the 2027–28 school year?

○ Yes (high school diploma) ○ Yes (GED or other state-recognized high school equivalent) ○ Yes (homeschooling under state law) ○ No, none of the previous

If the answer is "Yes (high school diploma)," provide the name, city, and state of the high school.

High school name

☐☐☐☐☐☐☐☐☐☐☐☐☐☐☐☐☐☐☐☐☐☐☐☐☐☐☐☐☐☐

Continue on next line.

☐☐☐☐☐☐☐☐☐☐☐☐☐☐☐☐☐☐☐☐☐☐☐☐☐☐☐☐☐☐

City

☐☐☐☐☐☐☐☐☐☐☐☐☐☐☐☐☐☐☐☐☐☐☐☐☐☐☐☐

State

☐☐

If the student will have a GED or other state-recognized high school equivalent, which of the following did or will the student receive, and from which state? ○ GED ○ TASC ○ HiSET ○ Other

Issuing state ☐☐

18 Federal Benefits Received

[See Notes page 22.]

▶ *See "Can I skip any questions?", on page 4.*

In 2025 or 2026, did the student, or anyone in their family, get benefits from any of the federal programs listed below?

A student's family includes their spouse, children, and other dependents. Select all that apply.

☐ Medicaid

☐ Supplemental Nutrition Assistance Program (SNAP)

☐ Free or reduced-price school lunch (based on income)

☐ Earned income tax credit (EITC)

☐ Lower premiums for a plan purchased through the health insurance marketplace

☐ Special Supplemental Nutrition Program for Women, Infants, and Children (WIC)

☐ Supplemental Security Income (SSI)

☐ Federal housing assistance (e.g., Housing Choice Voucher [Section 8] or public housing)

☐ Temporary Assistance for Needy Families (TANF)

☐ None of these apply.

19 Student Tax Filing Status

[See Notes page 22.]

Did the student file a U.S. federal income tax return for 2025 (or will they)? ○ Yes ○ No

The federal income tax form is called IRS Form 1040 or 1040-NR.

Did the student file a 2025 income tax return from Puerto Rico or another U.S. territory (or will they)? ○ Yes ○ No

If the answer is "Yes" to both this and the previous question, fill out the "Combined adjusted gross income" and "Combined income tax paid" fields in question 20.

If the answer is "No" to the previous two questions, which situation below applies for 2025?

○ The student earned income in a foreign country. ○ The student worked for an international organization and wasn't required to report that income on any tax return. *(International organizations include, for example, the United Nations, World Bank, and International Monetary Fund.)* ○ Neither situation applies.

▶ *If the student (1) is not married; (2) did not file a U.S. federal income tax return or an income tax return from Puerto Rico or another U.S. territory for 2025; and (3) answered "Neither situation applies," questions 20–22 can be skipped; however, if the student is also required to provide parent information on the form, question 22 must be answered.*

Did the student file their 2025 tax return jointly with their current spouse (or will they)? ○ Yes ○ No

20 Student 2025 Tax Return Information

[If the student had a spouse at any time in 2025 or later, see Notes page 23.]

Filing status

○ Single ○ Head of household ○ Married filing jointly ○ Married filing separately ○ Qualifying surviving spouse

[Question 20 continues on next page.]

Student 10

The above is a reprint of a draft of the 2027–2028 FAFSA. It is for informational purposes only. DO NOT SEND IN.

2027–28

20 Student 2025 Tax Return Information *[continued]*

▶ ***Convert all currency to U.S. dollars. If the answer is zero or the question does not apply, enter 0. If the answer is negative, completely fill the circle (⊖) before the answer box.***

Income earned from work

$ ___,___,___,___

IRS Form 1040 (or 1040-NR): line 1z + Schedule 1: lines 3 + 6. If a tax form line's value is negative, treat it as zero in your calculation.

Tax exempt interest income

$ ___,___,___,___

IRS Form 1040: line 2a

Retirement income: untaxed amount of IRA distributions

$ ___,___,___,___

IRS Form 1040: line 4a minus 4b

Retirement income: untaxed amount of pensions

$ ___,___,___,___

IRS Form 1040: line 5a minus 5b

Retirement income: IRA rollover(s)

$ ___,___,___,___

If IRS Form 1040: line 4c, box 1 is checked, enter the amount of untaxed IRA distributions moved to an IRA or other qualified plan.

Retirement income: pension rollover(s)

$ ___,___,___,___

If IRS Form 1040: line 5c, box 1 is checked, enter the amount of untaxed pensions distributions moved to an IRA or other qualified plan.

▶ *Use the "Combined adjusted gross income" and "Combined income tax paid" fields* ***only*** *if the student filed both a U.S. federal income tax return and an income tax return from Puerto Rico or another U.S. territory. Otherwise, use the "Adjusted gross income" and "Income tax paid" fields.*

Adjusted gross income

⊖ $ ___,___,___

IRS Form 1040 (or 1040-NR): line 11a

Income tax paid

$ ___,___,___

IRS Form 1040: line 24. If negative, enter a zero.

OR

Combine values from the U.S. federal tax return and Puerto Rico (or other territory) tax return. Report each dollar once. If any amount is reported on both the U.S. and the territory tax return, do not count it twice.

Combined adjusted gross income

⊖ $ ___,___,___

IRS Form 1040 (or 1040-NR): line 11a and Puerto Rico Form 482.0: line 5. For tax returns from other territories, use the equivalent line item.

Combined income tax paid

$ ___,___,___

IRS Form 1040: line 24 and Puerto Rico Form 482.0: line 26. For tax returns from other territories, use the equivalent line item. If negative, enter a zero.

Did the student receive the earned income tax credit?
IRS Form 1040: line 27a – Earned income credit (EIC)

○ Yes ○ No ○ Don't know

IRA deductions and payments to self-employed SEP, SIMPLE, and qualified plans

$ ___,___,___,___

IRS Form 1040 Schedule 1: total of lines 16 + 20

Education credits
(American Opportunity and Lifetime Learning credits)

$ ___,___,___

IRS Form 1040 Schedule 3: line 3 + IRS Form 1040: line 29

Did the student file a Schedule A, B, D, E, F, or H with their 2025 IRS Form 1040?

○ Yes ○ No ○ Don't know

[See Notes page 23.]

Net profit or loss from IRS Form 1040 Schedule C

⊖ $ ___,___,___,___

IRS Form 1040 Schedule C: line 31

Foreign earned income exclusion

⊖ $ ___,___,___

IRS Form 1040 Schedule 1: line 8d

Amount of college grants, scholarships, or AmeriCorps benefits **reported as income to the IRS**

$ ___,___,___

This question is typically answered with a zero because most of these items (including Federal Pell Grants) are not considered taxable income. If the student is married, include the amount their spouse reported.

21 Annual Child Support Received

▶ *See "Can I skip any questions?", on page 4.*

Enter total amount the student received in child support for the last complete calendar year. If the answer to question 3 was "Married" or "Remarried," enter the combined amount the student and their spouse received. If the answer is zero or the question does not apply, enter 0.

$ ___,___,___

22 Student Assets

[See Notes page 23.]

If the answer to question 3 was "Married" or "Remarried," enter the combined amounts held by the student and their spouse. If the answer is zero or the question does not apply, enter 0. Net worth is the value of the investments, businesses, or farms minus any debts owed against them.

Current total of cash, savings, and checking accounts

$ ___,___,___

Don't include student aid, retirement accounts, or investments.

Current net worth of investments, including real estate

$ ___,___,___

Don't include the home the student lives in or retirement accounts.

Current net worth of businesses and farms

$ ___,___,___

Don't include a family business with 100 or fewer full-time employees, farms where the family resides, or a commercial fishing business and related expenses.

Student

11

The above is a reprint of a draft of the 2027–2028 FAFSA. It is for informational purposes only. DO NOT SEND IN.

23 Colleges

[See Notes page 23.]

2027–28

Enter the schools that should receive the student's FAFSA information.

College 1
Federal School Code OR College 1 name / Address and city — State 1

College 2
Federal School Code OR College 2 name / Address and city — State 2

College 3
Federal School Code OR College 3 name / Address and city — State 3

College 4
Federal School Code OR College 4 name / Address and city — State 4

College 5
Federal School Code OR College 5 name / Address and city — State 5

College 6
Federal School Code OR College 6 name / Address and city — State 6

College 7
Federal School Code OR College 7 name / Address and city — State 7

College 8
Federal School Code OR College 8 name / Address and city — State 8

College 9
Federal School Code OR College 9 name / Address and city — State 9

College 10
Federal School Code OR College 10 name / Address and city — State 10

24 Student Consent, Approval, and Signature

[See page 6.]

Refer to the terms on page 6. By filling in the answer circle below and signing this form, you (the student) agree to the terms set forth on page 6. **If you do not provide consent and approval by filling in the circle below and providing your signature, you will not be eligible for federal student aid.**

○ Consent and approval to transfer federal tax information from the Internal Revenue Service (IRS)

Student signature

Handwritten original signature using full name is required.

Date signed

MM / DD / YYYY

Student

12

The above is a reprint of a draft of the 2027–2028 FAFSA. It is for informational purposes only. DO NOT SEND IN.

2027–28

Student Spouse +

► **See "Who must provide information on the FAFSA form?", on page 3, to determine if a spouse must complete this section.**

Questions 25–29 apply to the ***student's spouse****. Leave blank any questions that don't apply to the student's spouse.*

25 Student Spouse Identity Information

The student spouse's full legal name, for example, as it appears on their Social Security card.

First name

Middle name

Last name

Suffix *(e.g., Jr. or III)*

Date of birth

/ /

MM DD YYYY

Social Security number (SSN)

– –

If the student spouse does not have an SSN, enter all zeros.

Individual Taxpayer Identification Number (ITIN)

– –

If the student spouse does not have an ITIN, leave this field blank.

26 Student Spouse Contact Information

[See Notes page 21.]

Mobile phone number

– –

Email address

Continue on next line

Permanent mailing address

Continue on next line.

Include apt. number.

City

State

Postal (ZIP) code

Country

27 Student Spouse Tax Filing Status

[See Notes page 22.]

► *See "Can I skip any questions?", on page 4.*

Did the student spouse file a U.S. federal income tax return for 2025 (or will they)? ◯ Yes ◯ No

The federal income tax form is called IRS Form 1040 or 1040-NR.

Did the student spouse file a 2025 tax return from Puerto Rico or another U.S. territory (or will they)? ◯ Yes ◯ No

If the answer is "Yes" to both this and the previous question, fill out the "Combined adjusted gross income" and "Combined income tax paid" fields in question 28.

If the answer is "No" to the previous two questions, which situation below applies for 2025?

◯ The student spouse earned income in a foreign country.

◯ The student spouse worked for an international organization and wasn't required to report that income on any tax return. *(International organizations include, for example, the United Nations, World Bank, and International Monetary Fund.)*

◯ Neither situation applies.

► *If the student spouse (1) did not file a U.S. federal income tax return or an income tax return from Puerto Rico or another U.S. territory for 2025, and (2) answered "Neither situation applies," question 28 can be skipped.*

Student Spouse +

13

The above is a reprint of a draft of the 2027–2028 FAFSA. It is for informational purposes only. DO NOT SEND IN.

28 Student Spouse 2025 Tax Return Information

[See Notes page 23.]

2027–28

▶ See "Can I skip any questions?", on page 4.

Filing status

○ Single ○ Head of household ○ Married filing jointly ○ Married filing separately ○ Qualifying surviving spouse

▶ Convert all currency to U.S. dollars. If the answer is zero or the question does not apply, enter 0. If the answer is negative, completely fill the circle (⊖) before the answer box.

Income earned from work

$ ___,___,___,___

IRS Form 1040 (or 1040-NR): line 1z + Schedule 1: lines 3 + 6. If a tax form line's value is negative, treat it as zero in your calculation.

Tax exempt interest income

$ ___,___,___,___

IRS Form 1040: line 2a

Retirement income: untaxed amount of IRA distributions

$ ___,___,___,___

IRS Form 1040: line 4a minus 4b

Retirement income: untaxed amount of pensions

$ ___,___,___,___

IRS Form 1040: line 5a minus 5b

Retirement income: IRA rollover(s)

$ ___,___,___,___

If IRS Form 1040: line 4c, box 1 is checked, enter the amount of untaxed IRA distributions moved to an IRA or other qualified plan.

Retirement income: pension rollover(s)

$ ___,___,___,___

If IRS Form 1040: line 5c, box 1 is checked, enter the amount of untaxed pensions distributions moved to an IRA or other qualified plan.

▶ *Use the "Combined adjusted gross income" and "Combined income tax paid" fields **only** if the student spouse filed both a U.S. federal income tax return and an income tax return from Puerto Rico or another U.S. territory. Otherwise, use the "Adjusted gross income" and "Income tax paid" fields.*

Adjusted gross income

⊖ $ ___,___,___

IRS Form 1040 (or 1040-NR): line 11a

Income tax paid

$ ___,___,___

IRS Form 1040: line 24. If negative, enter a zero.

OR

Combine values from the U.S. federal tax return and Puerto Rico (or other territory) tax return. Report each dollar once. If any amount is reported on both the U.S. and the territory tax return, do not count it twice.

Combined adjusted gross income

⊖ $ ___,___,___

IRS Form 1040 (or 1040-NR): line 11a and Puerto Rico Form 482.0: line 5. For tax returns from other territories, use the equivalent line item.

Combined income tax paid

$ ___,___,___

IRS Form 1040: line 24 and Puerto Rico Form 482.0: line 26. For tax returns from other territories, use the equivalent line item. If negative, enter a zero.

IRA deductions and payments to self-employed SEP, SIMPLE, and qualified plans

$ ___,___,___,___

IRS Form 1040 Schedule 1: total of lines 16 + 20

Education credits
(American Opportunity and Lifetime Learning credits)

$ ___,___,___

IRS Form 1040 Schedule 3: line 3 + IRS Form 1040: line 29

Did the student spouse file a Schedule A, B, D, E, F, or H with their 2025 IRS Form 1040?

○ Yes ○ No ○ Don't know

Net profit or loss from IRS Form 1040 Schedule C

⊖ $ ___,___,___,___

IRS Form 1040 Schedule C: line 31

Foreign earned income exclusion

⊖ $ ___,___,___

IRS Form 1040 Schedule 1: line 8d

29 Student Spouse Consent, Approval, and Signature

[See page 6.]

▶ See "Can I skip any questions?", on page 4.

Refer to the terms on page 6. By filling in the answer circle below and signing this form, you (the student spouse) agree to the terms set forth on page 6.
If you do not provide consent and approval by filling in the circle below and providing your signature, the student will not be eligible for federal student aid.

○ Consent and approval to transfer federal tax information from the Internal Revenue Service (IRS)

Student spouse signature

Handwritten original signature using full name is required.

Date signed

___ / ___ / _____
MM DD YYYY

Student Spouse

14

The above is a reprint of a draft of the 2027–2028 FAFSA. It is for informational purposes only. DO NOT SEND IN.

2027–28

Parent

▶ ***See "Who must provide information on the FAFSA form?", on page 3, to determine if a parent must complete this section.***

*Questions 30–41 apply to the **student's parent**. Leave blank any questions that don't apply to the parent.*

30 Parent Identity Information

The parent's full legal name, for example, as it appears on their Social Security card.

First name

Middle name

Last name

Suffix *(e.g., Jr. or III)*

Date of birth

MM / DD / YYYY

Social Security number (SSN)

If the parent does not have an SSN, enter all zeros.

Individual Taxpayer Identification Number (ITIN)

If the parent does not have an ITIN, leave this field blank.

31 Parent Contact Information

[See Notes page 21.]

Mobile phone number

Email address

Continue on next line.

Permanent mailing address

Continue on next line.

Include apt. number.

City

State

Postal (ZIP) code

Country

32 Parent Current Marital Status

[See Notes page 21.]

- ○ Single (never married)
- ○ Unmarried and both legal parents living together
- ○ Married (not separated)
- ○ Remarried
- ○ Separated
- ○ Divorced
- ○ Widowed

33 Parent State of Residence

State, country, or military location

If the parent lives in Canada, enter the province code. For any other foreign country, enter FC.

Date the parent became a resident

MM / YYYY

If the parent was born in their state of residence and hasn't moved out of state since, enter the parent's date of birth. Otherwise, enter the date the parent moved to their state of residence.

Parent

15

The above is a reprint of a draft of the 2027–2028 FAFSA. It is for informational purposes only. DO NOT SEND IN.

34 Family Size

How many people are in the parent's family?

☐☐ *Include the parent (and spouse or partner), the student, the parent's dependent children (even if they live apart temporarily, such as due to attending college), and other people living with the parent now. Include these dependent children and other people only if the parent will provide more than half of their support between July 1, 2027, and June 30, 2028.*

35 Number in College

How many people in the parent's family will be in college between July 1, 2027, and June 30, 2028?

☐☐ *Do not include parent(s).*

36 Federal Benefits Received

[See Notes page 22.]

In 2025 or 2026, did the parent, or anyone in their family, get benefits from any of the federal programs listed below?

A parent's family includes their spouse, children, and other dependents. Select all that apply.

- ☐ Medicaid
- ☐ Supplemental Nutrition Assistance Program (SNAP)
- ☐ Free or reduced-price school lunch (based on income)
- ☐ Earned income tax credit (EITC)
- ☐ Lower premiums for a plan purchased through the health insurance marketplace
- ☐ Special Supplemental Nutrition Program for Women, Infants, and Children (WIC)
- ☐ Supplemental Security Income (SSI)
- ☐ Federal housing assistance (e.g., Housing Choice Voucher [Section 8] or public housing)
- ☐ Temporary Assistance for Needy Families (TANF)
- ☐ None of these apply.

37 Parent Tax Filing Status

[See Notes page 22.]

Did the parent file a U.S. federal income tax return for 2025 (or will they)? ○ Yes ○ No

The U.S. federal income tax form is called IRS Form 1040 or 1040-NR.

Did the parent file a 2025 tax return from Puerto Rico or another U.S. territory (or will they)? ○ Yes ○ No

If the answer is "Yes" to both this and the previous question, fill out the "Combined adjusted gross income" and "Combined income tax paid" fields in question 38.

If the parent didn't file a U.S. federal tax return for 2025, select the reason why:

- ○ They filed or will file a tax return in a country other than the United States.
- ○ They weren't required to file a U.S. federal tax return because their income was lower than the IRS filing threshold.
- ○ They earned income in a foreign country but will not file a foreign tax return.
- ○ They worked for an international organization and weren't required to report that income on any tax return. *International organizations include, for example, the United Nations, World Bank, and International Monetary Fund.*
- ○ They didn't and won't file a U.S. tax return for a different reason than low income.

Did the parent file their 2025 tax return jointly with their current spouse (or will they)? ○ Yes ○ No

38 Parent 2025 Tax Return Information

[If the parent had a spouse at any time in 2025 or later, see Notes page 23.]

Filing status

○ Single ○ Head of household ○ Married filing jointly ○ Married filing separately ○ Qualifying surviving spouse

► ***Convert all currency to U.S. dollars. If the answer is zero or the question does not apply, enter 0. If the answer is negative, completely fill the circle (⊖) before the answer box.***

Income earned from work

$ ☐☐,☐☐☐,☐☐☐,☐☐☐

IRS Form 1040 (or 1040-NR): line 1z + Schedule 1: lines 3 + 6. If a tax form line's value is negative, treat it as zero in your calculation.

Tax exempt interest income

$ ☐☐,☐☐☐,☐☐☐,☐☐☐

IRS Form 1040: line 2a

Retirement income: untaxed amount of IRA distributions

$ ☐☐,☐☐☐,☐☐☐,☐☐☐

IRS Form 1040: line 4a minus 4b

Retirement income: untaxed amount of pensions

$ ☐☐,☐☐☐,☐☐☐,☐☐☐

IRS Form 1040: line 5a minus 5b

Retirement income: IRA rollover(s)

$ ☐☐,☐☐☐,☐☐☐,☐☐☐

If IRS Form 1040: line 4c, box 1 is checked, enter the amount of untaxed IRA distributions moved to an IRA or other qualified plan.

Retirement income: pension rollover(s)

$ ☐☐,☐☐☐,☐☐☐,☐☐☐

If IRS Form 1040: line 5c, box 1 is checked, enter the amount of untaxed pensions distributions moved to an IRA or other qualified plan.

[Question 38 continues on next page.]

Parent

The above is a reprint of a draft of the 2027–2028 FAFSA. It is for informational purposes only. DO NOT SEND IN.

2027–28

38 Parent 2025 Tax Return Information *[continued]*

▶ *Use the "Combined adjusted gross income" and "Combined income tax paid" fields* ***only*** *if the parent filed both a U.S. federal income tax return and an income tax return from Puerto Rico or another U.S. territory. Otherwise, use the "Adjusted gross income" and "Income tax paid" fields.*

Adjusted gross income

⊖ $ ☐☐☐,☐☐☐,☐☐☐

IRS Form 1040 (or 1040-NR): line 11a

Income tax paid

$ ☐☐☐,☐☐☐,☐☐☐

IRS Form 1040: line 24. If negative, enter a zero.

OR

Combine values from the U.S. federal tax return and Puerto Rico (or other territory) tax return. Report each dollar once. If any amount is reported on both the U.S. and the territory tax return, do not count it twice.

Combined adjusted gross income

⊖ $ ☐☐☐,☐☐☐,☐☐☐

IRS Form 1040 (or 1040-NR): line 11a and Puerto Rico Form 482.0: line 5. For tax returns from other territories, use the equivalent line item.

Combined income tax paid

$ ☐☐☐,☐☐☐,☐☐☐

IRS Form 1040: line 24 and Puerto Rico Form 482.0: line 26. For tax returns from other territories, use the equivalent line item. If negative, enter a zero.

Did the parent receive the earned income tax credit?
IRS Form 1040: line 27a – Earned income credit (EIC)

○ Yes ○ No ○ Don't know

IRA deductions and payments to self-employed SEP, SIMPLE, and qualified plans

$ ☐☐☐,☐☐☐,☐☐☐,☐☐☐

IRS Form 1040 Schedule 1: total of lines 16 + 20

Education credits
(American Opportunity and Lifetime Learning credits)

$ ☐☐☐,☐☐☐,☐☐☐

IRS Form 1040 Schedule 3: line 3 + IRS Form 1040: line 29

Did the parent file a Schedule A, B, D, E, F, or H with their 2025 IRS Form 1040?

○ Yes ○ No ○ Don't know

[See Notes page 23.]

Net profit or loss from IRS Form 1040 Schedule C

⊖ $ ☐☐☐,☐☐☐,☐☐☐,☐☐☐

IRS Form 1040 Schedule C: line 31

Foreign earned income exclusion

⊖ $ ☐☐☐,☐☐☐,☐☐☐

IRS Form 1040 Schedule 1: line 8d

Amount of college grants, scholarships, or AmeriCorps benefits **reported as income to the IRS**

$ ☐,☐☐☐,☐☐☐

This question is typically answered with a zero because most of these items (including Federal Pell Grants) are not considered taxable income. If the parent is married, include the amount their spouse reported.

Parent

39 Annual Child Support Received

Enter total amount the parent received in child support for the last complete calendar year. If the answer to question 32 was "Married," "Remarried," or "Unmarried and both legal parents living together," enter the combined amount the parent and their spouse received. If the answer is zero or the question does not apply, enter 0.

$ ☐,☐☐☐,☐☐☐

40 Parent Assets

[See Notes page 23.]

If the answer to question 32 was "Married," "Remarried," or "Unmarried and both legal parents living together," enter the combined amounts held by the parent and their spouse or partner. If the answer is zero or the question does not apply, enter 0. Net worth is the value of the investments, businesses, or farms minus any debts owed against them.

Current total of cash, savings, and checking accounts

$ ☐,☐☐☐,☐☐☐

Don't include student aid, retirement accounts, or investments.

Current net worth of investments, including real estate

$ ☐,☐☐☐,☐☐☐

Don't include the home the parent lives in or retirement accounts.

Current net worth of businesses and farms

$ ☐,☐☐☐,☐☐☐

Don't include a family business with 100 or fewer full-time employees, farms where the family resides, or a commercial fishing business and related expenses.

41 Parent Consent, Approval, and Signature

[See page 6.]

Refer to the terms on page 6. By filling in the answer circle below and signing this form, you (the parent) agree to the terms set forth on page 6. **If you do not provide consent and approval by filling in the circle below and providing your signature, the student will not be eligible for federal student aid.**

○ Consent and approval to transfer federal tax information from the Internal Revenue Service (IRS)

Parent signature

☐

Handwritten original signature using full name is required.

Date signed

☐☐ / ☐☐ / ☐☐☐☐
MM DD YYYY

17

The above is a reprint of a draft of the 2027–2028 FAFSA. It is for informational purposes only. DO NOT SEND IN.

2027–28

Parent Spouse or Partner

▶ ***Do not complete this section if you are not the student's legal parent or stepparent. See "Who must provide information on the FAFSA form?", on page 3, to determine if the parent spouse or partner must complete this section.***

Questions 42–46 apply to the ***parent spouse or partner****. Leave blank any questions that don't apply to the parent spouse or partner.*

42 Parent Spouse or Partner Identity Information

The parent spouse or partner's full legal name, for example, as it appears on their Social Security card.

First name

Middle name

Last name

Suffix *(e.g., Jr. or III)*

Date of birth

MM / DD / YYYY

Social Security number (SSN)

If the parent spouse or partner does not have an SSN, enter all zeros.

Individual Taxpayer Identification Number (ITIN)

If the parent spouse or partner does not have an ITIN, leave this field blank.

43 Parent Spouse or Partner Contact Information

[See Notes page 21.]

Mobile phone number

Email address

Continue on next line.

Permanent mailing address

Continue on next line.

Include apt. number.

City

State

Postal (ZIP) code

Country

44 Parent Spouse or Partner Tax Filing Status

[See Notes page 22.]

▶ *See "Can I skip any questions?", on page 4.*

Did the parent spouse or partner file a U.S. federal income tax return for 2025 (or will they)? ○ Yes ○ No

The U.S. federal income tax form is called IRS Form 1040 or 1040-NR.

Did the parent spouse or partner file a 2025 tax return from Puerto Rico or another U.S. territory (or will they)? ○ Yes ○ No

If the answer is "Yes" to both this and the previous question, fill out the "Combined adjusted gross income" and "Combined income tax paid" fields in question 45.

If the parent spouse or partner didn't file a U.S. federal tax return for 2025, select the reason why:

- ○ They filed or will file a tax return in a country other than the United States.
- ○ They weren't required to file a U.S. federal tax return because their income was lower than the IRS filing threshold.
- ○ They earned income in a foreign country but will not file a foreign tax return.
- ○ They worked for an international organization and weren't required to report that income on any tax return.
  International organizations include, for example, the United Nations, World Bank, and International Monetary Fund.
- ○ They didn't and won't file a U.S. tax return for a different reason than low income.

Parent Spouse or Partner

18

The above is a reprint of a draft of the 2027–2028 FAFSA. It is for informational purposes only. DO NOT SEND IN.

45 Parent Spouse or Partner 2025 Tax Return Information

[See Notes page 23.]

▶ See "Can I skip any questions?", on page 4.

Filing status

○ Single ○ Head of household ○ Married filing jointly ○ Married filing separately ○ Qualifying surviving spouse

▶ ***Convert all currency to U.S. dollars. If the answer is zero or the question does not apply, enter 0. If the answer is negative, completely fill the circle (⊖) before the answer box.***

Income earned from work

$ ___,___,___,___

IRS Form 1040 (or 1040-NR): line 1z + Schedule 1: lines 3 + 6. If a tax form line's value is negative, treat it as zero in your calculation.

Tax exempt interest income

$ ___,___,___,___

IRS Form 1040: line 2a

Retirement income: untaxed amount of IRA distributions

$ ___,___,___,___

IRS Form 1040: line 4a minus 4b

Retirement income: untaxed amount of pensions

$ ___,___,___,___

IRS Form 1040: line 5a minus 5b

Retirement income: IRA rollover(s)

$ ___,___,___,___

If IRS Form 1040: line 4c, box 1 is checked, enter the amount of untaxed IRA distributions moved to an IRA or other qualified plan.

Retirement income: pension rollover(s)

$ ___,___,___,___

If IRS Form 1040: line 5c, box 1 is checked, enter the amount of untaxed pensions distributions moved to an IRA or other qualified plan.

▶ *Use the "Combined adjusted gross income" and "Combined income tax paid" fields* ***only*** *if the parent spouse or partner filed both a U.S. federal income tax return and an income tax return from Puerto Rico or another U.S. territory. Otherwise, use the "Adjusted gross income" and "Income tax paid" fields.*

Adjusted gross income

⊖ $ ___,___,___

IRS Form 1040 (or 1040-NR): line 11a

Income tax paid

$ ___,___,___

IRS Form 1040: line 24. If negative, enter a zero.

OR

Combine values from the U.S. federal tax return and Puerto Rico (or other territory) tax return. Report each dollar once. If any amount is reported on both the U.S. and the territory tax return, do not count it twice.

Combined adjusted gross income

⊖ $ ___,___,___

IRS Form 1040 (or 1040-NR): line 11a and Puerto Rico Form 482.0: line 5. For tax returns from other territories, use the equivalent line item.

Combined income tax paid

$ ___,___,___

IRS Form 1040: line 24 and Puerto Rico Form 482.0: line 26. For tax returns from other territories, use the equivalent line item. If negative, enter a zero.

IRA deductions and payments to self-employed SEP, SIMPLE, and qualified plans

$ ___,___,___,___

IRS Form 1040 Schedule 1: total of lines 16 + 20

Education credits
(American Opportunity and Lifetime Learning credits)

$ ___,___,___

IRS Form 1040 Schedule 3: line 3 + IRS Form 1040: line 29

Did the parent spouse or partner file a Schedule A, B, D, E, F, or H with their 2025 IRS Form 1040?

○ Yes ○ No ○ Don't know

Net profit or loss from IRS Form 1040 Schedule C

⊖ $ ___,___,___,___

IRS Form 1040 Schedule C: line 31

Foreign earned income exclusion

⊖ $ ___,___,___

IRS Form 1040 Schedule 1: line 8d

46 Parent Spouse or Partner Consent, Approval, and Signature

[See page 6.]

▶ See "Can I skip any questions?", on page 4.

Refer to the terms on page 6. By filling in the answer circle below and signing this form, you (the parent spouse or partner) agree to the terms set forth on page 6. **If you do not provide consent and approval by filling in the circle below and providing your signature, the student will not be eligible for federal student aid.**

○ Consent and approval to transfer federal tax information from the Internal Revenue Service (IRS)

Parent spouse or partner signature

Handwritten original signature using full name is required.

Date signed

__/__/____

MM DD YYYY

Parent Spouse or Partner

The above is a reprint of a draft of the 2027–2028 FAFSA. It is for informational purposes only. DO NOT SEND IN.

2027–28

Prearer

► *See "Who must provide information on the FAFSA form?", on page 3, to determine if a preparer must complete this section. Paid preparers are prohibited.*

*Questions 47–49 apply to the **preparer**. Leave blank any questions that don't apply to the preparer.*

47 Preparer Identity Information

First name

Last name

Social Security number (SSN)

Employer Identification Number (EIN)

48 Preparer Contact Information

Affiliation / Organization

Permanent mailing address

Continue on next line.

Include apt. number.

City

State

Postal (ZIP) code

49 Preparer Signature

[See page 6.]

Refer to the terms on page 6. By signing this form, you (the preparer) agree to the terms set forth on page 6.

Preparer signature

Date signed

MM / DD / YYYY

Mail Your FAFSA® Form

Make a copy of pages 7 through 20 for your records. Then mail the original of pages 7 through 20 to:

Federal Student Aid Programs, P.O. Box 70208, London, KY 40742-0208

Extra postage will be required. When mailing, include pages 7 through 20, even if some are blank.

College Use Only

○ D/O

Federal school code

FAA signature

Data Entry Use Only

○ * ○ @ ○ D ○ C

Preparer

20

The above is a reprint of a draft of the 2027–2028 FAFSA. It is for informational purposes only. DO NOT SEND IN.

Form **1040** Department of the Treasury—Internal Revenue Service
U.S. Individual Income Tax Return **2025** OMB No. 1545-0074 IRS Use Only—Do not write or staple in this space.

For the year Jan. 1–Dec. 31, 2025, or other tax year beginning , 2025, ending , 20 See separate instructions.

☐ Filed pursuant to section 301.9100-2 ☐ Combat zone ☐ Deceased MM / DD / YYYY Spouse MM / DD / YYYY

☐ Other

Your first name and middle initial	Last name	**Your social security number**
If joint return, spouse's first name and middle initial	Last name	**Spouse's social security number**
Home address (number and street). If you have a P.O. box, see instructions.	Apt. no.	Check here if your main home, and your spouse's if filing a joint return, was in the U.S. for more than half of 2025. ☐
City, town, or post office. If you have a foreign address, also complete spaces below.	State / ZIP code	**Presidential Election Campaign** Check here if you, or your spouse if filing jointly, want $3 to go to this fund. Checking a box below will not change your tax or refund. ☐ You ☐ Spouse
Foreign country name	Foreign province/state/county / Foreign postal code	

Filing Status

Check only one box.

☐ Single
☐ Married filing jointly (even if only one had income)
☐ Married filing separately (MFS). Enter spouse's SSN above and full name here:
☐ Head of household (HOH)
☐ Qualifying surviving spouse (QSS)
If you checked the HOH or QSS box, enter the child's name if the qualifying person is a child but not your dependent:

☐ If treating a nonresident alien or dual-status alien spouse as a U.S. resident for the entire tax year, check the box and enter their name (see instructions and attach statement if required):

Digital Assets At any time during 2025, did you: (a) receive (as a reward, award, or payment for property or services); or (b) sell, exchange, or otherwise dispose of a digital asset (or a financial interest in a digital asset)? (See instructions.) . . ☐ Yes ☐ No

Dependents (see instructions)

If more than four dependents, see instructions and check here . . ☐

	Dependent 1	Dependent 2	Dependent 3	Dependent 4
(1) First name				
(2) Last name				
(3) SSN				
(4) Relationship				
(5) Check if lived with you more than half of 2025	(a) ☐ Yes (b) ☐ And in the U.S.	(a) ☐ Yes (b) ☐ And in the U.S.	(a) ☐ Yes (b) ☐ And in the U.S.	(a) ☐ Yes (b) ☐ And in the U.S.
(6) Check if	☐ Full-time student ☐ Permanently and totally disabled	☐ Full-time student ☐ Permanently and totally disabled	☐ Full-time student ☐ Permanently and totally disabled	☐ Full-time student ☐ Permanently and totally disabled
(7) Credits	☐ Child tax credit ☐ Credit for other dependents	☐ Child tax credit ☐ Credit for other dependents	☐ Child tax credit ☐ Credit for other dependents	☐ Child tax credit ☐ Credit for other dependents

☐ Check if your filing status is MFS or HOH and you lived apart from your spouse for the last 6 months of 2025, or you are legally separated according to your state law under a written separation agreement or a decree of separate maintenance and you did not live in the same household as your spouse at the end of 2025.

Income

Attach Form(s) W-2 here. Also attach Forms W-2G and 1099-R if tax was withheld.

If you did not get a Form W-2, see instructions.

Attach Sch. B if required.

1a	Total amount from Form(s) W-2, box 1 (see instructions)	1a
b	Household employee wages not reported on Form(s) W-2	1b
c	Tip income not reported on line 1a (see instructions)	1c
d	Medicaid waiver payments not reported on Form(s) W-2 (see instructions)	1d
e	Taxable dependent care benefits from Form 2441, line 26	1e
f	Employer-provided adoption benefits from Form 8839, line 31	1f
g	Wages from Form 8919, line 6	1g
h	Other earned income (see instructions). Enter type and amount:	1h
i	Nontaxable combat pay election (see instructions) . . . 1i	
z	Add lines 1a through 1h	1z
2a	Tax-exempt interest . . . 2a — b Taxable interest	2b
3a	Qualified dividends . . . 3a — b Ordinary dividends	3b
c	Check if your child's dividends are included in 1 ☐ Line 3a 2 ☐ Line 3b	
4a	IRA distributions . . . 4a — b Taxable amount	4b
c	Check if (see instructions) . . . 1 ☐ Rollover 2 ☐ QCD 3 ☐	
5a	Pensions and annuities . . 5a — b Taxable amount	5b
c	Check if (see instructions) . . . 1 ☐ Rollover 2 ☐ PSO 3 ☐	
6a	Social security benefits . . 6a — b Taxable amount	6b
c	If you elect to use the lump-sum election method, check here (see instructions) ☐	
d	If you are married filing separately and lived apart from your spouse the entire year (see inst.), check here ☐	
7a	Capital gain or (loss). Attach Schedule D if required	7a
b	Check if: ☐ Schedule D not required ☐ Includes child's capital gain or (loss)	
8	Additional income from Schedule 1, line 10	8
9	Add lines 1z, 2b, 3b, 4b, 5b, 6b, 7a, and 8. This is your **total income**	9
10	Adjustments to income from Schedule 1, line 26	10
11a	Subtract line 10 from line 9. This is your **adjusted gross income**	11a

For Disclosure, Privacy Act, and Paperwork Reduction Act Notice, see separate instructions. Cat. No. 11320B Form **1040** (2025) Created 9/5/25

The above form is a copy of the IRS Form 1040. It is for informational purposes only. DO NOT SEND IN.

Form 1040 (2025) Page **2**

Tax and Credits

11b	Amount from line 11a (adjusted gross income)	11b
12a	Someone can claim ☐ You as a dependent ☐ Your spouse as a dependent	
b	☐ Spouse itemizes on a separate return **c** ☐ You were a dual-status alien	
d	**You:** ☐ Were born before January 2, 1961 ☐ Are blind	
	Spouse: ☐ Was born before January 2, 1961 ☐ Is blind	
e	**Standard deduction or itemized deductions** (from Schedule A)	12e
13a	Qualified business income deduction from Form 8995 or Form 8995-A	13a
b	Additional deductions from Schedule 1-A, line 38	13b
14	Add lines 12e, 13a, and 13b	14
15	Subtract line 14 from line 11b. If zero or less, enter -0-. This is your **taxable income**	15
16	**Tax** (see instructions). Check if any from Form(s): 1 ☐ 8814 2 ☐ 4972 3 ☐ ______	16
17	Amount from Schedule 2, line 3	17
18	Add lines 16 and 17	18
19	Child tax credit or credit for other dependents from Schedule 8812	19
20	Amount from Schedule 3, line 8	20
21	Add lines 19 and 20	21
22	Subtract line 21 from line 18. If zero or less, enter -0-	22
23	Other taxes, including self-employment tax, from Schedule 2, line 21	23
24	Add lines 22 and 23. This is your **total tax**	24

Standard deduction for—
- Single or Married filing separately, $15,750
- Married filing jointly or Qualifying surviving spouse, $31,500
- Head of household, $23,625
- If you checked a box on line 12a, 12b, 12c, or 12d, see inst.

Payments and Refundable Credits

25	Federal income tax withheld from:		
a	Form(s) W-2	25a	
b	Form(s) 1099	25b	
c	Other forms (see instructions)	25c	
d	Add lines 25a through 25c		25d
26	2025 estimated tax payments and amount applied from 2024 return		26
	If you made estimated tax payments with your former spouse in 2025, enter their SSN (see instructions):		
27a	Earned income credit (EIC)	27a	
b	Clergy filing Schedule SE (see instructions) ☐		
c	If you do not want to claim the EIC, check here ☐		
28	Additional child tax credit (ACTC) from Schedule 8812. If you do not want to claim the ACTC, check here ☐	28	
29	American opportunity credit from Form 8863, line 8	29	
30	Refundable adoption credit from Form 8839, line 13	30	
31	Amount from Schedule 3, line 15	31	
32	Add lines 27a, 28, 29, 30, and 31. These are your **total other payments and refundable credits**		32
33	Add lines 25d, 26, and 32. These are your **total payments**		33

If you have a qualifying child, you may need to attach Sch. EIC.

Refund

34	If line 33 is more than line 24, subtract line 24 from line 33. This is the amount you **overpaid**		34
35a	Amount of line 34 you want **refunded to you.** If Form 8888 is attached, check here ☐		35a
b	Routing number **c** Type: ☐ Checking ☐ Savings		
d	Account number		
36	Amount of line 34 you want **applied to your 2026 estimated tax**	36	

Direct deposit? See instructions.

Amount You Owe

37	Subtract line 33 from line 24. This is the **amount you owe.** For details on how to pay, go to *www.irs.gov/Payments* or see instructions		37
38	Estimated tax penalty (see instructions)	38	

Third Party Designee

Do you want to allow another person to discuss this return with the IRS? See instructions. ☐ **Yes.** Complete below. ☐ **No**

Designee's name | Phone no. | Personal identification number (PIN)

Sign Here

Under penalties of perjury, I declare that I have examined this return and accompanying schedules and statements, and to the best of my knowledge and belief, they are true, correct, and complete. Declaration of preparer (other than taxpayer) is based on all information of which preparer has any knowledge.

Your signature	Date	Your occupation	If the IRS sent you an Identity Protection PIN, enter it here (see inst.)
Spouse's signature. If a joint return, **both** must sign.	Date	Spouse's occupation	If the IRS sent your spouse an Identity Protection PIN, enter it here (see inst.)
Phone no.	Email address		

Joint return? See instructions. Keep a copy for your records.

Paid Preparer Use Only

Preparer's name	Preparer's signature	Date	PTIN	Check if: ☐ Self-employed
Firm's name			Phone no.	
Firm's address			Firm's EIN	

Go to *www.irs.gov/Form1040* for instructions and the latest information. Form **1040** (2025)

The above form is a copy of the IRS Form 1040. It is for informational purposes only. DO NOT SEND IN.

SCHEDULE 1 (Form 1040)

Department of the Treasury
Internal Revenue Service

Additional Income and Adjustments to Income

Attach to Form 1040, 1040-SR, or 1040-NR.
Go to *www.irs.gov/Form1040* for instructions and the latest information.

OMB No. 1545-0074
2025
Attachment Sequence No. **01**

Name(s) shown on Form 1040, 1040-SR, or 1040-NR | **Your social security number**

For 2025, enter the amount reported to you on Form(s) 1099-K that was included in error or for personal items sold at a loss . . . . ______

Note: The remaining amounts reported to you on Form(s) 1099-K should be reported elsewhere on your return depending on the nature of the transaction. See *www.irs.gov/1099k*.

Part I Additional Income

1	Taxable refunds, credits, or offsets of state and local income taxes			1	
2a	Alimony received			2a	
b	Date of original divorce or separation agreement (see instructions): ______				
3	Business income or (loss). Attach Schedule C			3	
4	Other gains or (losses). Check if any from Form(s): ☐ 4797 ☐ 4684			4	
5	Rental real estate, royalties, partnerships, S corporations, trusts, etc. Attach Schedule E			5	
6	Farm income or (loss). Attach Schedule F			6	
7	Unemployment compensation. If you repaid a 2025 overpayment (see instructions), check here ☐ and enter amount repaid: ______			7	
8	Other income:				
a	Net operating loss	8a	( )		
b	Gambling	8b			
c	Cancellation of debt	8c			
d	Foreign earned income exclusion from Form 2555	8d	( )		
e	Income from Form 8853	8e			
f	Income from Form 8889	8f			
g	Alaska Permanent Fund dividends	8g			
h	Jury duty pay	8h			
i	Prizes and awards	8i			
j	Activity not engaged in for profit income	8j			
k	Stock options	8k			
l	Income from the rental of personal property if you engaged in the rental for profit but were not in the business of renting such property	8l			
m	Olympic and Paralympic medals and USOC prize money (see instructions)	8m			
n	Section 951(a) inclusion (see instructions)	8n			
o	Section 951A(a) inclusion (see instructions)	8o			
p	Section 461(l) excess business loss adjustment	8p			
q	Taxable distributions from an ABLE account (see instructions)	8q			
r	Scholarship and fellowship grants not reported on Form W-2	8r			
s	Nontaxable amount of Medicaid waiver payments included on Form 1040, line 1a or 1d	8s	( )		
t	Pension or annuity from a nonqualifed deferred compensation plan or a nongovernmental section 457 plan	8t			
u	Wages earned while incarcerated	8u			
v	Digital assets received as ordinary income not reported elsewhere. See instructions	8v			
z	Other income. List type and amount: ______	8z			
9	Total other income. Add lines 8a through 8z			9	
10	Combine lines 1 through 7 and 9. This is your **additional income**. Enter here and on Form 1040, 1040-SR, or 1040-NR, line 8			10	

For Paperwork Reduction Act Notice, see your tax return instructions. Cat. No. 71479F **Schedule 1 (Form 1040) 2025** Created 7/25/25

The above form is a copy of Schedule 1 of the IRS 1040. It is for informational purposes only. DO NOT SEND IN.

Schedule 1 (Form 1040) 2025 Page 2

Part II Adjustments to Income

11	Educator expenses	11	
12	Certain business expenses of reservists, performing artists, and fee-basis government officials. Attach Form 2106	12	
13	Health savings account deduction. Attach Form 8889	13	
14	Moving expenses for members of the Armed Forces. Attach Form 3903. If claiming only storage fees (see instructions), check here ☐	14	
15	Deductible part of self-employment tax. Attach Schedule SE	15	
16	Self-employed SEP, SIMPLE, and qualified plans	16	
17	Self-employed health insurance deduction	17	
18	Penalty on early withdrawal of savings	18	
19a	Alimony paid	19a	
b	Recipient's SSN		
c	Date of original divorce or separation agreement (see instructions):		
20	IRA deduction. If you are married filing separately and lived apart from your spouse for the entire year (see instructions), check here ☐	20	
21	Student loan interest deduction	21	
22	Reserved for future use	22	
23	Archer MSA deduction	23	
24	Other adjustments:		
a	Jury duty pay (see instructions)	24a	
b	Deductible expenses related to income reported on line 8l from the rental of personal property engaged in for profit	24b	
c	Nontaxable amount of the value of Olympic and Paralympic medals and USOC prize money reported on line 8m	24c	
d	Reforestation amortization and expenses	24d	
e	Repayment of supplemental unemployment benefits under the Trade Act of 1974	24e	
f	Contributions to section 501(c)(18)(D) pension plans	24f	
g	Contributions by certain chaplains to section 403(b) plans	24g	
h	Attorney fees and court costs for actions involving certain unlawful discrimination claims (see instructions)	24h	
i	Attorney fees and court costs you paid in connection with an award from the IRS for information you provided that helped the IRS detect tax law violations	24i	
j	Housing deduction from Form 2555	24j	
k	Excess deductions of section 67(e) expenses from Schedule K-1 (Form 1041)	24k	
z	Other adjustments. List type and amount:	24z	
25	Total other adjustments. Add lines 24a through 24z	25	
26	Add lines 11 through 23 and 25. These are your **adjustments to income**. Enter here and on Form 1040, 1040-SR, or 1040-NR, line 10	26	

Schedule 1 (Form 1040) 2025

The above form is a copy of Schedule 1 of the IRS 1040. It is for informational purposes only. DO NOT SEND IN.

Glossary

ACADEMIC YEAR: A measure of academic work to be performed by the student, subject to definition by the school.

AGI: Adjusted gross income. In 2025, the AGI is listed on Line 11a of the IRS 1040 form.

AMERICAN COLLEGE TESTING PROGRAM (ACT): The administrator of a group of standardized tests in English, mathematics, reading, and science reasoning.

BASE INCOME YEAR (also known as the BASE YEAR): The second calendar year preceding the academic year for which aid is being sought. 2025 will be the base income year for the 2027–2028 award year.

BUSINESS/FARM SUPPLEMENT: A supplemental aid application required by a few colleges for aid applicants whose parents own businesses or farms or who are self-employed. The individual school's aid policy will determine if this form must be completed.

CAMPUS-BASED PROGRAMS: Three federal student aid programs that are administered directly by the school's financial aid office (the Perkins Loan, the Supplemental Educational Opportunity Grant, and the Federal Work-Study program).

COLLEGE BOARD: A nonprofit association that writes and processes the CSS/Financial Aid Profile form.

COOPERATIVE EDUCATION: A college program offered at many schools that combines periods of academic study with periods of paid employment related to the student's field of study. In most cases, participation will extend the time required to obtain a bachelor's degree to five years.

COST OF ATTENDANCE: A figure estimated by the school that includes the cost of tuition, fees, room, board, books, and supplies, as well as an allowance for transportation and personal expenses. This figure is compared to the Student Aid Index to determine a student's aid eligibility. Also known as the *student budget*.

CSS/FINANCIAL AID PROFILE: A need analysis application created and processed by the College Board. Also known as the CSS Profile and sometimes as just the Profile.

DEFAULT: Failure to repay a loan according to the terms of the promissory note.

DEPENDENT STUDENT: A classification for aid purposes for a student who is considered to be dependent upon his or her parent(s) for financial support.

DIRECT LOAN PROGRAM: Formerly known as the Stafford Student Loan program, this federally funded program provides low-interest loans to undergraduate and graduate students. In most cases, repayment does not begin until six months after the student graduates or leaves school, and there are no interest charges while the student is in school. For new loans disbursed after June 30, 2006, the interest rate is fixed. (Prior loans had variable rates.) There are two types of Direct loans: subsidized and unsubsidized. The subsidized Direct loan is need-based and the government pays the interest while the student is in school. The unsubsidized Direct loan is non-need-based and can be taken out by virtually all students. In many cases, students can elect to let the interest accumulate until after they graduate.

EMPLOYMENT ALLOWANCE: A deduction against income in the federal and institutional methodologies for two-parent families in which both parents work or a single-parent family in which that parent works.

FAFSA: See Free Application for Federal Student Aid.

FAO: See Financial Aid Officer.

FEDERAL METHODOLOGY (FM): The generally accepted method used to calculate the family's expected contribution to college costs for federal aid purposes. Depending on the individual college's policy, the federal methodology may also be used to determine eligibility for money under the school's control.

FEDERAL WORK-STUDY (FWS): A federally funded aid program that provides jobs for students. Eligibility is based on need.

FINANCIAL AID: A general term used to refer to a variety of programs funded by the federal and state governments as well as the individual schools to assist students with their educational costs. While the names may vary, financial aid comes in three basic forms: (1) gift aid (grants and scholarships) that does not have to be paid back (2) student loans, and (3) work-study jobs.

FINANCIAL AID OFFICER: An administrator at each school who determines whether a student is eligible for aid and, if so, the types of aid to be awarded.

FREE APPLICATION FOR FEDERAL STUDENT AID (FAFSA): The need analysis document written by the U.S. Department of Education. This form is required for virtually all students seeking financial aid, including the unsubsidized Direct Loan.

FSA ID: A new personal identification system for use with U.S. Department of Education websites, including the online FAFSA.

FOTW: FAFSA on the Web, the online version of the FAFSA.

401(k), 403(b): The names of two of the more popular tax-deferred retirement plans in which employees elect to defer part of their earnings until a later date.

GIFT AID: Financial aid, usually a grant or scholarship, that does not have to be paid back and that does not involve employment.

GRADPLUS LOANS: A federally sponsored educational loan program in which graduate or professional school students can borrow up to the total cost of attendance minus any financial aid received. Eligibility is not based on need.

GRANTS: Gift aid that is generally based on need. The programs can be funded by the federal and state governments as well as the individual schools.

HALF-TIME STATUS: Refers to students taking at least 6 credits per semester, or the equivalent.

INCOME PROTECTION ALLOWANCE: A deduction against income in both the federal and the institutional methodologies.

INDEPENDENT STUDENT: A student who, for financial aid purposes, is not considered dependent on his or her parent(s) for support. Also known as a self-supporting student.

INSTITUTIONAL FORMS: Supplemental forms required by the individual schools to determine aid eligibility.

INSTITUTIONAL METHODOLOGY (IM): An alternative method used to calculate the family's expected contribution to college costs. This methodology is generally used by private and a few state schools to determine eligibility for aid funds under the school's direct control. Colleges that use the institutional methodology usually require completion of the CSS Profile form.

NEED: The amount of aid a student is eligible to receive. This figure is calculated by subtracting the Student Aid Index from the Cost of Attendance.

NEED ANALYSIS: The process of analyzing the information on the aid form to calculate the amount of money the student and parent(s) can be expected to contribute toward educational costs.

NEED ANALYSIS FORMS: Aid applications used to calculate the Student Aid Index. The most common need analysis forms are the Free Application for Federal Student Aid (FAFSA) and the CSS/Financial Aid Profile form. Consult the individual school's financial aid filing requirements to determine which form(s) are required for that particular school.

NONCUSTODIAL PARENT'S STATEMENT: A supplemental aid application required by a few colleges for aid applicants whose parents are separated or divorced or who never married. The individual school's aid policy will determine if this form must be completed. If required, this form will be completed by the noncustodial parent. This is generally the parent with whom the child spent the least amount of time in the preceding 12 months prior to completion of the form.

PARENTS' CONTRIBUTION: The amount of money the parent(s) are expected to contribute for the year toward the student's Cost of Attendance.

PARENT LOANS FOR UNDERGRADUATE STUDENTS (PLUS): A federally sponsored educational loan program in which parents can borrow up to the total cost of attendance minus any financial aid received for each child in an undergraduate program. Eligibility is not based on need.

PELL GRANT: A federally funded need-based grant program for first-time undergraduate students (i.e., the student has not as yet earned a bachelor's or first professional degree). Funds from this program are generally awarded to lower- and lower-middle-income families. Years ago, this program was called the Basic Educational Opportunity Grant (BEOG).

PERKINS LOAN PROGRAM: This discontinued, federally funded need-based program provided low interest loans to undergraduate and graduate students with loans by the school's financial aid office. In most cases, repayment does not begin until nine months after the student graduates or leaves school, and there are no interest charges while the student is in school.

PHEAA: The Pennsylvania Higher Education Assistance Agency.

PLUS LOANS: See Parent Loans for Undergraduate Students.

PREFERENTIAL PACKAGING: The situation in which the more desired aid applicants get better aid packages, which are larger in total dollar amount and/or contain a higher percentage of grants versus loans.

PROFILE FORM: A need analysis document written and processed by the College Board.

PROMISSORY NOTE: The legal document which the borrower signs to obtain the loan proceeds and which specifies the terms of the loan, the interest rate, and the repayment provisions.

ROTC: The Reserve Officer Training Corps programs that are coordinated at many college campuses by the U.S. Army, Navy, and Air Force.

SAT: An exam, administered by the College Board, which has critical reading, writing and language, and math sections.

SCHOLARSHIPS: Gift aid that is usually based on merit or a combination of need and merit.

SELF-HELP: The portion of the aid package relating to student loans and/or work-study.

SEOG: See Supplemental Educational Opportunity Grant.

SIMPLIFIED NEEDS TEST: An alternative method used to calculate the family's expected contribution to college costs for federal aid purposes, in which all assets are excluded from the federal aid formula.

STANDARDIZED FORMS: The generic term used in this book when referring to any of the need analysis forms that must be sent to a processing service. The two most commonly used standardized forms are the U.S. Department of Education's Free Application for Federal Student Aid (FAFSA) and the College Board's CSS/Financial Aid Profile form.

STUDENT BUDGET: See Cost of Attendance.

STUDENT'S CONTRIBUTION: The amount of money the student is expected to contribute for the year toward his or her cost of attendance.

SUBSIDIZED DIRECT LOAN: See Direct Loan program.

SUPPLEMENTAL EDUCATIONAL OPPORTUNITY GRANT (SEOG): A federally funded need-based grant program for undergraduate students that is awarded by the school's financial aid office.

UNSUBSIDIZED DIRECT LOAN: See Direct Loan program.

VERIFICATION: A process in which the financial aid office requires additional documentation to verify the accuracy of the information reported on the aid applications.

WORK-STUDY: See Federal Work-Study.

About the Authors

KALMAN A. CHANY is the founder and president of Campus Consultants Inc. (www.CampusConsultants.com), a New York City-based firm that guides parents and students through the financial aid process. In addition to counseling thousands of families on the aid process, he has conducted workshops for corporations, schools, and other organizations. He also trains financial professionals regarding financial aid consulting. Kal is a frequent guest on television and radio shows across the country.

GEOFF MARTZ is a writer living in New York City.

NOTES

NOTES